OPIUM'S LONG SHADOW

Opium's Long Shadow

From Asian Revolt to Global Drug Control

◄ STEFFEN RIMNER ►

▐▐▐

Harvard University Press

Cambridge, Massachusetts
London, England
2018

Copyright © 2018 by the President and Fellows of Harvard College
All rights reserved
Printed in the United States of America

First printing

Library of Congress Cataloging-in-Publication Data
Names: Rimner, Steffen, 1983– author.
Title: Opium's long shadow : from Asian revolt to global drug control / Steffen Rimner.
Description: Cambridge, Massachusetts : Harvard University Press, 2018. |
Includes bibliographical references and index.
Identifiers: LCCN 2018012858 | ISBN 9780674976306 (hardcover : alk. paper)
Subjects: LCSH: League of Nations. Advisory Committee on Traffic in Opium
and Other Dangerous Drugs. | Opium trade—History—20th century. |
Drug Control—International cooperation—History—20th century. |
Social Reformers—History—20th century.
Classification: LCC HV5816 .R565 2018 | DDC 344.05/45—dc23
LC record available at https://lccn.loc.gov/2018012858

To my parents

Contents

Illustrations

INTRODUCTION

THE OPIUM TRADE was once the most official drug trade sponsored by states. Displacing it from its erstwhile privilege and dismantling its global legal protections were no small feat. Epitomized by the opium wars in the middle of the nineteenth century, defenders of the opium trade once spoke from positions of power, drowning out inferior critics. Sponsors of the trade at its prime did not forecast its demise. Observers were surprised or shocked to see it so dramatically challenged. Today, we have largely forgotten the immensity of mobilization and the profusion of networks that were responsible for discrediting the opium trade despite its clout. The process of discrediting required a geographically wider, socially more diverse, and logistically more multifarious process of raising opposition than was hitherto assumed.

As the cause of international drug control gained shape and augmented from the 1870s to the 1920s, Qing diplomats found unexpected support among European journalists; British social reformers among Hindu widows; colonial publicists among nationalist revolutionaries and medical drug experts. Chinese anti-opium activists joined forces with Indian colleagues; Dutch critics with American crusaders; British liberals with Chinese Confucianists. Anti-opium critics found a common voice with critics of human trafficking, leading to mutual sponsoring from Hong Kong to Germany. Humanitarians in Europe saw eye to eye with early anti-imperialist pioneers in East Asia. Their actions toppled, one by one, the local legitimacy, the national rationalizations, and the imperial justifications that had sustained the opium trade, run by empires and governments across Asia. The revolt against opium overturned the global legality of government-sponsored drug trading.[1]

The anti-opium movement, a composite rather than a uniform whole, laid the ideological and political foundations of global drug control through an almost mysterious confluence of interests, aspirations, and political agendas that defies historical explanations along familiar axes of loyalty, be it the state, an ideology, a political orientation, ethnicity, language, gender, or religion. Local variations, rather than hindering the global cause, composed it. Absent its local versions and adaptations to specific, social expectations and ideological demands, the global cause would have existed merely in word but not in deed. Yet in each new round of mobilization, ranging from anti-opium rallies, public speeches, and demonstrations to the distribution of anti-opium posters, pamphlets, books, and petitions to the public burning of opium balls and pipes, the cause showed a capacity for growth through transnational integration. Since most self-declared enemies of opium worked part time for this cause, other professional identities and private inclinations offered numerous opportunities to form compounds with partner causes, from the earliest calls for institutions of public health in Singapore and China to agendas of social reform and moral renewal from South Asia to Britain. As in other mobilizations of political opposition, such as the Ghadar movement that originated in California to overthrow the British regime in India, anti-drug mobilization did not do it all alone or in isolation. It was enriched by a wide, even dazzling array of partner causes that lent their social base and extended its public appeal to new audiences.[2]

Thousands of anti-opium protesters saw reason to prioritize cooperation among their growing ranks over conflict, galvanizing sufficient pressure to enact groundbreaking changes in the global politics of empire and of international law. In the vision forwarded by the critics, opium became the prototypical substance and symbol of imperialist malice: a poison to sabotage the coherence and stability of foreign societies with lethal success. Tracing the spread of anti-opium ideology, protest and politics in its foundational phase across cultures can help explain how transnational opposition formulated new norms of imperial political behavior—norms reassessed by recourse to their social purpose.[3] Anchoring drug control as a new political responsibility in international society involved a process of individuals gaining a stake in the international discourse and politics affecting their own livelihoods, a process that has by no means come to completion in the early twenty-first century.[4]

This book offers insight into how and why opposition to the opium trade and subsequent drug trades was spawned not merely within individual settings but across East, Southeast, and South Asia, western Europe, and North America in the period between the opium wars and the founding of the League of Nations after the First World War. It focuses on the transnational dynamics that proliferated protest from one setting to another, on the social connections that made the transmission of anti-opium critiques possible, and on the reasons why states around the world ultimately adopted an agenda initially directed against them.[5]

In order to understand the changing position of drugs in international society, the chapters that follow examine the political contestation, the popular mobilization, and, above all, the pervasive fear of impending disaster that triggered the global turn against opium and other narcotic drugs.[6] Sixty years after the end of the Second Opium War—that is, by the end of the First World War—states had turned their back on drug trading as an official privilege and instead chosen to become the principal stakeholders of global drug control. That they did so was less an act of state reasoning than a reaction to transnational pressure. This book argues that attacking the reputation of the trade played a key role in the withdrawal of states and empires around the world from the trade. To reassess the origins of global drug control calls for a focus on the multilayered conditions that turned the global revolt against opium from nineteenth-century utopia into twentieth-century reality.[7]

But unlike geographical distance, which could be bridged by mobility, political distance could not simply be reduced by communication, by someone's sole determination to speak truth to power. Protests in disparate locales did not simply issue global rethinking and political persuasion like rivers that merge effortlessly into a delta. A crucial role fell instead to the global representation of local opposition. Activists and their audiences, as judged by social and political reactions they provoked near and far, jointly produced a form of anti-opium representation that enhanced the reach and pressure of opposition beyond the immediate scene of protest, be it Beijing, Shanghai, or London. Anti-opium activists shrank the political distance to perceived perpetrators of the opium trade by producing and disseminating narratives of perpetration in pamphlets, fliers, booklets, news reports, journals, and entire protest books. Claiming long-distance perpetration and victimization were not only mutually constitutive tropes of criminalization. The claims and their repetition even appeared to make the act of an opium crime itself come true, not only in the eyes of critics but also in the eyes of those criticized. As a result of a globally growing base of support, moral capital accrued increasingly to those joining the criticism, displacing other criteria of recognition, such as nationality, cultural origin, or social status.[8]

It is no coincidence that the traveler of the twenty-first century passing through customs and the borders of China, Japan, Singapore, Malaysia, the United States, and many other countries that surface in this global history is inevitably confronted with tight drug-control regimes. These regimes testify to the resilience of the time when societies and states around the world felt compelled, like never before, to turn against the free movement of narcotic drugs. It would have hardly come to this if transnational, nongovernmental opposition had remained mere clamor. But policy makers from Beijing and Tokyo to London, Washington, Paris, and later Geneva perceived the intensity of outrage not merely because of the passions so amply on display. They saw and feared the global outcry of anti-drug opposition. And just as governments recognized the global momentum of simultaneous protest across cultures, anti-opium activists were emboldened by the perception that they shared not only political space but global time. Their reckoning aspired to be part of a historic change, evoking an hour greater than individual initiative and beyond political control and creating a mirage of magnified opposition.

The globality of anti-drug opposition, then, did not remain the lofty goal of anti-opium critics but compelled officials in Asian empires and beyond to see that they were indeed witnessing an overwhelming, irrepressible, and authentic sea change in international public opinion. The scale of this change was unanticipated and can be identified by recounting the opium discourse before the political impact of mobilization after around 1895. Defenses of the opium trade vis-à-vis an imperial or a domestic audience were rife up to the Royal Commission on Opium of 1895. British imperial defenders, rather than transnational, largely nongovernmental opium critics, spoke globally at the vanguard of the opium debate. They showed a preference for responding to anti-opium criticism by downplaying the addictiveness of opium consumption, denying that it posed any serious health hazard. Drawing a long-lasting analogy to the West, they averred that opium was the alcohol of the East. "Excess in opium, so far as the individual consumer is concerned, may probably be as bad as excess in alcohol; it cannot be worse, and its effects upon his neighbours are comparatively harmless," as the British reporter on economic products with the government of India put it in 1891.[9]

Contradicting the alcohol analogy, opponents pointed repeatedly to a different parallel: the opium trade in Asia as analogous in social damage and historical weight to the slave trade in Africa. Both impinged on minds and bodies with untamable force, they argued, degrading the relations between different cultures and ethnicities into unethical infractions of human inviolability. The anti-drug cause was never a wholly independent force, and perhaps even less so because of its circulation. From Asian metropoles, such as Shanghai and Singapore, to China-based international newspapers, European parliaments, and American pamphlet literature, opium emergencies manifested themselves as rallying points for opposition. Encounters of the anti-opium movement with compatible causes of social suffering, similar reckonings with perceived imperial abuse, and related dynamics of international publicity drew on the human horror of distant political decisions as the immediate causes for social suffering here and now.[10]

The precedent of abolitionism and humanitarian discursive interventionism could have warned those backing the Royal Commission on Opium of 1895 that its six-volume final report would not be enough to shield the trade from future backlash. After 1895, the criticism emanated with unforeseen vigor not from within but from without the British empire, intruding into the debate in order to seek a political confrontation. This also explains why the transnational scope of anti-opium mobilization cannot be seen as coterminous with either imperial ideology or anti-imperial tropes of criticism.[11] Even though fundamental changes of opinion may appear inadmissible to much of the human psyche and staying one's course maintains dignity and authority, this change of international public opinion attained political visibility at the time. Its traces can be pieced together through numerous archives around the world. Anti-opium criticism reconfigured the politics of adjudicating the opium trade through new diagnoses of opium's toll on minds and bodies, individuals and families, societies and nations. Anti-opium circles committed to radical reinterpretation were the social sites where medical and moral narratives depicting the opium trade as a form of aggression—as a threat to life itself—first appeared.

Covering the broad spectrum from the scientific to the conspiratorial, the anti-opium movement used both social evidence and speculation to deduce the political malice of Western powers. By contrast, even concerned and critical social reformers in European societies did not succeed in gaining transnational support for the view that consumption of opium in the form of laudanum or other liquid drugs was inextricably and inevitably tied to moral and social corruption. In China, it felt far worse than Charles Baudelaire's allusion that opium in France created "a meditative nation lost within the heart of the busy nation."[12] Perhaps closer came Zionist and Socialist Moses Heß, who in 1843 stated that opium robbed a person of the ability "to respond consciously and independently against harm and to liberate oneself from evil."[13]

But in the Asian anti-opium cause, the darker and starker the vision, the greater the emotional mass effect. Through opium, the story of China's victimization moved front and center. Unlike Chinese critiques, which followed the anti-opium movement from the 1920s to the 1940s to target imperialist privileges like the unequal treaties—including, in legal disputes, extraterritoriality—the anti-opium movement itself brought the damage to the Chinese people, not the Chinese state, front and center.[14] On that basis, a focus on the transnational, nongovernmental dimension of anti-opium mobilization seems merited.

Unfortunately, no reliable opium statistics were available to even the most dedicated researchers at the time, but we do know that in 1890, between 15 and 40 million people in China were opium smokers, corresponding to between 3 and 10 percent of China's total population. The United Nations in 2009 estimated that China had 21 million opium smokers in 1906. The International Opium Commission suggested at least 13.5 million opium smokers for 1909. In fiscal terms, China's own interregional trade around 1900 saw opium worth 130 million taels in circulation, compared to 100 million taels each of salt and rice.[15] This translates into an estimated 85 to 95 percent of global opium for smoking purposes destined for China.[16] Like the data of the historical anti-opium sources from which it was compiled, this calculation was limited to Asian consumption of "smoke opium" and excluded western European or North American consumption of opium in a variety of liquid forms, such as laudanum. Non-Asian consumption of opium, although existent, remained marginal in the essentially Asia-focused construction of global anti-drug knowledge.

But in contrast to the figures and their scientifically unsatisfactory approximations, the narratives of opium have survived almost intact to this day. Most prominent among them is the trope of opium taking aim to poison an entire people. The harrowing imagery and political symbolism of the emerging anti-opium discourse dragged the opium trade into new meanings. With ever more dire images of opium victims, the trade's political legitimacy began to waiver in the 1870s, and became subject to diplomatic scrutiny in the 1900s and to international legal constraints in the 1910s. Thus, decades before postcolonial nationhood, international political legitimacy came under the influence of grassroots mobilization. Opium's long shadow from the late nineteenth century forward, from transnational mobilization into international law and politics, from Asia to a worldwide covenant of drug control, was the product of a political and ideological change of what a state, even if powerful, could and could not do. Through mobilization of public opinion, drug trading became an inalienable factor of a state's international reputation. The activity once blessed by international law was now cursed as a crime.[17]

Even though it was heavily concerned with opium consumption and its mental, physical, and societal consequences, anti-opium mobilization was not simply victims speaking for themselves. Far from autobiographical, the process of mobilization brought to the fore proponents of drug control who claimed to speak on behalf of opium victims, with varying degrees of intimate familiarity. But it would be inaccurate to describe their cause as simply giving voice to the opium consumer. Rather, they enacted new social and political representations of opium consumers. This turned the well-established social practice of opium consumption from a hapless, private penchant into a serious public problem. Anti-drug opposition conquered international public opinion not exclusively due to the conviction, ambition, and even desperation of those who spoke out. Politicization of opium suffering across Asia served as the means of enacting official disapprobation of the trade.

The trade acquired its stature as a state-sponsored business of almost matchless attraction. Although this book is not an economic history of the opium trade and although anti-opium mobilization did not align itself—geographically or chronologically—with the highs and lows of the trade itself, let us first recount the scale and significance of the opium trade. So prized was the Asian opium trade in the age of imperialism that it became part and parcel of Asia's political economy in the nineteenth century.[18] As the British, French, Dutch, American, and Japanese empires descended in various forms on Asia from the mid-nineteenth to the mid-twentieth centuries, they coveted this trade for state business, folding it into the economically legitimate and politically legal repertoire of state practice. Of all the large-scale trades in narcotic drugs that have permeated the nineteenth and twentieth centuries, the global opium trade was the earliest.

The existing historiography has taught us much about early anti-opium activism stemming from a distinct strata of Anglo-American Protestant missionaries, whose own transnational lives put them on the ground in China. Missionaries take center stage as protagonists with the ability to cross geographic and social borders between East and West. But the familiar focus on missionary initiatives, ambitions, accomplishments, and impediments owes less to a careful comparison between their influence and the transnational influence of Asian anti-opium activists. Instead, the preference on missionary histories appears increasingly to be the result of a contextual choice: the abiding concern among China scholars outside Asia, especially in the 1950s and 1960s, to deliberate the twists and turns of China's modernization in response to the encounter with the West. In this perspective, it made perfect sense to highlight how Western pioneers enlarged their own civilizing footprint by compelling forward-looking Asians to rid their societies of strange and harmful Oriental habits, such as opium consumption.[19] The governmental anti-opium initiatives of Britain and the United States from the 1910s onward offer a supplement to the Anglo-American focus on missionaries, crediting in effect London and Washington for accomplishing the objectives of their own religious proselytizers overseas.[20]

A second line of research in cultural and social history has taken note of anti-opium perceptions in connection to what was known as the Yellow Peril. As a xenophobic sentiment, the Yellow Peril experienced its own proliferation across North America, Germany, France, Britain, and Russia.[21] Chinese opium addiction, especially among the Chinese living in those societies, became an easy target of imperialist ideology, coming to signify both Chinese moral and social inferiority and Western vulnerability through contact with those deplorable Chinese. Inserted into the broad palette of Western stereotypes of Chinese society, Chinese opium consumption appeared to confirm key tenets of earlier cultural criticism: that the Chinese were an unchangeably backward, shiftless, and feeble collectivity devoid of national integration, under a weak Qing state vacillating pettishly between despotic rule and political incompetence. Assuming China's civilizational inferiority, the image of the opium-smoking Chinese lying on the sickbed of his opium den symbolized the worst in China: the "sick man of Asia," both unwilling and unable to protect his health and that of his society at "civilized" "Western" levels of productivity. From such people, one kept a healthy distance. By contrast, Asian anti-opium sentiment targeted producers rather than consumers and, accordingly, came in the guise of opposite social relations: projects of transnational integration rather than nation- or race-based exclusion.[22]

A third line of research, turning in many ways against the Anglo-American dominance of the first, highlights Chinese national genealogies of anti-opium activism in an effort to marginalize the foreign contributions to Chinese social change since the first major Imperial Anti-Opium Edict of 1905. This disregards the pronounced transnational response, in Asia and overseas, to Chinese opposition since the 1870s, which is uncovered here. Furthermore, national explanations of Chinese anti-opium opposition, in the simplest sense of restricting the inquiry to a national arena of sociopolitical action, owe much to the backdrop of Chinese nationalist opposition itself. In 1911, one close observer of early anti-drug politics claimed, "China's crusade to free her people from the opium curse may be justly reckoned one of the greatest moral achievements in history—a challenge to our Western world."[23] But by treating Chinese and Western drivers of change as mutually exclusive and by virtually denying the possibility for their mutual involvement, our understanding of one dimension almost got lost: the reverse direction of border-crossing influence from Asia into metropolitan societies of imperial powers—or, more broadly, Asian influences on a global shift of political attitudes toward drugs. Perhaps power is commonly considered the guiding, even exclusive, principle of world politics; we tend to equate power with influence, assuming that both necessarily flow in the same direction. We still have a much better understanding of the waterfalls of influence by the West on "the rest" than grasping why there are geysers of "non-Western" influence on the West, seemingly defying gravity with subterranean force.

In the history of East Asia's various opium encounters with the wider world in the late nineteenth and early twentieth centuries, we have become accustomed to a dichotomy of historical influence: either Western influence on Asian societies or Asian self-referential influence on their own societies.[24] In fact, even in the China-centered approach, the Chinese legacy of anti-opium opposition has revealed another state centrism. This state centrism brings it in line with the dictates of the current Chinese state to privilege the past and present of anti-drug crusading far above popular narratives—for instance, of human rights. In the case of China, this observation is admittedly more notable for the high priority attached to anti-drug politics than to the no-longer-surprising low priority attached to human rights.[25] But even the human rights dimension has not always helped in moving historical approaches beyond the already observed state centrism, and for good reasons.

Beyond China and Asia, the historiography on Central and Latin America's past and present encounters with narcotic drugs has favored explanations of why the War on Drugs became excessively authoritarian, inhumane, and ineffective. Partly as a result of this worthwhile focus, suspicion haunts anti-drug narratives as being driven by political self-justification more than by critical explanation. Anti-drug representations themselves have been decried as complicit in social ostracism and ultimately the carceral state. Within this historiography, drug use is no longer considered inherently criminal but plotted across a varied spectrum of cultural and social experience apart from the grip of the state, an interpretive trend also found in histories of British India and to some extent republican China. It may be fair to say that the history of anti-drug politics has become increasingly enmeshed with the politics of anti-drug histories.[26] This book makes the case that prior to the drug-control commitments by states around the world that appear paradigmatic today, states were a secondary pressure group, lagging behind transnational opponents of narcotic drugs.

Readers might wonder what is to be gained from taking a critical distance to the above lines of research and opening up a new one. The point is explicitly not about taking a normative stance and gauging a new scale of moral evaluation. This book aims neither to accuse nor to exonerate. It is neither conceived to praise nor to condemn. Instead, it examines the process of proliferation that augmented the scale of anti-drug opposition beyond local and national settings; the dynamics that expanded anti-drug thought, lobbying, and politics on a transnational scale. The following chapters take normative decisions as objects of analysis, not as method.

In substance, the anti-drug opposition that rose in the late nineteenth century differed quite fundamentally from the War on Drugs in the United States, Mexico, and the Philippines today. Its chief criticism was reserved for producers, not consumers. This important difference of argument effectively reversed the understanding of the political economy of drugs, turning the charge of ethical neglect against state suppliers rather than private consumers. In the process of vilification, states not only became guilty of transgressing against Qing and other Asian legislation—a critique that would have emphasized the damage to an Asian state. Instead, examinations of what drugs did became a distinctive sort of social disputation, an interrogation into how and why opium transgressed against the norms of society, whether written or unwritten.

If the first generation of anti-drug discourse obsessed over anything, it was not drug control as an index of a newly empowered state or a state strategy of social suppression. Instead, its nongovernmental activists overwhelmingly interpreted the opium problem as unstoppably contagious and criticized the lack of state control. Those most successful in the transnational proliferation of protest diagnosed opium consumption as a societal malfunctioning caused by political neglect, not by the accretion of the state's power to punish. In many ways the perceived causalities of a drug problem in the early twenty-first century and a drug problem in the late nineteenth century were reversed. In the long term, this may point to a cyclical development of the global drug problem, proceeding from drug legalization in 1860 to control after 1912 and renewed calls for legalization in recent years.[27] But importantly, proponents of the recent return to legalization rarely call it a return and do not seem to be attuned to the historical precedent of legalization and the lessons of that precedent. In short, the story told in this book shows that first, states were cornered to take up drug control, then later learned to use it to their perceived advantage. The drug opponents with transnational leverage thought too much about the political causalities of the global marketplace, not too little.

To appreciate the political and normative downfall of the opium trade, it is worth remembering how tall it stood as an economic privilege of empires across Asia. Since the early eighteenth century, opium rose to become one of the most lucrative sources of colonial and imperial revenues across the Asian region. The political economy of the opium trade expanded in volume, geographic scope and administrative sophistication long before international legal guarantees were woven into the Asian regional economy in 1860. As part and parcel of European imperial expansion, the opium trade carried economic weight and brought political leverage. As a commodity trade of light weight and high value, its profits beckoned empires with an almost magnetic attraction.

Embedded in the project of European expansion and its intercolonial economy in Asia, opium revenues were prized on every register of local and maritime investment, despite the chaotic workings of its political economy. Opium traveled on junks plying from offloading vessels ashore the creviced coastlines of China, passing noticeably through customs offices, tariff stations and tax commissions and unnoticed by nighttime. The opium trade connected commercial profiteers to opium connoisseurs with the majority of commercial expansions in Asia.[28] In 1842, at the end of the First Opium War, few if any British officials would have had nightmares of global drug control, even though by 1921 the scenario had become a fact of political life.

The Second Opium War moved international society further away from any prospect of drug control or regulatory oversight. The Treaty of Tianjin and the Peking Convention of 1860 legalized unlimited drug trading, trusting that any regulation would be ensured by the market. With the unremitting support of international law, the opium trade became a legitimate government enterprise of European empires as well as a market for private investment. With the forceful entry of the British empire into Asia's Qing-centered trading system, the opium wars defined how the Qing and the succeeding Republic of China could engage with the world of the great powers, notably Britain, France, the United States, Russia, and Japan.

But as drug trading became an inalienable factor of state reputation, states began recalculating the political costs attached to self-incrimination. From the 1880s onward, governments from Japan to the United States and China gradually converted to the paradigm of drug control. The International Opium Convention of 1912 expelled the free trade in opium and other narcotic drugs from the legitimate repertoire of state conduct. Imperial, national, and subnational constituencies responded to transnational and international pressures by institutionalizing an ever-expanding array of anti-drug legislation, which has continued beyond the Cold War. After the First World War, Germany, the Netherlands, British India and others followed the course set by Japan, the United States, and China in subscribing to the global regime of drug control under the League of Nations. But the increasing political exposure of the trade from the 1870s to the 1920s did not yet end drug trading itself, despite contemporary expectations to the contrary. In 1931, Basel-based economist Edgar Salin, mentored as a student by Max Weber's brother Alfred and later serving as dissertation adviser of Talcott Parsons, commissioned the first comprehensive study of the opium problem in the global economy, to be published in a series on Problems of the Global Economy by the Institute for Global Economy and Maritime Commerce in Kiel. Combining Royal Commission evidence with the British Indian government's annual "Opium Statistics," he showed that India's total opium output persisted on high levels until the 1910s. Except for the cessation of the direct Indian-Chinese opium trade in 1917, drug trading continued beyond the 1920s, an economic fact without which the League of Nations regime of global drug supervision would have been superfluous.

The anti-opium movement sprang from multiple sources rather than from one center, mirroring earlier projects of mobilizing international public opinion like abolitionism, and later projects of nationalist anti-imperialism.[29] But in contrast to movements like the Risorgimento or philhellenism, the anti-opium cause itself became an international rallying ground.[30] In 1909, the International Opium Commission (IOC) convening in Shanghai became the first multilateral summit committed to formulating principles of global drug control. Not only did the IOC respond to the demands of transnational anti-opium activists to open official negotiations of the "opium problem," as it became known in English, Chinese, Japanese, German, French, Dutch, and other languages, but transnational activists themselves served as many of the delegates at the IOC. The IOC of 1909 held more than symbolic importance. Its range of participants pointed to the fact that the foundational phase of global drug control revealed the centrality of Asia and its global repercussions. Participants represented all powers with colonial or imperial interests in Asia, plus China and Japan: in the original order, America, Austria-Hungary, China, France, Germany, Great Britain, Italy, Japan, the Netherlands, Persia, Portugal, Russia, and Siam (present-day Thailand).

The China focus of early drug control, so often observed, was part of an Asia focus that sprang almost ineluctably from the Asian conceptualization of the opium problem by critics since the 1870s. But even if the history of anti-opium mobilization cannot be reduced to a Chinese dimension, the Sinocentrism of public memory of opium in China and abroad can be explained. Beginning from the end of this book, in the 1920s, several strands of the anti-opium movement shed their internationalist convictions in favor of an increasingly exclusivist Sinicization, for reasons that shall be analyzed in Chapter 8.[31] And perhaps most tellingly, the politics of recounting the history of drug control today has embraced a novel form of Sinocentrism that displays, at least publicly, a rare, broad, and stable consensus between China and the international community.

One hundred years after the IOC, in February 2009, the gradual disillusionment over global drug control that had emanated from Central and Latin America's reckoning with the War on Drugs gave way to an extravagant display of how global drug control of the past can still cast a spell on the present. The scene was the Shanghai International Conference Center on February 26, just before nine a.m. Chinese and foreign guests of the Chinese government and the National Narcotics Control Commission flocked into the hall to participate in an act of multilateral commemoration. From the stage, five Chinese characters announced *wanguo jinyan hui*, the International Opium Commission of 1909.

It could not have been coincidence that the displayed map placed China at the center of the world. Rising some eighteen feet in height and stretching across forty feet in length, the map depicted the People's Republic of China in conciliatory light blue. Hovering below was Southeast Asia; to the left, the Indian Ocean; and to the right, Japan and the Pacific Ocean. China's neighbors were held in darker blue, visually enhancing their immediate proximity. The West Coast of the United States was in the process of fading away on the right edge, mirroring the sad fate of western Europe on the left edge. Not unlike an afterimage, the evocative map covered a presentation wall, which in turn crowned the festive stage of the elongated conference hall. But the centennial of 2009—half ceremony, half summit—refrained from heaping praise on an individual nation and celebrated global drug control as a breakthrough of collective, multinational crisis management. The speeches refused a Whig reading of history that would have declared the political, social, economic, and cultural challenges of global drug control overcome. With the flags of the international community standing at attention, the centennial reaffirmed ownership of a global past that carried duties and responsibilities into the future, under the aegis of the United Nations Commission on Narcotic Drugs (UNCND), an arm of the United Nations Economic and Social Council (ECOSOC).[32] Eyes and ears focused on the global regime of drug control, which the global renunciation of the opium trade had made a moral deterrent.[33]

By raising the UN regime—usually doing its quiet work from tucked-away Vienna—to unprecedented world attention, the centennial illuminated aspects of how the global regime of drug control had emerged. In February 2009, the recourse to public opinion as a potent barometer of political legitimacy, so well-rehearsed around 1909, stretched across international and Chinese society. Like the Qing ahead of the IOC, the Chinese government had ordered nationwide media announcements of the centennial since the fall of 2008, from Beijing to Yunnan.[34] The centennial concluded with the Shanghai Declaration, which kept its historical praise anonymous and uncontroversial, "paying tribute to those who made unremitting efforts and even dedicated their lives to the international endeavor to countering the problem of illicit drugs, and appreciating their great visions and important contributions."[35] Whatever editorial disputes yielded this narrative, the shining 2009 version of drug control remained undimmed by historical humiliation and perpetration.[36] Likewise, Sinocentrism kept its discreet reserve, discernible only to the eye wandering across the choreography that framed the celebrants. This served the purpose of the ritual: to display a historical consensus as an international accord, in line with the United Nations as composed of nation-states. At the same time, the example highlights the limitations of official memory, both of nation-states and of international organizations. After all, examining, analyzing, and assessing the influences on public and political opinion that cross borders can be construed as undermining the authority of an institution, be it one state or a combination of them. Political memory is a choice and serves political functions of remembrance.[37] To grasp where those political functions come from and why they are so stubbornly adhered to may no longer elude the reader who keeps reading to the end.

CHAPTER ONE

THUNDERS BEFORE THE STORM

UNWIELDY OBJECTS LIKE the opium trade are not easily removed, even if their foundations shake and objections all around begin to mount. Understanding the size, weight, and economic significance of the opium trade that contributed to its force in international politics helps create the backdrop against which later opposition arose. Especially given the swiftness of opposition, let us remember that neither the trade under attack nor the politics that tried to absorb the shock could be taken lightly. The opium trade in Asia can be described in terms of two major shifts in the position of narcotic drugs in international society. The first attracted empires to the opium trade like flies to a flame. The second turned the flame against empires, leaving them with the black stains of a burnt reputation.

Before that happened, the first human traces of opium were not all that auspicious. Some four thousand years ago, opium was spotted in the southwest of Switzerland, close to Neuchâtel. Thirty-one hundred years ago, opium appeared in the Cueva de los Murciélagos, in the Spanish province of Córdoba. In the sixth century, long-distance trade brought it to the Tang dynasty, although nothing seemed to suggest that the palliative fueled the commercial appetites of the Arab traders for conquest, subjugation, or, in Chinese perceptions, an opium threat.[1] For centuries to follow, opium did not yet become synonymous or synchronous with imperial expansion. As a commercial practice, the opium trade preceded the age of British-European imperialism without attracting the social or political controversy for which it is known today.

Around 1700, however, a mixture of tobacco and opium began spreading from the Mughal empire to Java, the East Indies, Taiwan, and especially Fujian Province, then part of the Qing empire.[2] At the time, signs that a long imperial embrace of the opium trade would follow were still inchoate, just as its ties to colonial and imperial expansion were still tenuous. During the nineteenth century, Britain, France, and later the Netherlands and the United States as empires targeted Southeast Asia for revenues, territorial resources, and adventure. The opium trade offered satisfaction across all three domains. But before the opium wars brought Asian and British trading paradigms and practices head to head in a political clash, market competition revealed British ambitions on the rise. The British, however, started out from an initial position of inferiority vis-à-vis Asian opium traders. Despite the attractiveness of the opium trade, its complexity resisted the metaphor of a ready harvest. Before it could be harnessed as an investment opportunity of strategic proportions, opium's political economy posed a managerial conundrum. Its internal, intra-Asian organization remained quite inscrutable to the British, French, and Dutch colonial administration up until the late nineteenth century, when they took hold of it across Asia.

But as the opium trade exposed the limited epistemic reach of imperial aspirants, some were determined to meet the challenge of incomprehension with early analytic footwork on the maritime coordination of opium and its regional market composition. The drug traversed rather erratically the formal divide between official and unregistered trade, vacillating as a source of revenue for both British official trading and Chinese smugglers. Caught in an interdependence that could neither be politically unacknowledged nor socially welcomed, British and Chinese opium traders became trading partners, ever since British captains ordered their Indian opium shipments in defiance of the Qing ban. Indian opium shipments were not offloaded directly onto Chinese territory but first offshore by Chinese "fast crab" boats to gigantic opium hulks, the floating warehouses plying the harbor. There, opium shipments were transferred to boats that brought them ashore for Chinese consumption.

The major turning point came in 1757, when the British East India Company (BEIC) received the opium monopoly from the government. This step precipitated international commercial recognition that an Asian opium market existed, seemingly open to those who were able to develop the logistics and infrastructure of long-distance trade. In South Asia, an increase in opium supplies fed the BEIC's opium monopoly, testing the reliability of the British conduit to Chinese opium smokers.[3] The opium trade spurred the rise of the BEIC, making it arguably the financially and territorially most powerful, non-Asian market force within Asia. By the early nineteenth century, the Gujarat coast was under BEIC control, enabling its administration of maritime exports from Malwa in the northwest to the Portuguese ports of Daman and Diu. Inter-imperial cooperation in the opium trade may have begun with the British-Portuguese experiment in prohibition by Marquis Wellesley and the Portuguese Viceroy of Goa, in exchange for British military defense assistance to Portugal against Napoleonic France.[4] By the early nineteenth century, economic opium interests were prominent enough to be traded with military strategic gains in the domestic heartlands of empires. Within the triangular economy between soaring British demand for Chinese tea, paid for by Chinese silver, the BEIC moved opium auctions in Calcutta into the center of its efforts to regain a trade balance with the Qing. The tea that British traders carried from Guangzhou to India thus directly corresponded to the British return trade in opium to the Qing, parked offshore to be carried into the interior by Chinese opium smugglers. In a global perspective, the Latin American movements for independent statehood became a complicating external factor of risk by creating a shortage of silver exports. While Qing silver exports increased during its silver-copper coin crisis in the early decades of the nineteenth century, this came at a cost, with Qing opium imports serving as a substitute for former silver imports. The resulting Qing exposure to the Asian opium economy increasingly dominated by Britain was embedded in a global restructuring of commodity trades.[5]

Lest we understand the advance of the imperially sponsored opium trade as a purely commercial initiative absent any political valence, it is worth taking note of long-standing Asian regimes of opium prohibition prior to imperial claims of the Asian opium market. The BEIC role of expanding the Asian opium economy are by now well known. So is the Qing's comprehensive commitment to opium control across the imperial domain, not only at coastal borders but also crucially at the continental frontiers in the West.[6] But a cross-cutting perspective on less-known opium policies between present-day India and present-day China reveals a different face of opium proponents and opponents across the main region of opium transport between South Asia and East Asia. Bordering on the east coast of the Bay of Bengal and almost bordering the Qing dynasty, Siam, which corresponds to present-day Thailand, presents one window into the Asian opium economy and attempts to rein it in.[7] Buddhist injunctions decreed anti-opium laws as early as 1360. Ayutthaya's Law of the Three Seals (*Kotmai Tra Sam Duang*) subjected violators of the law to severe ostracism. For three days, opium consumers were paraded "around the city on land and on

FIGURE 1.1. The first phase of opium consumption (English pamphlet).

Source: The Chinese Opium Smoker (London: S. W. Partridge & Co., ca 1880). Widener Library, Harvard University.

FIGURE 1.2. The first phase of opium consumption (Chinese pamphlet).

Source: Jie yan xing shi tu. Fuzhou: Min bei sheng shu hui yin fa, Guangxu 26 (1900). Harvard-Yenching Library, Harvard University.

water," imprisoned until presumed detoxification, then sent home on the condition that relatives proved willing to retrieve the culprits from jail. The family would monitor the abstinence of a former convict to enable life after crime. Tellingly, this state system of drug control put a high premium on the family, turning it into the strongest available constraint on social behavior short of prison.[8]

But social law like this stopped at the water's edge, and state control was never as easily asserted in the maritime realm off the coast. Siamese oversight of maritime opium distribution continued to pose a challenge, causing King Ramathibodi I to enact a ban in immediate response to Chinese opium traders, skilled in the opium trade since at least 1282. By the 1510s, opium traders had linked up with Siamese return voyages from Malacca, stepping up the influx of opium into the kingdom. The political capacity to keep the drug literally at bay showed its constraints early, with economic incentives holding the upper hand and state intervention struggling to keep up.

Deficient political controls illustrate how the superiority of economic stimuli over time encouraged supplies from more distant supply regions, leading to elongated trading routes and exacerbating the political dilemma of maritime interdiction. In 1511, after the Portuguese capture of Malacca, opium entered Siamese ports under Ayutthaya not only from Bengal but also from Arabia, as reported by sea captains and envoys to Duarte Barbosa, the brother-in-law and fellow circumnavigator of Ferdinand Magellan.[9] With the Siamese state losing its grip, conflicts with the increasingly assertive presence of imperial commercial fleets sharpened. From the 1710s to the 1730s, Siamese maritime inspectors expressed frequent suspicion over Dutch opium trafficking, leading to confrontations between Siamese patrols and Dutch defense actions and finally the withdrawal of the Dutch East India Company (VOC) from Siam in July 1740.

In Siamese-British relations, it probably did not help that the ship carrying the new British governor of Bengal in 1733 was exposed as a smuggler of opium.[10] Tellingly, with the 1839 outbreak of the First Opium War between China, Siam's close trading partner, and Britain, Siam's long-term foe, the Siamese government promptly decided to step up opium prohibition to the highest level—to include the death penalty.[11] In the 1840s, the Siamese government hired a British missionary, Dr. Dan Beach Bradley, to print nine thousand copies of the royal anti-opium edict, an unprecedented commitment to public anti-drug policy.[12] More than a mere block to imperial market intrusions, Siamese prohibition reflected the personal duty, demanded by Buddhist codes, to cultivate the disciplined exercise of mental concentration. On the flip side, prohibition was part of the state's concern with condemning delirium as mental and moral obstacles. Injunctions in the fifth precept and in the Mangala Sutta against fermented liquors and spirits were well established in Siam and other Southeast Asian settings with Buddhist characteristics, suggesting early social criticism of alcohol and narcotic consumption, centuries before the U.S. Christian version of temperance and prohibition achieved global fame.[13]

In continental Southeast Asia, Siam's resistance was no secret to the British, despite subsequent disavowals of knowledge and responsibility regarding Siam's preferred opium policies. Furthermore, Siam's prohibition regime was not alone. Burma, its northern neighbor, made opium prohibition a top policy priority as well. As in Siam's case, Burma's opium prohibition responded directly to British commercial expansion. During the Konbaung dynasty (1752–1885) of what is today Burma and Myanmar, King Bodawpaya—an expansionist into the kingdoms of Arakan, Manipur, and Assam between 1784 and 1817—backed up the ban on intoxicant and stimulant consumption with the threat of capital offense, paralleling Siam. From both a political and a Buddhist religious perspective, these measures taken by states, although succeeded by anti-opium movements of the social reform type, bore conservative, authoritarian features during the first generations of interdictions.[14] After Burma's defeat by the British in the First Anglo-Burmese War (1824–1826), King Thibaw, the last of his dynasty, ordered the opium ban in 1880. The raison d'état of opium prohibition, however, was not to survive the collapse of the state itself. Burma's unwilling presentation to Queen Victoria as a "New Year's gift" in 1886 put an end to the project of prohibition, a gift presented by none other than Randolph Churchill, the future prime minister's father.[15] Economically, imperially motivated opium trading was too haphazard and punctuated by Asian counterefforts to earn the epithet of an opium strategy.

The First Anglo-Burmese War not only reversed political fortunes but also beckoned with profits for some. Asians participated in the trade, exemplified by prominent Parsi family enterprises, like that of Hormusji Bhicajee, whose ships offered a transport infrastructure even through the disruptions of the Anglo-Burmese clash. With at least equal vigor, other Parsi family enterprises had set their hopes on the China market as a mass consumer for Indian opium, even before the war. Leading Parsi merchants discovered the China market in the 1810s and 1820s, joining the widening participation in the Indian-Chinese opium trade that would become the economically and politically dominant supply route of Asia. Connections between the British and Indian opium trading were closely linked. Ships like the *Ernaad* and the *Ternate* were purchased by pioneering Parsi merchants from the BEIC, evidencing another facet of Asian capitalism before imperial capitalism.[16] Many of Bombay's Parsis shared their commercial success with the Hindu gentry of Calcutta.[17] The lineages of local support for British imperial enterprises that had started with the financial backing of Hindu and Jain banking families for British armies gained maritime extensions in the decades preceding the First Opium War.

A glimpse into episodes of the burgeoning South Asian opium business offers a vivid illustration of opium's significance as a social and political practice beyond happenstance. Caught in rough seas between Bombay and Guangzhou in 1827, Dadabhai Rustomjee was forced into an emergency landing at the island of Huiling San, southwest of Macau. He made good use of the crisis to gather information about the China commodity market. Although a rough sea provided the initial conditions, the result of Rustomjee's inquiries with Chinese maritime authorities served as immediate inspiration for his own decision to join the drug trade. In 1830, Rustomjee's first major opium shipment made its way along the same route, from Bombay to Guangzhou. Even environmental factors, such as storms raging off the China coast, brought unpredictable opportunities for the Indian-Chinese opium trade.[18]

In 1835, Rustomjee's *Sylph*, famed as one of the fastest "opium clippers" of its kind, able to rush opium from Calcutta to Macao in a mere sixteen days, experienced a second episode of escaped shipwreck. Stranded on Bintang Island, the incident triggered an elaborate rescue operation. The opium consignment on the *Sylph*, in Rustomjee's name, was rescued from distress and refloated by the warship *Clive* of the BEIC. The opium, readily recognized as precious cargo that could not be sacrificed, was brought by the *Clive* to Singapore to be dried, repacked, and reshipped to China. According to the account that has survived in the *Parsi,* the cargo consisted of twelve hundred chests. Dadabhai and Manockjee Rustomjee collaborated with Dent and Company to offer the rescued drug at a joint, public auction, "with instructions to remit the net proceeds to the Bank of Bengal," where the commander of the *Clive* could claim them. The Supreme Court of Calcutta duly cooperated in ensuring proper compensation. Drawing on the urgency and dedication visible in opium rescues, it is fair to say that principal Parsi and British opium trading firms were firmly embedded in opium partnerships, including support by the best-placed institutions of the financial sector and judiciary. In turn, comprehensive, cross-institutional support for the political economy of opium trading raised expectations for greater commercial security. To ward off "not merely the perils of the sea but the lurking pirate, the hostile war junk, the insidious smuggler," and Chinese men-of-war, Rustomjee's proudest ships were equipped with guns and a European crew. The first signs that the opium trade was worth guarding by military means did not appear on the battlefield. It became visible on ship decks.[19]

As the opium trade grew for more than a hundred years before the First Opium War, British knowledge of its operations improved, along with the burgeoning determination to claim it for themselves. Indeed, recounting its expansion profiles opium as a highly mobile commodity, compared to other high-demand trades in silver, cotton, or human forced labor. The unique suitability of the opium trade to revenue maximization and commercial expansion heightened the sense of competition between established Asian opium traders and younger, imperial participants in the trade. Thus, at the eve of the First Opium War, many British aspirants to the opium trade liked to believe reports that "practically the whole of the Indo-China opium trade" was "in the hands of Parsis, and as the profits had hitherto been colossal." When Lin Zexu, the Qing's opium commissioner, seized opium from local warehouses and hulks, Parsi losses were thought to be "proportionately great." Other competitors were hit worse.[20] As the First Opium War became the death knell to many Parsi family enterprises of long standing, the opium trade moved still closer into the British imperial fold.

Meanwhile, British supremacy in the expansion of the Asian opium trade began growing beyond the Indian-Chinese nexus. Amid its expansion, the British had become keenly aware of the necessity to rely on a whole array of local divisions of labor in what was a multiplex trading enterprise. British merchants themselves had benefited from Dutch generosity when Dutch opium prohibition applied to VOC merchants but not to their British colleagues frequenting the same ports and markets.[21] Inter-imperial collaboration alerts us to the fact that bilateral trade statistics were less-than-optimal efforts at documentation and in many ways fictions of transparency. The trade volume even of well-known transshipments, complicated by illicit diversions, remains largely obscure today.[22] Prior to the rise of prohibitionist perceptions, imperial administrations often equated opium destinations with potential opium markets and deduced the capacity of those markets from reported estimates of opium demand. Asian opium smuggling flourished around the Dutch East Indies, in Sumatra, Borneo, the Celebes, the Moluccas, and Singapore, territories where the volume of licit and illicit opium flows remained roughly on a par, up to the 1910s. When "the amount smuggled" was "admitted to be large," as at the Royal Commission on Opium of 1895, the comment was given short shrift and consigned to a footnote of the report, like an embarrassing discovery.[23] It is no exaggeration that opium's political economy grew into dimensions that "battled the organizational strategies of all governments globally."[24]

British administrators in India could be cavalier with opium statistics because other imperial, opium-trading powers in the Asian region behaved similarly. The French Indo-Chinese government imported "to Saigon direct from Calcutta," a dimension incompletely captured in British statistical reports. Occasionally someone would cryptically admit that "France participates indirectly in the opium trade in China."[25] But against all appearances, the British and the French could trace their opium cooperation to the immediate aftermath of their war from 1756 to 1757. Imperial stories circulated that the British East India Company had paid the French government one million francs, known as the mythical "million of Chandernagor," in return for the French limitation to sell two hundred opium chests per year at the market price.[26] In a different version, Britain paid a tribute of three hundred opium cases to France in return for guarantees that the French would not intervene in the British opium monopoly.[27] In the course of British and European imperial expansion into Asia, interimperial cooperation never disappeared, enabling the opium trade to flourish between British India, Siam, Burma, and French Indochina, to Singapore, British Malaya, Hong Kong, the Dutch East Indies, and the Spanish, later American, Philippines, then north along the China coast to Formosa (Taiwan), before and after Japanese colonization, and Manchuria. All colonial opium regimes in the region helped integrate this massive drug trade and augment its unprecedented scope and complexity.[28] Across Asia, Meiji Japan alone remained unscathed by the waves of opium trading that washed across Asian societies, for reasons that will be explained later.[29]

AGAINST the background of Siamese and Burmese efforts to stem the influx of opium, the Qing effort to maintain opium control does not appear as exceptional as national histories would oftentimes have it. Outright prohibition during the Qing dynasty responded to rising consumption and found expression in the opium ban of 1729, the now legendary precedent set by the Yongzheng emperor. Up to the mid-nineteenth century, the Qing's western frontier became a focal point of imperial control efforts.[30] In practice, however, the Qing state struggled to achieve a level of political control that saturated the empire's territory and social behavior. Illicit but tenacious poppy cultivation survived on its continental frontier in the west. Across its extended coastline in the east and south, illicit opium imports from India seeped in. Under the inescapable impact of the British Indian opium economy, Qing monitoring of maritime imports remained haphazard and became a politically convenient limbo preferable to confronting a superior merchant force on terms likely to be even more disagreeable. On the other hand, British cultural arguments at the time blamed Manchu corruption for a deficient rule of law. Meanwhile, few Chinese knew that British control over its maritime borders at home did not provide a shining example of British rule of law. In reality, smuggled imports of tea were just as responsible for producing a British tea culture as opium imports were responsible for producing a Chinese opium culture.[31]

British objections to and violations of the Qing opium ban did not give open support to British contraventions. Instead, British justifications for opium trading came in the guise not of political convenience but of the higher logic and ethic of free trade, with its lofty aspirations of social advancement for all participants. On the level of British parliamentary and diplomatic debate, an economic paradigm cast the opium trade largely as a nonpolitical phenomenon of an ethically neutral market playing to Chinese consumers. Importantly, a consensus was discernible whereby demand fueled foreign supply, and "so long as there is a demand" for opium in China, "it is certain to be brought."[32]

AFTER DECADES of historiographic debate on the Qing's opium position at the eve of the First Opium War, most historians now see 1836 as the key date when Qing deliberations to possibly relax opium prohibition collapsed. In that year, the junior minister of the Court of Imperial Sacrifices, Xu Naiji, failed to obtain sufficient support for his proposal to flex the existing prohibition regime. Like other aging empires, the Qing's political volatility was reflected in policy debates on the opium trade and opium consumption. What they revolved around was that the status quo of nominal prohibition had become untenable and had failed to deliver in terms of policy implementation across maritime trading provinces. The sharpest conflict of opium interpretations was not within the Qing administration but pitted the growing Qing perception of a foreign threat against British professions of political innocence. When the two interpretations of an opium problem clashed irreconcilably, many agreed with one of China's most prominent chroniclers of both opium wars, Xia Xie, who argued that opium had arrived because foreigners, frustrated by the inability to import opium by fair means, were driven to seek profits by foul means, implying the violation and circumvention of Qing legislation and coastal authority.[33] Qing emperor Daoguang himself had long perceived British Indian opium imports as a violation of China's domestic opium ban. The exposure of Prince Zhuang's opium smoking in the heart of the Forbidden City alarmed the emperor.

But even if rampant illegal British supplies off the coast were to blame for the spread of opium use up to the highest echelons of the Qing administration, it took political measures to escalate the British-Chinese relationship toward an open confrontation. The key role fell to the imperial anti-opium commissioner, Lin Zexu. Others, to be sure, shared his determination, be it Qishan, the main lobbyist behind the imperial anti-opium promulgations, who launched his own opium crackdown in Tianjin from August to November 1838 and confiscated 150,000 taels; Deng Tingzhen, who seized 260,000 taels in Guangdong; or the officials who supported them at court.[34] It was Lin Zexu, however, who incurred the wrath of Britain by destroying a major opium shipment, an act that more than a century of Chinese nationalism has now elevated into the annals of Qing's encounter with imperialism. Hailed as one of modern China's premier national heroes, precisely because of the tragedy attached to his role, Lin's now iconic status owes much to Chinese anti-opium mobilization from the 1870s, perhaps more than to his supposed supremacy among prohibitionist officials at court.[35] But in national and nationalist memory, Lin's legendary fame in the late 1830s put his actions on a par with the United States' most desperate, symbolic, and, in hindsight, foundational show of nationalist resistance: the Boston Tea Party of 1773.

Certainly, the scale of Lin's action did not pale in comparison. More than 20,000 opium chests surrendered by the British to the Chinese, with an average 140 pounds per chest, amounted to 3 million pounds of opium. It took five hundred workers; three trenches, each of which was 150 feet long, seventy-five feet wide, and seven feet deep; unknown amounts of salt and lime; and twenty-three days in June 1839 to send the drug to the bottom of the sea.[36] If anything, the amount of opium destroyed by Lin offered irrefutable evidence of British commercial determination to sponsor the drug trade relentlessly. At its core, British opium trading was characterized by a maximalist investment strategy.

It was the disruption of this strategy by the Qing state that led to the conflict known as the First Opium War. Lin Zexu prayed to the spirit of the Southern Sea to avert the divine wrath provoked by maritime pollution through opium. The intensity of his religious invocation reflected the depth of his political revulsion: "But alas, poison has been allowed to creep in unchecked, till at last barbarian smoke fills the market. . . . If it [opium] had been cast into the flames, the charred remains might have been collected. Far better to hurl it into the depths, to mingle with the giant floods." Lin prayed, to continue in Arthur Waley's evocative translation, that "cryptic influences may rid China of this baleful thing."[37] The sea spirits may not have been pleased, but at least they could not blame him for a lack of political zeal. The public, too, had to recognize in the ceremonial spectacle of opium destruction that this defense of Qing opium control made a charismatic case for the emperor's commitment to banish the drug from the imperial realm. What made the dispute boil into a full-fledged war was the Qing blockade, which deprived British ships off the coast of food and other supplies.

On September 4, 1839, the Battle of Kowloon unleashed the First Opium War. The question of whether opium was the casus belli remains subject to alternative historiographic priorities. Long- and short-term explanations chart distinct developments of political escalation, all of which were historically merged into one another, without yielding one overarching teleology. A key element explaining the conflict is that Qing assertions of its own maritime order backfired. Britain retaliated with the cannon, attacking the legitimacy of that very order. The clash between Qing and British policy positions and cultural priorities found a conclusion in 1842, when the Qing was forced into defeat. Ceding Hong Kong and opening extraterritorial and extrajudicial treaty ports to foreign residents were unprecedented acts in Chinese history. Alongside severe curtailments of what today would be called national sovereignty—the ability of a state to decide the terms of economic, social, and political encounters across its borders and the international recognition of that ability—the conflict from 1839 to 1842 ushered in the age of imperialism and, for some, the beginning of the end for the Manchu regime.[38] Regarding the opium issue, the Qing was forced to pay an indemnity for the opium destroyed by Lin. The detailed chronicling of military operations and wartime diplomacy has been ably summarized elsewhere.[39] What is important here is that the peace treaty refrained from legalizing the trade officially.[40]

However, once the international politics and the international law concerning opium entered a period of disconnect, there was much consternation on both sides. In Chinese national history, the familiar picture does not quite capture these complexities. The opium wars are recognized as China's zero hour, as points of no return, revolutionizing the Qing dynasty's relations with the world of Western maritime empires. Twice the Qing dynasty was defeated, each time leading not to greater isolation but to an incremental and forceful integration into the world trade system of global imperialism. But contrary to the passionate pioneers of British free trade, the Qing's unwilling, even imposed, centrality to the economic aspirations of global empires was a perilous one. And importantly, the opium trade drew the Qing economy on terms not of their own into a transformative process of the Asian region: the opium trade was never a neat bilateral commerce, running, say, between Britain and China, with none of China's immediate neighborhood of Asia being centrally affected.

As the opium wars have come to signify China's zero hour in national history, passionate drug aversions, so frequently revived in rounds of mobilization throughout China's twentieth century and into the twenty-first, have often blurred the line between memory revival and historical analysis. In at least one crucial respect, however, Lin did not lay the basis for anti-opium movements to come. On July 5, 1839, Lin himself explained his rationale behind opium destruction. Reporting on his communication with American observers of opium destruction, he told them through his interpreter: "Now that the Heavenly Court has banned opium and that new regulations of a very severe kind have been agreed upon, you people who have not sold opium in the past and who will no doubt never think of bringing it in the future, must do more than that. You must persuade the foreigners of every country to devote themselves from now onward to legitimate trade, by which they can make immense profits, and not seek to enrich themselves in defiance of the ban, and so wantonly cast themselves into the meshes of the law." Lin reported that the foreigners understood and respected the admonition, although British sources remain silent on this event.[41]

Certainly Lin's explanation showed that he overestimated foreign assent. Contrary to future anti-opium movements that mobilized a perpetual front of opposition, he put high hopes in international leadership by powers other than China. Curiously, this very early proposal for a U.S.-China alliance against drugs went unheeded for the moment, only to find some fulfillment seventy years later. Beyond the opium issue as such, the type of Western encroachments of the peace of 1842 came to characterize Qing relations with the British and European overseas empires. Backed by a growing system of formal foreign enclaves, gunboat diplomacy, and informal imperialism, opium became a firm pillar of Britain's free-trade regime in China.[42] In the Qing perspective, the expansive array of British demands at war's end confirmed earlier suspicions. Opium very much appeared to be the casus belli and remained an economic objective of the peace order.

No longer could British imperial finance be ignored as a prerogative of imperial power and opium as a prerogative of imperial finance. Reversely, anti-opium voices in China, and on a smaller volume in Britain, Europe, and North America, became the subject of sad ridicule. With its victory, Britain eliminated opium control from Qing China's repertoire of feasible policy options. The Qing realization of this new predicament would shape its political calculus for decades to come.

To the Qing, the British victory of 1842 also failed to clarify many questions of political norms. That perception sprang less from a British diplomatic gamble than from British domestic opinion. One of the numerous news commentators in Britain who rushed to support Viscount Palmerston, Britain's foreign secretary and future prime minister, argued in the *Times* that "notwithstanding all our affected or virtuous self-denial of the opium trade, we have no power to control the acts of other European or American traders in China."[43] This spoke to the fact that the vocal British assessments of American opium interests diverged significantly from Lin Zexu's assessment. On these grounds, opium prohibition in British India appeared futile. In opium policy, the famed panache of British imperial administrators suddenly collapsed with resignation before forces greater than themselves. It almost appeared as some structural necessity that absolved them of political initiative and discussions of political accountability.

In this context, Britain's critique of China's ineffective control became a serious argument: "If China can prevent her subjects from buying and consuming opium," Palmerston claimed, "the trade in it would cease at once of itself."[44] China's rule of law, by contrast, was lackluster at best: "But as long experience has shown that the Government of China has not the power of putting down the use of opium, and is equally unable to prevent its being smuggled into the Empire." To Palmerston, the impossibility of drug control narrowed the range of policy options to one: "for the Emperor to legalize the sale by barter, and to fix a duty on it."[45] Here, opium legalization came to constitute the only feasible remedy to an international problem of chiefly economic concern.

This fit well with what Henry Pottinger—the superintendent of British trade in China, whose victories in the First Opium War earned him the first governorship of the new British colony of Hong Kong—had stated in 1841. If there was an "opium evil," he averred, it affected distribution rather than consumption. Deploying a later famous comparison, he insisted that the use of opium was "not a hundredth portion of the evils" from those arising "in England from spirituous liquors."[46] Pottinger's personal experience had not yielded "one single instance of its decidedly bad effects." This critique strategically made a forceful care for highlighting the operational efficiency of the opium economy while downgrading its social effects.[47]

Meanwhile, the political economy of the Asian opium market continued to attract colonial powers just below Britain's preeminence: Spain, Portugal, the Netherlands, France, the United States, and, in the early twentieth century, Japan. The sprawling opium trade was now acknowledged as a multi-imperial enterprise, underpinned by Chinese overseas syndicates that reached Siam, Cochin China, the Philippine Islands, Java, Borneo, and "all the islands and territories in the Eastern seas." The multiplicity of Southeast Asian destinations, transshipment ports, and sale opportunities, an expert argued at the time of the First Opium War, were the means by which "so certain and lucrative a trade as that of opium will surely find a vent."[48]

Simultaneously, global candidates in rival opium production were identified by the British as Turkey and Persia. On a more experimental basis, Mexico and South American states aspired to join "where the plant would assuredly find a soil and climate suitable to its propagation and growth; where adventurers would readily avail themselves of the profitable production which we so heedlessly sacrificed, and traders possessed of no scruples about its transit, to supply the places where it would meet a certain and lucrative demand."[49] These British imperial assessments testified to a new stage in global assessments of opium's attractiveness. This Asian commodity trade now attracted global economic attention.

The First Opium War had passed only for a few years when its consequences provoked the vision of China as an opium market in some American eyes. The U.S. secretary of the navy, John P. Kennedy, derived his hopes from China's opium, pushing for a transpacific expansion of the U.S. steamship industry by incorporating archipelagos such as Hawai'i as coaling stations. But Kennedy's loftiest fantasies did not come to fruition: the Chinese people did not convert en masse from Indian opium to his beloved American tobacco. Long after Kennedy, under the People's Republic of China, tobacco consumption in China would indeed fill the lungs and lives of a new generation, the ancestors of whom had often been drawn to opium.[50]

It took far less time in the aftermath of the First Opium War for Qing-British relations to draw the drug into new political roles and functions. A central development was the search for policy convergence, shared between London and Beijing. The basis on which opium legalization in 1860 emerged was laid in the British-Chinese negotiations between the two opium wars, covering the 1840s and 1850s. The key series of exchanges on the opium issue were inconspicuously titled *Correspondence Relating to China* and *Papers Relating to the Opium Trade*.[51] The compilation itself served a diplomatic purpose. There was "no chance of effecting anything as to the legalization of the opium trade," one British official remarked, "except by transmitting the whole of the correspondence on that subject direct to Pekin [*sic*]." Perhaps for the same reason, the correspondence skirted the profit-making aspects of the trade. Viscount Palmerston, Britain's secretary of state for foreign affairs, insisted as early as February 1841, with the First Opium War still raging, that British interest in opium legalization be presented as a diplomatic preference rather than a brute *diktat*. Legalization was not to be pursued at any cost. Palmerston ordered Rear-Admiral George Elliot and his cousin, Captain Charles Elliot, "to make some arrangement with the Chinese Government for the admission of opium into China as an article of lawful commerce." But crucially, in taking the initiative, they were to bring "this matter before the Chinese Plenipotentiaries" but "state that the admission of opium into China as an article of legal trade, is not one of the demands which you have been instructed to make."[52]

Much misunderstanding has haunted posthumous interpretations of Qing-British opium relations, not least due to the politicization of the issue since the late nineteenth century, to a point where attributions of political motivation are accepted without much regard for documentary evidence. It is therefore well worth considering original key statements in some detail. To prevent a British-Chinese misunderstanding, Palmerston explicitly emphasized a second time what the Elliots were to convey: "You will not enter upon the subject of it in such a way as to lead the Chinese Plenipotentiaries to think that it is the intention of Her Majesty's Government to use any compulsion in regard to this matter."[53] In May 1841, Palmerston continued to demonstrate awareness of the high sensitivity of legalization when reiterating in his directive to Henry Pottinger, who succeeded Charles Elliot as British superintendent of trade. This time, his terms were more direct than tactical and expressed the official position: "Her Majesty's Government make [sic] no demand in regard to this matter; for they have no right to do so. The Chinese Government is fully entitled to prohibit the importation of opium, if it pleases; and British subjects who engage in a contraband trade must take the consequences of doing so."[54] Palmerston wanted the Qing government to "make up its mind to legalize the importation of opium upon payment of a duty" for their own benefit, as he argued patronizingly, noting "the considerable increase of revenue" into the Qing's "public coffers." On the greater revenues flowing into British coffers, his instructions kept silent.[55] In sum, legalization, according to this British position, was only acceptable as the outcome of negotiations and not as a result of imperialist imposition.

The Chinese response to the elaborate British proposal was curt and covered one-eighth of Palmerston's main letter. "On the withdrawal of the prohibition against opium it is not expedient at this time hastily to make any representations to the Throne," the Qing imperial commissioners declared. Imperial opium prohibition, they reassured the British, would target the limited range of "the soldiery and people of the country" and leave "the merchant vessels of various countries" outside its jurisdiction.[56] Qing opposition to British legalization remained firm. Palmerston's hope to entice the Qing to a voluntary renunciation of its imperial opium ban failed to pay off.

In the British-Chinese interwar period between 1842 and 1856, the British Indian opium economy continued its growth unimpeded. The Bengal Commission reports recorded an increase from 30,108 Calcutta and Bombay opium chests in 1842–1843 to 68,003.5 chests in 1857–1858, equaling a margin of value from 28,203,520 rupees to 72,410,318 rupees. The trade's concurrent bloom made the distanced formalism of the Chinese-British negotiations all the more conspicuous.[57] There is little evidence that British aloofness to trade dynamics was an exercise in diplomatic evasiveness. Information on Indian opium exports in Whitehall remained more a prospect than documentation. It could and should have been much more readily available. In 1843, Pottinger thanked Vice-Admiral William Parker for "having brought the subject of the recent increase in the opium trade to my notice, although I had before heard of it." Pottinger had to press for the recognition of this fact: "The revenue derived from India," he wrote, "must not, in a discussion like the present, be lost sight of." His emphasis spoke to the increasing priority of opium revenues within Britain's empire of finance. On the political record, Pottinger noted that he had "spared no pains or exertion to persuade the Government of China to legalise it, but hitherto without effect." Meanwhile, the British considered the Chinese practice of receiving and rejecting opium at will "beyond our control."[58]

Imperial commissioner Qiying, a Manchu official of the Plain Blue Banner and powerful viceroy of Liangguang Province, acted as the Qing negotiator in both opium war treaty settlements, serving as a key figure of Qing foreign relations during the most taxing crises facing the dynasty. Given his direct line of communication with the British in the specific opium correspondence that followed the First Opium War, it is particularly instructive to follow his engagement with the international dispute and joint Qing-British attempts to find a resolution. On the subject of opium smuggling—the central point of contention in early British communications—Qiying professed as little sympathy as the British. But he placed the responsibility for distribution and for Indian supplies on the British side. The Qing's principled insistence on prohibition remained unimpressed by British legalization pressure. The "proposed measure" of legalization "cannot be carried into operation," and "it is therefore useless to discuss the point."[59] He acknowledged a British proclamation that prohibited British subjects from selling opium "in the inner waters" but noted that Britain's record of coastal law enforcement was as lackluster as the Qing's. Qiying knew that the problem of controlling opium distribution in the administrative gray zone between British delivery ships anchoring off the coast and smugglers taking opium the last distance ashore dated back to the days of the East India Company's opium trade.[60]

However, neither the Qing nor Britain was ready to recognize the embarrassing fact that both had been unable to rein in the unregistered trade, what would today be called drug trafficking. Neither party, locked into the accusatory mode of diplomatic shaming, acknowledged this reciprocity, which was central to the dilemma of opium imports into the Qing empire but more basically a shared dilemma that fell short of political expectations on both sides. Keeping face emboldened each antagonist in the insistence on self-justification. Mutual combativeness moved both sides deeper into diplomatic deadlock, while the political facades of each turned into mirror images.

Not to "go over the old story again" was Qiying's plea to end a British-Chinese debate over opium legalization that had turned wearisome. Qiying did object to free trade as such. With four Chinese treaty ports now open as per the Treaty of Nanjing, he acknowledged, "The merchants of all nations" could reap "an ample harvest of profit" if they "would only content themselves with bringing legal articles of traffic to China. . . . Why should they persist in selling this baneful opium," necessitating legal barriers to the trade?[61] In this perspective, the prospect of allowing the free trade paradigm to orient foreign commercial relations was realistic. The question, then, was no longer free trade as one of the oldest objectives of British imperial pressure. It had become a question of how indispensable opium was as a prime commodity of free trade in Asia under imperialism.

On the British side, going over the old story again became a diplomatic strategy of its own, signaling that whether in war as in 1839 or in peace as in 1842, opium priorities did not just fade away. Contrary to Qiying's hopes, the British pressed ahead to push for legalization "by the continual repetition of such representations" to induce "the rulers of China . . . to legalize the trade."[62]

In the first few years after the First Opium War, British frustration over unfulfilled expectations neared obsession rather than relinquishment of the legalization agenda. The British described legalization as a "desirable measure, the only one, in fact, that is now wanting to render safe and permanent the newly-established system of foreign trade in this country," based on the Nanjing Treaty of 1842.[63] The claim to inevitability meant to boost political support: "There can hardly exist a doubt," Pottinger informed the foreign secretary in 1844, that economic and political developments "will lead to its eventual legalization."[64] Internal government correspondence urged "to push the subject" in the years to come, much like prophets of revolution who enact the change that, they claim, has to happen.[65]

Whitehall saw little risk in the boldness of this pursuit. Britain's spectacular victory over Lin Zexu and other Qing anti-opiumists had "removed," some opined, "nearly all, if not the whole," of the "odium."[66] But as far as opium legalization was concerned, Britain's political and symbolic superiority lacked a legal corollary. The Nanjing Treaty did not legalize opium, and the Qing were adamant that this arrangement "cannot be changed under any circumstances."[67] Against the backdrop of Qing resistance, British policy positions after the First Opium War were strikingly volatile. When 1842 was "adduced as a sort of argument against the legalization" by the Qing, British realpolitik charged ahead, leaving any traces of legalism in the dust.[68]

Fighting over the causes of the opium trade, each side used its own explanation to identify different drivers of opium's half-illicit political economy. In British statements, the argument of supply as a response to demand continued undeterred: "Where there is no demand or market . . . merchants . . . will not go."[69] As for Chinese opium consumption as a cultural habit, it fit the dominant Western clichés of Chinese social depravity and deficient self-control. Beyond British perceptions and claims, the question of Chinese consumption became central to the opium debate itself. The Qing as mandated guardian of the people's moral integrity was "obliged to issue prohibitions in order to put a stop to it; for prohibiting smoking is to preserve life." If "instructions" alone failed to deter consumers, "punishment due to their crime and transgression" would "make them more careful for the future." In other words, just because a social problem persisted or grew, it did not mean that the government had to surrender its principles stance and give in. Smokers had become "almost innumerable." Still, social ethics held that "opium is a commodity injurious to man," and "those who traffic and smoke it, do it from a want of self-love." This made opium consumption first and foremost a threat to society itself. A society with rampant drug consumption was its own worst enemy. Legal compromise, Qiying argued, could serve as a sophisticated political solution to a problem spurred by foreign economic supplies and exacerbated by domestic patterns of consumption. Opium responsibilities should be determined by the nationality of the offender: British law for British offenders and Qing jurisdiction for Chinese offenders.[70]

Far from isolationist or inward looking, the Qing deployed representatives like Qiying to have an active role in the international analysis of Chinese domestic opium consumption and, which is virtually forgotten today, of the British Indian opium system. The results of this proactive Qing commitment to untangle the opium problem in its international complexity can speak for itself. "Among the different countries that furnish opium," Qiying informed Pottinger, "we find that Bengal, Bombay, and Madras, supply the most . . . which are subject to your honourable nation." Qiying used his knowledge of India to press Britain into a coalition of Western powers—the exact opposite of the proverbial divide and rule. "We must look up to the Honourable Plenipotentiary first and foremost to prohibit English merchants to engage" in opium sales, to "set a bright example to all other nations." Addressing the abiding British imperial concern with its own glory, Qiying encouraged Pottinger to take the lead in international control to ameliorate the bilateral relationship: British "difficulties" would become "infinitely less" and "our labour infinitely lighter," with "our friendship . . . very much strengthened and cemented."[71] Pulling together foreign policy knowledge and a renewed proposal for a multilateral anti-opium accord was reminiscent of Lin Zexu's call for U.S. leadership against drugs. It also defied the British and European caricature of the Qing mind-set as defined by ignorance.

But unimpressed by what was effectively a template of today's global drug control, Pottinger argued: "The many large kingdoms and provinces of Hindoostan . . . not immediately under the British Government" marginalized rather than highlighted British responsibility. And where Indian poppy cultivation was under British supervision, it served the best interests of the Indian farmers, who could "acquire a subsistence for themselves and families." Once again, let us correlate these statements with what was left unsaid. Pottinger remained silent on the active British inducements, financial or by brute force, to make this crop an integral part of Indian agriculture.[72]

Although incompatible, the two rationalizations hardened into a Sino-British retrenchment despite established communications and even the physical transmission of the correspondence documents. Every new round of negotiations drifted toward increasingly predictable discordance. Communications became less and less an effort to represent goodwill or acknowledge good faith. Half of the vicious cycle was self-referentiality. Like two wrestlers unable to disentangle, the dispute moved from clinch to deadlock, narrowing the scope of political imagination on each side.

Looking ahead, the wider world of empires failed to respond to Qing calls for international cooperation in drug control, which did not lack in originality. The reputational context first suggested by Qiying in the 1840s fell into the proverbial dustheap of history, at least for the time being. In the same vein, Guo Songtao, the Qing's first diplomatic representative in Britain, made a third attempt in the 1870s to convince British anti-opium

FIGURE 1.3. Opium smoker admitting guilt to his parents (English pamphlet).

Source: The Chinese Opium Smoker (London: S. W. Partridge & Co., ca 1880). Widener Library, Harvard University.

FIGURE I.4. Opium smoker admitting guilt to his parents (Chinese pamphlet).

Source: Jie yan xing shi tu. Fuzhou: Min bei sheng shu hui yin fa, Guangxu 26 (1900). Harvard-Yenching Library, Harvard University.

organizations that "other countries beside England" and Qing "must co-operate in order to make the abolition possible."[73] The analogy to slavery was not lost in this choice of words, as we shall soon see in related contexts.

But it took more than sixty years, until 1909, for a U.S.-Chinese initiative to make the old Qing dream of international drug control come true. Arguments alone, however congruent with twentieth-century priorities, did not carry the clout to bring about international political change. As the agenda of international control stuttered across more than half a century, it required a more encompassing change to render an idea once thought fruitless a resounding success. That change shifted the terms, levers, and stakes of the opium debate from the domain of international diplomacy to the less charted terrain of transnational mobilization. But before that resolution entered the difficult birth of global drug control, the pendulum had to swing back entirely, toward outright legalization. For that to happen, the opium problem underwent an emergency unprecedented even by the First Opium War: a crisis of two wars folded into one.

THE EXTERNAL CHALLENGE that tipped the context of the opium debate in favor of legalization, more than any diplomacy, did away with most political rationalizations by the Qing and by the British. Six years before the Second Opium War, the Qing was already plunged into a state of war. With the dynasty's strength already undermined, the Second Opium War cut into a damaged regime in 1856. Despite its name, a focus exclusively on the Second Opium War fails to bring into relief the conjoint domestic and foreign crisis. Prolonged and multipronged, the twin challenges of civil war and foreign aggression mutually constituted each other in their simultaneous assault on the Qing's sovereign control.

The opium emergency that hit the Qing dynasty was a product of one of its most severe civil wars. In 1850, the Taiping Rebellion targeted nothing less than the Qing's raison d'être by mounting a brutal and sustained crisis. The rebellion's mission was to shake the dynasty to its very core by offering, indeed demanding, a spiritual alternative to the Mandate of Heaven. The Taiping fight for a "heavenly kingdom" aimed to replace the Manchu regime with an incarnate political megaproject inspired by the charismatic and occasionally wordy Taiping leader Hong Xiuquan. His metaphorical self-enthronement as the son of the Christian God gave license to unprecedented manslaughter, with those caught by the imagery of his eschatological utopia following the enactment of his vision with fierce determination. While historians have been divided about Hong legacy in the context of

Chinese national history, many have argued that his radicalization was not foreordained. In the early stages of his self-initiated conversion, Hong did not have "the faintest inkling, as he began during the 1840s to preach to small groups of farmers and migrant workers . . . , that the trail of events set in motion by his visions would lead to the deaths of millions of people, and would require a decade of the concentrated military and fiscal energies of some of China's greatest statesmen to suppress."[74] But ultimately Hong committed to popular savagery to topple the Qing regime because it was the only sociopolitical order standing in the way of his newly aggrandized divinity.

A serious practical consequence of the military and spiritual havoc wrought by Taiping armies was the financial depletion of Qing coffers. The ensuing wartime crisis sapped state resources to force a radical change of direction in state thinking and practice regarding the opium problem. The unraveling threat of political destabilization made Qing wartime taxation of opium one of the very last remaining sources of emergency revenue to the Qing's provincial governments along the coast, impelling a change of position that decades of British diplomatic pressure had failed to achieve. To this, the military success of the Taiping insurrectionist armies was key. With ranks swelling to half a million, they expanded their social and territorial control from Guangxi Province to the northeast, invading the wealthy provinces of Jiangxi, Zhejiang, southern Anhui, and eastern Hubei. Among the less direct victims, Lin Zexu, the Qing's legendary anti-opium pioneer, died en route to the anti-Taiping front. Ironically, opium policy was one of those areas where Qing and Taiping visions of social control matched rather than clashed. The Taiping's own opium ban rather resembled the prohibitionist edge of the Qing policy repertoire. Extending the parallels from principle to practice, the Taiping—like the Qing—struggled to enforce the ban effectively. The "consumption of opium was enormous, and the vice universal," reported John Bowring, the governor of Hong Kong on the Taiping, surveilled "immediately under our eyes and observation." Save for a biographical continuity, little seems to connect this criticism with his later unleashing of the Second Opium War and his order to have Canton shelled. Bowring insisted that "the chiefs" were "particularly addicted to it, while, among the junks, whether piratical or patriotic . . . opium smoking prevails, without, as I believe, a solitary exception."[75]

Across law, social custom, and the contradictions between them, the Taiping encountered the same opium dilemma as their declared enemy, the Qing. Interestingly, neither the Taiping's nominal opium ban nor their likely violations have become prominent parts of their historical legacy. Even Communist celebrations of the Taiping as proto-revolutionaries do not credit them with the noble cause of opium suppression.[76] Meanwhile, Bowring's critique indicates that the British-Qing cleavage was as deep as the British-Taiping cleavage. Neither Taiping nor Qing prohibition impressed the British. Within this triangle, no one opium policy could serve as a point of orientation, even by way of a counterpoint, for the others.

The war induced a concerted effort of information gathering. British diplomats monitored Qing opium policy planning through its official correspondence with the emperor, the imperial censors as overseers of official integrity, and the provincial administrations along the coast. On January 4, 1853, a paper trail emerged, which, albeit less conspicuous than the Pottinger-Qiying exchange, offered a glimpse of a new legalization opportunity. On that date, a memorial revealed that its author "does not hesitate to point out the mine of wealth which lies unworked in the opium trade, and defends the policy of making it contribute to the expenses of the State."[77]

Through Consul Rutherford Alcock, Bowring learned that the initiative stemmed "from a high authority." The proposal appeared in the Qing's foremost government paper, the *Peking Gazette*, which presented "the daily record of Imperial decrees and rescripts, and of reports or memorials to the throne together with a brief notice of Imperial and official movements, forming a species of Court Circular."[78] The *North China Herald* translated the issues of the *Gazette*, known in Chinese as *jingbao*, into English. As a result, the *Gazette* was hailed as far as the United States as "the oldest newspaper in the world . . . established in 911," and "the formal record" unraveling "the movement of the administrative wheels" of the Qing's vast political system.[79] If official dissent in wartime was already unusual, its prominent publication merited even greater attention.

The author of the memorial was Wu Tingpu. His document, "very long and elaborate," appeared revolutionary to the British but fell in fact into his regular responsibilities in the Military Affairs section of the Imperial Censorship Office in Beijing. Wu responded to the imperial edict of September 15, 1852, on raising military funds against the Taiping threat.[80] Contrary to the cliché among British politicians and pundits who decried Qing policy making as helplessly lost in an arcane Oriental ritual, established Qing procedure paved the way to the first serious legalization proposal after the First Opium War. An earlier proposal of January 16, 1851, by Tang Yunsong, the imperial censor of Huguang, was ignored by the emperor, by the *Gazette,* and by the British, although its emphasis on rampant abuse under the guise of opium prohibition—from wrongful accusations of opium smoking for extortion to banditry under the pretext of official opium investigations—would have strengthened Wu's case.[81]

Wu's legalization proposal can be analyzed as comprising two levels. One unraveled a programmatic exercise in political ethics; the other presented a sober assessment of prior prohibitionist policy performance. "Of two advantages you must choose the greatest; of two injuries, exclude the deepest," the proposal opined. Political maxims had to adjust to current political conditions, even if the latter changed radically and swiftly. As Wu averred, if even Confucius himself "did not attempt to stop the fixed course of events," then "a new policy has to be adjusted to the altered state of things." Political flexibility of this kind did not jeopardize but actually secured strategic interests. The object of a pragmatic opium policy was, after all, the "assurance of permanency." Anticipating later, analogous arguments in the Atlantic world, Wu believed in a comparative approach to drug toleration. "Tobacco and spirituous liquors," he explained, had been "prohibited by the Ming dynasty" but "now yield a large revenue"—a precedent that could justify a reversal of opium policies from prohibition to legalization. Crucially, the social damage wrought by opium was overdrawn, according to Wu. To the perception that the drug rendered users "incapable of business and induces disease," he responded that "there is nothing in the world but what proves injurious in excess. . . . It is self-control alone that will obviate baneful effects."[82] With moral education, the politics of prohibition would become obsolete.

So unorthodox was Wu's reinterpretation of the opium problem that a trail of newspaper coverage reached via Hong Kong all the way to Munich in southern Germany.[83] More importantly, British political attention would decide whether or not Wu's proposal would open up a diplomatic initiative. "For us," the British consular interpreter Thomas Taylor Meadows commented, "the chief point is, that he ultimately proposes a duty of 1 tael on each 'piece' (ball of opium, which, he states, weights, on an average, three catties and of which thirty-three go to a chest)." Meadows immediately followed with a calculation of the financial benefits in response to Wu. "The price of a chest he estimates at about 300 taels. This proposed duty would be about 11 per cent." China as an opium market, access to which had for so long been refused by the Qing, now became the focus of British commercial and geopolitical strategy. If all ports "from Kwan-tung to the Yellow Sea" were to enter the system proposed, it could yield an "annual revenue of 7,000,000 taels," Meadows augured. This revenue was presently lost to unregistered traffickers.[84]

Wu's own strategic considerations cannot be reduced to their British reception, of course. The most desirable function of a liberalized policy, in his view, was the harmonization of cultural and social relations between Britain and China: "Doubts and contradictions in the intercourse between

Chinese and foreigners will be removed, and the germs of trouble extinguished."[85] This aim was as welcome to the British as was the prospect of financial profit maximization. But Wu formulated it in a manner that, although justifiable in Chinese eyes, risked the wrath of British official readers. With fatal candor, he closed on an anti-foreign note, provoking British commentators to dismiss the entire proposal as "ludicrous nonsense."[86] A proposal moving closer to the terrain of British legalization interests than any other fell victim to the intercultural fallout it was meant to alleviate.

The false start pointed to two new trajectories. British receptiveness to Qing policy reforms was scant. This British disinterest reflected misperceptions. For example, they failed to recognize that Wu's proposal moved within growing support for legalization, including the emperor himself. At the same time, the Qing's official guardian of prohibition, Xianfeng, had requested the rank and file of his Grand Secretariat, the Privy Council, nine heads of the independent bureaus, and Censor Zhang Wei to scrutinize two legalization proposals between mid- and late December 1852, only weeks before the date of Wu's memorial. Furthermore, the emperor's response to Wu was earlier and more favorable than the British response.[87]

Wartime heightened the pressure on prohibition. Taiping armies advanced into the wealthy outskirts of Shanghai, making the emergency as much military as financial.[88] By summer 1855, the Qing was forced to take countermeasures: the purchase of offices and titles (*juan shu*), compulsory loans to the government, and the hasty imposition of internal transit and sales taxation—dubbed "the tax of one-thousandth" (*lijin*) and known to the British as "likin."[89] To the British, the likin became the single most objectionable Qing legislation of the crisis. At the same time, its establishment showed a Qing regime creating its own financial prerogatives at a time of critical vulnerability.

Among Qing governors along the coast, faith in the desirability of maintaining the opium ban began to fray. Ying Qi, the provincial treasurer of Hunan Province, memorialized to the emperor that legalization of opium imports would ameliorate the scarcity of silver flows in the interior as well as stem piracy. Official domestic poppy cultivation could yield a less delicious and also less harmful drug than the Indian product, replacing the social disorder under prohibition with actual state control. Tentatively, ideas of opium import substitution were floated under the duress of the Taiping Rebellion.[90]

Official communications evidence this change of perception in shrinking intervals. In 1855, the *Peking Gazette* revealed that the emperor had once more ordered his Council of Ministers to deliberate opium duties as a remedy for the war expenditure, only to have the proposal rejected. The governmental split between prohibitionists and legalizers that featured in the First Opium War did not simply disappear. Increasingly, support for prohibition from its Guangdong base became isolated on the highest levels of policy planning in the capital.[91] Provinces most affected by the Taiping onslaught saw themselves beleaguered by fiscal shortages, social destabilization, and military enervation, desperately in need of wartime funds but blocked by the political center to resort to some of the most lucrative ones.

Wartime gave rise to a second pressure with the disruption of foreign opium deliveries. Starting in the summer of 1855, Chinese purchasers could no longer reach the receiving ships at Shanghai's opium station in Wusong. Europeans stored the drug in their own warehouses. A mob of protesters pressed the Shanghai Daotai, the chief magistrate and superintendent of customs, to order confiscation by the foreign inspectorate of customs, overriding opposition by the French and American consuls. In port cities like Ningbo, foreign opium began bypassing British consular and customs authorities altogether, in exchange for Chinese rice. Between April and August 1855, estimates projected $283,000 of rice aboard English vessels, followed by $72,500 on American vessels and smaller freight on German, Dutch, Danish, and Swedish vessels. Along with rice, saltpeter, and sulfur, these smuggled goods found their way into Taiping army stocks. The increasing frailty of the import market was enabled by the illicit collaboration of foreign merchants, as the Daotai Duan of Ningbo alerted Consular Sinclair.[92] To the British, this meant that opium deliveries under formal prohibition could no longer be guaranteed. To the Qing, wartime piracy continued to make prohibition more ineffective than it had been in peace. The sharpening commercial precariousness of opium trading became, although for different reasons, a political problem shared by the Qing and the British in collective misfortune.

In April 1855, John Bowring legalized opium imports into Siam, present-day Thailand—the kingdom southwest of the Qing empire. The Treaty of Friendship and Commerce, the so-called Bowring Treaty, achieved in Siam what the British still hoped for in China.[93] Siam had assented, fearing the same fate as Burma, its northwestern neighbor, which was defeated three years before.[94] Bowring had a free hand to work opium sales into a special arrangement, which included Chinese opium farmers as intermediaries. This arrangement helped blur British responsibility for the drug business and echoed the managerial distance by which the East India Company had played an active yet aloof role in expanding the opium trade of the eighteenth century.

Analogies across South and East Asia very much guided Bowring's own policy planning, especially in comparing opium governance across Asian settings. "The license system in the Colony of Hong Kong has been altogether successful," he explained in late 1855, pointing to precedents of opium legalization "in a somewhat similar manner" in Singapore under the BEIC, Macao under the Portuguese, the "islands of the Indian Archipelago" under the Dutch, "and I believe the Spaniards in the Philippines." In the same breath, he spelled out his conclusions. All of them, Bowring observed, had adopted the system of opium licensing like Siam, the "least pernicious" policy to follow, "nor am I aware that any European or Colonial Government has objected to make opium a subject of revenue."[95]

If legalization was so undeniably aligned with European expansion in Asia, then the regional context made China the only missing piece in an emerging system across the Asian region. By 1855, this British desideratum was no longer the stuff of confidential diplomacy. Transnational observers within China took notice and sometimes sided with the Qing. In September 1855, missionaries in Ningbo lamented the failure of a memorial that forewarned that if pressure on the Qing for legalization went too far, "no amount of professions of amity will suffice to disabuse the Chinese mind of the idea that we have no wish to reciprocate advantages, or any desire except that of enriching our country, even though it might be by the dismemberment of their Empire, and the destruction of their people."[96] How true would those words sound by the 1880s, 1900s, or 1920s!

In Britain, Lord Shaftesbury, chairman of the long-named and short-lived Committee for Relieving British Intercourse with China from the Baneful Effects of a Contraband Trade in Opium, attacked Bowring's legalization agenda, with the support of the Earl of Chichester. In November 1855, Benjamin Hobson—the son-in-law of Robert Morrison—and the London Missionary Society proclaimed that "several leading statesmen in China are favourable to its legalization, with a fixed duty of about 5 dollars on every 100 catties (133 lbs.), by which they say the public finances would be improved."[97] But opposition failed to produce a political effect.

Nowhere, however, did political conditions for legalization change as dramatically as on the China coast.[98] Even though Bowring was "heartily glad to see the importation of opium legalized," he did "not feel authorized to take any official action" and reaffirmed that "extreme displeasure" over smuggling was shared by Britain and China.[99] By November 4, 1856, a daily opium duty raised 20 taels of sycee (equivalent to about $20 at that time) for every opium chest entering Shanghai, less than a month after the *Arrow* incident of October 8 had unleashed the Second Opium War.[100] The first legalization of opium imports predated the legalization clause of the Tianjin Treaty of 1858 by two years and its ratification in 1860 by four years.[101] Legalization was on its way long before the British could secure it as the spoils of war—not a Pyrrhic victory but more precisely no victory at all.

This time, the step toward legalization was more than episodic. In March 1857, the opium duty received the emperor's endorsement. The small boats transferring opium from the Wusong ships to the mainland started flying official flags. Of the duty, now reduced to 12 taels, 10 went into Qing coffers. Institution-building followed suit. An opium office with two subordinates of the Shanghai Daotai and the County Magistrate's Office (*zhi xian yuan*) was opened "near the Catholic Cathedral" in Shanghai.[102]

Understandably, Qing official reluctance to publicize radical policy changes reflected the abiding concern with a long history of factionalism over opium. The Shanghai Daotai himself denied the existence of the collectors' office and dismissed the taxing scheme as unauthorized fund-raising by Cantonese guilds for anti-Taiping militias. But in private, the tone changed. The Qing government, the Daotai claimed, had never directly authorized opium trading guilds to raise the opium duty, but neither were they barred from fund-raising for the official Qing military. Thomas Francis Wade, the scholar-statesman and mastermind of the Western transcription system of the Chinese language named after him, understood the relevance of these private representations and conveyed them to Bowring.[103] In response, the British made the political choice to silently collaborate with the Qing's sensitive modus vivendi, retreating from traditional accusations of Chinese duplicity and realizing the strategic gains of official ambiguity.

Narrowing the previous gaps between British and Chinese perceptions of opium policies was not just about a change of minds; it became integral to the practice of policy enforcement itself. Daniel Brooke Robertson, the British consul in Shanghai, refrained from enforcing the new opium duty.[104] Even half a year after Sino-British hostilities commenced, economic convenience trumped legalism. As John Fairbank once put it, the Daotai "wanted to tax the trade, and the Consul to legalize it. But officially, the former kept his hands off and the latter closed his eyes."[105]

When in February 1857 a new Chinese legalization drive emerged in Ningbo, the Daotai used two intermediaries—a confidential agent and a special deputy of Zhejiang Province—to communicate it to Thomas Meadows. Meadows, in turn, used the opportunity to explain to his government that it was "impossible" for an imperial official and subject of the emperor "to sanction the trade as such." Instead, "the present measure [would] amount practically to a permanent legalization of the opium trade." Imperial consent could be obtained by petition, but "the name of opium is to be avoided." Only close communications could keep track of the swift changes of what was politically legitimate. Just months earlier, the first opium duty had been carefully enacted. Now, revenue discussions already cited the Shanghai example as a policy precedent.[106]

Qing initiatives of legalization accelerated and multiplied. A month had merely passed before the transfer of legalization policy reached from Shanghai and Ningbo to Fuzhou in May and June 1857. There, too, Chinese initiative preceded British action. Ye Yongyuan, the prefect of Fuzhou and local superintendent of customs, learned of the Shanghai and Ningbo duties through Viceroy Wang Yide and his provincial treasurer and approached British vice-consul Hale the following day, warning that any delay in adopting the same regulations would be "peculiarly inadmissible."[107] Ye enjoyed the support of Fujian's Committee on Military Affairs, the treasurer, the judge, the rice commissioner, and the salt commissioner, all of whom had a stake in the military finance of the province. When Bowring received the news, he hastened to respond that "Her Majesty's Government would be gratified by the legalization of the import of opium at a moderate fixed duty." Lord Clarendon, Britain's secretary of state for foreign affairs, added in a cautious, scribbled remark that formally, "the Emperor's consent is not yet obtained."[108]

Growing official support also allowed for greater institutional visibility of legalization. Compared to Shanghai, Fujian used two opium offices: one close to the Pagoda Anchorage, seven miles from the foreign settlement, and a second one for the city of Nantai at Zhongzhou, staffed with more than two dozen clerks and equipped with official seals to accredit each transaction. The new institutional setting of legalization shows that the Qing chose greater transparency than did the British. Bowring, on the one hand, proposed a Foreign Inspectorate modeled on Shanghai's, but when the question was whether to appoint a British Consulate staffer as the opium official, he refused.[109] The Qing proceeded undeterred. Indian opium from Patna and Benares yielded $1 per opium ball and an average $40 per chest. The lower-grade opium from Malwa yielded between $20 and $40 per chest.[110] Each collecting station was ordered to "act in concert."[111]

The domino effect of provincial opium duties spoke to the depth of interprovincial consultation. Provincial opium duties reached Daotai Shi of Amoy (today's Xiamen) through the General Provincial Committee in November 1857, followed by Bowring's support.[112] Each province falling under the sway of legalization made the overall direction of policy change more inexorable. Even so, Britain stayed put. In 1857, Meadows, the interpreter, still opined that "her Majesty's Government has but to let things take their own course, and then the much desired legalization of the Opium trade will quietly take effect; not as a boon solicited by us, but as a favor accorded by the Imperial Authorities." Lying low was seen as imperative for political success: "Only the matter will for some time be kept a secret, carefully guarded," as Meadows believed, "from the Imperial Court and the general public."[113]

By spring 1858, the tables had turned, and the source of pressure emanated on the Chinese side. Daotai Shi pressed Bowring to clarify the British position. Would they follow suit in accepting opium as a legitimate import? Before answering, the British had a counter-question: Would ships carrying opium "be called upon to enter in the manifest?"—to which the Shi answered with an emphatic "yes!" He could afford to be straightforward—he had received the emperor's endorsement, unbeknownst to the British.[114]

In sum, at least five ironies prevented the Taiping provocation of Qing legalization to be recognized by the British as a diplomatic opportunity for peace negotiations. First, the Taiping, while welcoming the wartime emergency wrought on the wartime Qing, were unlikely to see opium legalization as a social success, since, as discussed before, the opium ban was officially included in their vision of a new society. Second, the Qing were unlikely to announce legalization under wartime pressure, since it so obviously ran counter to the prohibitionist prewar policies. Third, the British did not fully appreciate the Qing's wartime legalization as a comprehensive point of no return and continued to believe in the Qing commitment to prohibition. And fourth, even if some British officials were informed of Qing legalization, they were unlikely to give credit to the Taiping for a Qing policy change that they had urged for decades in vain. Thus, no party involved was immediately likely to give official recognition to a political fait accompli. Fifth, and finally, posterity has rarely if ever recognized the Taiping onslaught as the primary influence behind Qing legalization. And although Britain saw its goals accomplished by a third party, they were as unlikely as the Qing to give the Taiping any credit whatsoever.

Beyond the ironies, the context of peace negotiations obscured many conditions of its own making, just as the Treaty of Tianjin, true to its genre, remained silent on what enabled it and focused on what the treaty settlement itself enacted. The Taiping rebels, moreover, were losing the attempted civil war and hence absent from the Peace of Tianjin. Outside the negotiations themselves, British expressions were more forthcoming. Palmerston had once more lamented missed opportunities of legalization in March 1857.[115] Foreign Secretary Lord Clarendon presented it as a top priority among Britain's "commercial aims" but could not speak to its political feasibility. One month into the negotiations, in July 1858, Bowring stated the problem as a fait accompli: "The legalization of the opium trade is the removal of one grave difficulty in our treaty negotiations."[116]

But given that Britain, China, France, Russia, and the United States all played a part in the treaty settlement, where should postwar consensus-building begin? The only individual who chronicled those conversations was Samuel Wells Williams, the interpreter of the American Legation in China since 1856, in a journal addressed to his wife, Sarah Walworth, and later published by his son, Frederick Wells Williams. The journal details the twists and turns that consolidated piecemeal provincial legalization into a permanent framework in international law. Tracing the tortuous road toward legalization may appear arduous to the reader because it appeared arduous to the protagonists at the time. With that caveat, it still deserves a careful reconstruction and explanation.

Qing diplomats played an active role in identifying the legal obstacles to consensus-building. Imperial Commissioner Ye Mingzhen had alerted Bowring as early as June 1856 to a fundamental discrepancy between Chinese-British treaties and, on the other hand, Chinese-U.S. and Chinese-French treaties. The 1844 treaties of Wangxia and Huangpu with the United States and France included provisos for treaty revision, whereas the 1842 Treaty of Nanjing with Britain did not. The French and U.S. treaties also disagreed over the separation of criminal and civil jurisdiction.[117] Qing insistence on the absence of a Western consensus could keep imperialist interests at bay by keeping them apart. He Guiqing, governor-general of Liangjiang since July 1857, reiterated the proven strategy of divide and rule: "It should not be hard to separate then, and using barbarians to control barbarians, sow mutual disaffection and gradually weaken them." And many the barbarians were: Participants in the system of unequal treaties also included the Belgians, the Swedish, and the Norwegians, making it perhaps the closest approximation and institutional expression of comprehensively "European," even Scandinavian, imperialism in Asia.[118]

In more than a geographic sense, Russia was well positioned to mediate in the rifts between China and a divided West. The Russian delegates at Tianjin were eager not to be left behind. It helped that Chinese assessments honored them with a reputation of greater inscrutability than the British, French, or Americans.[119] Respect, however, did not equate a warm welcome. The *North China Herald* and the *Times* decried the Russians and Americans as "intrusive neutrals," provoking outrage in the *New York Times* and in the Californian press.[120] Privately and in view of British intransigence, however, a Russo-American coalition enjoyed qualified American support: "Now of course the Russian and American are partners," Williams stated, "but if the Englishman were more *bon homme* and open he might readily have the Yankee to his aid against the others, were there any need of that kind."[121]

Within China, the Russian position was firm and old. The Russian Orthodox Church mirrored the Euro-American presence of religious establishments and, like them, acquired social and cultural knowledge through intimate Chinese contacts. Russian territorial ambitions could even exceed the European hunger for maritime and inland access, far beyond the Manchurian region east of the Ussuri. Count Nikolai Muraviev, the governor-general of Eastern Siberia, had earned British and Ottoman respect at the Fortress of Kars in the Caucasus in September 1855, hailed as the last major operation of the Crimean War.[122]

In the Tianjin negotiations of 1858, the precedent of interimperial observation and competition left an unmistakable imprint on legalization alliances. On June 7, 1858, Count Efimii Vasil'evich Putiatin, head of the Russian delegation, first aligned his opium policy position with Britain. He "altered one of the articles to please the English by erasing the special mention of opium among the contraband articles of import."[123] Although "the Count is strong in his views as to the bad policy and results of the trade in the drug," Samuel Wells Williams noted in his journal, a Russo-British rapprochement was defined as imperative, overriding personal ethics.

This Russo-British synchronization of policies became the first in a series. The British made "the same request" to William Bradford Reed, the American envoy extraordinary, who at first "declined to alter the clause in his projet [sic] of a treaty" and only gave in later.[124] After all, the Sino-American Treaty of Wangxia from 1844 stipulated bilateral opium prohibition. Chinese provincial governors had stepped up their U.S. relations beyond anything Sino-British relations had seen. The Middle Kingdom and the American Republic caught the first glimpses of their transnational entanglement. In a meeting on September 26, 1858, He Guiqing, the governor-general of Liangjiang, announced his plan to visit the United States—an unprecedented move.

The strategic principle behind this initiative was "to employ soft and manage hard," the very opposite of the clichéd American "impact" and its Chinese "response." Prince Gong, soon to be China's foremost foreign policy voice, even identified this "self-evident" principle as "the present policy for the management of barbarian affairs."[125] This opening up of the Qing diplomatic outlook, one of many more to come, did more than narrowly manage to imagine an American ally. He Guiqing asked Williams "many questions," including "what sort of people the Japanese are," knowing that Williams himself was a veteran of Commodore Perry's mission to Japan in 1853 and 1854. Qing's diplomacy in the 1850s was far from self-enclosed or isolated, as its posthumous image would have us believe.

But even familiarity did not rule out misunderstanding. When the American delegation arrived, Chinese "flageolets and kettle-drums sounded oddly amidst the deep tones of our bass drums and other instruments," Williams recalled, until "a salute of three guns" brought the ominous overture to a speedy close.[126] Some personal relations evolved, as between W. A. P. Martin and the Chinese junior deputy Yushan.[127] On the American side, Chinese agency could be overestimated, as in the misperception that the Russo-Chinese agreement on religious toleration in 1880 had been initiated "by the Chinese Commissioners themselves."[128] On the Chinese side, too, amity bent sober assessments. The opium conversations led the postwar Qing Foreign Ministers to judge that "the American barbarians are pure-minded and honest in disposition and have always been loyal to China and are not allied to England and France."[129]

Williams appreciated Governor-General He Guiqing as "a sprightly man of forty-four from Yunnan" and "the most interesting personage" alongside Grand Secretary Guiliang, the head of the Chinese delegation. The amity of U.S.-China relations directly influenced legalization, as the U.S. delegation co-created the final version of the tariff articles on November 13, 1858, which included opium.[130] As the Chinese were absent from that meeting, Williams delivered the copies to the Chinese commissioners in person the following day. "By this tariff, you will perhaps be surprised to learn that opium is legalized and pays thirty taels per picul as import duty," Williams recorded in his journal to his wife. "The Chinese government has yielded in its long resistance to permitting this drug to be entered through the custom-house, the opium war of 1840 ending in the treaty of Nanking has triumphed, and the honorable English merchants and government can now exonerate themselves from the opprobrium of smuggling this article." Like Count Putiatin earlier, Williams was at pains to point out that American assent to British preferences did not equate moral endorsement. "Bad as the triumph is, I am convinced that it was the best disposition that could be made of this perplexing question; legalization is preferable to the evils attending the farce now played, and throwing ridicule on the laws against it by sending the revenue boats to the opium hulks to receive a duty or bribe from the purchasers."[131] Elgin's American colleague William Reed learned that Elgin simply "could not reconcile it" to his "sense of right to urge the Imperial Government to abandon its traditional policy in this respect, under the kind of pressure which we were bringing to bear upon it."[132] Gone was Western discord, along with forgotten critiques like that of an American Presbyterian missionary, who likened British actions to the nightmare of the Russian fleet sailing up the Thames River.[133]

Skepticism informed Elgin's take on opium legalization, the area in which he, like Count Putiatin and William Reed, was a more reluctant imperialist than in any other.[134] Before the actual negotiations, Elgin disclosed British official instructions "not to insist on the insertion of the drug in the tariff, should the Chinese government wish to omit it."[135] He emphasized in a report: "In my recent discussions . . . , I have merely sought to induce them to bring the trade in opium from the region of fiction into that of fact, and to place within the pale of law, and therefore under its control, an article which is now openly bought, sold, and taxed by them beyond that pale."[136] The position was credible. Even the opium trading giant of Jardine and Matheson would be rebuffed on the same grounds in the spring of 1859.

Great confusion, however, arose in the meeting on October 13, 1858, on tariff revisions. It was triggered by Chinese nonchalance. The Qing delegation simply stated that "we have resolved to put it [opium] into the tariff as yang yeh (foreign medicine)," a policy position that would bewilder the British for decades to come.[137] Huan Xue, the appointed "Judge" and Commissioner of Finance for Jiangsu Province and Shanghai Daotai until October 1857, explained in more detail: "China still retains her objection to the use of the drug on moral grounds; but the present generation of smokers, at all events, must and will have opium."[138] He Guiqing had advised the emperor that removing prohibition laws would simply provoke the Taiping to "collect in bands to convoy it and breed serious troubles." Thus, legalization would mean "the advantage will be with us and there will be neither loss nor gain to the barbarian merchants."[139] These steps were in an uneasy relationship with the emperor's warning against subservience to foreign demands, although he referred to the customs question in general without specifically highlighting opium. Significantly, legalization became a policy of financial consolidation and anti-Taiping stabilization. It was juxtaposed to British financial interests, not a direct Qing financial concession to British pressure. There was less humiliation involved in supporting policies that benefited yourself more than anyone else, especially if they prevented a crisis-ridden dynasty to collapse.

Xue also posited that the inevitability of Chinese demand could be part of the very logic of legalization. Formally, he still pressed for discreetly separating the opium legalization from other duty regulations. Article 26 set the ad valorem duty at 5 percent and was given higher priority than Article 28, exempting opium from transit duties, and Article 9, on the rights of foreign passport holders who imported opium into China. On Xue's insistence and with Guiliang's authorization, opium became "an article brought into China by the Chinese alone." This was seen as the solution to British property claims on opium, as at the outbreak of the First Opium War. This decision took the political economy of opium and the moral hierarchies of that political economy in a different direction than the First Opium War. Twenty years before, the Qing had destroyed British opium, only to face massive British compensation claims. In 1860, however, the Taiping crisis impelled the opposite direction of Qing policy. As the Manchu officials explained to the British, the duty would be "more easily evaded at the Barrier Custom-houses, and collisions with their establishments more probable; but besides this, . . . the value of the article is such as to offer great temptation to the lawless, and that the convoy of it by foreigners would expose the Chinese Government to constant risk of discussions, arising out of loss of property, and perhaps of life."[140] Legalization placed the opium business into Chinese hands because foreigners could not be trusted.

But amid the tumult of peace negotiations, whose cross-cultural character would have made a neat consensus a surprise, the novelty of these policies led almost immediately to narrative distortions and blatant misinterpretations. False stories started circulating almost immediately, with reports from overly partial witnesses. Williams's journal failed to record the detailed negotiations, possibly because he was traveling in Japan until October. W. A. P. Martin, another chronicler, misrepresented the facts in his account: "The treaty contained nothing about the opium trade, though there was an article denouncing it in the first draft," he wrote. "Well do I remember the blank surprise of the Chinese deputies when I informed them that the anti-opium article had been withdrawn." In 1898, he claimed, "The reason for this backward step I was not at liberty to disclose, but I am now." Had U.S. minister William B. Reed "discovered the nugatory nature of such a stipulation[,] he would have deserved credit for perspicacity. Without making that discovery, he backed down under a menace from Lord Elgin to introduce into the British treaty an article in favor of opium."[141] Martin's personal dissatisfaction may have clouded his judgment. He had been heavily invested in compiling a comprehensive opium survey since 1856, spending "much time," certainly months, on a manuscript that was never published and whose unlucky fate—especially in the face of legalization— remains unknown.[142] In May 1858, Martin presented his own anti-opium tracts, rife with biblical exegesis, to Chinese officials in private meetings. As Williams noted, the sixth commandment ("Thou shalt not kill") struck one official named Qian as incongruous. The English, he reasoned, could not possibly be Christians, "for they killed the Chinese with opium merely for gain." There as elsewhere, Martin relished in conveying Chinese imputations of English hypocrisy to Anglophone readers: "How strongly England and opium are connected in the minds of these people," his journal expressed, "can only be appreciated after long acquaintance with them."[143] Auspicious words indeed!

A more glossy account was given by William B. Reed, the head of the American delegation, who told Elgin, of all people, of voluntary U.S. assent to legalization: "In our brief conversations on this subject at Tientsin, I frankly stated . . . what the views of the Government of the United States were on this subject and that I was instructed to inform the Chinese authorities, if the opportunity offered, that the United States did not seek for its citizens the legal establishment of the opium trade, and would not uphold them in any attempt to violate the laws of China by the introduction of the article into the country." Reed, too, claimed to have made personal representations to Chinese officials prior to official negotiations: "I am not quite sure whether I mentioned to you that on one occasion, at least, in my intercourse with the Commissioners in the north, I did state these views to them, going even further, and assuring them that the United States would sustain any lawful attempt their Government made to suppress the traffic. I have said something to the same effect to the Taoutae [*sic*] here, but in both instances the suggestion met with no response."[144]

Elgin had noticed Chinese apprehension among provincial daotais in the Taiping emergency: Their "reluctance . . . to talk on the subject may be easily accounted for; but the indifference of those who more directly represented the Emperor could only be explained on the ground that it was indifference, or, as has been suggested, by their fear even to talk on a subject which they thought had once involved them in a war, and which might (so they reasoned) give them trouble again." The specter of the First Opium War haunted foreigners, too. Reed argued, "My deliberate judgment was, and is, that the trade must go on as it is with all the mischief and disgrace, unless your Excellency will undertake to adjust and regulate it." In this version, the Americans almost requested the British lead toward legalization, failing to anticipate that the Qing, once derided as too slow, would anticipate the British.

Unlike Martin's report of British intimidation, Reed told Elgin that "at your Excellency's instance, while the American Treaty was in progress at Tien-tsin, I struck out from the draft the express prohibition of opium, which as you are aware is in the Treaty of Wanghia," a notable departure from the precedent of American national legislation in favor of an Anglo-American legalization consensus.[145] It is unlikely that Reed misrepresented his interactions with Elgin to Elgin himself. Instead of British bullying, American motivations entered the picture here and may be quoted in full, to illustrate their nuances: "The reason for doing so, aside from my acquiescence in the views which your Excellency suggested, was that I was conscious that in its operation in China it was a dead letter, and, as such, had only a place in the Treaty for mischief. I beg to assure you that I do not at all regret my decision, and have reason to believe that what I did will be approved by my Government."[146]

Reed as an American representative understood the meaning of the change from status quo to legalization: "Opium now is expressly contraband. In the new Treaties (for I understand them in this to correspond) it is contraband or not according to the laws of the Chinese Government," a reference to the medical or nonmedical status that formally categorized opium imports. Legalization, in Reed's eyes, fit rather than infringed Qing legislation. Even so, he was frustrated at his limited grasp of the complexities he faced: "I am at a loss to understand why this inconvenient masquerade—the English Treaty being silent on the subject, and the Chinese laws virtually abandoned—is kept up."[147]

After these intractable, diplomatic maneuverings, the final opium legalization clause brought much-desired clarity:

> Rule V. The restrictions affecting trade in opium, cash, grain, pulse, sulphur, brimstone, saltpeter and spelter are relaxed, under the following conditions: §1. Opium will henceforth pay thirty taels per picul import duty. The importer will sell it only at the port. It will be carried into the interior by Chinese only, and only as Chinese property; the foreign trader will not be allowed to accompany it. The provisions of Article IX of the Treaty of Tientsin, by which British subjects are authorised to proceed into the interior with passports to trade, will not extend to it, nor will those of Article XXVIII of the same Treaty, by which the transit dues are regulated. The transit dues on it will be arranged as the Chinese Government see fit; nor, in future revisions of the Tariff, is the same rule of revision to be applied to opium as to other goods.[148]

The legal technicality and not exactly prosaic quality of these terms may have repelled readers in subsequent decades, to give way to the imputations that gained such shocking popularity in subsequent years.[149] Misinterpretation did not necessarily emanate from distant sources; they could stem from sources conceivably close to historical events. In 1893, Elgin's former Chinese secretary, Horatio Nelson Lay, attacked Elgin for having admitted to "bullying the poor Chinese." Lay's dismissal of Elgin's position could not have been more poisonous: "He was then getting his treaty too easily, and could afford to indulge in the luxury of sentiment." Airing breezily, he added, "I am China's friend in all this."[150]

The unintended effect of the Taiping crisis succeeded where British pressure on Qiying had foundered. Just as the Taiping effect outlasted the demise of the rebellion itself in 1864, it transcended the rebellion's local impact with the international consequence of legalized opium trading.

The myth of opium legalization as a British achievement enhanced in credibility with serial Qing tragedies. When the British sacked one of the sacrosanct imperial sites called Yuanmingyuan, the Summer Palace, this Qing defeat stemmed definitely from British intervention.[151] As Charles Gordon, the man responsible for razing the palace to the ground, put it: "We were so pressed for time, that we could not plunder them carefully."[152] Despite significant empirical differences in British might and Chinese inferiority, nationalist memory has lumped much of it together in the "century of humiliation," citing the opium wars, Yuanmingyuan, and later national tragedies in the canon of China's national humiliation. Concerning the legacy of the Second Opium War, it did not help that Lord Elgin left town on a ship, amid four other steamers, named *Furious*.[153]

With all its vagaries, contentions, and surprises, the opium trade became an economic success story. Why the political safeguard of opium legalization could not secure Chinese or international acquiescence, pushed into the crosshairs of a global political affront, will be explored in Chapter 2.

CHAPTER TWO

THE POROSITY OF INTERNATIONAL LAW

V ICTORY AND DEFEAT serve as markers of national development and international hierarchy, orienting historical chronology. Each of them is almost universally recognized to represent a moment defining one country's future relations with another. The Qing's double defeat in the two opium wars is no exception, having yielded in Chinese and international history the predominant narrative of the postwar superiority of Britain in direct relation to the inferiority of the Qing. Cultural corollaries confirm British imperial expansion and Chinese national subjugation as leitmotifs. In architecture, an apt example might be Shanghai's Bund promenade, towering over the old Chinese society and welcoming foreigners on imperialist terms and with imperialist tastes. In allegory, an equally citable case might be China as the melon carved up by great and greedy powers all around.

But despite the unquestionable forcefulness of legalized opium trading as a political, economic, and social routine of imperialism in the Qing dynasty after 1860, foreign control over the maintenance of imperialist privileges never became absolute. International law, although designed as a long-term guarantee of political settlements, as in the case of opium legalization, exposed over time its porousness and permeability by transnational dissension. Overwhelming power to prevent the undoing of one's own might may be a fantasy inhabiting the imperialist and the nationalist imagination, but it resides in few other domains of the human experience.

The lack of control practically affected the imperialist capacity to cling to power arrangements won through war. In the specific case of the legalized opium trade—the arrangement established in 1860 after diplomatic headaches since the early nineteenth century—caused a renewed bout of controversy within less than a decade. But this time, the dispute would differ in kind and scope from all preceding protests, unshackling the discussion of opium legalization from the stuffy officialdom of diplomatic negotiations and entering the new, versatile, and unpredictable playing field of transnational public debate. There, even similar arguments would acquire different functions, develop different effects, and cause a different kind of damage. In diametric opposition to diplomacy's restricted circles of communication, the international level of public contestation knew no bounds, and governments had few if any means to restrict, channel, or influence the debate according to their own interests. It is here that the designation of the debate as "transnational" establishes an empirical and analytic distance to the "international" histories on the actions that states pursue abroad. In the transnational opium controversy, participants didn't wait to get permission from states to join in.

In July 1869, the Qing chief secretary—known in English as Prince Gong, in Chinese as Yixin, and in Manchu as I Hin—launched a combination of demarche and tirade that would have momentous, sustained, and long-term consequences. An individual protest would not deserve an entire chapter were it not for the enormity of its intellectual universe, the unprecedented range of thematic strings, and the rhetorical tropes of its anti-opium critique. Furthermore, the protest's sustained and comprehensive reception by audiences from Asia to western Europe and North America made it the first stimulus behind a mobilization of anti-opium sentiment on a global scale, revealing the unusual capacity of anti-opium arguments to garner strong sympathies among social, political, intellectual, and professional identities that were quite dissimilar, from French scientists to American China watchers.

The setting where the momentous speech was first heard was not that conspicuous. A private meeting in Beijing brought Prince Gong together with Rutherford Alcock one last time before the British minister's return home. Not unlike Yixin's emergence from the First Opium War, Prince Gong emerged from the cauldron of the Second Opium War. His half-brother, Emperor Xianfeng, had ordered him to negotiate the Peace of Tianjin. Enduring that ordeal brought a reward. It appears that no other Qing veteran of the peace negotiations—besides Wenxiang—carried comparable weight in key postwar decisions of Qing foreign policy. Certainly nobody save Prince Gong did so in his twenties.[1]

Prince Gong's individual initiative of 1869 was conveyed both as a conversation and as a written memorial by him, Wenxiang, and three senior
Manchus at the Zongli Yamen. It may have taken the British minister by
surprise. But the very fact of informal consultations with the British and
less with European continental diplomats was the product of careful and
strategic institution-building. Prince Gong had been personally responsible
for overriding an isolationist contingent of Qing ministers in 1860, when
he divulged tentative plans for a new Qing Foreign Ministry to Britain's
Chinese secretary, Thomas Francis Wade, who was reported to be "ex-
tremely pleased."[2] For the Qing, revamping the entire social purpose and
physical space for postwar Qing-British interactions was an unprecedented
initiative. When the new Office for the Management of Foreign Countries
(*zongli geguo shiwu yamen* or *zongli yamen*) materialized, it took the place
of the much more minimalist Office for Calming Down the Barbarians
(*fuyiju*). It operated under the aegis of the Grand Council, increased mutual accessibility, and opened direct lines of communication between Qing
officials like Prince Gong and foreign officials stationed in the diplomatic
quarter of Beijing.[3] The British supported the creation of the ministry so
strongly that the tone bordered on a demand, but combined with the level
of Qing interest set the Zongli Yamen apart from other, more punitive elements of the postwar order after 1860.

Beneath the creation of the ministry, unofficial communication was
considered important enough to be integrated into the Peace of Tianjin.
Article 5 of the Treaty of Peace, Friendship, Commerce and Navigation
between the Queen and the Qing emperor, dated June 26, 1858, and ratified on October 24, 1860, set forth the terms by which the Qing emperor
"agrees to nominate one of the Secretaries of State, or a President of one
of the Boards, as the high officer with whom the Ambassador, Minister, or
other Diplomatic Agent of Her Majesty the Queen shall transact business,
either personally or in writing, on a footing of perfect equality."[4] This
corresponded with Article 8 of the American-Chinese Treaty of June 18,
1859, ratified on August 16, 1859. Both arrangements forestalled "any
pretext for declining these interviews," the great Western frustration of
prewar times, and stepped up the potential to liaise tout court.[5]

Without a Qing foreign service yet established, the Zongli Yamen acted
as the only global platform where Qing and foreign officials enjoyed con-
tinuous and legally guaranteed access to each other, with no restrictions on
the themes and problems discussed. This was not a Qing concession to communicate grudgingly; both Chinese and British opposition were responsible for blocking alternative venues, such as Qing overseas missions in the
1860s, an innovation emerging only by the mid-1870s.[6] Since 1867, the

ministry strove to put "the earliest, official Chinese exchange of views regarding foreign policy on record." Seventeen provincial and higher officials compiled the so-called secret correspondence on possible revisions of the Tianjin Treaty. The secret questionnaire's six sections included the claim by foreign diplomats to the right of an audience with the emperor; the stationing of Chinese embassies in the capitals of the treaty powers; the foreign construction of telegraph and railway networks in China; the establishment of foreign warehouses and business offices in China outside the treaty ports, and inland travel on foreign steamships; foreign investments in China's salt and coal mining industries; and the expansion of foreign missionary activities. Opium was not part of it.[7]

When Prince Gong raised the opium issue with Alcock, he still spoke from a position of weakness. By 1869, the opium issue was hampered not only by the historical weight of the controversy, as in 1858 or 1860, but also by the legal fact of its official resolution. On the face of it, neither the law nor the political relations between the Qing and Britain suggested that raising objections to the newfound framework of legalization would have any discernible influence, while a backlash was very much in the cards. "That opium is like a deadly poison, that it is most injurious to mankind, and a most serious provocative of ill-feeling, is . . . perfectly well-known to his Excellency," Prince Gong started. "The object of the treaties between our respective countries was to secure perpetual peace," he continued, "but if effective steps cannot be taken to remove an accumulating sense of injury from the minds of men, it is to be feared that no policy can obviate sources of future trouble."[8]

What made the argument at least worth paying attention to was its functional emphasis on the social costs and intercultural fallout, the intensity of which could be beyond political remedy—a nightmarish scenario particularly for an official. But even before such a state of affairs could imperil Chinese-British popular relations, Chinese social stability—even goodwill—was required for a smooth functioning of British-Chinese free trade. Prince Gong enunciated that he did not oppose a free trade as such. But the opium trade, he insisted, constituted an exceptional commodity trade: "The Chinese merchant supplies your country with his goodly tea and silk, conferring thereby a benefit upon her, but the English merchant empoisons China with pestilent opium. Such conduct is unrighteous. Who can justify it? What wonder if officials and people say that England is willfully working out China's ruin."[9] From the outset, Prince Gong showed himself by no means inimical to British profit maximization, stressing that the drug trade was "prejudicial to the general interests of commerce."[10]

But in Chinese popular perception, of which Prince Gong declared himself to be a representative, the opium trade represented by definition a political act rather than an abstract market at play. Prince Gong's premises were as important for the effective communication of his demarche as the words themselves. His explanations to Alcock implied, whether strategically or sincerely, that the Chinese and British views on the opium trade differed fundamentally. The Peace of Tianjin had adjudicated the opium trade behind diplomacy's proverbial closed doors. But Chinese society, even though shut out from high-level international decisions, reinforced the debate while changing its terms fundamentally. In other words, the Qing-British political consensus on legalization after the Taiping opium crisis in 1860 was nothing more than an accord floating on the political surface of Chinese-British relations, but a surface populated only by officials. In the terminology of today's historians, the international dimension of opium legalization was not backed up by the transnational dimension required for social acceptance—and disregarding this insufficient resolution could doom all levels of the relationship: the political top level from state to state and the social level from people to people.

In Chinese eyes, the opium trade was still what it had been before 1860: malevolent in conception, harmful and frequently fatal to the individual, corrosive in its societal effect. In turn, the injury caused by opium harmed Britain's own international reputation, an outcome Prince Gong lamented with demonstrated sympathy: "The wealth and generosity of England is spoken of by all. She is anxious to prevent and anticipate all injury to her commercial interest. How is it then she can hesitate to remove an acknowledged evil?"[11] Chinese popular misperceptions had simmered for many years now, he averred. Both officials and the Chinese people "cannot be so completely informed on the subject," opening the door to the further risk of misperceptions which, vice versa, heightened the need for a political message of goodwill. "All say that England trades in opium because she desires to work China's ruin."[12] This phrase, as we shall see, would become one of the most unforgettable of the anti-opium campaign. Where the cause repeated itself, it was more often than not in confirming China's ruin through opium.

The popular and less predictable plane of Chinese emotional perceptions and mass belief was the level that fed the dominant opium debate in China, with its sense of desperation and overdue outrage. Contradicting the British perception of Chinese opium smoking as an inescapable habit, Prince Gong argued that its affront was in fact escalating. What the opium trade symbolized for the Chinese people was by turns horrifying yet politically reversible. In this, Prince Gong's signature protest anticipated what Emperor

Guangxu in the Qing's closing years would identify as Chinese public opinion, a recognized social lever of domestic policy change.[13] Through Prince Gong's radical reinterpretation, the opium trade became inseparable from its perception by its enemies, whose numbers grew in proportion to the social, cultural, and moral damage perceived—a vicious cycle that fed itself as long as politics did not find a way to break it.[14]

Rutherford Alcock, for his part, had good reason to listen closely to Prince Gong's representations. The massacre of Christians in Sichuan, reports of which reached the British in June 1869, just one month previous, testified to the costs exacted by Chinese ill will. Elsewhere in Britain's Asian empire, security threats of "rebellions" and "unrest" by "fanatics" straddled colonies from India to Singapore to Hong Kong.[15] The young age of legalization did not yet allow the risk of unrest to be gauged, but if the risk existed, as Prince Gong claimed, that alone would raise the political cost of inaction. Massacres were not the only prospect. Popular discontent was compounded by the unknown amounts of additional supplies that reached consumers by escaping Qing oversight. The British opium trade, then, appeared besieged from two sides: the outrage of righteous anti-opium activists and the cunning of unrighteous traffickers. A "strict enforcement of the prohibition," Prince Gong cautioned, "would necessitate the taking of many lives"—this time he meant Chinese offenders—and worsen social polarization. Had he lived until the 1900s, he would have seen his fears come true in the human lives lost in clashes around the opium bans of the 1900s and 1910s.[16]

It spoke to Prince Gong's political prudence to address Chinese opium traffickers in his demarche to Alcock. After all, Chinese traffickers had been the oldest target of British counteraccusations, from before the First Opium War. Rather than protecting them or denying their actions for fear of losing face, Prince Gong discussed them straight away. Although traffickers could only fault themselves for punishment when caught, "bystanders would not fail to say that it was the foreign merchants who reduced them to their ruin by bringing the drug." Adding to the existing damage of Britain reputation, "it would be hard to prevent general and deep-seated indignation; such a course would indeed tend to arouse popular anger against the foreigner."[17] Chinese popular opinion took issue with British political accountability for a multiplicity of reasons, from Britain as a drug peddler to Britain as a manipulator of social harmony within Chinese society itself.[18]

The political accountability of the Qing state stretched in two directions, relating to the people below and to spiritual ethics above. Accordingly, the dynasty, "most unwilling" to lift the ban on Chinese poppy cultivation, insisted "that a right system of government should appreciate the beneficence

of heaven, and (seek to) remove any grievances which afflict its people."
On the other hand, "to allow them [the people] to go on to destruction,
though an increase of revenue may result, will provoke the judgment of
heaven and the condemnation of men."[19] With the Mandate of Heaven
and the mandate of the people linked, opium legalizers found themselves in
a bind, whether Qing, British, or otherwise.

But social representations like Prince Gong's demarche virtually on behalf of the Chinese people did not come foolproof or reflect sincerity in and
of themselves. Sincerity, the linchpin of any argument, had to be displayed.
Breaking with precedent and dogma, Prince Gong opted to openly discuss
dissent within the Qing administration: "There are others again," he conveyed, who advocated a lifting of the Qing's domestic ban on poppy cultivation. "They argue that as there is no means of stopping the foreign (opium)
trade, there can be no harm as a temporary measure in withdrawing the
prohibition on its growth. We should thus not only deprive the foreign merchant of the main source of his profits, but should increase our revenue to
boot."[20] Facts backed up the case. In October 1869, Alcock learned of incipient poppy cultivation by the two ruling brothers in the provinces of
Huguang and Zhejiang, Li Hongzhang and Li Hanzhang. Qing calls for
opium import substitution beckoned with rising revenues, growing official
support and conjuring up an economic competitor to British Indian opium
imports, with grave effects to British trade, not to mention the diplomatic
opportunity of the Opium Agreement of 1907 that we shall discuss later.[21]

Representing a diversity of Qing positions, Prince Gong seemed to understand, did not automatically invalidate the Qing position as weak or
self-contradictory. Instead of diagnosing the administration's approach as
fragmented and torn apart from within, the move communicated Qing
political reasoning as a comparative method, a weighing of different policy
options. Needless to say, this flexibility moved his own policy position—at
the very least the non-endorsement of domestic cultivation—closer to Alcock's, relative to the Qing colleagues who favored cultivation. More generally, offering several policy options within the administration also prepared
the ground for extending the comparative method to a diplomatic conversation with the British, the precondition for any rapprochement. Disagreement within the Qing administration did not necessarily form an admission
of incompetence, nor did it have to be kept under wraps at all costs. Instead,
referencing it signaled political flexibility, put openness above orthodoxy,
and, at the very least, pointed to the political competence of the speaker,
who through the act of referencing an existing disagreement moved above
it. Gone, for a moment, was the old adage of domestic unity as the key to
divide and rule the pugnacious barbarians from the West.

Instead, Prince Gong played with open cards, which was itself a play, moving rhetorically and analytically above his factionalist colleagues and anchoring his explanations in the concerns and trajectories of Chinese societal perceptions, all of which amounted to more than the agonies of an emotional man flying into a rage. By ingeniously acting as a representative of Chinese public opinion, Prince Gong's adopted position allowed for more substantive controversy than an expression of personal ill feeling, which would have restricted his argumentative leeway. Without alienating Alcock, which would have derailed the entire purpose of the demarche, Prince Gong continued with a radical proposal: "To stop the evil at its source, nothing will be effective" but prohibition enforced by a joint Qing-British accord.[22]

A template of political steps to be taken contrasted the earlier reference of Chinese popular grievances with the role officials held so dear: the ability to solve complex problems with the detached ingenuity of superior understanding. Memorialize your government, Prince Gong urged in an obvious analogy to policy change in the Qing administration, to give orders for India and other territories to start the process of substituting opium with cereals and cotton. Next, make sure to align prohibition across all three dimensions of opium's political economy: cultivation, distribution, and consumption. Finally, see for yourself how Britain's reputation, by abstaining from such a great evil, would be marked instead by great virtue: "She would strengthen friendly relations and make herself illustrious." Do so before it is too late, because the Qing government's reach into the minds and hearts of the people was limited: "They may be unable to cause the people to put aside all ill-feeling." The memorialists on whose behalf Prince Gong spoke and wrote to Alcock had given opium legalization "most earnest thought, and overpowering is the distress it occasions them."[23]

More than establishing a contrast between the place of opium in the predominant Chinese and British political imagination for mere comparison's sake, Prince Gong clearly aimed at something that British propagandists of free trade, Christianity, and other gospels had made part of their own effusions: the objective to convert the mind-set of others to one's own. Astonishingly, the demarche took audiences, readers, and other recipients in different cultural milieus and far-off settings by storm. Immediately following the demarche, Alcock gave the protest much attention in official correspondence, in private conversations, and on the parliamentary floor. Prince Gong's words became the defining expression of both Qing and Chinese popular thinking on the opium question, "China's ruin" an almost canonical reference point. Conversion to anti-opium views started with Alcock himself. Before 1869, the British minister had been unconvinced by the anti-opium statements of Wenxiang. After Prince Gong's demarche, Alcock

urged to "reconsider the step taken" in the Treaty of Tianjin, which removed
opium from the list of prohibitions.[24] The vehicle that made anti-opium
conversions beyond Alcock possible was premised partly on the existence
of a vigorous international press abroad but, more importantly, on the
existence of the international press in China. Through the Anglo- and
Francophone communities in Qing treaty ports, information flowed in and
out. This is not the place to recount the history of the Qing's relations with
transnational journalism. But to give a sense of perspective, let us not forget
in the years of the demarche's most conspicuous reception overseas, the
Qing espoused a strong interest in receiving international information in
China, the flip side of reaching outlets beyond Chinese borders. In March
1876, seven years after the demarche, when it had already achieved some
prominence overseas, Prince Gong—most likely impelled by unrelated
motivations—ordered the systematic sharing of foreign newspapers with
"all the high officials in the Northern and Southern Treaty Ports." Thereafter, translations of English-language reportage crossed the desks of the
Zongli Yamen regularly.[25] In 1878, aided by China's first diplomat in Britain,
Guo Songtao, the Zongli Yamen began formally cooperating with the four-
year-old Anglo-Oriental Society for the Suppression of the Opium Trade
(SSOT).[26] And by 1884, Prince Gong was "quite aware" that "the opium
trade has long been condemned by England as a nation," an awareness also
known in England.[27] Anti-opium sentiment consolidated not only within
societies but between them, with flows of information intensifying rather
than diluting the message. It almost appeared as if shedding the peculiari-
ties of each local context, in Prince Gong's case the demarche meeting with
Alcock, helped radicalize reportage. Ironically, the more unintended the
distant recipients of Prince Gong's demarche, the greater was their contribution to the enlargement of the cause. The remainder of this chapter will
explore the astonishing longevity of the demarche by following the phases
of its reappearances around the world.

China's Ruin: Global Anti-Opium Conversions

Prince Gong's unprecedented protest of 1869 predated the oft-cited missionary momentum from the 1880s onward, superseding the latter in its
multifarious appeal to most diverse audiences.[28] This discursive intervention also preceded, by about twenty-five years, Western initiatives to elicit
official Qing statements on the opium problem.[29] This observation flips the
line of inquiry pursued by John King Fairbank and influential in Anglophone as well as Sinophone academia on the question "exactly how the

heritage from the past and the influences from abroad have interacted within Chinese society" as "the nub of our problem."[30] But here, anti-opium publicity spread from China to the West to impel a massive sensitization to the social suffering and political precariousness of the opium trade, explicitly on the terms laid out in Prince Gong's critique.

Reports of his demarche proliferated in waves of affirmation, beginning in East and Southeast Asia. Throughout, writers who had never met or known Prince Gong, who was anything but a global political celebrity, found themselves in agreement. When comparing his influence with that of supposedly better-placed voices of opposition, such as the London Anti-Opium Association, Prince Gong's unwitting global prominence does not really diminish. Prince Gong knew of the association's existence, even though he knew less about its effectiveness to act as a lever in British democracy.[31] *Punch,* if it is any indication, quipped that "so frequently" did "the Reverend Gentlemen" of the association "induce on their mesmerised hearers a state of coma" that the phenomenon earned fame as "oratorial opium."[32] More seriously, social and political intransigence marred attempts by the association to convert key officials to an anti-opium view on legalization. Its impetuous entreaties to the secretary of state for India in 1858 and the secretary of the treasury in 1860 never achieved any political breakthrough. Neither did anti-opium speeches in parliament. London was not a central location for political lobbying, which was sometimes more inhibited than enhanced by its closeness to power. Speaking from a distance, however, carried its own advantage.

Bridging the social and political distance to the expansive world of international public opinion began with small steps. In December 1869, the *Shanghai News Letter* and the *China Overland Trade Report* somewhat moderated the July meeting to Gong "bidding adieu" to the prince, a version transmitted to the *Straits Times Overland Journal,* based in Singapore. In the context of a colonial public setting, the anti-opium protest easily exposed British official vulnerabilities. The *Straits Times Overland Journal* condemned the protest for "about as cool and unwarranted an insult as it is possible to conceive, the meaning clearly being: we are glad to see the last of you, and should be still better pleased if you would take away your Opium and Missionaries too."[33]

That was exactly the point, and British disagreement from Singapore could not stop Alcock from recalling the charge of opium "forced upon China" in 1871, when speaking to the British government's Committee on Indian Finance. Worse still, Alcock extrapolated that the entire Treaty of Tianjin had been "extorted from its [China's] fears," echoing a combination of the 1869 demarche and Elgin's 1859 argument.[34] By backing the prince in an official setting, Alcock conveyed a Qing position where Qing diplomats never got to speak: in internal government consultations at the heart (or brain) of the empire in London. Tellingly, Alcock never dismissed the protest on the grounds that it was "Manchu," "Chinese," "Oriental," or some other cultural particularism. Subsequently, the Committee on Indian Finance remained the chosen venue for repeated anti-opium representations. It was there that in 1873 Indian economist Dadabhai Naoroji announced his theory of India's drain and opium as a primary factor in the imperialist sabotage of Indian national finance.[35]

As for the demarche, it received its next endorsement in January 1872 by Sir Robert Hart, head of Imperial Maritime Customs in China, who cited the protest's "take away your opium and your missionaries and you will be welcome," echoing Wenxiang's similar call for the removal of extraterritoriality. Hart's American colleague Hosea Ballou Morse followed suit in his 1918 voluminous synthesis of Qing-Western relations, titled *The International Relations of the Chinese Empire.*[36] Following, Westel W. Willoughby prolonged the life of the demarche in his *Foreign Rights and Interests in China* of 1927, a standard reference work for policy makers around the world.[37] Each of these affirmations helped make the demarche the most widely cited reflection of what the Qing state and Chinese society thought of opium legalization, and why the consequences could not be ignored.

Invisible to contemporaries but surfacing in hindsight, a group of global endorsers used the thread of the demarche to draw global circles of influence and opinion formation. Soon this group, united by little else than their sympathy for Prince Gong's representations, grew to incorporate others beyond high-placed protagonists of British imperial history.

Popular journals joined the chorus of support, such as the London-based *Food Journal* in 1873, self-described as "A Review of Social and Sanitary Economy." The journal was founded in 1870 by John Morris Johnson, born to a chief rabbi in Sweden and head of the printer and international exhibition agent J. M. Johnson and Sons. Social sensibilities were a conspicuous orientation of Johnson's social engagement as the guardian of the poor in the City of London, in his founding of the Western Free School for Girls.[38] In the *Food Journal,* four series of essays engaged with the "Horrors of Opium." We do not know whether any readers took issue with the journal's motto in this context: "Appetite runs, whilst Reason lags behind."[39] What is certain is that the journal alerted readers to the magnitude of opium damage among the Chinese people. Millions of Chinese bodies and brains, by no fault of their own, were being destroyed while British readers sat in the comfort of their homes.

Beyond the Anglosphere, French journals rushed to attest to the validity of Prince Gong's protest, allowing its virtual extension to global expressions of anti-opium empathy. The *Revue des deux mondes,* so named to reflect its commitment to Atlantic reportage, voiced energetic support, building on the precedent of an anti-opium article in 1870. According to the *Revue,* numerous French travelers in China reported that there was no "more terrible scourge in the world than opium."[40] It is reasonable to assume that French testimony added considerably to the persuasiveness of Prince Gong's arguments in French eyes.

But even if conspicuous, the proliferation of anti-opium references, along with the disproportionate centrality of Prince Gong in this proliferation, does not explain itself. Nor did it occur in a vacuum of global indifference. The *Revue*'s anti-opium coverage attracted a second round of favorable reviews in newspapers and books outside France and the French empire. In 1873, the opium writings of French scientist Fernand Papillon in the *Revue* caught the attention of Yale sinologist Samuel Wells Williams.[41] In the 1890s, the *Revue* discussed Thomas de Quincey's opium writings, with a new edition of his *Confessions of an English Opium-Eater* recommended as further reading.[42] Simultaneously, Charles Richet, winner of the Nobel Prize in Physiology or Medicine and later editor of the *Revue scientifique,* presented one of the first rigorous comparisons of addictive substances in 1877. Based partly on self-experiment, partly on observation of patients, Richet's perspective compared the effects of hashish, opium, and coffee. His results, published in English in 1879, introduced the scientific concept of physical and emotional hypersensitivity. Richet explained sedative effects of opium alongside the effect of hashish on the loss of temporal and spatial recognition and the extreme ambitions fueled by coffee. Richet, too, confirmed Chinese popular alienation by British attempts to provoke the habit by all means possible, even though he disputed their physiologically lethal effects. In terms of long-term resilience, this French commentary survived as long as Robert Hart's anti-opium reference. Several of them fed into the report of the Philippine Opium Commission of 1903, others from the *Revue des deux mondes* into critiques of opium policy in the French Indo-Chinese Customs Office in Saigon, while Richet's publications found their place in the United Nations Bulletin of Narcotics in the 1950s.[43] As to be shown later, the confluence of Chinese anti-opium publicity and European drug research appeared in recurrent combination, in the 1870s and again in the 1910s. Across British and French publication markets, anti-opium sympathies mobilized a diversity of professions, languages, and incentives to create Atlantic support for a Qing protest of seemingly universal appeal. Further following the trail of princely promoters through time illuminates that this broad-ranging, Atlantic interest in Chinese anti-opium opposition moved from the belletristic to the scientific and medical worlds of thought.

These connections were not as random as they might appear in an exclusive focus on transnational sequences of supportive citations. Starting simultaneously in the 1870s, the publicity nexus linking scientific knowledge from China with incipient European opiate research led to open displays of Chinese domestic opium samples at the Paris World Fair in 1878. British "commissars" of the Statistical Department at the Imperial Maritime Customs in Shanghai had received the samples from Yinkow (Niuchang) in Manchuria, Wenzhou in Zhejiang, Sichuan, and Guangdong. A German journalist took note of the irony of a British representation of the Qing Chinese exposition while gratuitously ignoring the fact that the World Fair celebrated the recovery of France from its war with Prussia in 1870 and 1871. The contradictions that seem self-evident today were not necessarily seen at the time. Writers and readers appeared oblivious to the divergent meanings that opium acquired in political mobilization. Discussions could mention in one breath Chinese opium samples and the anti-opium literature inspired by Prince Gong, one seemingly as indisputable as the other, endorsed by authorities like the former president of the Swiss Association of Pharmacists, Friedrich August Flückiger.[44] After the World Fair, the Chinese opium samples were transferred to pharmaceutical institutes in Paris.

Reminiscent of the *Food Journal*'s anti-opium series in 1873, British newspapers organized an 1876 essay competition on the theme of Britain's opium policy. Coinciding with a parliamentary anti-opium intervention in defense of Prince Gong by Henry Richard, the competition fueled the ambitions of Frederick Storrs Turner, the secretary of the Society for the Suppression of the Opium Trade, established in 1874. Turner's resulting essay took its cue from Prince Gong's insistence on some parameters of ethical governance. This could be seen as confirming both the righteousness of Chinese protest and liberal expectations of an empire uplifting not only others but also itself. Turner plunged into a veritable rage and accused the British government of enriching its treasury, "regardless of the consequences to China." Offering perhaps the most scathing critique of the opium trade to be offered by a historian, he decried the institution as nothing less than "an anachronism in this nineteenth Christian century."[45]

While the elongating series of transnational support for Prince Gong's interpretation demonstrates emotional mobilization as a historical event, the context in which each show of support emerged pointed to broader networks of publicity and social and cultural agendas at moments of recalibration. Cultural journals like the quarterly *Contemporary Review*, founded in 1866 by Alexander Strahan, a staunch supporter of Christian liberal reform and publisher of Alfred, Lord Tennyson, did not take long to chime in. In 1876, the *Contemporary Review* was edited by Sir James Thomas Knowles, the founder of the Metaphysical Society, Tennyson's architect, and later founder of the *Nineteenth Century* literary magazine.[46]

The intellectual and social domains of science, religion, and society endowed Prince Gong's one-time protest with a long legacy that could move far away from the original message. Turner's anti-opium article struck a distinctly patriotic tone to radicalize rather than moderate the critique: "We are not now planning to save China," he called out, "but to save England; we are not consulting how the Chinese may be cured of an enslaving vice; but how we may extricate ourselves from an unjust and dishonourable policy."[47] Here, Chinese anti-opium sentiment triggered British imperial self-criticism, evidencing that even the soul searching of the powerful can draw on transnational reflexes.

THE DISTINCT WORLD of social reform as a domain of shared sentiment driven by social dissatisfaction may help in delineating the following phase of anti-opium adoptions, especially since it functioned as a key conduit of the anti-opium agenda to an audience of states. Publishing agencies and houses acted as primary producers of public sentiment. In addition to the *Contemporary Review*, the SSOT's own house journal enlarged the voice of Prince Gong. In 1875, that voice reappeared at the top of China headlines.[48] In February, the murder of Augustus Raymond Margary, a British diplomatic interpreter, briefly eclipsed the anti-opium cause, culminating in the Chefoo Convention of 1876.[49] In 1876, Turner's own book, *British Opium Policy and Its Results to India and China*, reached the printers, laying the early foundations only to be refuted, and feebly so, by the Royal Commission from 1893 to 1895.[50]

Members and affiliates of the SSOT undertook their lobbying against the opium trade by honing strategies of information sharing and refashioning the language of politicization. Turner, as both institutional beneficiary and socially active sponsor of anti-opium publicity, transmitted Prince Gong's protest to the *Church Missionary Intelligencer and Record* and the *London Quarterly Review* in 1876.[51] These outlets, he knew, communicated British domestic public opinion to missionaries in Asia, the Middle East, East Africa, North America, the Pacific islands, and New Zealand. As a global bulletin board of missionary problems and prospects, the *Church Missionary Intelligencer and Record* was dedicated to refer indigenous and "native" perceptions of social problems to English readers. The *London Quarterly Review,* of the same age as the *Revue des deux mondes,* had first brought Charles Darwin's *Origin of Species* (1859) to public attention, before the adoption of Darwinist ideas into a series of imperialist projects. In 1865, it skyrocketed to fame with the publication of David and Charles Livingstone's *Narrative of an Expedition to the Zambesi and Its Tributaries.* (Incidentally, the publishing house that ran the *London Quarterly Review,* John Murray, recently published the opium-themed Ibis trilogy by celebrated novelist Amitav Ghosh.) In content, the *Review* voiced support for a variety of causes that shared the theme of social abuse. From the gradual abolition of slavery to the improvement of prison conditions and mental asylums, it was preoccupied with the socially destitute by no fault of their own. Preexisting sympathies shared a strain of sentiment with the anti-opium cause: the humanitarian duty to empathize with socially disconnected groups, the effort to represent those whose suppression prevents them from speaking for themselves, the political focus on state intervention as a solution—all of it would have a familiar ring to anti-opiumists. Those subscribing already to one of the above causes did not have to stretch their sensibilities to empathize with the opposition to the opium trade.

The Politics of Public Opinion

Channeling the combined work of agendas, outlets, and broad audiences was the belief that public opinion, in its national, imperial, and international scopes, functioned as a salient force of political criticism. Prior to Gallup, public opinion was surely ill defined and yet it worked precisely when taken for granted and explicitly not the product of partial interests, be they journalistic producers of news or activist circles of criticism. At odds with the analytic murkiness of public opinion, it was never easy to ascertain who speaks for it, how to determine its direction, or, in the case of Prince Gong, how to pinpoint the time and place where a proliferation of opinion originated. But since the 1870s, both civic producers and state targets of public opinion seemed to accept that imperial foreign policy was ineluctably accountable to international public opinion. Perhaps because of its anonymity and indeterminacy, it could not be brushed aside.

International public opinion became the proxy of antidrug lobbyism, an imagined yet powerful realm of global public adjudication. But unlike anticolonial lobbyism solely aimed to reach the movers and shakers of empires, this lobbyism rotated back to the origins of anti-opium protest in Beijing. Within the identifiable circle of the Chinese foreign ministry and the foreigners in its orbit, anti-opium inspirations, references, and influences turned in many different directions. In 1875, Scottish doctor John Dudgeon penned an anti-opium article in Beijing. Usually, Dudgeon tended to the 120 patients in his care and taught as a professor of anatomy and physiology at the Tongwenguan, the Qing's preeminent school of governance, aiming at national renovation by instructing the next generation in mathematics, international law, German, chemistry, astronomy, and physics. No doubt thanks to the social milieu of this work, Dudgeon's anti-opium article was received favorably at the Zongli Yamen, where it received full "interest and approval."[52]

In the same year of 1875, six years after the Gong-Alcock meeting, the Zongli Yamen became the nodal point and confluence of anti-opium cooperation. This time, the conveyor was a transnational Chinese. Chen Laisun had pledged to communicate "the sentiments" of the SSOT to the Qing, acting much like a courier of anti-opium perceptions. Chen had studied in the United States and now, as a freshly minted graduate, stopped over in Britain on his journey home, where he met with the SSOT. Thus, Chen appears to have become the first person to bring together two major orbits of influence. He brought the lengthening legacy of Prince Gong to the SSOT and the SSOT's vote of confidence to the Zongli Yamen.[53] As for Chen's own role, his mobility propelled anti-opium opposition from one social and cultural setting to another, but it hinged on Qing support. At the same time, the Qing sponsored the Chinese Educational Mission in Connecticut, where Chen was enrolled. The government reaped strategic benefits from this overseas platform of China's Self-Strengthening Movement. Chen advanced to become an interpreter at the Fuzhou Navy Yard School and later personal secretary to Li Hongzhang, the powerful viceroy of Zhili Province. Meanwhile, the significance of the SSOT–Zongli Yamen interface did not escape contemporary observers, such as Dutch legal scholar and later colonial minister Baron Willem Karel van Dedem, active in the incipient Dutch anti-opium debate.[54]

Therefore, both the Qing and the British government faced the sea change in international popular discontent with the political status quo of unlimited opium trading from British India to Qing China. In 1876 and 1880, Henry Richard, a member of parliament from Merthyr Tydfil in Wales, once again referred to Prince Gong in the House of Commons, backed by Richard Cobden, among others. The opium trade, in Richard's words, was a trade "in pestilence, poverty, vice, madness, and death." What an uproar followed! Samuel Small Mander, cofounder of Mander Brothers, the British empire's leading manufacturer of varnishes, voiced unqualified support.[55] Lewis Appleton, the honorary secretary of the British and Foreign Arbitration

Association, joined in the effort, hoping for British-Chinese reconciliation and peace.[56]

Richard's confrontation was not just a rerun of familiar accusations, reference points, and demands. In his representation, the Zongli Yamen, and specifically Grand Secretary Wenxiang, became figureheads of legitimation. Alcock, "the statesman who had the most intimate acquaintance with, and the longest experience of, Chinese affairs," had been "pressed hard" by Prince Gong and Wenxiang "to release them from the obligation to admit opium at all." This also meant that Whitehall's failure equaled Alcock's tragedy. "Sir Rutherford had been powerless to assent to that demand." In fact, Richard seemed to raise his finger, the British government was "yielding to the clamour" of the China merchants, the pressure group most closely approximating the anti-opium movement's enemy number one. The opium trade, Richard concluded in entire agreement with Prince Gong's early warning, was a "good-bye to our reputation for good faith in China and everywhere else."[57]

This "everywhere else" included Philadelphia in the United States, a hub of Quaker financing, publishing, and lobbying on the East Coast, which should have raised flags among anyone familiar with the Quakers' success in the cause of international abolitionism. In 1877, Prince Gong's premonition of China's ruin debuted in the *Penn Monthly,* a journal similar in intellectual orientation as the *London Quarterly Review,* "devoted to Literature, Art, Science and Politics."[58] In total, Britain saw three full-fledged anti-opium books published between 1877 and 1882.[59] The young journal *China's Millions* and Hudson Taylor's China Inland Mission even used Prince Gong to press for proselytizing the poor heathen Chinese, resembling the *Evangelical Magazine and Missionary Chronicle.* Hudson Taylor's childhood friend and secretary of the *Mission,* Benjamin Broomhall, published *The Truth about Opium-Smoking* in 1882, followed by Alcock's renewed plea before parliament.[60]

Elongated as it had become, the series of anti-opium adaptations may be less impressive for its inner, ideological, or argumentative coherence than for its globally variegated linkages to local, national, and imperial partner causes. Few attacked publicly the demarche as incredulous or overdrawn. Over time, the cascade of support flowed into a routine of mobilization, temporarily for its own sake, neither limited to missionary supporters nor wholly streamlined toward missionary objectives. The protest transitioned through missionary circles but was never absorbed by them.

To take stock of the anti-opium cause in the mid-1880s—ideologically, culturally, and socially—makes us realize that the cause had morphed into something more global than any of its individual or collective supporters could fathom without the benefit of twenty-first century archival research. Spencer Hill's *The Indo-Chinese Opium Trade* of 1884 considered the controversy "in relation to its history, morality, and expediency, and its influence on Christian missions. The author, a scholar at St. John's College at Cambridge University, had composed it as an essay that won the Maitland Prize at Cambridge in 1882. In 1844, two years after the end of the First Opium War, the prize was initially proposed for an "essay upon some subject connected with the propagation of Christianity in India," with an initial £1000 as a handsome reward and named, ironically, after a leader of the British army in India, Sir Peregrine Maitland.[61] Its publication received endorsement through a preface by Right Hon. Lord Justice Fry. But circulation, reception, and readership did not confine themselves to auctorial intentions. Instead, the book of more than one hundred pages, printed by Pickard Mall and Horace Hart at the University of Oxford, strengthened the secular focus of mobilization by moving from the world of Cambridge into the wider readership of social reform in Britain and beyond, like so many anti-opium writings pouring out of Paternoster Row in London, where the book's publisher, Henry Frowde, was based. A largely secular reception and citation legacy was not the only irony of Hill's account. As he confessed in the introductory "advertisement," he "commenced with strong prejudice against the Anti-Opium agitators; but my investigation of the facts and arguments on both sides of the case compelled me to adopt their views, and forced me to the conclusion that our connection with the traffic is wholly unjustifiable." Perhaps Hill's elaborate, indeed complete, reproduction of Prince Gong's demarche played a not insignificant role in his own conversion to the anti-opium cause.[62]

In fact, by 1900, the book *A Cycle of Cathay* by China hand W. A. P. Martin paraded the first strains of anti-missionary sentiment.[63] One of the most quoted anti-opium books, Joshua Rowntree's *The Imperial Drug Trade*—a Quaker-commissioned monograph—ran its second edition in 1906 and remained unsurpassed in reprints by any other anti-opium book.[64] In 1907, David Ekvall, a longtime resident at the Qing's western frontier, more proficient in Chinese than in English, had his *Outposts, or Tibetan Border Sketches* published by Alliance Press in New York to keep Prince Gong's protest alive.[65] In 1915, California-based historian and bibliophile Hubert Howe Bancroft, who today has a Berkeley library in his name, went even further. In Bancroft's visionary *The New Pacific,* Prince Gong's dark warning became an early announcement of the twentieth century as the Asian century.[66]

Considering that Prince Gong's demarche made him the foremost Chinese voice in the anti-opium cause, perhaps we may even describe him as the first international authority on China's official and popular opium perceptions. Reproductions and confirmations overseas turned his diplomatic protest into something of a literary commodity, catering to a global audience of ever more politicized consumers for more than forty years. Across religious creeds, professions, political orientations, cultural identities, and geographical networks of publishing, the demarche became a reference point like few others before, superseding in global serviceability even Lin Zexu's precedent. It is significant that without a center of command or a teleological agenda to coordinate them, the chain reactions to a single protest served to radicalize the social, cultural, and political meaning of the opium trade to hitherto unknown levels of intensity. As such, the chain reactions did not act in the vanguard of one identifiable political interest, a distance to state power that propelled the momentum of augmenting support. They all insisted that no society deserved opium's inflictions and no empire warranted its design. The scale of global anti-opium affirmations revealed how deep the fissures ran in the international law of opium legalization, rendering the Treaty of Tianjin more porous than ever before.

The First Anti-Opium Alliance

Although separated by biographical background, professional profile, and competing ideological commitments, journalists, intellectuals, publicists, policy experts, advisers, and many others connected through the virtual bond of extolling Prince Gong as an anti-opium hero. Yet they never formed an institutional group. However, several proved capable of institutionalization below the global commons, enabling the first anti-opium alliance to form in 1877. The Cantonese K'euen Keae Shay (*quanjie she,* or KKS)—the Association for the Promotion of Abstinence—merged nongovernmental, non-missionary groups of transnational mobilization. Emerging on the Qing empire's southern edge, it identified Chinese diagnoses of opium consumption as not merely an economic liability for the state but a popular risk of public health.[67]

Recruitment was the first step in KKS-driven mobilization. Formally based in Guangdong, the KKS drew members from Jiangsu, Sichuan, and Jiangnan provinces. A second tier of transnational cooperation gained British partners, including from the SSOT, now two years old.[68] The KKS-SSOT partnership echoed central arguments developed by Prince Gong, which may serve as a good reason to consult its own publications for the original words. "It is certain that a reversal of the policy pursued by our Government hitherto," the SSOT admitted to the KKS, "would remove a great scandal, and exalt Britain in the eyes of all mankind . . . that it would conciliate the Chinese nation, and do more than anything else in our power to promote beneficial intercourse between the two nations." A two-pronged, Chinese-British, anti-opium representation, even with its political demands yet unspecified, "would remove two serious dangers, the danger to India of a sudden and unexpected collapse of the opium revenue at a time when it would be most inconvenient to meet it, and the danger of a rupture with China, which is always imminent so long as this scandal continues."[69] Reversing legalization while ensuring a Sino-British rapprochement anticipated the dynamics of effective anti-opium campaigning in the 1900s.

KKS-SSOT propaganda drew on *The Friend of China* to advertise partnership correspondence at "One Penny, or Seven Shillings per hundred," and to celebrate an emerging counter to the British Indian opium lobby.[70] Transnational cooperation was pitted against colonial interest groups, opening cleavages among British imperial administrators and observers and allowing, in turn, the closing of ranks around a cause rather than culture, ethnicity, or even language. National representation stood in no obvious contradiction to the transnational agenda and could be incorporated. Like Prince Gong, the KKS functioned as a virtual spokesperson of the "Chinese" national anti-opium sentiment, promoted when it was barely visible to foreign observers. The KKS emphasized that Chinese willingness to curb opium consumption was gaining force. The Qing's opium duties were pilloried as mere commercial convenience and as responding to British opium imports, not an authentic expression of political will. These core claims by the KKS-SSOT partnership began reaching American anti-opium writers and publishers beginning in 1882.[71] Two years later, American Methodists read about the KKS-SSOT work in their house journal.[72]

Such ambitious transnationalism to undermine an international legal settlement did not fail to spawn further Sino-British anti-opium partnerships. In 1881, twelve years after Prince Gong's demarche, Li Hongzhang, as viceroy of Zhili Province, arguably one of the Qing's most influential posts, added his name to invigorate the SSOT: "Opium is a subject in the discussion of which England and China can never meet on common ground," he told Frederick Storrs Turner, the SSOT secretary. Speaking on behalf of China, he expressed popular and governmental frustration with the two "Opium Wars" as by now a cultural fact: "China views the whole question from a moral standpoint; England from a fiscal."[73]

These cycles and iterations sketched an expansive array of political demands in the international public sphere. In new anti-opium views like those espoused by the SSOT, the opium trade was detrimental to Western missionaries in China and the British government alike. Chinese anti-Christian sentiment claimed that this religion was "professed by those who force upon them opium," and while Westerners previously felt confident to trace Chinese destitution to civilizational defects, now "the conduct of our Government" became directly responsible for "the physical and moral degradation of thousands of Chinese subjects."[74] Dissenters in China and the West strategically chose to pose in unison, revoking official policy, willfully ignoring geographic distance or proximity as determinants of loyalty, and, most importantly, denying international law's unchangeability.

In February 1881, four years after the first publication of KKS-SSOT correspondence, Qing officials occupied diplomatic positions in Britain, a considerable advance for representing Chinese social issues overseas with political potency. Zeng Jize, Qing ambassador to London, Paris, and St. Petersburg, made good use of his credentials. The son of Zeng Guofan, one of China's preeminent heroes for having militarily defeated the Taiping, he had scored a decisive diplomatic victory in the Russian negotiations that had yielded the Treaty of St. Petersburg and returned Yili to China. Writing to the SSOT, Zeng testified to the toxicity of Chinese perceptions of Britain as provoked by opium legalization. The SSOT's new secretary, Joseph Pease, an active anti-opium publicist in his own right, ensured that Zeng's backing of Prince Gong's demarche would not fall on deaf ears.[75]

An in-depth look into the social engineering of anti-opium lobbying conveys some of the multiplier effects that gave propaganda international traction. Joseph Pease reported proudly in 1881 that Zeng had established personal communications with him to "prevent anyone from falling into the mistake of considering that the Chinese Government has ceased to view the consumption of opium by its subjects otherwise than as one of the most grievous evils which ever befell a nation." Summarizing repeated anti-opium protests by China, its officials, and its people, Pease adopted the role of representing Chinese opposition: "We have, therefore, in 1860, 1869, 1880, and 1881, proofs of the way in which the Chinese people have been always protesting against the opium trade."[76] Other British members of Parliament added the official U.S. distance to the opium trade and China's prohibition treaty with the United States of 1844, showing "that the Chinese are still honest in their desire to induce this country to discontinue the trade."[77] Even if American infringements of prohibition were rife, the fact of legal prohibition sufficiently exonerated the American republic, putting the onus in Chinese eyes even more on Britain. Here, the U.S. comparison fulfilled a similar function as later prohibitionist Japan. International comparisons did not relativize but radicalized the debate.[78]

SSOT connections made sure that Prince Gong's ghost kept haunting the British public sphere. The opening chapter of *Chinese Writers on Opium* appeared in an acerbic collection of pamphlets, dedicated to a council member of the SSOT. The publisher, Partridge and Company, a historian, bibliographer, and sales manager, reprinted Frederick Storrs Turner's *British Opium Policy and Its Results to India and China:* "In view of the increasing attention which is being given to this important subject, Messrs. P& Co. confidently anticipate that the work will be deemed worthy of a notice by the Editor of Allen's Indian Mail."[79] Alcock did his part in 1883: "We forced the Chinese Government to enter into a treaty to allow their subjects to take opium." The Zongli Yamen had "at different times officially or privately . . . shown the greatest readiness to give up the whole Revenue, if they could only induce the British Government to co-operate with them in any way to put it down."[80] This diplomacy of scandal worked hard to stir up a greater international outcry than the Treaty of Tianjin could withstand. In a sense, the peace settlement grew worse as it grew older. The strengthening momentum of mobilization rendered the military, diplomatic, and legal victory of 1860 weaker as the years passed: Nothing in international law could set in stone future perceptions that threatened the fundamentals of legalization.

Tellingly, the missionary body in China, a group beholden to agendas of social reform for the spiritual and physical betterment of Chinese society, admitted in 1884 that the opium problem was made of history and politics, giving carte blanche to the missionary establishment itself. The popular Chinese view, the pamphlet insisted, was "a permanent badge of their defeat in several wars, and the sense of humiliation aggravates their dislike for the 'outer barbarians.'" As a consequence of this perception, a political solution became imperative: "So that we can believe Prince Kung's wish, expressed to Sir Rutherford Alcock, to have been a heart-felt one: 'Take away,' he said, 'your opium and your missionaries, and we need have no more trouble in China.'"[81] If Chinese, British, Russian, and American caution at Tianjin left opium formally at the margins of Chinese-foreign relations, now it became an uncomfortably central agenda. To right old wrongs, lobbyists shaped the anti-opium agenda into a panacea for all major ailments of Sino-British relations. Finding a political alternative to legalization had to be made to appear less and less optional.

Simultaneously in the Francophone world, the anti-opium agenda reappeared with a different face in 1884. Journalist, librarian, and educator Philippe Athanase Cucheval-Clarigny felt certainly fully aligned with the debate. Two years before his induction into the Académie des sciences morales et politiques, he, too, rushed to Prince Gong's defense. French being the world's most influential language, alongside English, Cucheval-Clarigny's attestation reached beyond the confines of one colony or empire. Through the global distribution network of the *Revue des deux mondes,* where his article appeared in September 1884, readers could access Prince Gong's protest in Paris, London, Brussels, Liège, and The Hague; in St. Petersburg, Moscow, Tiflis, Leipzig, Berlin, Vienna, Lisbon, Milan, Florence, Madrid, Barcelona, Sweden, and Norway; as well as in Odessa, New York, Boston, San Francisco, Havana, and Buenos Aires.[82]

Cucheval-Clarigny was editor and director of *Le Constitutionnel* from 1845 to 1856 and *La Presse* from 1864 to 1870, author of *Histoire de la presse en Angleterre et aux États-unis* in 1857, and member of the Académie des sciences morales et politiques since 1886. These roles included him in a European exchange of reform ideas and letters that was intellectually cognate.[83] His fifty-page article paraded the main thesis in its title: "La déclin de la puissance Chinoise." Here, a causal link was established to explain the decline of China as a civilization through the rising power of the West.[84] So compelling did it appear to German sinologists that they took note of Cucheval-Clarigny's opinion piece in their major journals.[85] Whether an English, French, or German press, Prince Gong's demarche instilled it with the odium of opium.

To interrogate when a space for political change became conceivable, we have to shift the perspective to other core charges of the demarche as they came into the focus of the opposition. American Methodist support in 1886 welcomed the demarche warmly if belatedly. But the pro-Meiji paper *Japan Weekly Mail* in Yokohama offered words of caution in 1889, eight years after a fleeting engagement with the demarche.[86] "It seemed fair to hope that the 'coercion' argument was at an end, and that, China herself having elected that the opium trade should continue, we should at least hear no more about her scruples and her sufferings. . . . It was felt that the old platform was gone and that the bottom had been knocked out of all agitation on the old lines." The SSOT, the paper claimed, had plunged into crisis "towards the end of 1885," facing financial cuts, a slackening publication schedule from monthly to quarterly issues, and the retirement of Turner as secretary.

Just what had the SSOT really achieved, the *Japan Weekly Mail* challenged its readers, besides assuming "merely a position of observation"? Institutional fragmentation was rife; "its offices were joined to those of another Society; and generally there was withdrawal all round." With the SSOT virtually vanished, the paper pronounced its disappearance: There was "little theoretical use, and no practical benefit, in discussing the opium trade to revert to the doings of our predecessors in the Far East between 1800 and 1860. Opium is now an article of daily consumption by a large portion of the inhabitants of China, who, if they cannot be supplied from abroad, will get it at home."[87] Politics, this diagnosis suggested, did create new facts on the ground, uninhibited by the transnational quibbles of a budding NGO.

But ironically, the determination of these dismissals testified to the existing strength of the anti-opium sentiment, a strength visible in growing venues of support and coalition-building between anti-opium organizations. Indeed, playing down Prince Gong's arguments sparked a new debate of its own. The demarche benefited from the attention by its opponents. In 1893, the *First Report of the Royal Commission on Opium* targeted the firestorm of anti-opium protesters within Britain. And yet Prince Gong's "affecting appeal" converted even some former proponents of the trade, not only the likes of Hill but also Thomas Wade.[88] Outlasting, certainly in vigor, the Royal Commission of 1895, the demarche then reached Herbert Giles, the accomplished sinologist in Cambridge. Giles's contact with the demarche, in turn, became so famous that the British Consul at Ningbo included it as a defining feature of Giles's life in the *Chinese Biographical Dictionary*.[89] The list of luminaries in support continued. After the Boxer War in 1900, Sir Robert Hart still remembered the demarche and Wenxiang's addition: "Do away with your extraterritoriality clause, and merchant and missionary may settle anywhere and everywhere; but retain it, and we must do our best to confine you and our trouble to the treaty ports." To the director of Chinese Maritime Customs, "In these two utterances may be found the key-note of China's attitude to the missionary question."[90]

Even if the protest of 1869 became an unrivaled article of faith for anti-opiumists around the world, that left the meaning of their globality still unanswered. We may be impressed with Prince Gong's skills as a wordsmith, but the external effects beyond the circles of support remained out of sight for several years, with government constituencies remaining the most stubborn audience of all. Economically, the successive realization of the Qing's own poppy cultivation program in the 1880s risked rendering any talk of prohibition null and void. Socially, only a minority of those supporting Prince Gong ideologically became professional activists.

On the level of ideological mobilization, however, repeated confirmations of Prince Gong's righteous cause made his protest emblematic of the injustices inherent in Chinese-Western relations.[91] It is true that the accumulation of affirmations becomes visible only in hindsight. None of the demarche's supporters engaged in even an attempt to delineate the demarche as an icon of the cause. What became visible at the time was a radicalized understanding of opium in the Tianjin peace settlement, leaving the legalization clause in a trail of bitter politicization. Like never before, the opium trade

acquired an ominous transnational prominence through the global recep-
tivity of the demarche.[92] An American medical doctor represented a spectrum of opinion broader than he knew when stating in 1882, "There has
been too great readiness to accept all evils happenings to the Chinese individual, or nation, as the certain result of indulgence in this vice."[93]

The spectacle of his successful protest reminds us of Lin Zexu, whose
similar protest had crumbled into the disaster of the First Opium War. It
speaks to the ironic eclecticism of collective memory that Lin's failure en-
joys today, after generations of nationalist incantations, a more legendary
and representative statement than Prince Gong's success, an event too counterintuitive and implausible to fit nationalist narratives of imperialism. Engineering the protest required an elaborate Qing initiative. Like Lin, Prince
Gong used the allure of political predictions to argue that the opium trade
was corroding the Sino-British relationship beyond repair. But unlike Lin's
diagnosis of a British violation of political ethics in China and Britain, Prince
Gong couched the fallout as the inevitable result of a social deterioration
between Chinese and British people, rather than between their states. In this
new, nongovernmental focus, power politics appeared bereft of one power
essential for its maintenance: the capacity to appear legitimate in the eyes
of the suppressed and the ability to shield itself from the alienation of their
hatred.

When comparing the demarche with Lin Zexu's famed anti-opium protest to Queen Victoria, it strikes us again that the latter never reached its
recipient. Captain Warner of the *Thomas Coutts,* Lin's courier to the British
government, wrote to Lord Palmerston on June 7, 1840, to deliver Lin's
letter, but the Foreign Office refused to receive him.[94] Lin's protest, while
becoming a rallying point of nationalist memory, failed to resonate across
cultures and societies.[95] It fell to Lin's own descendants to raise his historical profile, just as in Britain the First Opium War has remained a warning
only to some.[96]

The memory of opium suffering, then, did not constitute an exclusive
cultural monopoly of the Chinese people. "If the drug had been as beneficial as it has been baneful," another non-Chinese anti-opium protagonist
wrote in 1905, "its history to patriotic Chinese would still be a history of
overflowing humiliation." Memory is not so much a mirror of historical
experience, as is commonly assumed, but the product of how we in the
present imagine past experience. Foundational tropes of China's national
victimization appeared sporadically. "The linking of the religion of Jesus
of Nazareth with the British opium trade is as bitter an irony as professing
Christians have ever brought on themselves, which is saying much," Rowntree wrote. "To the Chinese, they came together, spread together, have been

fought for together, and finally legalised together. Nor can the natives know that the humiliation of the combination is felt by many on Western shores as keenly as it is in their own land."[97] Jumping ahead to 1918, H. B. Morse published *International Relations of the Chinese Empire,* arguably unchallenged as a reference on Chinese international history until John Fairbank's 1953 *Trade and Diplomacy on the China Coast.*[98] And only then, after forty-nine years, did Prince Gong's demarche come to a temporary halt and cease to attract cyclical and serious attention. From 1869 to 1918, a plethora of anti-opium articles, pamphlets, and books in Singapore, Britain, the United States, Germany, France, Japan, and elsewhere had endowed the original protest with propagandistic glory. We have to assume that the complete global number beyond these estimates must be even higher, considering the logistical limitations of historical research.

For the first time since the abolitionist upheaval in the Atlantic world of the early nineteenth century, British imperial policies were targeted by a massive global accusation of having perpetrated the crime of a foreign society's abuse. Recognition of this interpretation proliferated, showing how mobilization across borders could forge a shared understanding across disparate social settings and political motivations. The global anti-opium campaign that sprang from these connections was disproportionate to the initial momentum and audience of the demarche, shaping instead a multifarious movement of its own. Propagated in East and Southeast Asia, western Europe, and North America, the opium trade became one of the leitmotifs of an inter-cultural affront.

THE SECOND OPIUM WAR, then, encapsulated larger dilemmas of how to relate to a controversial past. The contradictions between the diplomatic experience of opium legalization at war's end and the mobilization of political memory call into question the discontinuity in postwar perceptions of what the Tianjin settlement had accomplished, at whose initiative and at what cost. Major wars, like every human experience itself, change their meaning over time dramatically. Even the most decisive victory or defeat cannot fix its own interpretations or project them into the future. Like politics itself, memories forage the past for friends and foes, victims and perpetrators. The fiat of the Peace of Tianjin was not able to settle its legacy and afterlife. As an event once deemed irreversible, it fell prey to transnational politicization. Tellingly, a simplified view of the past easily became the handmaiden of politicization in the present. Politicized postwar generations sought to establish not only what happened but whether the results could be lived with. It was successive generations, rather than warriors themselves, who made memories of war act with social and political force. The contestation of memory remade history in the image of the present.

Although the Treaty of Tianjin of 1858 and the Peking Convention of 1860 established the legality of this peace settlement, its legitimacy in Chinese memory split off into its own development. Debate over the verdict of Tianjin, its meaning and its effects, is reflected in competing efforts to name the war itself. The English term "Arrow War" takes the casus belli to be the defining feature.[99] The term declares the British imperialism of free trade, referring to the commercial and administrative conquest of the China market, as the primary priority.[100] By contrast, Lord Elgin regarded "that wretched question of the 'Arrow'" an embarrassment at best and, confiding to his wife, "a scandal to us."[101] Some aggressors at the time considered the Arrow incident a "brutal injustice" and an undesirable aspect altogether.[102] Thus, even protagonists of the aggressor nation would have disagreed with the designation chosen by their postwar compatriots.

Critiques of the Arrow incident lent greater support to the term "Second Opium War" and its emphasis on the British desire to expand the opium trade. In this suspected opium strategy, "Britain was the sole master, India was its instrument and China was the ultimate victim."[103] The opium trade as a core interest of British war and peace objectives permeates non-English histories. In Chinese, "Second Opium War" (*dierci yapian zhanzheng*) has become the only politically accepted and unchallenged designation in China. Here, opium legalization acquired an outsized prominence compared to its formal marginality in the peace treaty documents.[104]

Despite the historical layering of political baggage, the ideological implications of a Second Opium War stand for a global rather than an exclusively Chinese accumulation of emotional historical memory. The understanding that a political opium interest pervaded all of British imperial expansion was too simple not to believed. This may explain why it enjoyed such a remarkable global career and justified the term "Second Opium War" in Japanese, French, German, and Spanish historiography.[105] Multilingual historians often choose the "Arrow War" for their English books but use "the Second Opium War" for the Chinese translations, despite substantive reservations to the term in the English text.[106] Opium may be related to the war's "origins" and "genesis," but its status as a war goal remains overcast by memory rather than underpinned by documentation. "How exactly was opium related to the *Arrow* War? Their lordships did not say."[107]

The terms "Arrow War" and "Second Opium War" capture marginal aspects of the war as well as the peace. Western peace aims secured commercial, political, and social privileges: diplomatic missions in Beijing, unlimited passport travel into the Chinese hinterland, the opening of eleven more ports to commerce (in addition to the five ports guaranteed by the Treaty of Nanjing), the opening of the Yangzi River for foreign civilian and military navigation, the right of Christian proselytizing (including Protestant, Catholic, and Russian Orthodox denominations), and extraterritorial protection through an entire system of foreign jurisdiction, all against the backdrop of a hefty Qing indemnity of five million taels.[108] Each of these privileges required extensive Chinese collaboration rather than territorial colonization, giving the peace settlement the imprint of "informal empire"—or, in Chinese, "unequal treaties" (*bupingdeng tiaoyue*).[109] In most other domains of foreign diplomatic and trade privileges, the opium issue excepted, continuity held sway as intended by the peace settlement. Extraterritoriality continued until the early 1940s; complete Chinese control over foreigners' legal rights and privileges was only restored in 1949, upon the establishment of the People's Republic of China.

Of all aspects denoting victor's justice, none was more fiercely and earlier under attack than opium legalization. Opium, as more than one critic came to assert, "was ham-stringing the Chinese Nation."[110] Karl Marx, writing as a journalist in his London exile, had a different take: "The first opium-war," he tried to prophesy, "succeeded in stimulating the opium trade at the expense of legitimate commerce, and so will this second opium-war do if England be not forced by the general pressure of the civilized world to abandon the compulsory opium cultivation in India and the armed opium propaganda in China."[111] The next chapters will demonstrate how the scripted legacy of this new anti-opium ideology gathered international political force.

CHAPTER THREE

GROUNDS OF OBJECTION

India, America, Asia

NOT ALL FORMS and phases of anti-opium mobilization shared the sheer placelessness of global endorsements of a Qing demarche. The 1890s featured a different kind of cooperation against the opium trade, characterized by locally intimate coalitions forged between globally oriented pressure groups. Indicative of the logistical challenges these linkages involved, in late May 1891, it was a typo in a Western Union Telegraph Office in Maharashtra in western India that threatened the survival of one group. We may never know whether it was the heat of the early summer, the fatigue of a late night, or simple carelessness that caused a clerk to telegraph the price of an attractive estate in Pune at $20,000 instead of $12,000.[1] The consequences of the typo encapsulated the risks of transnationalism for a new anti-opium cause in India. The Pune estate was eyed by the core organization campaigning for two movements at once: the Sharada Saran, the Home of the Goddess of Learning. Devised as a refuge and a school to offer shelter and higher education to Hindu widows and girls, it was conceived in March 1889 in Bombay, once the chosen seat of the opium-trading British East India Company.

Initially, the Sharada Saran opened its doors only to widows of the Brahman, Kshatriya, and Vaisya castes of "priests," "warriors," and "agriculturists and merchants." Its female residents appropriated this social space "without fear of losing their caste, or of being disturbed in their religious belief." By 1891, the school was considered "no longer an experiment," housing forty-three pupils, thirty widows, and other girls.[2] By the 1900s, it had grown into six partner institutions and boasted twenty-five hundred residents across India. It has survived to this day as the Mukti Mission.[3]

Compared to the Chinese anti-opium appeals in Anglo- and Francophone international public opinion, Indian anti-opium activists launched their own campaign under different though equally global auspices. The Indian anti-opium movement sprang from the movement to empower ostracized Hindu girls with the assistance of capital from women supporters in the United States. Much like humanitarian nongovernmental organizations (NGOs) today, circles of financial support spread from Boston to the Pacific seaboard, affirming the Sharada Saran as a nominally Christian institution while remaining quite indifferent to its actual practice of syncretism, including Hindu teachings.[4]

But local conditions could jeopardize global intercontinental partnerships literally at a stroke, reminding us of the quotidian vulnerability and precariousness of the global anti-opium cause. The most immediate context for anti-opium campaigning was the strategic extroversion of the Sharada Saran curriculum and its cosmopolitan embrace of ideas from any discipline and country within reach. Students enjoyed access to "libraries, containing the best books on history, science, art, religions and other departments of literature . . . for the benefit of their inmates, and other women in their vicinity who may wish to read." In interdisciplinary spirit, lecturers pledged to "embrace in their topics, hygiene, geography, elementary science, foreign travel," inspired by the noble cause "to open the eyes and ears of those who long have dwelt in the prison-house of ignorance."[5] Unlike government schools, the Sharada Saran offered education as a form of social empowerment. The institution "combined the training of the hand with that of the head," protecting both in equal measure.[6]

But to alleviate the suffering of Hindu girls and widows through education and address social abuse in other than an escapist manner, the Sharada Saran required a permanent base as a launch pad. The problems attached to abuse outside the institution were rife, from persecution to paternal opium addiction by Indian husbands and fathers. With that in mind, the Sharada Saran had been founded by an energetic widow named Pandita Ramabai. Between age sixteen and twenty-one, Ramabai's parents, sister, brother, and husband had all fallen victim to famine and cholera. In contrast to these private calamities, she excelled early as a Sanskrit scholar and in her studies in England. With equal determination, she dispelled the financial confusion following the typo by Western Union. It took her two telegrams and a midnight train from Bombay to Matheran. That "forest crest," a British votary had once quipped, had been in deep sleep until "one day an Englishman came and woke her up."[7] Like the British political and commercial elite, upper-class Indians went there for physical and emotional recuperation in a mountain resort, including the owner of the coveted property in Pune. The contrast to Ramabai's cause could not have been starker. Arriving at the foothill in the wee hours of the morning, at five o'clock, the widow hired a horse to ride the sixteen miles up to her destination. Exhausted, she was received by the estate's owner in the morning and negotiated successfully, but not before she had explained her institution and the owner had consulted with his wife, for a reduction of the price down $9,000, or 27,500 rupees. Ramabai descended the mountain again, as reported, now "under a scorching sun, and, though weary and sore from her long ride, took the afternoon train to Bombay for the purchase money awaiting her there, and which the next day was deposited in a bank." Quite an effort for a widow close to deafness.[8]

The funds were in an account registered under the Sharada Saran in Bombay and boasting receipts of $36,285.70. Its sources stretched across seventy-two Ramabai Circles across the United States and Canada. Two years of lobbying by Ramabai had yielded those hard-won sympathies, with 113 lectures yielding start-up capital of $3,320, ten scholarships, numerous donations, and a weekly average of twenty-five letters in her mailbox. Such overseas backing was nearly the institution's only hope.[9] Helen Dyer's biography of Ramabai, published in 1900, reflected her personal investment in the publishing business. Her husband, Alfred, having continued her family tradition in publishing, would become a vocal advocate of the anti-opium cause. Alfred later liaised with a British reform publisher to contact Ramabai's colleague Soonderbai Powar to forge one of the first Indian-British anti-opium coalitions.[10] More broadly, Ramabai's existing prominence, proven by a plethora of biographical portraits, became perhaps the most important security for the survival of her school.[11] Contemporary Indian pioneers related themselves to Ramabai to gain attention and share, perhaps, some of her reputation.[12] Overseas support in conjunction with local reformist humanitarianism made the Sharada Saran a proud conjunction of "Eastern and Western civilization and education."[13]

Local conservative opposition, however, tried to impede transnational support for Hindu women, whether moral or material.[14] To Ramabai, this dilemma exerted its influence through the malleability of public opinion abroad and at home, a force seen as arbitrating between local elites and overseas donors. In the last decade of the nineteenth century, affirmations specifically over the causal difference that public opinion made in addressing social problems were not limited to India, Britain, the United States, and Canada but spread back to China and French Indochina.[15]

In spring 1889, Ramabai's address for the inauguration of the Sharada Saran pointed to the way ahead: "Let the newspapers and the general public say what they will, there is not the least doubt that the condition of the women of our country is heart-rending in the extreme," she exclaimed. "It is we, and we only, who can ever have a real knowledge of the welfare of our people. Foreigners can never know." But crucially, claiming to know better did not go much beyond maintaining institutional sovereignty. Turning to the few British men in attendance, she continued: "Gentlemen, in your parliament no one has allowed one of us sisters to plead the cause of India's unfortunate women; I am fully convinced that you men have no better idea of the oppression and woe suffered by Hindu women than the British Parliament has of the misfortunes of Hindustan."[16] But the way that public opinion impinged on the Sharada Saran's capacity to pursue its agendas old and new carried risks of its own, as proven by conservative Marathi newspapers like the *Kesari*. The tide of public opinion, however, turned in 1891, when Bombay became a metropolitan hotbed questioning the Sharada Saran's right of existence. Given this contested climate, every crisis had to be searched for its opportunities. In this manner, moving the Sharada Saran to Pune, although initially a relocation to rescue the school from precarious local criticism in Bombay, was turned into a publicity feat of its own, complete with Ramabai's story. Without both, it is by no means certain whether Indian anti-opium campaign could have developed beyond a lofty and utopian idea.

Indian Poverty Meets American Affluence

Readers must have guessed already that institutional publicity, at times bordering on Ramabai hagiography, did not tell the entire story. But a closer look at Sharada Saran activities betrays the fact, unsurprisingly, that Ramabai could not curry favor with local and overseas public opinion single-handedly. "Bai," as her students called her, gained a staunch ally in "Ukka," or elder sister: the impressive personality of Soonderbai H. Powar, one of the most visible reformers in Hindu women's protection, who had previously worked with Christian missions in Bombay. Like Ramabai, Powar had personally encountered the hardship she decided to help tackle as a social cause. The Kunbis, the workers toiling in Bombay factories, displaced from their rural origins by poverty and migrants in new centers of productivity, left a lasting if bitter impression on Powar. To alleviate the physical exhaustion and mental stress of overwork, men took to alcohol and opium. Their female coworkers told Powar of these newly acquired habits when Powar visited factories for preaching the gospel over lunch or dinner.[17] Not only did she subscribe to an emerging female critique of industrial conditions as a direct cause of male opium addiction, but Powar's previous engagement as a zenana teacher had sensitized her to male-induced social evils of all sorts, from opium and alcohol consumption to spousal abuse and financial mismanagement as the cause for prostitution.

But Powar as well as Ramabai knew that given the strength of a missionary establishment in India, as in other South, Southeast, and East Asian societies under imperial influence, being seen primarily as an importer of foreign support could undermine the validity of their local work. Instead, Powar took her lobbying overseas, from India to Britain.[18] A first Indian-British partnership formed in response to Powar's inaugural anti-opium tour in 1889. The initiative arose out of the transnationalism of publishing networks that gained an interest in Powar. The newspaper *Bombay Guardian* had a branch in London, headed by Alfred Stace Dyer, the owner of Dyer Brothers publishing. When the *Bombay Guardian* asked journalist Maurice Gregory to invite her, Powar was taken by surprise.[19] Less so Gregory himself who saw analogies in his and her work in social reform, having authored anti-opium pamphlets since 1900, such as *Britain's Crime against China: A Short History of the Opium Traffic*. Gregory's anti-opium engagement culminated in a pamphlet whose title summarized all aspects of his critique: "The stand for righteous rule in India: a thrilling chapter of anti-opium history: the opium traffic illustrated by the imprisonment of missionaries in Bombay, in consequence of exposing official subterfuge and criminality in connection therewith."[20] At the same time, Gregory's parallel preoccupations extended beyond the anti-opium cause, as evidenced by his scandalous exposure of prostitution in the service of the British Indian military, analogous to Powar's findings in Bombay. As for the mediation between the two by Dyer Brothers, the publisher was poised to become a major transnational funding source for mobilizing the public against social abuses specifically in South Asia, western Europe, and Britain. In many ways, Gregory's promotion of Powar corresponded with the U.S. promotion of the Sharada Saran.

Powar's signal chronicled her coalition with the British anti-opium circles around Dyer Brothers in an extended pamphlet titled *An Indian Woman's Impeachment of the Opium Crime of the British Government: A Plea for Justice for Her Country People*.[21] On the front page, a harrowing sketch conveyed the central charge. An Indian mendicant widow kneels in a gutter, two downtrodden children huddle around her. A little child sleeps in her arms—or is it dying? In a plea for help, the widow's arm stretches out to draw the eye of the reader to a snake, which, surrounded by black smoke, arises threateningly from "an Opium Smoker's Lamp." No help or alleviation in sight, the illustration captured the gruesome inevitability of social vulnerability, with the widow's hand raised to denote the attention denied and the complaint ignored (fig. 3.5).

Powar's indictment reached from newspapers like the *Bombay Guardian,* the *India Watchman,* and Madras's *Eastern Star* to Cornish Brothers publishers in Birmingham, Andrew Stevenson in Edinburgh, and Robert Stewart in Dublin. At Ludgate Hill in London, four retailers printed Powar's pamphlet, with Dyer Brothers being joined by Morgan and Scott at the Paternoster buildings, John Kensit at Paternoster Row, and the office of the *Christian Commonwealth.* Together, they enlarged an individual initiative into international print propaganda.

Anti-opium speeches formed the basis of Powar's pamphlet, having previously captivated British audiences at rallies organized with the support of Gregory and like-minded sympathizers. At least one American transnational observer, too, was present and rendered Powar's memorable appearance in such vivid detail that it is worth chronicling here: "[She] brought most pathetic appeals from both Hindu and Mohammedan women. One of these messages from a mass meeting of Mohammedan women in Lucknow was: 'We will thank the government to take the sword and kill the wives and children of opium smokers, so as to rid us of the agony we suffer!' When these bitter cries from outraged heathen women were repeated to Christian England the verdict of 'shame! shame!' was heard again and again, but will public sentiment be strong enough to induce the British government to forego this blood money which swells her revenues?"[22]

This was not just any American observer but the head of another premier lobbying group in the anti-opium movement, Wilbur F. Crafts, the head of the International Reform Bureau. Crafts's reaffirmation of Powar's influence extended her legacy into the 1900s, if not longer. In sharp contrast to Prince Gong, Powar's sympathizers and audiences not only took part in the proliferation of her views but came face to face with a protagonist of anti-opium mobilization, a physical encounter with a palpably intensified effect.

Others who witnessed Powar's anti-opium tour in 1889 and 1890 were positively enraptured by her declamations. No less than 116 of her public addresses dotted the extensive British press coverage. Sponsors included the Secretariat of the Women's Anti-Opium Urgency League, an NGO affiliated with the Quakers.[23] Paralleling a trope developed to great effect by Dadabhai Naoroji, when he analyzed the Indian economy being drained by strategic British financial manipulation, Powar argued that opium sapped men of their strength. But the social damage did not stop there. Women

FIGURE 3.1. Opium smoker in homelessness and poverty (English pamphlet).

Source: The Chinese Opium Smoker (London: S. W. Partridge & Co., ca 1880). Widener Library, Harvard University.

FIGURE 3.2. Opium smoker in homelessness and poverty (Chinese pamphlet).

Source: Jie yan xing shi tu. Fuzhou: Min bei sheng shu hui yin fa, Guangxu 26 (1900). Harvard-Yenching Library, Harvard University.

used the drug as an anti-depressant. Children were exposed to it when their mothers used it as a tranquilizer. Opium risks ranged from public health to family coherence, held together by the malfunctioning of social hierarchies.

These grievances mirrored Chinese opium dilemmas. Absent Indian-Chinese kinship in the circles observed here, it was kindred interest that aligned Chinese and the Indian anti-opium lobbying overseas with each other from a historical perspective. The analogies ran deep and wide. Victimization emerged as a central contention in Indian and Chinese mobilization. But triangulating Indian and Chinese mobilization networks reveals some biographical connections, as through missionary to China Frederick Howard Taylor, the son of Hudson Taylor.[24] His sister-in-law, Lucy Guinness, held both Ramabai and Powar in high esteem, honoring them with a double frontispiece in her account of India.[25] Finally, in both Indian and Chinese mobilization, the British government was made responsible for excessive opium supplies as the root cause of local and national social problems, from discrimination to gender relations.[26]

In the case of Indian women's lives, opium was presented as a fundamentally disruptive force, typifying the emerging leitmotif of oppression in India by problematizing the agency of Indian husbands and fathers.[27] To move from anti-opium speech to anti-opium action, Powar came to act, like Prince Gong before, as a representative of all Indian women at home. In many ways, this facile construction of transnational influence in the eyes of her audiences seemed necessary to justify the intensity of her attacks. Her vociferous criticism targeted the "English Christian Government" with arguments on its own cultural terms, adducing from the malicious consequences of the opium trade that the government must have surely intended it all and therefore be "in the clutches of the father of sin." Powar implied that the opium trade in its multifarious sprawl was inseparable from an empire run from the center and that the center in turn was inseparable from its avowed religious identity. Thus, the perceived combination of financial greed—"the government wants the money and nothing else" and exploitation "our poor India is suffering much"—led to the charge of hypocrisy as the only logical conclusion. According to this form of Indian opposition, British imperial belief undermined British imperial practice.[28]

At her transnational anti-opium rallies, Powar also saw plenty of opportunity to observe the extraordinary contagiousness of outrage. "Another woman rose," she reported, "and said in her Oriental way of speech, but full of sad meaning: "Tell the English Government that if they will stop the Opium curse, I and other women in India will willingly take off the skin of our bodies to make shoes for the English Government and people." As in Chinese perceptions of relations with Britain, Indians felt their relations with the empire to be poisoned almost beyond repair—unless, of course, political steps were taken to avert more radical opposition yet. "We will be very grateful if the Government will help us out of our sorrow. Our children and our dear ones die of Opium. Have pity on us, and stop the trade." Imperialism was to be reassessed by scrutinizing the legitimacy of its economic practices: "If the Government will stop the Opium, we will worship the Government."[29] Even when desperate to a point of aggression, the political purpose of the anti-opium cause never got entirely out of sight. In these ways, anti-opium arguments traced an interesting layer of political contestation located between anti-imperialist inclination and imperial self-reform.

Although falling short of a coherent political ideology of program, Powar's commitment to the anti-opium cause drew on identifiable sources of social reform, particularly the feminist strain that sought to empower women to speak up, at the very least, as a step toward improving their integrity against social victimization. But for the anti-opium cause to widen support overall, it was equally imperative to signal openness to and support for non-feminist parallels of anti-opium opposition. Powar was fortunate to be able to draw on parallel mobilizations in her own time and country that could be nominally incorporated into her anti-opium representations. In such a case in October 1891, Powar reported on several hundred anti-opium protesters meeting back in India, in the Baradari of the Kaisar Bagh in Lucknow: "A grand pavilion holding a thousand persons . . . was crowded to over-flowing with Mohammedans, Hindus, and others," emphasizing the capacious embrace of anti-opium protest beyond dividing lines of religion, gender, and geography.

In February 1892, Rao Bahadur Narayen Govind Deshmuk, the vice president of the District Local Board of Sholapur, convened yet another anti-opium rally. This time, anti-opium memorials appealed to Lord Robert Cecil, the acting British prime minister, with an impassioned plea using similar words as Prince Gong. The British prime minister was urged "to consider the ruin caused in India by the Opium traffic," to realize a bright future for this "vast country." Legislation in the form of opium prohibition across the three major tiers of opium's political economy in India—poppy cultivation, opium production, and sale—would bring "peace and prosperity." The petition anticipated a form of drug control restricting all three to medical and scientific purposes, demanding that "the proper place for medicine is in chemists' shops. That is what we want." As in Lin Zexu's famous anti-opium letter to Queen Victoria, the petitioners believed legal restrictions in Britain to be in place and sought to align colonial with British domestic legislation.

FIGURE 3.3. Sale of an opium-afflicted family estate (English pamphlet).

Source: The Chinese Opium Smoker (London: S. W. Partridge & Co., ca 1880). Widener Library, Harvard University.

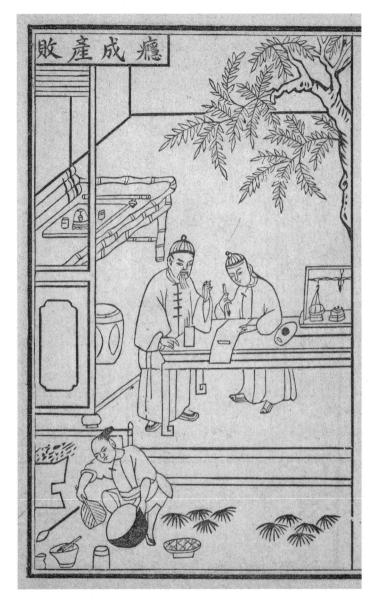

FIGURE 3.4. Sale of an opium-afflicted family estate (Chinese pamphlet).

Source: Jie yan xing shi tu. Fuzhou: Min bei sheng shu hui yin fa, Guangxu 26 (1900). Harvard-Yenching Library, Harvard University.

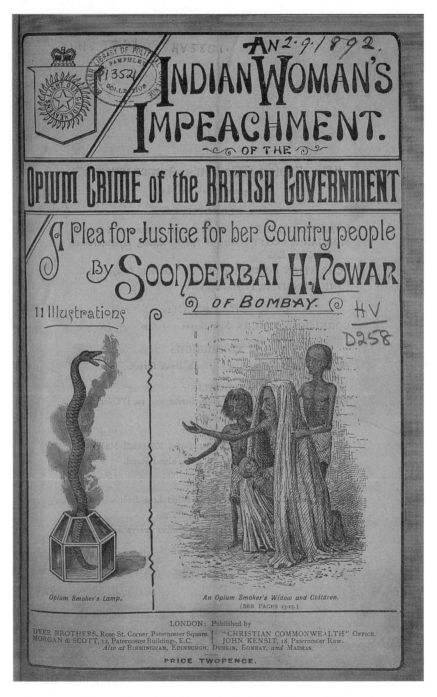

FIGURE 3.5. Cover of Soonderbai Powar's *An Indian Woman's Impeachment*.

It did not escape them that financial considerations were key to this policy change, urging that "no additional taxation be laid on the people of India, but that any loss to the revenue might be made up by the Crown Exchequer."[30] As in earlier protests in Britain as well as India, here the protesters kept a distance to blatant anti-imperialism: "No doubt it is great audacity for my countrymen—no matter how qualified and experienced—to differ from highly decorated, paid and pensioned Anglo-Indian officials, who do not want revelations that would foul their nest." The point was to not underestimate the Indian determination to take an active role in forging public opinion. "Patriotic Indians will not be brow-beaten into silence. I also think the British public will not always be deceived."[31] Not giving in to the status quo and bridling against unwarranted social victimization put the autonomy of the Indian mind before the autonomy of the British state.

Adding a fourth facet to the feminist, syncretic, and legalist strains of anti-opium lobbying, medical anti-opium opposition joined in through the publication of *The Voice of Fifty Indian Medical Men*. This anticipated the American-sponsored counter to the Royal Commission on Opium's *Opinions of over 100 Physicians on the Use of Opium in China* of 1899. By comparison, this extended Indian pamphlet situated clinical diagnosis within a broader appeal to several addressees across British politics and society: to Lord Cross, the secretary of state for India, as well as "to many thousands of people in England, Scotland, and Ireland." Powar perceived them as "sympathetic audiences who listened to the sad story of the wrong which is being done not alone to my people, but to other peoples of Asia by the iniquitous trade in Opium."[32] This may be one of the first glimpses into the realization that Indian, Chinese, and other opposition movements against the opium trade were indeed an "Asian" project in the making and more than a splintered assortment of coincidentally parallel expressions of sentiment. In fact, Powar's own recounting and reinforcement of protests other than her own served to unify anti-opium initiatives that at first lacked coordination or even cognizance of one another.

Signs that the activity of lobbying enhanced not only public visibility but also the sense of purpose among protesters joined increasingly by an awareness of one another surfaced at several occasions. In Bombay, anti-opium supporters drew on ranks from across professional and ethnic identities: At the university's Grant Medical College, several protesters holding licentiates in medicine or in surgery emerged as a stronghold of anti-opium opinion. The large majority of supporters bore Indian names, but several of the petitioners' names suggest their Portuguese origin.[33] Medical anti-opium experts in India practiced among Indians wielding greater local legitimacy. As Powar put it, "Unlike certain Anglo-Indian medical partisans of Opium," they were to be commended for not having spent their time "curing British officials and European residents," all of which, we seem to be meant to understand, would have merely distracted from the real problems the Indian population was facing. Powar saluted the heroism of physicians serving Indians: "Here then is the judgment of men who are real authorities."[34] Even at this stage, the Dyer Brothers connection still held: Brigade-Surgeon Pringle of Bengal and Deputy Surgeon-General Partridge, formerly presidency surgeon in two Bombay prisons, supported Powar with anti-opium testimonies on the pages of the *Bombay Guardian* and the *Banner of Asia,* an outlet later edited by Gregory.

Heralding some dynamics of international mass media, the symbolism inherent in the public representation of single events played its own role in shaping very individual modes of anti-opium opposition.[35] Specifically within the Ramabai-Powar-Gregory nexus, it is noticeable that Gregory abstained from writing his life into anti-opium mobilization, as Ramabai and Powar did. Instead of projecting intimate commitment, Gregory enlisted existing social reform networks to convert journalistic success into a diplomacy of its own, the art of negotiation developed by transnational anti-opium experts, as a glimpse forward in time illustrates.

In 1907, the influential Religious Society of Friends in London, the Quakers, proposed Gregory as a potential delegate for the first multilateral opium summit, the International Opium Commission in Shanghai of 1909. Gregory did not take up the nomination. In summer 1922, the Quakers tasked Gregory with Quaker lobbying at the League of Nations in Geneva, through Dame Rachel Crowdy (1884–1964), the chief of the league's Social Section who oversaw international social reform in committees on the Traffic on Opium, the Traffic in Women and Children, and the Promotion of Child Welfare.[36] Thus, beyond its foundational links, the Indian-British network extended its reach into the global politics of alleviating the human toll of perceived imperialist malpractice.

Social Reform Propaganda in Europe and Asia

The intensity of anti-opium mobilizations drew partly on its own emotional energies and partly on the benefit of global simultaneities beyond the skills of even the most able networks. For a historical interpretation, synchronicity poses the unresolved challenge of refusing a historical narrative along a linear chronology and of giving equal attention to activities taking place simultaneously. Unlike music, no written text can render simultaneity as it is. Instead, a more kaleidoscopic ambition may at least offer the reader an appreciation of anti-opium mobilization as a trajectory of over-lapping but by no means contradictory aspirations, each with its own lines of dissemination.

One line of disseminating anti-opium influence, which may be defined as the strategic harnessing of social observations, modes of accusation, and political demands, was the mediation of publishing networks as nodes of mobilization. Thrown into relief particularly in the 1890s, different forms of trafficking appeared to join partner causes of mobilization. The most important of these partnerships emerged between critics of drug trafficking and critics of human trafficking.

Dyer Brothers not only connected Gregory and Powar but also brought the Ramabai network into the scope of British Quakers, who financed the prominent Society for the Suppression of the Opium Trade (SSOT). The SSOT, we may remember, had linked up with the Qing's Zongli Yamen in 1878. Dyer Brothers became one of the vanguards of social purity litera-ture in Britain and India in the 1880s and 1890s. The spate of anti-trafficking publications began in 1880 with *The European Slave Trade in English Girls: A Narrative of Facts,* alleging forced prostitution in Bel-gium in six editions within six months, becoming a bestseller overnight and causing almost allergic alarm of British legislators.[37] Its publication coincided with *The White Slavery of Europe: From the French of Pastor T. Borel, of Geneva: With Supplement relating to the Foreign Traffic in En-glish, Scotch, and Irish Girls,* which featured the findings of the French-speaking, Swiss-based pastor Théodore Borel—a Belgian citizen—in collaboration with Donat Sautter.[38] A German translation of *The Euro-pean Slave Trade in English Girls* was commissioned and published in 1881, and of Borel's work in 1882.

Here, the twin genealogies of human trafficking and drug trafficking ap-peared in demands for social protection and international legal reform be-fore they entered the agendas of international organizations. Dyer Brothers was not alone in raising the issue of white slavery—the traffic of women and girls for prostitution—to a level of scandal across Europe. Early on, the level of mobilization was epitomized by Silesian-born activist Gertrud Guillaume-Schack, who indicted the traffic as a "question of public mo-rality" at the Town Hall in Berlin in 1880.[39] In France, Guillaume-Schack fought the same fight with a new target: the discriminatory punishment of prostitution as an expression of legal inequality between women and men. After fighting another private battle for her divorce, she worked closely with her newly founded Der Deutsche Kulturbund (German Cultural Associa-tion), an NGO and subsidiary unit of Josephine Butler's International Ab-olitionistic Federation of 1875.[40] Dyer Brothers' commitment in India and

Britain to exposing and fighting the opium trade alongside the white slavery trade could not be at all considered idiosyncratic but was tied to close mobilizations on the European continent.

Across anti-opium, anti-prostitution, and anti-slavery agendas, the legacies of defending the oppressed intersected. In 1887, Dyer Brothers added the anti-slavery repertoire to its Indian publications. The text *Slavery under the British Flag: The Iniquities of British Rule in India and in Our Crown Colonies and Dependencies, to the Friends of Social Purity* appeared in print while Alfred and Helen Dyer were moving to Bombay. Social reformism, so commonly treated as a uniquely western European liberal vintage, did not necessarily advance more easily or quickly in western Europe than in South Asia. Guillaume-Schack found herself more marginalized in Europe than Soonderbai Powar in India, with censorship regimes cracking down more vigorously in France and Germany than in the British Raj. It appeared as though in the case of women's protection from social abuse, socialism as well as its foe, conservative state control, impinged more strongly on European than South Asian mobilization.

Guillaume-Schack's sharply censored and consequently short-lived *Die Staatsbürgerin* (*The Woman Citizen*) of 1886 reflected a predicament that moved from the professional to the personal. Acquiring Swiss citizenship in 1886 facilitated her extradition and escape to England. There, Friedrich Engels—her seasoned friend and coauthor of the *Communist Manifesto*—tried to slow her down; in a letter, he wrote: "I must confess that I am more interested in the health of the coming generation than in absolute, formal equality between the sexes during the final years of the capitalist mode of production. True equality between men and women can, or so I am convinced, become a reality only when the exploitation of both by capital has been abolished, and private work in the home been transformed into a public industry."[41] Given Guillaume-Schack's temperament, Engels does not appear to have been successful in restraining her. Much more compelling, in fact, was his confidential clarification in the same letter that the anonymous author of the preamble of the French Workers' Party's election manifesto went by the name of Karl Marx. As for the idea of religion as the opium of the people, it famously engaged Marx more than Engels, falling short of another interface of crosscutting mobilization. What historical memory has split into separate and disconnected thematic agendas of international and global history appears here in greater proximity than commonly thought. Competing profiles of mobilization (such as capitalism versus socialism), which may have been highly visible in one region, like Europe, did not necessarily replicate themselves in another, like Asia, or, for that matter, on a global scale.

Dyer Brothers continued its publishing crusade largely uninhibited, combating the symptoms and presumed causes of abuse, oppression, and exploitation. In 1883, male readers on both continent, were admonished to practice ascetic self-discipline, moral purity, and plain health. Elsewhere, societal safeguards repeated the calls for men to heed safeguards against immorality and listen to plain words to young men on "an avoided subject," selling 150,000 copies. In 1897, Britain's imperial military came once again under scrutiny "in regard to their morals" and—was it more sparingly or less?—their health. Even the margins of publications illuminated the frontiers of mobilization. Back-matter advertisements offered further insight on publication strategies, initiatives,, and replications. Pamphlets revealed how the same tropes of exploitation and oppression recurred in newly conjoint agendas as in anti-opium and anti-prostitution publicity. As for Soonderbai Powar, she retained centrality in *What Indian Women Suffer through British Greed: Women of India Commission One of Their Number to Plead with the British People against the Opium Traffic*. And back at the Sharada Saran, Ramabai reported that her pupils "were not backward in sending their petitions to the government in favor of the necessary reforms and in aiding the work of progress as far as lay in their power."[42] Male greed, lewdness, and violence all seemed to become elements of a greater specter of social abuse and an outgrowth of imperialist forces of corruption.

It did not take many years for Indian-Chinese parallels to draw attention outside Britain. In Bombay in 1890, Asian parallels of opium suffering produced indictments of Chinese Christians and the "ravages of the opium plague," while others spoke of "the great plague of Asia" in 1891 and summarized the opium trade as a British imperial crime. Thus, the criminalization of the drug problem started with an unambiguous focus on the imperial system of British control of Indian supplies, long before the political logic of criminalization started haunting drug consumers first in the China of the 1930s and with renewed vigor in the United States of the 1970s. For now, the Dyer publishing network was one of the most transnational of its kind. It juggled with a variety of thematic causes, from human trafficking to male crime and the opium problem, with tropes from social victimization to the willful oppression by men and empires, and with lobbying centers from Bombay to London.

In this sense, the protest movement against the opium trade formed a composite rather than a unitary protest movement. Produced by interpretive critiques of the opium trade, Chinese and Indian victimization came closer than ever before to an alignment of the two anti-opium discourses. This alignment did not remain just an interpretive exercise but began

merging into the lobbying of political support. Alfred Dyer used his established profile as an anti-opium publisher to garner and disseminate the anti-
opium position by Qing officials and confronted the virtual heirs of Prince
Gong's demarche with the democratic will of the British people. To ensure
attention, availability had to be guaranteed first. Dyer Brothers calculated
demand to justify the mass production of anti-opium literature, as evidenced
by the advertisement that "larger quantities" could be obtained "at 12S.
per 1000."[43] Political pressure and popular outrage became available at bar-
gain prices in the quest for a maximized readership. As a result of dumping
rising amounts of propaganda at the lowest possible price, soon the question was no longer about the social effects and political intentions of the
opium trade. Instead, anti-opium criticism from Asia had turned into a force
in its own right, composed of nongovernmental and official strands of
opposition. Confronted with this far-flung Asian opposition, the question
was increasingly how British public opinion and the British government
would respond to a criticism whose very expansion appeared to have justified
itself. The pamphlet collecting interviews with Qing officials around Li Hongzhang had been organized by a British Indian anti-opium deputation.[44]

This transition from publicity work to political lobbying closed distances
on several levels: between Dyer Brothers as a Bombay-based British reform
publisher and the Qing administration and later between Maurice Gregory
and the League of Nations. On April 21, 1890, Dyer and Reverend W. E.
Robbins became the first members of a transnational anti-opium delegation ever to be received by a high-placed Qing official. Their hosts were Li
Hongzhang, the grand secretary of the Qing and its most powerful viceroy,
and Zeng Jize. Zeng is best known today as Qing minister to the Court of
St. James and the composer, together with his wife, of China's first national
anthem. As a son of Zeng Guofan, the celebrated victor over the Taiping,
he was among the first to speak of "unfair aspects" in British-Chinese treaties after the Opium Wars—a direct forerunner of the full-fledged nationalist concept of "unequal treaties."[45]

Li Hongzhang received Dyer and Robbins "cordially" in a rare interview
in the port city of Tianjin, close to Beijing. Both guests were convinced that
"the confidential information they had previously had as to the Viceroy Li's
sincere antagonism to the opium trade" was accurate. In response, they submitted two memorials to Li, one representing ten thousand Christians in
India and another representing "between six and seven thousand Christian
ministers and others in Scotland." The Indian memorial expressed "sorrow
at the moral and physical havoc" inflicted on the Chinese people by the
British opium policy, "which has been totally at variance with the principles of the Christian religion." Following this skeptical self-criticism and

perhaps anticipating that Li was not as interested in religion as in law and diplomacy, the memorialists urged him to embark on a diplomatic initiative to terminate the Chefoo Agreement's legalization article and "secure the execution of a new treaty repealing the Tientsin treaty, as far as it relates to opium," alongside "prohibition of the legalized importation of opium into China." This nongovernmental policy proposal, however, ran counter to Li's understanding of the premises on which the opium problem existed. Qing political leverage was not the same as Britain's, he explained to Dyer and friends: "We are not free; we cannot take the first step." Still, Dyer felt free to publicize the lamentable constraints of the Qing administration, rather than giving up or keeping silent. The resulting pamphlet honored Li's policy stance in its very title: *Will Not the Demand for a Prohibition Treaty with Great Britain Bring on Another War—a Third Opium War?*[46]

Dyer and Robbins admitted that the tragic opium wars, which demonstrated the "duplicity of foreigners," justified sustained Qing suspicion up to that day. Elsewhere, Dyer was even more outspoken: the opium wars displayed "shameful outrages which British histories do not record" and were nothing short of a "national crime."[47] Beyond the polemics, however, Li did express "his satisfaction at receiving this memorial" and promised political action. From the viewpoint of lobbying, such initiatives undermined Chinese acquiescence as a psychological outcome of the opium wars.

More moderate minds would have rested at the level of politicization now achieved. But the Dyer mills of anti-opium propaganda were relentless in perpetually radicalizing the anti-opium message. Soon, China's ruin through opium, so eloquently proposed by Prince Gong in 1869, found its equivalent in the question of whether India would also be ruined by opium, whether Britain's "poisoning policy" would continue indefinitely regardless of the social cost, whether opium consumption would keep growing to distort the face of society itself, and whether the public opinion expressed by the Indian press would have any political impact by protesting in the strongest possible terms the "Anglo-Asiatic opium curse."[48]

Given the prevalent emphasis on missionary ideas, initiatives, and networks in the existing historiography of anti-opium expressions, it is worth pointing out that missionary critiques were, by comparison, surprisingly scarce. Some financial critiques argued that the opium trade from India to China was commercially inefficient, draining not only Indian but also British resources. Others mused in a theological fashion on biblical exegesis geared toward the anti-opium cause. But despite the terms used to describe the genres of this proliferating anti-opium discourse—from "testimony" to "anti-opium tracts"—this was a markedly secular political opposition, focused on imperial abuse in Asian societies from Asian perspectives and not geared toward proselytizing.[49]

The expansion of anti-opium publicity across a widening array of genres served as an indication of the information used. Maps of poppy cultivation supplemented written critiques. Educational journals like the *India Medical Record* and the Medical Missionary Training Institution in Agra carried anti-opium information into closer contact with universities and training programs.[50]

Newspapers came closest to contesting official opium information with outlets such as "*Anti-Opium News,* a supplement to *The Sentinel,* the organ for Social Purity and National Righteousness." The announcement of "current information of the agitation and demand for the abolition of the Opium Traffic" was increasingly shared on the desks not only of activists but of officials.

In terms of longevity, the abolitionist analogy to opium trading outlived the partner cause of white slavery. Many Quaker grandparents of Quaker anti-opiumists had fought the "real" slave trade to much acclaim. Reverend Thomas Evans evoked in an extended piece for Dyer Brothers on opium slavery in India the image of the Indian and Chinese "opium slave." In contrast to British Orientalist and later American Yellow Peril depictions of inferior Asian subjects with strange appetites, here the causality of the moral economy was reversed, blaming supply for demand rather than demand for supply. Prince Gong would have approved.

By the same token, Western imperial rule became the enabling condition for a sustained process of social sabotage inflicted by foreigners in power, rather than a domestic social problem deserving collective self-pity. In this sense, the Indian-Chinese campaign against opium recast the trade as a force of Asian oppression and predated later charges of nationalist upheavals against imperialism, colonialism, and capitalism.[51] In sum, anti-opium activism cannot be said to have produced an entire world of interlocking movements of social revolt and political protest but was born into it.

Tagore and the Death of India

Set apart by space but joined in time, a distinct anti-opium momentum originated where few would have suspected. "In Geneva and Paris, a French translation of my Opium Trade will be published these days which you might wish to draw to the attention of your French friends." The innocuous postcard written about 140 years before the publication of this book, on New Year's Eve 1878, was addressed to Eduard Schaer, a professor at the Polytechnic Institute at Zurich trained in Berlin, London, and Paris. Since 1877, he was also an honorary member of the American Pharmaceutical Association. By 1892, he was appointed director of the Pharmaceutical Institute of the University of Strasbourg.[52] The postcard continued: "In America," where several of Schaer's former students practiced, "the little book has already become quite popular, thanks to several reprints (10,000 copies). I have [received] further enthusiastic and encouraging assessments, also from colleagues in the field of medicine, especially in England and Russia."[53] In this miniature of global information-sharing for the anti-opium cause, the postcard requested from Schaer an opium tract authored by "the Spanish minister," if a revised edition of his own book should become "necessary."[54] He most likely referred to Don Sinibaldo de Mas's defense of the trade, *L'opium*, extracted from his *L'Angleterre, La Chine, et l'Inde*, first published in Paris in 1857, with frequent reissues in English until at least 1884.[55]

A few weeks before, the postcard had been sent off by a devout German theologian based in leafy Bonn, in the western part of Germany, Theodor Christlieb. Having produced one of the most extensive book-length indictments of the British opium trade to date, endorsements in German, English, French, and Swedish abounded in response to numerous editions and translations.[56] In London, the SSOT's house journal praised it as a "wholesome" lesson "to see ourselves as others see us," an assessment praised in turn for "the expressed approbation of the author's moral indignation."[57]

The *Church Missionary Intelligencer* had given the initial impetus for Christlieb by communicating to him Prince Gong's demarche.[58] Appropriating the principal tenets of the Chinese protest, Christlieb confirmed the "forcing of opium upon" China as the only explanation of opium legalization through the Treaty of Tianjin.[59] The trope of victimization brought this anti-opium vision close to the anti-opium movements of Indian women and international reform publishers. Adopting the same accusation of British malice as the principal lever behind opium suffering, Christlieb's treatise extended the arguments across a historical survey of several hundred pages. The treatise offered a synthesis of the trade's historical development, moral implications, and political intentionality. It pointed to the risks and costs of the trade for India, England, and China (in that order), climaxing with a policy proposal: to substitute Indian poppy cultivation with food crops and renounce British drug trading. Compared to preceding anti-opium propaganda, the vocabulary radicalized further. The opium trade, decried as one of the "monsters of immorality," Christlieb wrote, hardly differed from "wholesale murders." Blame met "the unquenchable thirst for gold" had driven the mass murders that "have long stained the pages of international history," a striking characterization of the nineteenth century. As to Britain's world role, he reminded readers that this was the country that "in the first half of the present century, did her part in putting an end to the wholesale destruction of human life, by heroically abolishing in her colonies the curse, not only of the slave-trade, but of slavery itself." Alas, "this same country it is, which, in spite of the protest, in spite of the earnest entreaty of China, and the cry of the Christian conscience from her own midst, by her opium trade, sacrifices ever-increasing multitudes of Chinese to her greed of gain."[60] Once again, the abolitionist analogy sharpened the alleged brutality and, in a chronology of imperial progress, the global anachronism of the opium trade.

This human-inflicted suffering had created vicissitudes across cultures: "America, Africa, and many, how many! other smaller lands have seen, still do see, murders committed wholesale by the avaricious hands of Christians."[61] If Christlieb's reference to abolitionism as a global humanitarian precedent deepened the political urgency, it also widened his audience beyond self-declared anti-opiumists. Incorporating the incipient opposition against the opium trade in a new genealogy of international humanitarianism welded this movement to existing Anglo- and Francophone abolitionism. This partnering of protest movements stretched its global profile and self-declared significance beyond Asia and the North Atlantic world to Brazil and other South American societies since the 1880s.[62]

Linking anti-slavery and anti-opium into one grand opposition against global humanitarian violations enhanced the international historical legitimacy of each constitutive part. Elias Schrenk—pietist preacher and theologian from the German southwest—used Christlieb's perspective to call for a global mapping of missionary tasks. At the General Conference on Foreign Missions in London in October 1878, Schrenk advocated transferring the Basel Missionary Conference from the Gold Coast in western Africa to the western coast of India in 1834, as "the mode of work" in either locale "is much the same."[63] Likewise, Africa and Asia became the two mutually supportive causes of a global mission through stories and representations of suffering and human degradation.[64]

These were not purely theoretical deductions of a humanitarian sensibility. Christlieb's father-in-law, John James Weitbrecht (born Johann Jakob Weitbrecht), had encountered opium suffering in his Bengal service and conjectured that opium and famine were causally connected: "While one monopoly deprives or stints a hundred millions of Hindoos of an essential ingredient in their food, a second, viz. that of opium, is poisoning, by its effects, three hundred million of souls belonging to a distant nation." Christlieb senior's missionary colleagues in Bengal added financial information: "The monopoly of opium is exclusively belonging to the East India Company," he had written in the early 1840s, "and yields them an annual income of two millions and a half sterling."[65] With father as with son, local anthropology inflected the analogy between slavery and opium, enriching the rhetoric with secular empiricism and diluting the role of theological dogma.

But the figure who contributed most to the Asian legacy of Christlieb's book, across a vast distance and a three-year lapse in time, was Rabindranath Tagore. Transnational reception forged ties where they had previously been inconceivable. In May 1881, one month after his twentieth birthday, Tagore penned the article "The Death Traffic in China" ("Chine Maraner Byabsa," in its original Bengali), an attack pioneering some of the most pervasive and long-lived anti-opium arguments in the context of Indian intellectual and social engagement with the issue. The Bengali magazine *Bharati*, under the editorship of his brother Dwijendranath, served as the venue for Tagore's opium critique.

In contrast to the continuity of anti-opium thought in the Christlieb family, Tagore's engagement bore some elements of the vehemence of personal frustration. Tagore's father was an opium trader himself, deepening the poet's commitment to an intimate subjectivity not unlike Ramabai's and Powar's. The biographical context directly informed the timing of the article. One year before Tagore had just returned from England. Now he used Christlieb's book to condemn the British drug trade on his own terms, becoming one of the most prominent proponents of Prince Gong's argument, even without explicitly referencing the Qing official: "We have never before heard such a revolting story of Thuggism, as is contained in this book by Doctor Theodore Christlieb, which lies before us for review," he started out. "A whole nation, China, has been forced by Great Britain to accept the opium poison,—simply for commercial greed."[66] China's oppression through opium meant, to this Indian observer, a quasi-national victimization inflicted by British brute force: "Both the hands of China were tightly bound. Opium was forced down China's throat with the help of guns and bayonets, while the British merchants cried, "You have to pay the price of all the opium you take from us."[67] In contrast to the concept of social death on an individual basis, Tagore conceived of society's death as a shared, lethal fate.[68]

In sharp contrast to racist anti-opium visions by Westerners, who deduced the opium trade from the inferior and essentially Chinese opium craving, Tagore expressed his discontent with excessive supply, like Prince Gong and many other predecessors in the anti-opium cause.[69] Instead, opium supplies became the crux of the opium trade's political economy: "The article, which the customer does not want, is shoved into one pocket by force, while the money to pay for it is forcibly extracted from the other pocket, and its full price realised. Such a method of carrying on business and accumulating wealth can only by courtesy be called by the name of traffic," he added at a time when *traffic* did not yet possess the connotation of illicit transactions. Conversely, Britain's "sheer brigandage" provoked Tagore's call for Sino-Indian mutual empathy, at a time when his expressions to this border- and mountain-crossing affinity were still few and scarce in between. Admiration for the Chinese heightened their tragedy: "Such a great people," Tagore exclaimed, "has become of so little worth!"[70] Tagore wrote these scathing lines more than thirty years prior to his prominent visit to China in 1925.[71] Hinting at an early recognition of Indian-Chinese shared suffering and cooperative resistance allowed for a tentative consensus shared by two Asian societies, a consensus building on the shared experience of British imperial abuse, preceding their nationalist reincarnations since the 1920s.[72] Tagore married cultural admiration of Qing China, extolled as "one of the greatest and oldest countries of Asia," with social empathy. "The poison of opium," he continued, was "eating at the vitals" of India's neighboring empire and "has been spreading like an infection over the whole body politic."

Here, abolitionism became the lesson that the British empire had refused to learn: "The very nation which had become an object of gratitude to thousands of African negroes," Tagore wrote, "by removing from the chains of slavery, is now saying to China: 'I want more money, and therefore you must take opium.'"[73] By separating two of its most lucrative trades into disparate responsibilities and geographies, Britain had failed in the global humanitarian ethics that Christlieb, Tagore, and many others espoused. Abuses in Africa and in Asia pointed to two perfidious if complementary illustrations of global ethical inequality as directly causing the social suffering of the weak.

The elements of Tagore's critique that went deeper than those of his predecessors in anti-opium protests elsewhere spoke to the medical, somatic, and mental depth of the opium injury. In the trail of its destruction, opium had been "killing slowly by inches mind and body alike." Tagore expressed the firm conviction that "a strong nation, like Britain, is using its strength to sell death and destruction to a weak nation, and thus make profit."[74] The imputation of imperial abuse of power hinged on a newly posited disproportionality.[75]

Tagore's historical perspective on the opium trade did not soften the charge. "After this Second Opium War," Tagore taught his Bengali readers, "the trade flourished to such an extent that in the year 1875 as many as 90,000 chests of opium were imported into China from abroad."[76] Like Prince Gong before him, Tagore predicted that massive popular discontent "against the red-haired foreigners" was to follow—a derogatory term he adopted from various Chinese dialects, as in "*hong mao*" in Putonghua and "*ang mo*" in Hokkien. British conciliation had long become a political urgency, Tagore insisted. "The English people are really sustaining a great loss in moral prestige owing to the utter distrust" of the Chinese people. The British opium trade was not only "immoral" but "shortsighted."[77]

The pervasive force of the British-sponsored opium trade had damaged India twice, as a victim as well as a perpetrator of the opium crime against millions of Chinese men and women. The established presence of opium smoking in Chinese rituals of daily life, however, was no grounds for defending it. On the contrary, a danger unknown was more threatening than a danger exposed. "Just as in our country of India, we offer the hookah to a guest on his arrival, so wealthy people and rich merchants in China offer their visitors and their customers opium to be smoked." Nanjing in 1881, Tagore wrote, was "so notorious for opium-smoking that the inhabitants lie intoxicated during the day and work at night." Ningbo counted 2,700 opium shops "in the poorest quarters." Quite apart from Orientalist prejudice that diagnosed shiftlessness as an innate characteristic of the Chinese race, it was opium that made them "lazy and inactive" yet exonerated them as social beings.

The socioeconomic consequences of opium consumption matched the incidence of famine, Tagore argued, with poppy cultivation displacing rice and corn.[78] Thus, Asian consumers, planters, and producers of opium became trapped in a cycle of perpetration and victimization that none of them had chosen. It was key that in social victimization, India did not lag behind China. The opium evil indicated Britons' "universal fear on account of the dependence of revenue." On this basis, the notorious famine of 1877 and 1878 had robbed the lives of "one million men . . . in Bengal alone." Likewise, opium as a threat to life manifested itself in Rajputana, the region northwest of the opium hub Malwa, where opium cultivation amounted to collective economic suicide. Opium did, as the title of his essay suggests, amount to nothing less than a "death traffic," something much worse than lamentable economic malpractice.[79]

As with China, India had suffered a loss of industriousness under the direct impact of opium, Tagore claimed. "It is hard indeed to think of such a brave and chivalrous people becoming stolid and inactive, lazy and lifeless," Tagore averred. "Whereas the ancient kingdom of Rajputana was a kingdom of noble dreams," at present it resembled "a kingdom of dull

FIGURE 3.6. Wife and child weep, an aged mother serves tea to an opium smoker (English pamphlet).

Source: The Chinese Opium Smoker (London: S. W. Partridge & Co., ca 1880). Widener Library, Harvard University.

置若罔聞

FIGURE 3.7. Wife and child weep, a mother serves tea to an opium smoker (Chinese pamphlet).

Source: Jie yan xing shi tu. Fuzhou: Min bei sheng shu hui yin fa, Guangxu 26 (1900). Harvard-Yenching Library, Harvard University.

FIGURE 3.8. Wife and child turn away from an emaciated opium smoker (English pamphlet).

Source: The Chinese Opium Smoker (London: S. W. Partridge & Co., ca 1880). Widener Library, Harvard University.

FIGURE 3.9. Wife and child confiscate an opium pipe and are chased away (Chinese pamphlet).

Source: Jie yan xing shi tu. Fuzhou: Min bei sheng shu hui yin fa, Guangxu 26 (1900). Harvard-Yenching Library, Harvard University.

sleep."[80] Similarly, Assam in India's northeast joined the community of opium victims, augmenting it along the Arakan coast. Here, physical and mental enfeeblement appeared not as a cultural weakness from within a society but as a sociopolitical vulnerability produced from without, as in the American or Japanese accounts of social Darwinists like Herbert Day Lamson and Harvard-educated Japanese-born Maejima Yutaka, for whom Chinese pathologies invited Japanese expansion.[81] In West India, too, the anti-opium stance dovetailed less with liberal convictions or Indian nativism than with several decades of discontent over British opium trading. In the regions of Portuguese Goa, Diu, and Daman, "freedom of trade meant particularly freedom to trade opium."[82]

In conclusion, Tagore's global comparisons extended the evocativeness of analogies further to the North American history of the British empire. Expansionism from the angle of popular health seemed to showcase another example here: "But we know well this 'Christian' nation! These Christians have exterminated the aboriginal Americans. By their 'Christian' method, they confiscate 'heathen' lands, whenever their covetous eyes fall upon them." Absent a political conscience, an empire could pursue the accumulation of wealth at the expense of formerly great nations, among whom Tagore assumed the Chinese excelled.[83] In other words, for Tagore, opium stood for the denial of a civilizing mission.[84] If imperialism pulled inferior societies in a historical direction, India and China showed that this direction pointed downward, not upward.

Tagore's critique gained a second lease of life at the League of Nations Opium Conference in 1925. When the British Indian delegation clashed with Indian anti-opium representatives in Geneva, the confrontation stirred up an international public scandal over British Indian opium interests. The anti-opium delegation, anticipating a form of representation today called civil society, used Tagore's critique in an English translation by the Calcutta-based *Modern Review,* founded in 1907. Its editor, Ramananda Chatterjee, was a close friend of Tagore and was commonly considered the founding father of modern Indian journalism. The work started by publicity networks, to carve out an expansive public sphere by inventing, radicalizing, and disseminating new tropes of anti-opium mobilization, also carried Tagore's influence into the new arena of global public politics. From the original publication of Tagore's essay review of Christlieb in 1881 to the 1920s, Bengali readers in India and world leaders in Switzerland confronted the recurring vision of Asian victimization as a bitter struggle of opponents who conceived of the opium trade as a matter of life and death.[85]

Naoroji and India's Economic Drain

Indian women saw the Indian nation maltreated just as they were. Tagore foreboded the death of Indian and Chinese society by opium. A contemporary of Tagore, who was more than thirty years his senior, appropriated the anti-opium discourse for yet another purpose: to trace the effects of opium through the Indian economy. Born in 1825, Dadabhai Naoroji made his name as an ambitious intellectual, particularly in mathematics; as a political figure at home; and as the first Asian Liberal member of the British Parliament in the early 1890s. In 1867, he helped establish the East India Association, the predecessor of the Indian National Congress, an organization committed to enhancing the public and political representation of Indian interests vis-à-vis the institutions representing British rule. In 1876, the association sponsored Naoroji's most celebrated contribution to Indian anti-imperialist thought.

Like Tagore, Naoroji highlighted the effects of opium as a trail of destruction. However, in his rendering, the fatal drug exerted its force as chiefly a malign and plural influence of economic imperialism. What he called the drain of Indian finance through British imperialism became chiefly responsible for "the poverty of India."[86] If Powar's plight for downtrodden individuals had been eclipsed in Tagore's national account, Naoroji returned to it via an analysis of the insidious logic and financial dynamics of the trade. On October 16, 1880, his memorandum on "The Moral Poverty of India and Native Thoughts on the Present British Indian Policy" explained to the Marquess of Harrington, Britain's acting secretary of state for India: "There is the opium trade. What a spectacle to the world! In England no statesman dares to propose that opium may be allowed to be sold in public houses at the corners of every street, in the same way as beer or spirits."[87] Parliament, he criticized, reserved "opium and all preparations of opium or of 'poppies,' as 'poison,' be sold by certified chemists only, and every box, bottle, vessel, wrapper, or cover in which such poison is contained, be distinctly labeled." But in India, no such regard for the social well-being and according legislation could be seen.

Like others before him, Naoroji assailed these perceived double standards of legislation on the grounds of religion as the official placeholder of Britain's normative order and identity. A rendering of his original words conveys the eloquent passion and intensity of feeling in his attack. "At the other end of the world, this Christian, highly civilised, and humane England forces a 'heathen' and 'barbarous' Power to take this 'poison,' and tempts a vast human race to use it, and to degenerate and demoralise themselves with this 'poison'!"[88] This belied the British aspiration to further "the good of the conquered as a duty," provoking the question of Britain's real purpose. "And why? Because India cannot fill up the remorseless drain; so China must be dragged in to make it up, even though it be by being 'poisoned.'" Cynicism was difficult to restrain. "It is wonderful how England reconciles this to her conscience. This opium trade is a sin on England's head, and a curse on India for her share in being the instrument."[89] Like railway imperialism in China, opium imperialism in India offered itself polarized zero-sum interpretations, with the benefits flowing to Britain and the brunt being born by subjugated Asia.

Tellingly, these lines were written while Naoroji lived in Britain. His transnational perspective stood in no conflict with depicting Britain within a mind-set far removed: as the foreign tyrant from a different world wreaking havoc across cultures and societies other than itself. Having arrived in England in 1855, Naoroji penned these attacks at 32 Great St. Helens, less than three miles east of the secretary of state's office in London. It "may sound strange," he expressed, "as coming from any Natives of India, as it is generally represented as if India it was [sic] that benefited by the opium trade." But his cultural origin made him insist that India was "nearly ground down to dust, and the opium trade of China fills up England's drain." Indian trade profits, "several millions from her very produce," and even opium profits all appeared to escape to England—the destination of the drain. The problem was that India's economy could not flourish as long as this financial abuse of British imperialism remained in place. As for Indian-Chinese relations, Naoroji had observations to share as well: "Only India shares the curse of the Chinese race. . . . This trade," he concluded with unmistakable furor, "has prolonged the agonies of India."[90] In this Indian indictment, Britain's Asian empire could preview the international anti-opium criticism that would peak in the 1890s and 1900s.

However, as with Ramabai's fight for local as well as global legitimacy, the Indian press was not immediately impressed with Naoroji's arguments. Global supplies of raw opium hailed not only from British India but also from Persia, the Ottoman Empire, and Qing China, questioning Naoroji's notion of British unilateral responsibility.[91] But while neither the political or social arguments of Tagore and Naoroji was beyond reproach, their normative interventionism came out as their forte. Opium, once grudgingly accepted as a fact of life there, turned into a new and potent symbol of British oppression. These early Indian anti-opium critiques refashioned the moral meaning of the British empire based on controversial practices. They can be seen as part of the ambition not to sever India entirely from British rule but to bring the Raj on a par with British dominions like Canada or Australia.[92]

Countering the British official genre of imperial reportage on the "moral and material progress of India,"[93] Naoroji pursued two perspectives on India and China to enlarge the image of Asian opium damage. In his *Poverty and Un-British Rule in India,* published in 1901, he took aim at both British statistics and their ethics. India's economic emaciation through opium drew on the early drain arguments by Bhaskar Pandurang Tarkhadkar and Ramkrishna Vishwanath's *Thoughts on India's Past, Its Present Condition and Their Impact on the Future of 1843.*[94] Naoroji found another precursor in Robert Montgomery Martin, a cofounder of the East India Association in 1867.[95] Within this intellectual pedigree, the Indian empire appeared very much as an empire of opinion, as Sir John Malcolm had warned in 1824.[96]

Other Indian critics targeted the place of indigo in the Indian economy, its most valuable commodity alongside opium until the mid-nineteenth century. But unlike opium, indigo featured primarily in the moral economy of farmers' having an ethical stake in making decisions about the choice of crops, the terms of their cultivation, and rural relations in general.[97] Between 1859 and 1861, conflict pitted Bengal's elite and educated *bhadralok* against British authorities over farmers' loss of status and subsistence. Alcohol, British cloth, and most famously salt became commodities of contestation in Indian-British relations. But the core of Naoroji's critique remained the financial system, similar to his skepticism toward British railway policy, where the British repatriation of loan interests fared unfavorably in comparison to U.S. railway projects favoring the interests of local investors.[98] But whether Naoroji employed comparisons between commodities or economic systems, a preoccupation with the seeming ineluctability of gradual, incremental economic crisis remained a guiding concern. Ever since his publication on *England's duties to India* in 1861, Naoroji had worked on evidence of British deviations from the promise of benevolent rule.[99]

Like Tagore's "death traffic," Naoroji's criticism was widely received—by, among others, Subramania Iyer [Aiyar], a member of the constitutional drafting committee of the Indian National Congress. Iyer, too, could claim a background in the publicity profession, having edited prominent journals such as the *Hindu, Swadesamitran,* and the weekly *United India,* not unlike Naoroji's embrace of his Hindu, Musulman, Parsi, and overseas Indian identities.[100] Following Naoroji in 1903, Iyer adopted the anti-opium cause in first book, *Some Economic Aspects of British Rule in India.* Addressed to India's "public men," the book reaffirmed the broadening aspiration of

Indian anti-opium critics to reach a public sphere beyond India with political narratives of opium suffering. It is no coincidence that international public opinion appeared at that time less elusive than ever before, with the "new global journalism" simultaneously crisscrossing the Ottoman Empire, French North Africa, colonial Southeast Asia, and late Qing China, with shared spheres of global attention.[101]

According to Iyer, British rule had produced "great economic evils," with "the people's material well-being" pointing to "a dismal failure."[102] Like Christlieb, Iyer saw the opium trade as a symbol of British greed, violating mercantilism and absorbing Indian tribute in Britain. Directly building on Naoroji, he calculated that "about £500,000,000 . . . England has kept as its benefit. . . . Towards this drain, the net opium revenue contributed by China amounts to about £141,000,000. The balance of about £360,000,000 is derived from India's own produce and profits of commerce." Opium was at the center of this drain, with an Indian deficiency of nearly £200,000,000, all of which Iyer considered as a drain. "It is the exhaustion caused by the drain that disables us from building our rail roads & c., from our own means."[103] Under the pens of anti-opium critics, even statistics became vehicles for mobilizing anti-opium opposition and sources of political meaning.

In Iyer's reception, Naoroji spoke alongside premier figures of Indian politics and higher education, such as Hindu scholar Gopal Krishna Gokhale, who denounced the British opium trade as psychologically humiliating and socially corrupting, complementing the Chinese trope of opium as *guochi* (national shame). "I confess," Gokhale stated in 1907, when the Indian-Chinese opium connection reached the beginning of its end, "I have always felt a sense of deep humiliation at the thought of this [opium] revenue, derived as it is practically from the degradation and moral ruin of the people of China."[104] For Naoroji, Iyer, and Gokhale, anti-opium campaigning diversified existing commitments of Indian national reform and turned out to be, whether intended or not, beneficial to the posthumous tassels of national esteem.[105]

Gokhale was also the member of the Indian National Congress responsible for nominating Alfred Webb as its president. Webb, too, recalled in his autobiography the combination of philanthropic and reform movements, naming temperance, women suffrage, and contagious diseases as causes that roused his enthusiasm for "those concerning people oppressed who could not help themselves—such as slaves, women deprived of the franchise, the Indian people, practically without a voice in the government in their own country." To Webb, that tied these victimizations together, a history whose explicit recognition served to sharpen the message further.

The Second Opium War, Webb concurred implicitly with Prince Gong, brought unrighteous oppression and created British imperial victims, notably "the Chinese with the use of opium almost forced on them."[106] He openly denounced "the wars waged by England to keep open the opium trade with China as the greatest (in their consequences) political crimes ever committed. The total massacre of population by the Romans was less barbarous than the aiding in planting a vice like opium smoking in the vitals of a people."[107]

The historical and ideological concatenation of social causes did not mean that they all balanced one another in terms of urgency. Even against the backdrop of other causes, however, Webb saw his anti-opium motion in parliament in the summer of 1893 as "the most important part I ever took. a motion on the opium traffic." He was convinced that the Indian people "ought not to be called upon to bear the cost" of the opium trade, including the political responsibility for social damage in China.[108] Given what we know about the origins of these tropes of anti-opium interpretation, these echoes of Indian opposition are hard to ignore. Since the 1880s, British imperial opium ventures became the object of severe debates, sustained analysis, and far-reaching politicization among English-speaking Asian activists.

In these examples of complementary Asian proto-nationalist sentiment and critique, the potential of transnational influence on public opinion was already visible in the fact that they wrote in English. This transnationalism was still germinant compared, for instance, to more proactive transnational overtures to Irish circles in London twenty years later. But the ideological fermentation of anti-opium tropes and their political explosiveness was, after so many rounds of adaptation, reaffirmation, and replication, an enlarged voice with growing sociopolitical clout. However, that leverage was not easily translated into effective political pressure. Across opium's intra-Asian political economy, select Qing governors appear to have been the most conspicuous elements of change, as in the case of Tan Zhunpei in Jiangsu and Suzhou. But piecemeal provincial efforts could not be effective in combating the lack of interprovincial border control until a regional system of control was found.[109] Toward that end, much of the above radicalization, politicization, and scandalization had worked with relentless determination. This determination would not show signs of abating until policy makers came up with a solution to the perceived perpetration of opium victims across Asia.

The Anti-Opium Tour: American Women
and Asian Temperance

Before it morphed into the glib expression of mobility, physical dislocation was, despite its discomforts, essential to transnational mobilization. In 1891, Soonderbai Powar was not quite out of the picture. She embarked on a second anti-opium tour, supplementing the Indian-British alliance with a third anti-opium circle in Hong Kong. Leaving "my sunny India to spend nearly six months upon your cold, wintry soil," Powar's publicity tour mirrored Ramabai's crossing of the "wintry ocean" on her way to the United States in the spring of 1886. The act of dislocation itself, we should remember, symbolized the refusal of male restrictions to the domain of the family or domestic society, a refusal well understood by overseas supporters like the Ramabai Association. There, the "defiant women" were celebrated, just as "another movement in the interest of stopping the terrible opium traffic" was congratulated.[110]

In 1883, Frances Willard, founder of the Woman's Christian Temperance Union (WCTU) in 1874, underwent a traumatic experience, three years before Ramabai encountered her "opium curse." Willard remembered the shock in San Francisco well: "We there saw the opium den in all its loathsome completeness, and next door stood the house of shame." And in the blink of an eye, it seemed, the parallel between drug trafficking and prostitution looked to her as credible as it did to European reform publishers and Indian critics. This, Willard affirmed, was "the most flagrantly flaunted temptation" she had ever witnessed.

Willard's personal awakening was credited by the WCTU as the cause for the organization's internationalization in response to a perceived social emergency in Asia. To Willard, the Pacific Ocean represented explicitly the interdependence between Asia and America, one issuing immediate moral demands of a different sort than the civilizing mission with its colonial trappings. "It was borne in upon my spirit, as I breathed the ozone of the Pacific coast, that except for an interval of water the shores of China and Japan abutted against our own, with that concept, the determination was fixed to extend the work of the white ribbon women to those opium-cursed shores."[111] Here, it was no longer the grievance of victimization, suffered by Asian women or Asian nations, but instead the potential to enact change that came into focus. Resignation and protest gave way to a new exercise in global public representation.

The passion of the WCTU's global progressivism soon joined the North American lobbying tour of Pandita Ramabai. In December 1887, Chicago's *Daily Inter-Ocean* held an interview with Ramabai, giving her the opportunity to act as the first Indian anti-opium advocate in the United States. The oppression shared by American and Hindu women, Ramabai argued, grew out of different combinations of imperialism, alcohol, opium, and the males who produced all three: "Missionaries are showing by their precepts and example that Christianity does not mean going into other countries and taking possession of them, putting taxes upon the people, introducing the liquor traffic, and gaining a great deal of revenue from the infamous traffics in rum and opium."[112] Despite these overt anti-imperialist motives, however, the WCTU platform of anti-drug lobbying and the winning of American sympathies in this particular case cannot be unreservedly interpreted as a reflection of Ramabai's Christian sentiment. In India, Ramabai preferred leaving out the attribute "Christian" when referring to the WCTU. Even when lobbying spread globally, the message changed with the location.[113]

Chicago in those days was the headquarters of the Woman's Temperance Publication Union, known in the 1880s as "the largest publication society of women in the world." Its postage bill ran over $10,000, its printing output over 135,000,000 pages.[114] The "good, diligent and upright women" of the Union and especially their skills in NGO institution-building were deeply admired by Ramabai: "The administration of the Union is the very replica of that of the United States," she wrote in *The Peoples of the United States* of 1889. "It has four levels—local, county, state, and national—and an excellent system of administration. Each local union has a president, a vice president, a secretary, a treasurer, and a board of management as well as subcommittees appointed for specific purposes. At each annual function the officers are elected, and take office. . . . The Union has over 10,000 chapters in the United States, and about 250,000 women members." In 1885, the WCTU had set up a foreign department.[115]

To Ramabai, the success of the WCTU offered lessons on how to consolidate disparate reform groups across divides of opinions and agendas and multiply the effect of protest. "The many different capabilities possessed by the female sex had earlier been scattered among individuals and dissipated like vapor in the sky, being unregulated and ineffective," she reported. "When they were collected together in this Union, they became activated in various ways like steam concentrated and controlled by a steam engine," she commented with a notable demonstration of her technological knowledge. "Thanks to it, the harmful differences of opinion and class animosity among women of different opinions and classes have disappeared. . . . I have no hesitation in saying that this is the best and greatest of all the associations prevalent among all civilized countries."[116] Yet the impending initiatives of the WCTU extended far beyond the pretensions of a White, Protestant, Western circle of "civilization."

Preceding the Women's League for Peace and Freedom by more than thirty years, the scope and force of the WCTU was unrivaled at the time. Its achievements withstood global comparisons to similar lobby groups. No male anti-opium group had ever launched a comparable fight for its voice.[117] As if this ambition required a symbol and trophy, one WCTU product embodied its success, its agenda, and its global aspirations. The Polyglot Petition was half document, half commodity, made of white cloth and bound at the edges with white and blue ribbons. Signatures were "pasted to the cloth . . . in three columns."[118] About one hundred names fit in each one-yard column. Unlike any written document, the petition contained the representations of people from dozens of cultures and languages at the time; it came to boast over seven million names, alternatively by signature or endorsement, and ran across no less than seven thousand yards. "It is the largest petition ever presented on behalf of any object, and is the most international in its proposed reforms." As an exuberant display of a distinct grassroots cosmopolitanism, the rolls of the petition were ecumenically straddled: "Catholic and Protestant, Gentile, Jew, Hindoo and Mohammedan have found the Polyglot Petition a common ground of faith and works."[119]

And captivating it was. In addition to forty-four states and five territories of the United States, the petition represented Alaska, Nova Scotia, New Brunswick, Prince Edward Island, Quebec, Ontario, Manitoba, British Columbia, Newfoundland, Jamaica, the Bahamas, Tasmania, New Zealand, Queensland, New South Wales, Victoria (in Australia), Micronesia, Madagascar, South Africa, France, South Australia, Belgium, Burma, Chile, Congo, Denmark, Holland, the Madeira Islands, Mexico, Norway, Sweden, Spain, Uruguay, Brazil, England, Scotland, Ireland, Wales, Bulgaria, Ceylon, China, Japan, Corea, Egypt, Finland, Russia, Turkey, Hawaii, India, Martinique Island, Siam, West Africa, Angola, and Transvaal.[120] The loving detail in descriptions of the petition noted the artistry, technology, and ideology of this physical mobile symbol of protest. Abolitionism became once again an ideological resource for the women's movement, just as the women's movement became an explicit form of global political engagement.[121] The Polyglot Petition espoused causes of universalist social improvement that extended across the separation of sex, nation, religion, language, culture, or nation.

Like Ramabai's strategic reliance on American funds for the Sharada Saran, the WCTU underpinned its work with long-term fund-raising. In 1894, it covered the costs of Elizabeth Andrew and Kate Bushnell's anti-opium tour to Shanghai. Hinting at global financial consultations among leading anti-opium lobbies around the world, the WCTU knew that the

FIGURE 3.10. The Polyglot Petition.

Source: Frances E. Willard, *Do Everything: A Handbook for the World's White Ribboners* (Chicago: The Woman's Temperance Publishing Association, 1895). Widener Library, Harvard University.

funds of anti-opium societies like the SSOT were insufficient for covering expensive telegrams to correct "one-sided reports from India day by day." This swipe drew attention to the real disadvantage of Indian anti-opium protesters in terms of resource competition with the British Indian government.[122] On the Chinese end, too, institution-building and the collection of anti-opium news overcame a certain paralysis. In June 1896, the foundations were laid for a new Anti-Opium League to represent all missionary communities and anti-opium supporters throughout the Qing empire. The Anti-Opium League in China was the only organization of that name, although some papers, such as the *New York Times,* referred erroneously to the SSOT as a (capitalized) Anti-Opium League, while decrying that "a poison administered to one-half of the population of Asia can hardly be the vital principle of a system of imperial finance."[123] As a fitting counterpoint, half the costs for the female anti-opium tour were covered by Chinese private donations, supplementing WCTU funding.

This was about more than women rallying against opium as a root cause of social injustice. Influential anti-opium organizations like the WCTU enacted a new momentum of cross-institutional integration, docking with one another through targeted projects of cooperation. The perception of compatibility across preexisting causes of social reform reoriented Powar's and Willard's institutions, respectively, from India to Britain and from the United States to Asia. The WCTU decided to put a women's delegation in charge of the journey around the world, with the specific aim of collecting support and signatures for the petition that urged "governments of all nations to separate themselves from all legal complicity with the trade in opium and alcohol."[124]

In the process of garnering signatures, the United States ended up taking the lion's share with 480,000, though unfortunately without indicating any social subcategories along gender or ethnic lines. Ramabai had rallied Indian support while the WCTU sought support from the *issei,* Japanese descendants in the United States, through joint American and Japanese mediation.[125] Crossing languages and writing systems was not inconceivable in the cosmopolitan project of producing a material manifestation of global public opinion.

Even so, the American sponsors of the petition lacked the cultural understanding for the signatures collected. "There are columns of Chinese women's signatures that look like houses that Jack built," Willard reported. "There is a list of Burmese signatures that looks like bunches of 'tangled worms.'" Thousands of signatures from Ceylon were thought "to make a short-hand man shudder; the incomprehensible but liquid vowels of the Hawaiian Kanaka jostle the proud names of English ladies of high degree; the Spanish of haughty *senoras* of Madrid make the same plea as the 'her mark' of the converted woman of the Congo." Orientalist attraction to the unknown mixed with the cosmopolitan imagination of intimate encounters across cultural spheres. "There are Spanish names from Mexico and the South American republics, French from Martinique, Dutch from Natal and English from New Zealand, besides the great home petition from the greater nations."[126]

Spending so much effort, ink, cloth, time, and money for the sake of global grassroots representation was designed to measure up with the considerable scope of the audience. The petition addressed them as "Honored Rulers, Representatives, and Brothers: We, your Petitioners, although belonging to the physically weaker sex, are strong of heart to love our homes, our native land, and the world's family of nations," as the opening lines read. "We know that clear brains and pure hearts make honest lives and happy homes, and that by these the nations prosper, and the time is brought nearer when the world shall be at peace." Unlike Willard's private quips, jest was in short supply in official pronouncements of opposition. Women, the petition asserted, knew that male indulgence in alcohol, opium, and "other vices" disgraced social life and caused misery for "us and for our children."[127]

Law and government, traditionally the exclusive domain of males, were called to political action. Stimulants and opiates filled the pockets of governments through "legal guarantees," they charged, a thinly veiled attack on opium legalization in the Treaty of Tianjin. "We know with shame that they are often forced by treaty upon populations, either ignorant or unwilling."[128] And if the WCTU knew all this and, by extension, the global public knew, one had to wonder why governments were the only parties apparently oblivious to these deficiencies of international political control. Much like in a public relations campaign of the twenty-first century, states around the world were addressed and urged to "redeem the honor of the nations from an indefensible complicity" in the unlimited supply of opium and alcohol.[129] Although still a distant hope in 1895, by 1912 this demand had become enshrined in the International Opium Convention. Nicknamed the "Magna Charta of the home," the petition did not anticipate such success.[130]

As GRANDILOQUENT as the petition's diction sounded, the practicalities of lobbying involved logistical planning to reach and unite "women of every race."[131] Lobbying on this logistical scale exceeded the level of institutionalization in global diplomatic cooperation. But the effort did not lag behind. Even photographic technology was harnessed to advertise the Polyglot Petition, with pictures showing off the massive rolls on a global tour.[132] Thanks partly to the assistance of Mary Clement Leavitt and Jessie Ackerman, Frances Willard became known as the "most widely travelled woman of the world."[133]

With the Polyglot Petition in tow, Leavitt embarked on her own world tour in the fall of 1883. From California, she proceeded across half the Pacific to Hawaii, then Australia, New Zealand, South Africa, Madagascar, Burma, India, China, Madeira, Mauritius, Ceylon, Siam, the Straits Settlements, Korea, Japan, and Europe.[134] Eight years later, Leavitt returned to the United States to attend the first World's Woman's Christian Temperance Union Convention, held in Boston's Faneuil Hall on November 10 and 11, 1891. Before an astonished convention, Leavitt reported on the "ninety-seven thousand miles" she had traveled and the services of "more than two hundred interpreters" in forty-seven countries. A month later, Leavitt turned up in South America, "meeting with many difficulties in establishing the work there; the next winter was passed at Honolulu, in regaining physical strength." In her own exulting words, her journey led her not only "around the world, but well-nigh all over it."[135]

The feat of Leavitt's true tour de force was not an isolated event. Before Leavitt returned to the United States, Elizabeth Wheeler Andrew and Kate C. Bushnell set out on yet another women's tour for the cause of anti-opium legislation. Andrew worked as editor of publications at the Woman's Temperance Publication Association.[136] In the 1930s, she was among the most vocal advocates of anti-drug campaigning, with an explicit focus on women. At the World's Congress of Representative Women; in all schools of the District of Columbia; and in all national, military, and naval academies, she spoke on the need of having anti-narcotic education, ultimately reaching an estimated twelve million children.[137]

Complementing Andrew's eight years on the editorial staff of the *Union Signal* journal, Bushnell had worked in the social purity section of the WCTU for five years. More than an evangelist, Dr. Bushnell was also known as "a thoroughly educated physician," with a degree from Chicago and medical missionary service in China. Bushnell also mingled in the circle of Alfred and Helen Dyer. In the United States, she had worked in "a good practice" in Denver, Colorado. She had founded the Anchorage for Women in Chicago and explored the "dens of white slave women in the northern pineries."[138] Both women were hailed as secular round-the-world missionaries.

On the U.S. East Coast, where the WCTU had staked out its biggest claim, the first wave of addiction centers were being built. The Massachusetts Home for Intemperate Women gained a reputation as a site where those "addicted to the use of opium are received and successfully treated." New York established its Christian Home for Intemperate Men for "curing" alcohol and opium addiction "by religious teaching and complete rest."[139] And while these "culprits" rested, the crusaders could not have been more restless.

Thus, it came as little surprise when they left the East Coast in early 1891, spending subsequently six months in Britain, then "Africa" (without further specification), traveling across the western and eastern halves of the Indian Ocean to India, followed by Australia. Thereafter, the route led back via Ceylon to Egypt and Syria before returning to England in March 1893. The Andrews-Bushnell itinerary covered "eighty-seven thousand miles, crossed the equator four times," and "took sixteen sea voyages," during which they delivered "six hundred and seventy addresses to an estimated attendance of forty-five thousand people." Noted enthusiastically by the *World's Progress*, "In all this journeying by sea and by land, no money was supplied them from the home treasury." All costs were covered by the private donations of their hosts.[140]

Approaching Hong Kong via Burma and Singapore, Bushnell and Andrew's all-female American delegation met a much larger all-male group working in social welfare reform on February 25, 1894, at the headquarters of the Po Leung Kuk Society. This Society for the Protection of the Young and Innocent (also known in English as "the Society for the Protection of Women and Children") was located next door to the Tung Wa Hospital. Established as one participant in a string of partner institutions—notably the Po Leung Kuk in Singapore, established in 1888, and further branches in Penang since 1889 and Kuala Lumpur since 1895—the Hong Kong branch of 1880 was the oldest. Here, agendas of transnational social work stretched beyond the protection of women and children, specifically against trafficking, prostitution, and abuse, starting a legacy that has survived until today.[141]

By bridging geography and gender in their cooperation, the Bushnell-Andrew duo extended previous WCTU initiatives in Canada, Sweden, Finland, Germany, Bulgaria, Turkey, India, Siam, China, Japan, South Australia, Queensland, New Zealand, Victoria, the Hawaiian Islands, South Africa, and Mexico.[142] This global context of anti-opium lobbying was further encouraged by lobbying outreach provided by Dyer Brothers, who published the first account of Bushnell and Andrew's transnational campaign by women against the Asian opium problem in 1894, produced "for private circulation among Specialists." Their colleagues in Hong Kong received a particularly glowing narrative: "They were a fine looking set of men, sitting in a grand, spacious chamber, covered with a handsome Oriental carpet, and furnished with carved ebony cabinets, sofas and chairs, and massive tables," the report documented. "A gorgeous shrine was at one side, with candles burning to their god, and many ornaments and offerings." Bushnell and Andrew took much interest in their male collaborators. "The men themselves were elegantly dressed in native fashion, and had an air of proud superiority." The report continued in high spirits: "Our entrance through the open doors in front (for the whole of this apartment was thrown open to the verandah by swinging black and gilt doors) produced quite a sensation."[143]

Moving from splendor to the substance of their work, it is important to realize that the moral entrepreneurs in Hong Kong could match the American ladies' experience and expectations, even though those expectations had been raised by recent achievements. Calling to task neglected government responsibilities and demanding colonial welfare policies were reminiscent of the duo's campaign from late 1891 to early 1892 against the British colonial regime in India and its inaction over prostitution in the military. When the two women produced an original prostitution "ticket" from India as evidence there, the government had promised to abolish the system. When that promise remained unfulfilled, the commander-in-chief, Lord Roberts, apologized to the American women activists and "acknowledged his fault in neglecting to see that Army discipline had been carried out." In a further show of the dependent quality of public ethical adjudication, Lord Roberts submitted an official apology to journalist William T. Stead.[144] In Hong Kong, Andrew and Bushnell drew on this boost of self-confidence and reported the successful precedent in the *China Mail.*

The organization hosting them, the Po Leung Kuk, had battled criticism by members of the Legislative Council as an alleged Chinese secret society with subversive political intentions.[145] Not unlike the Sharada Saran, the Po Leung Kuk provided physical shelter to women and children when it took up the anti-opium cause, raising greater controversy still than in the *mui tsai* question over female, low-cost domestic household servants.[146] But the Po Leung Kuk's recognition by the WCTU was quickly earned, boasting as it did in about a hundred of the "wealthiest and most influential Chinese residents of Hong Kong."[147] Assistants led Andrew and Bushnell for personal inspections to Hong Kong opium dens in search of evidence that was perceived to enhance the scientific credibility of their anti-opium arguments. They visited opium and prostitution houses on Hong Kong's Square Street, Queen's Road in West End, Cochrane Street, Stanley Street, and the small Kuw (or Kwah) Lane. With the help of translators (and Bushnell's skills in Mandarin Chinese, acquired as a medical missionary), they interviewed "child slaves" who had been trafficked to Guangzhou. In Singapore, they visited the establishments on Tringanu Street. An "immediate connection" was claimed between opium smoking and "impurity," namely the forced prostitution of girls, their "hair dressed elaborately, like married women."[148]

As a result, they documented 322 interviews with 184 opium smokers, 41 "degraded girls and women," 5 opium den keepers, 18 brothel keepers and "pocket-mothers," 5 physicians, 8 missionaries, 23 officials, and 38 "respectable persons in various callings, mostly natives." This information was drawn from Burma, Singapore, Hong Kong, Guangzhou, Shanghai, Zhenjiang (in Jiangsu Province), Nanjing, Zhejiang, Tianjin and Chefoo (Yantai). To confront British colonial officials, Bushnell and Andrew communicated sixty pages of testimonies, statistics, and reports, ranging from "Reasons for beginning the Habit" to "Physical Effects" of consumption to "the Effects of the Withdrawal of Opium from Habitual Consumers." They engaged in sociological interpretation of what it meant to lose one's reputation as a social consequence of opium consumption. Diametrically opposed to the glamor of their elitist welcome, the Po Leung Kuk offered its guided access to the most despised establishments in Hong Kong.

On the basis of this new exercise in anti-opium anthropology, the American–Hong Kong network started outlining the first comprehensive study of the opium-prostitution nexus across the South China Sea, Hong Kong's southern gateway. The president of the Po Leung Kuk urged them to go beyond "an expression of their opinion in regard to opium and its effects upon the people," precisely because it did not supersede governmental methods of investigation: "This had already been requested by the Hong Kong Government."

British government officials beyond Hong Kong did react. The results of this inquiry were discussed by the Royal Commission on Opium in a massive countereffort to outdo anti-opium documentation. With the Po Leung Kuk's lobbying support, the American–Hong Kong meeting closed with the pledge to press for "co-operation between the British and Chinese Governments" as a political guarantee for the cessation of British Indian opium supplies to China. The histories of abolitionism and the opium wars now fit comfortably into one sentence: "England ought to take the lead in abolishing the trade in opium, because the Chinese Government would be afraid of offending the British Government, the latter being very strong, and the former weak in comparison."[149] If a political settlement on these terms came to fruition, the Po Leung Kuk would pride itself in having played a crucial part. Hard work, planning, and commitment was extending women's cooperation against opium to "more than forty countries," with "many thousands of women and children . . . standing in the ranks."

As Leavitt, Willard's assistant, described this successful test run of mobilization: "The white ribbon has belted the world. . . . The World's Christian Temperance Union is an accomplished fact."[150] Much like suffragists, White Ribboners symbolizing the WCTU's global outlook paraded and marched on the streets and on paper. "Lady Henry Somerset's name at the head, leads the procession with its 350,000." Canada followed with 67,000, Burma with 32,000, and, in descending order, Ceylon, Australia, Denmark, China, India, and Mexico.[151] By 1895, the petition had grown to include 1,121,200 names. The WCTU did not record how long it took them to count them all. Expectations for Asia's sign-up to the conjoint agenda of anti-opium and temperance were high. "Hundreds of thousands of names" were "yet waiting to be added to the long roll." The numbers directly stimulated the WCTU's ambitions. "Nor will we ever rest until we have 2,000,000 actual names, besides the present 5,000,000 additional signers by attestation."[152]

Women's activism and anti-opium activism informed each other in a conscious closing of ranks, enriching the pool of reform ideas and rhetoric and, crucially, adding funding infrastructures of transnational scope to the methodical work of mobilization. Willard once noted that while pondering over Leavitt's peripatetic work life and reading about "the opium trade in India and China," she felt to be "under the impulse of its unspeakable recitals" and hence urged for a Polyglot Petition.[153] But global recognition for "breaking down . . . the system of legalized vice" in British India and exposing "the hidden things of darkness in the opium trade of India and China" she ceded to Andrew and Bushnell.[154]

As part of the wider surge of Asian anti-opium movements in the late nineteenth century, British territories around the South China Sea, from Singapore to Hong Kong, featured with particular intensity the theme of women's vulnerability within the family and within society writ large. This discovery made the region particularly amenable to anti-opium mobilization. Hong Kong served as a case in point. The first British Crown colony since the First Opium War showcased the success and failures of the British colonial administration and professed benevolence. The influential Chinese elite, rooted in comprador families, lent their names to causes of social reform where they saw the colonial state neglecting its self-professed duties.

What made these developments a continuing effort of mobilization rather than a repetitive complaint was the diversification of agendas and participants. Regional variations in the pairing of social-reform agendas formed the basis, not the impediment, of a transnational mobilization of protest and legislative demands. As shown by the American–Hong Kong alliance against opium and prostitution, global cooperation restored to local reformers the notion of global humanitarian progress, for now in terms of mobilization and expanding support. In Hong Kong, the exploitation of the most vulnerable members of society contradicted Confucian ideals of a harmonious family. It illustrated the potential of societal corruption by pointing to problems where society had seemingly lost its own sense of direction. The tropes of political causation and the teleology of winning public opinion until a tipping point of legislative change were thought to compensate for this and reorient, aided by perspicacious observation, unremitting documentation and a rhetoric of irrefutable universalism.

CHAPTER FOUR

BRITAIN'S LAST DEFENSE

The Anti-Opium Cause on Trial

If you're pestered by critics and hounded by faction
To take some precipitate, positive action
The proper procedure, to take my advice, is
Appoint a Commission and stave off the crisis.
By shelving the matter you daunt opposition
And blunt its impatience by months of attrition,
Replying meanwhile, with a shrug and a smile,
"The matter's referred to a Royal Commission."

C ONCLUDING a concerted, government-sponsored, three-year project
from 1893 to 1895 to quench anti-opium criticism once and for all,
the final report of the Royal Commission carried the physical and
moral imprimatur of the British government with ostensible weight. It was
the most determined and elaborate effort of its kind, a project of political
self-rehabilitation meant to restore legitimacy to the opium trade from
British India to China. However, the bureaucratic scale and comprehensive effort to find representative defenders of the opium trade for the Royal
Commission inescapably testified to the degree to which the opium trade
had been tarnished by the preceding influence of anti-opium opinion.

In 1893, the commission was facing an anti-opium opposition honed in
social work, discursive innovation, and even an internal diplomacy of its
own. The first nongovernmental anti-opium delegation had reached high
Qing officials. Criticism of the Second Opium War, legalization, and unlimited drug supplies being forced down China's throat had gathered force
ever since Prince Gong's signal protest of 1869. It would border on the plati-
tudinous to state that it was only a matter of time until governments would
take notice and devise a political response to antidrug criticism. What is
noticeable, however, are at least three points. First, the political response

of the Royal Commission intended to meet its challenger on the same scene, albeit an imagined one, where the attack had arisen: in the domain of public opinion. Second, engaging the attack on those terms over three sustained years showed that the government could win that battle, raising the question of why it did not. Third, both the mobilization against drugs and the first international answer by a state saw itself as at an overdue initiative, an effort that should have been taken long before, which itself represents an effective tool of political rhetoric to add drama, draw attention, and attract moral support. This begs the question how and from which sources the imperial urgency of the Royal Commission had emerged. The commission as a response cannot be properly understood without a comprehensive view on what preceded it, what it responded to, and what it ignored.

In 1890, a pamphlet by the Pekin [*sic*] Anti-Opium Society, authored by Shao Kangji, Rong Lin, Xue Beiqing, and Pan Zhen and dated August 2, 1890, fervently called on "all lovers of virtue in Great Britain," in which "the enormity of the crimes" that "our country is perpetrating upon the people of China" caught the moral and political attention of its readers, culminating in the accusation of "Britain's attitude and blood-guilty complicity in this debasing and ruinous traffic."[1] The reports were transmitted by Scottish press references to the *Sentinel,* a Dyer publication to which we shall return later. An estimated fifteen million Chinese opium consumers were increasingly difficult to ignore.[2]

As the ambition of anti-opium campaigners multiplied, the Pekin Anti-Opium Society addressed its appeal "to all lovers of virtue in Great Britain," producing tropes inflected by medical imagery on a par with new knowledge of opium's impact on Chinese agriculture: "Since Opium came to China, it has been like an evil ulcer, daily spreading and putrefying, infecting the whole body from head to foot."[3] The lack of British familiarity with Chinese economic predicaments caused by poppy cultivation was squarely addressed by raising the level of systemic agricultural risk, which linked seamlessly to the immoral economy of opium. "Opium stops the cultivation of the soil, squanders property, ruins a man's prospects, makes him lazy, hungry and cold, destroys his good example, causes him to lose his virtuous heart, makes thieves and robbers, estranges brothers and makes enemies of parents." In short, opium "causes every sort of crime, destroying body and soul."[4]

Opium as the root cause of familial disintegration and moral decline, however, was not a self-enclosed Chinese problem but instead symptomatic of the intercultural alienation between British and Chinese that Prince Gong had predicted decades ago. "Frequently men say of the Missionaries: "Your word exhorts us to virtue, but your heart conceals poison, since you kill us with Opium and carry our money to your own country."[5] Would mass mobilization turn the tide? "Alas! We cannot see you; and pen and ink cannot paint the terrible reality. One man can not move 10,000 lbs., but one hundred men can." The appeal did not say whether those mobilized should preferably represent the Chinese, the British, or both. But whoever took up the cause, the situation called for political action to "stop the curse, cast out from China this giant evil, and prohibit the traffic."[6] The prospect of closer Chinese-British cooperation that emerged from such communications lent activists a renewed sense of common purpose under political strain. Of all levels, progress of policy pressure seemed most difficult in a domestic setting, whether British or Chinese. Transnational anti-opium reports refreshed anti-opium activism because it felt, in this period at least, unfettered by ideological loyalties to surrogate causes, from political party to national belonging. In this respect, the Pekin Anti-Opium Society occupied a position and function equivalent to that of the British SSOT.

Meanwhile, in London, April 10, 1891, would be a date well-remembered by generations of anti-opiumists. Domestic anti-opium opposition brought the House of Commons, ever alert to scandalous press reportage of political importance, to carry the anti-opium agenda to its first historical victory in the very heart of an empire. Whereas 130 members of Parliament (MPs) voted against it, 160 voted in favor of the resolution declaring that "the system by which the Indian Opium Revenue is raised is morally indefensible."[7] By having this breakthrough on the parliamentary floor rather than in British India or another colonial setting, anti-opium campaigning had reached the metropolitan halls of power, the place where the desired decisions could be made. Their hopes high, anti-opium lobbyists were soon joined by English newspapers and journals that relished in the same enthusiasm. The press anticipated that before long the poppy would follow the fate of slavery, that the age of opium was "a black and blurred page of our national history," and claimed that the House of Commons vote "dooms the opium traffic to extinction at no distant date." In its eyes, this was "a decisive victory" for "the friends of national morality."[8] However, with the tragedy that often haunts formalism, the resolution never passed officially due to the lateness of the hour.

Still, the 1891 verdict of opium revenues as "morally indefensible" was indebted to various anti-opium forces with transcontinental ties, an attribution that cannot be underestimated in its recognition of transnational anti-opium pressure as real, serious, and dramatically on the rise. The Bombay Anti-Opium Alliance was one of the forces credited with the parliamentary victory, in line with its mission to promote "the total severance of the Government of British India from its connection with the Opium traffic" and to "endeavour, as its finances shall allow, to disseminate pamphlets, &c., putting the Opium question in a true light before the people of this Presidency."[9] Likewise, any careful reader of the British government's Blue Book on *Consumption of Opium in India* of 1892 would have noticed the growing acceptance of Indian anti-opium information disseminated by the SSOT, which had established contact with the Zongli Yamen and other Asian anti-opium supporters. With the entrance of anti-opium information into British policy planning, the neat separation between governmental and nongovernmental camps of opium interpretation showed the first signs of dissolution. Anti-opium criticism could no longer be ignored or kept at bay.

In 1892, one year before the Royal Commission opened its sessions, a wide spectrum of British official opinion on opium still tried to defy giving in, despite the 1891 resolution vote—or perhaps because of it. As president of the SSOT, astute anti-opium critic Joseph Pease brought further pressure on Viscount Cross, the secretary of state for India, by confronting him for neglecting "the very decided advice of the Executive in Upper and British Burma as to further and stronger measures for stopping the consumption of opium."[10] Cross had cited the Blue Books in Parliament himself, opening him up to the charge of willfully ignoring anti-opium opinion evidenced in the government's own documents.

Pease's position was further strengthened by the fact that defenders of the political status quo of the government-owned, supply-driven opium business ran into opposition among British officials in Asia who, like Alcock in one of his last meetings with Prince Gong in 1869, took a local version of Asian anti-opium opposition seriously. While most perspectives have sought signs of change in India and China, the search for the origins of British imperial rethinking of the Asian opium problem leads to the less known settings in between. Burma appears to have been the pioneer in this context, featured here before with its centuries-old legacy of prohibition. Although commonly neglected in discussions of anti-opium opinion on the eve of the Royal Commission and the Royal Commission's position vis-à-vis South and continental Southeast Asia, it was from Burma that a chief commissioner, Sir Alexander Mackenzie, warned in a report included in the Blue Book that "the average quantity of opium sold" in the opium shops of Lower Burma was increasing. The growth of consumption was accompanied by the spread of diverted opium deliveries—a typical conundrum of what is today called drug trafficking: "In spite of all precautions the licensees arrange to hawk their opium about the country." Mackenzie had recommended closing all opium shops as the most sensible solution.[11] The loss of opium revenue could be offset by raising taxes elsewhere. With an astonishing affirmation of intense, popular anti-opium sentiment, he argued that "Burmese opinion would accept a moderate increase of the land tax or the rice duty as a small price to pay for the withdrawal of the drug which is ruining so many of their race."[12] In these ways, direct lines of anti-opium influence can be traced from Burmese opposition at the eastern seaboard of the Bay of Bengal via British local officials to the SSOT, using both to make representations in Parliament.

More than a mere episode, this official reassessment of the opium problem built partly on the insights of the preceding colonial administration. The first time a former chief commissioner in Burma corroborated Burmese anti-opium opposition to London with urgency was when Sir Charles Aitchison informed London in 1880, the last year of his posting, that "native opinion is unanimous in favour of stopping the supply altogether, and no measure we could adopt would be so popular with all the respectable and law-abiding classes of the population."[13] Colonel Hildebrand, late deputy commissioner of Sandoway, agreed: "I am entirely of the same opinion as the Burmans I have consulted, and I think nothing short of absolute prohibition will cure the evil, which I look upon as of the gravest description."[14] Colonel Street from Burma expressed that he "would gladly see the sale, possession, and the use of opium (save for medical purposes) absolutely prohibited." The officiating commissioner of Arakan, Mr. Hodgkinson, concurred that "the importation, possession, use, or sale of opium, save for medicinal purposes, should be prohibited." He defended the suggestion as reminiscent of the Dutch opium monopoly under the ethical policy, despite the latter's factual extension far beyond medical purposes.[15] But like Dutch arguments of opium policy as a debt to the Javanese, Hodgkinson posited, "We owe this measure to the people, who have for years suffered grievously from our licensed shops, which are supplied with Government opium, and which," he added in diametrical opposition to the official function of the license system, "foster and spread the use and abuse of the drug." Hodgkinson, too, stated "that all respectable Burmans would be in favour of such abolition."[16]

Likewise, opium information from the highest levels of the British imperial bureaucracy in China had arrived at diverging assessments for decades, occasionally merging into administrative self-criticism. The public availability of these British imperial opium assessments further undermined the Royal Commission's position that it was preserving a status quo of opium trading that had remained politically unchallenged. In 1881, Sir Robert Hart, at the helm of Imperial Maritime Customs (IMC), had issued his famous Circular No. 64, the first large-scale information-gathering on specifically opium *consumption* in China, including the drug's addictive capacity. One of his instructions (no. 8) to all British customs officers in

China was to "ascertain the general opinion as to the length of time—months or years—a man must smoke before the habit takes such a hold on him as to be very difficult, if not impossible, to be given up." Measuring the time "to enslave a man" to opium smoking, the commissioner of customs in Hankou reported to the IMC in 1879, "depends so greatly on the constitution of the person that it is almost impossible to fix any period." On that basis, he continued: "When the smoker is of a robust constitution, he will resist the effects of the drug, naturally, for a much longer time than he would were he weak and sickly." Opium consumption was a variable, as was the politics of its reportage. "Great stress is laid by my informants on the regularity or irregularity observed in the daily hours for indulging in the habit. If the same times be observed, then a beginner will develop into an habitual smoker in about three or four months; but if, on the other hand, he smokes daily, but at uncertain hours, he may smoke for years, and then even be able to give up the habit without effort or inconvenience."[17]

As for medical assessments of opium consumption, preexisting health figured as perhaps the greatest cause for variability. "It is to the strong and healthy that this remark applies," the customs officer continued in critical distance to Chinese observations, "for when once a weakly person becomes a confirmed smoker, it seems next to impossible for him to give up the artificial stimulus that supplies him with life and energy, without a prostration very difficult to combat."[18] Likewise, the customs officer at Zhifu (today's Yantai) noted that, even though a powerful man may give up smoking after four or five years, the "general opinion" among the Chinese "appears to be that a man who has smoked two years becomes a slave to the drug, and that weakly constituted persons cannot give it up after six months' consumption."[19] Prior to the opium controversy further polarized by the Royal Commission, British opium observations did differ from "anti-opium fanatics," while reaching similar conclusions.

Imperial memoirs furnished similar evidence of British officials being very much aware of local, long-standing grounds of anti-opium opposition. As early as 1878, the Christian "Elders of Bassein" were "unanimous in their condemnation of opium in every shape. Burmese anti-opium sentiment extended to secular and Buddhist strands. The Burmese curse *bein-sa*, meaning "opium eater," was among "the most opprobrious epithets that can be applied to anyone," as the British knew. The British administration was also aware of the royal opium ban in precolonial times, an anti-opium legacy that would outlast the Royal Commission on Opium.[20] In the 1910s, Ledi Sayadaw—Burma's most famous Buddhist preacher and, as such, "more powerful than the Lieutenant Governor himself"—earned British praise for his "passionate eloquence," which "drew immense congregations."[21] Sir Herbert Thirkell White, the British lieutenant governor from 1905 to 1910, claimed after more than thirty years of service in Burma that Ledi Sayadaw's immense following was due to "the ethical part of his sermons," namely "fervent denunciations of intemperance, drinking, gambling, opium-smoking"—put differently, "the pleasant vices most devastating among Burmans." British authorities respected him, and his anti-opium remonstrations to Colonel Maxwell—as with Prince Gong's 1869 remonstrations to Alcock—not only found open ears among officials but lodged themselves in British officials' memory.[22]

In sum, the British received sufficient evidence that native Burmese opinion was overwhelmingly opposed to opium. The question, then, concerned not the existence or availability of anti-opium opinion but whether the government wanted to go so far as acknowledging anti-opium information and its perceived political pressure in its official decision making. In Upper Burma, the British position was particularly precarious, as the queen had issued a proclamation declaring never to derive revenue from the sale and use of opium. The SSOT was able to access an official Chinese translation of this proclamation through a member of the China Inland Mission named Mr. Stevens. The contradictions between existing British policy practices and the insistence on the status quo were bewildering, not merely from an opponent's point of view.[23] But to expose those contradictions effectively, anti-opium information could not just flow from Burma to London but had to be rerouted through anti-opium channels (like the SSOT) via missionary NGOs (like the China Inland Mission) before reaching its destination in London.

Network influence of this kind became perhaps the most significant consequence of sprawling decades-long mobilization against opium across the borders of Asia and Europe. We can detect today that in the 1890s, the first swivels of a political turn against opium added to network influence through nongovernmental mediators a second strand of influence that has been much ignored because of its supposed geographic and historic subsidiarity. But in the political economy of the opium problem as an Asian regional dilemma, the notion of international master narratives—big giants measuring up to one another—can fall short of social, political, and ideological realities. In addition to network influence and geography, the far from cold fact of chronology points to these new settings and their historical importance in preparing a British political turn against opium.

The region now notorious for compelling Rohingya refugees to escape since 2016, Rakhine State in Myanmar, was called Arakan in the 1890s and played a special role in the British political turn against opium. Several British officials from Arakan expressed their anti-opium positions in almost identical terms as anti-drug officials in the upcoming decades in Asia, Europe, and North America. Colonel Sladen, commissioner of Arakan, expressed that "the best of all opium reforms would be to prohibit its sale, or possession, or use (save for medical purposes) throughout Burma," further served as anti-opium support.[24] G. D. Burgess, commissioner of the Arakan division in 1886, agreed that "it would on the whole be better, and more for the advantage of the people and the administration," in that order, to implement a policy of opium prohibition "than to persist in the course which is now being followed," adding that "the present plan is one of inconsistency, and can never prove satisfactory."[25]

In total, more than two dozen officials, some of them in revenue collection, took a decidedly anti-opium stance, as Joseph Pease documented dutifully on behalf of the SSOT. A petition signed by five thousand medical experts in India was added to strengthen the SSOT representation, as if to prove that officials were yet being outnumbered by civilian anti-opium voices.[26] The British government's Blue Book, however, decided to conclude that as "the unanimous opinion of our responsible officers," it was "impossible to devise any machinery by which the consumption could be wholly suppressed, even if it were desirable on general grounds to do so." Meanwhile, "the attempt to enter upon any such policy of suppression would involve gigantic evils of which the Society for the Suppression of the Opium Trade can have no conception from their experience of the wholly different conditions of life and society in England."[27]

The government's accusation that the SSOT suffered from blinkered nationalism was clearly ill-informed about the SSOT's reach across Asia, despite abundant publications that proved that point. So irreconcilable was the charge with the facts that the government even rebuked the SSOT for information on India and Burma drawn from the government's own printed record. The bulk of Pease's documentation, used in his public letter to Viscount Cross, came from the government's own publications: the Blue Book of 1892, the Financial Statement (East India), the Moral and Material Progress and Condition of India, the Statistical Abstract of India, and the East India Accounts, not SSOT "agents" in India, as alleged in government attacks. Locked into an emerging information battle with the SSOT, the government made further mistakes, exposing weaknesses that were in turn identified by the SSOT as geographical misnomers—placing Lahore in the North-Western Provinces and Lucknow in the Punjab—all evidence of the government's "imperfect acquaintance with India and its conditions."[28] In a prequel to familiar Cold War debates, an early form of area-studies expertise played out as a competition between government critics on the one hand and officials on the other. As for the government's claim to "the unanimous opinion of our responsible officers," opinion was at best divided.[29]

Caricaturing the SSOT as provincial also stood at odds with its existing modus operandi as a transnational hub of anti-opium mobilization, including partnerships with the Qing government. Its contribution to the anti-opium debate questioned the British government's professed incapability as a practical objection to control. If the "entire extirpation of the habit is beyond the powers of Government," an SSOT memorial declaimed cynically, "it is no compliment to the integrity and ability of British officials to place them in this respect on a level with the agents of a sovereign like Theebaw," Burma's last king. Legal prohibition had "for generations" made a difference in "Burma, Siam and China," the SSOT knew and confirmed. Likewise, drug control had been "encouraged and supported by the British Government in Corea and Japan" and therefore "cannot owe its origin to the mere caprice of arbitrary monarchs, who might rather be expected to catch at so fair an opportunity of obtaining money from their subjects." Instead, these historical precedents across the Asian region spoke to "their perception of what the moral and religious sense of their people requires of them"—in other words, a democratic impetus that British officials should have recognized and honored long ago.

Anticipating some of the American admiration that would flatter the Japanese government a few years later, the SSOT stated, "Even though no Asiatic government, perhaps not all the vigour and honesty of British rule, can ever entirely prevent the illicit sale and consumption of the drug, still we believe that the imperfect operation of a prohibitory law is far less harmful than would be the introduction of licensed sale."[30] London, the argument went, paid a price, willingly or unwillingly, for failing to grasp the significance of anti-opium protest beyond Britain and the opium problem as not only a British Indian but a wider Asian sociopolitical controversy. The British government needed an outside party to interpret the opium problem for it, the SSOT intimated. "So fatal" had the opium habit appeared "in the Chinese Empire and in the Dutch Colonies of Java and Sumatra" that the historical risk was high, indeed likely, for a spillover effect into British India. The SSOT, true to its lobbying scope in Asia, explained that reframing the opium problem along regional rather than merely colonial lines was "especially fascinating."[31] Just how fascinating, the upcoming years would reveal.

The SSOT's priority to use the analytic benefits of an Asian comparative perspective on the opium problem did not go unnoticed, being faintly discernible in the way the Blue Book of 1892 mentioned diverse opium policies across Asia as options. However, the British government decided to reject the idea of borrowing policies in whole or in part from other Asian states, insisting instead on India's exceptionalism. "We do not consider it incumbent on us to enter on an elaborate exposition of the fallacy underlying the suggestion that a policy which may be practicable in such places as Japan, the Corea [sic], Java and the Philippine Islands," in its last years under Spanish rule, could be "adopted by a stroke of the pen in the enormous continent of India." The imagery, as compelling in sound as it was misleading in substance, was judged as incompatible by definition. "The whole circumstances of the history, geographical position, nationality, and habits of the people" were so "essentially different" that it obliterated the need for further explanation. Concluding this swift rebuttal presented the Indian government's attitude as uncompromising and unique. "No useful purpose would be served by a purely academic discussion which failed to take into account the primary conditions with which we have to deal in India," the Blue Book closed its rejection of intercolonial lessons.[32]

Despite the notable success of an anti-opium resolution receiving a majority of votes in the House of Commons, none of these tussles for opium information, government accountability, public legitimacy, or interpretive superiority could be resolved effectively in Parliament, the classic political battleground of British Indian interests. But the controversy over the Blue Book on Indian opium consumption in 1892 proves at least two things. First, British official acknowledgment both of local anti-opium opposition and of opium control as a commendable policy started not in China, the main recipient of the Asian opium trade, or British India, its main supplier, but in Burma and Arakan, at the eastern edge of the Bay of Bengal. First signs of political rethinking were voiced in the spaces between the giants. Second, transnational anti-opium lobbyists played only one part in fashioning available information on Asian anti-opium positions.

The very idea of the Royal Commission, a bureaucratic ritual replayed in more than 380 instantiations between 1830 and 1900, aimed to draw public support for existing policies, rather than forge a new strategy of opium administration.[33] What allowed it to ignore transnational SSOT and intraimperial communications on anti-opium sentiment in South and Southeast Asia was an increasingly exposed politics of contextualization. Anti-opium reportage itself had become a game into which the Royal Commission and its gigantic documentation from 1893 to 1895 would throw its weight.

The Politics of Anti-opium Reportage

At odds with the multipronged impetus of opposition, now along nongovernmental as well as governmental lines of influence from Asia, the Royal

Commission simplified the framing of the opium problem itself by targeting the anti-opium party as if it would constitute a marginal and exclusively nongovernmental position, as if it lacked any constituency of opinion within the government. Tying Burma's and Arakan's anti-opium influences to the new projects of anti-opium publishers helps establish to what degree the upcoming Royal Commission reduced what had preceded it.

Dyer Brothers had taken a hit in the 1892 Blue Book on Indian opium consumption, dismissed as "the sensational descriptions drawn by Messrs. [Maurice] Gregory, Dyer and Sessions."[34] But without too much effort, anti-opium information kept becoming available from new sources, enabling Dyer Brothers to fortify its positions. The same circle that had sponsored Powar's international publicity ran the journal the *Sentinel*. In 1890, it transmitted anti-opium protests from Melbourne, Australia, where a Chinese Christian named Cheok Hong Cheong addressed the Victorian Alliance to criticize opium consumption "in this colony" spreading even "among the European population" and to demand that opium be declared "among the deleterious articles of human consumption." Against all of them, like the WCTU, the Victorian Alliance "declare[d] war."[35]

In Singapore and the Straits Settlements, the *Sentinel* reported, over eleven thousand residents had signed an anti-opium petition, read to parliament on April 9, 1891, against "the terrible evils of opium-smoking among so many of the thousands of Chinese who crowd to these parts of the British possessions to make a livelihood for themselves." The British administration, "generally fraught with so many blessings to those under its rule," could surely do something if willing. Chinese laborers on British soil were being ruined morally, physically, and materially by "this most pernicious drug." In Singapore, too, it was time to enact the "immediate prohibition of the growth of the poppy, and the traffic in opium, in and from any of Her Majesty's dominions, except for strictly medicinal purposes." The petition testified to organized anti-opium opinion in Singapore and included Chinese overseas leaders like Song Ong Siang, then an undergraduate at Cambridge University and ten years later a pioneer of Singapore's first anti-opium organization.[36]

Serving as the platform for the *Anti-Opium News*, an "Organ of Movements for Social Purity and National Righteousness," the *Sentinel* offered, in addition to rhetorical propaganda, fresh anti-opium statements combined with reprints of recent press cuttings to form one of the most international anti-opium press reviews of its time. Orders were received through the London and Bombay offices "or through any bookseller."[37] Through its agency in India and joint headquarters with the *Bombay Guardian*, the Dyer network built up a regular exchange of anti-opium information between Asian sources and European audiences.

In 1893 and 1894, the first standoff between the government and anti-
opium forces emerged. The half-hearted closure of licensed opium dens in
the Bombay Presidency remained under the pressure of criticism in the
Bombay Guardian.[38] Yet these measures did not reflect a governmental turn
against opium, as Dyer learned from a confidential circular by the commissioner of excise, which ordered staff *not* to prosecute the opening of
new, officially illicit dens, a development confirmed by the chief inspector
of the Opium Department, who counted about 150 opium dens "known
to the police" in late 1893.[39] At that moment, Dyer launched a joint publication with three like-minded publicists: American A. W. Prautch, a
longtime resident of the Philippines, currently at the Methodist Episcopal
Mission in Thana; Thomas M. Hudson, of the same mission's Bombay
branch; and Man Sukh Lal, editor of the *Banner of Asia*, where his colleague,
Maurice Gregory, had published Powar.[40] Lal also served as a pugnacious
officer of the Salvation Army and the author of forceful Dyer Brothers
pamphlets, including *Opium and the Gospel in Indian Villages*, which
cross-referenced the *Sentinel* and the *Bombay Guardian*.[41] Although the
name Man Sukh Lal masked a British missionary by the name of R. Ward
gone native, the representations were indeed in line with "native" anti-
opium opinion.[42]

In a show of the power of transnational protest, the quartet of anti-
opiumists participated in an Indian anti-opium deputation to the Conference Representing Protestant Missions in the Indian empire. Moving toward
repressing anti-opium dissent, the government had warned Dyer not to go.
Held in Bombay in early 1893, the conference led to a declaration signed
by 1,112 Indian missionaries denouncing the "demoralizing traffic in
Opium, and we record our conviction that it is a sin against God, and a
wrong to humanity."[43] The press exposure of January 1894 radicalized the
tone of the declaration into a political impeachment. It indicted the corruption of the government's Opium Department in Bombay; the police in
Mahim, a suburb of Bombay; and the opium contractor in the Mahim district, Damji Lakhmichand. The latter had been informed by the government that he would have his permit restored to run his opium dens on the
condition that he would support the prosecution of the libelous anti-opium
journalists. This governmental generosity he could not refuse. In court for
his opium dens, Lakhmichand received direct counsel by the government
Opium Department, with the chief inspector "seated side by side with the
counsel" and "the nominal prosecutor himself standing at the back of the
Court, and being on some occasions actually absent."[44] As for the quartet
of Prautch, Lal, Dyer, and Hudson, they were arrested and likewise dragged
into court, but with less auspicious help. They refused to pay the fine of

their sentences, and all except Hudson were subjected to a month's imprisonment for contempt of court (Hudson was bailed out by an affluent friend). Anti-opium publicity had made a hitherto invisible line of government tolerance visible—in negative proportion to its tolerance of the drug.

Putting the male protagonists of the Indian-British anti-opium fight behind bars brought their tenacious wives to the fore. Helen Stace Dyer took control of publications at the *Bombay Guardian* and the *Banner of Asia*. As the anti-opium lobby was pleased to note later, the government had failed to foresee "the energy and resourcefulness" of Ms. Dyer. "Descended from the Huguenot ancestors, she inherits a goodly share of their bravery under oppression, and their tact in overcoming difficulties." Maurice Gregory gave her full recognition for her anti-opium service, praising "the heavy debt owing by this generation to women in moral reform."[45] The WCTU would have been pleased. Phulbai, "the educated Gujerathi wife" of Man Sukh Lal, took refuge with Ramabai, a "heroic friend of the child widows of India." With the support of Powar, the trio of women continued their work and traveled 119 miles from Poona to Bombay "to greet" the trio of men "on their liberation from jail."[46] So much for female domesticity!

Mr. Prautch reportedly "lost six pounds in weight in four weeks"; all of them were "neither allowed to write nor receive letters." But imprisonment also created opportunities and deepened anti-opium loyalties. Producers and consumers of anti-opium publicity closed deals on covering the expenses of their convicted leaders. While the readers of the *Bombay Guardian* covered Prautch's legal expenses and even his lobbying tour to England in September 1894, following his release, the readers of the *Sentinel* covered the expenses for Man Sukh Lal and his wife, Phulbai. The burgeoning financial strategy of anti-opium networks to transform readers into donors gave a boost to the transnational potential for mobilization, just as the less visible emotional consolidation compensated for the temporary institutional damage of the anti-opium lobby. The title of Gregory's collection of pamphlets and press cuttings used a reference to the biblical trope of "suffering for the Truth," making spiritual heroism soar in times of secular failure.

The anti-opium element in border-crossing projects of mobilization widened its circles in response to state repression. Thanks to Ms. Prautch's Canadian origins, missionaries there published a resolution in support of the anti-opium cause, along with nearly fifty missionaries traveling sixteen hours from Berar to give evidence in Mr. Dyer's defense in Bombay. Telegrams of sympathy from England were suppressed until his release.[47] S. C. Kanaga Ranam, assistant master of the London Missionary Society High School at Belgaum and already president of the local YMCA at age twenty-five, joined Man Sukh Lal. Crisis augmented anti-opium cooperation.

No wonder that the Royal Commission kept a wary eye on Kanaga Ranam and Man Sukh Lal. With Prautch—an early protagonist in the British publicity campaigns around Dyer Brothers—Man Sukh Lal, Hudson, and Alfred Dyer, the "anti-opium gang" further exposed the state control that they had criticized in the first place. The *Bombay Gazette* celebrated the prosecution as a precedent "in which amazing fictions palmed off on the good faith of the English people by a certain class of missionaries had been tested in a court of justice, and they had been proved up to the hilt to be based on barefaced and impudent lying."[48]

Using political persecution as an achievement, not a defeat, Rustom Pestonji Jehangir had the full proceedings of the trial published, warning anti-opium activists in India and elsewhere. In the aftermath of the scandal, Prautch, Lal, and Hudson noted with alarm that Jehangir adopted the same methods of transnational travel and social mobilization that they had championed. Twice he visited England to propagate a defense of Indian opium consumption. In revenge, the anti-opium gang uncovered four illegal shops opened with his "full knowledge and consent" as chief opium inspector, charging Jehangir "with personally taking a staff of Opium Department Police to Mahim, to supervise the illegal smoking shops." The painstaking detail of anti-opium investigations reached the level of detective work, reporting that there was one *madak* shop for prepared smoke opium in Kassibarri, Mahim, "kept open for eight days by one Aga Mahomed and a woman named Saddi," further "a *chandul* shop, open for five days on Mahim Bazar Road by one Karim Jetli and Khuda Bux; another *chandul* shop, open for ten days by Rahimtulla in Mahim also, and a *kasumba,* an opium-drinking place, open for seven days by Haji Ahmed near Kassibarri in Mahim."[49] International public opinion now had the power to connect and attack, to encourage and intimidate.[50]

In response, colorful vignettes of opium victims and social portraits of their addictive suffering gained a quality of intimate immediacy. Hand-drawn sketches furnished by Man Sukh Lal for Gregory's *Suffering for the Truth* helped convey what a social problem inflicted from abroad meant to those most closely and more than just politically affected.[51] Stories of the addict's pitiably ruined wife and children evoked the impression that society writ large could fall or had fallen victim to social, economic, and moral decline, with opium as the root cause. Beyond mere illustration, eliding and withdrawing the voice of visual interpretation is reminiscent of the early days of photojournalism, exploiting the assumption that pictures speak for themselves and more truthfully than statements.

British Quakers became the principal sponsors of the SSOT, operating with specially reserved funds of "Anti-Opium Committees," which enabled the first Chinese-British anti-opium coalition. Reverend Yan Yongjing partnered with colleagues during an extended visit to England from late 1893 to September 1894. Like Powar in 1889, his lobbying tour in England earned roaring applause, contrasting with earlier disappointments of Chinese-British transnationalism. Most dramatically, in spring 1872, Du Wenxiu (alias "Sultan Suleiman")—leader of the Chinese Muslim "Panthays" in China's southwestern Yunnan—sent his son Hassan to England. Even though an official guest of the British government, the visit failed entirely, with a London reception falling far short of the homage paid in Constantinople.[52]

But in 1893 and 1894, the Quakers hosted Yan to satisfaction, as an "eloquent Chinese Christian of good repute throughout the Churches there," all expenses covered.[53] The financial backing of the British Anti-Opium Urgency Committee of the Religious Society of Friends totaled £1081 in 1894 and showed how core elements of the anti-opium camp could weather the financial strain experienced by the SSOT. That organization, in turn, abandoned its earlier rules for local lobbying on the principle of self-sufficiency. The financial bonds of anti-opium mobilization stretched across institutions, space, and time.[54]

Not for the first time, Yan Yongjing experienced transnational appeal. Descending from a family of prominent Chinese Anglicans in Shanghai, Yan was the first Chinese to receive a college degree in the United States, graduating from Kenyon College in Ohio in 1861. Seven years later, in 1868, he founded in Wuchang the first in a series of schools, indicating his pioneering contribution to reformist higher education in the years to come. In 1879, it culminated in St. John's University in Shanghai, the most internationalist Chinese university during the Qing dynasty. In 1890, Yan and his wife were the only Chinese delegates at the Shanghai Missionary Conference. His nephew Yan Huiqing, a graduate of the University of Virginia, later became China's premier—five times—and, as another anti-opium campaigner, fought the bureaucratic battles over opium at the League of Nations in Geneva.

In turn, the SSOT and allied British transnational lobbyists caught the attention of the Qing's Zongli Yamen, where Zhang Yinhuang—having served as the Chinese minister in the United States, Spain, and Peru in the 1880s—was eager for contact at the time, far beyond the anti-opium cause. Like Ramabai, Yan, and many others, Zhang shared a commitment to transnational institutions of higher education, establishing the first Sino-Western schools in the United States, Peru, and Cuba, with Havana starting in 1886.[55] The Qing's originality in building transnational networks in its foreign policy was limited neither to Cuba nor to the Americas or Asia. In 1886, Zhang took an entire year "to investigate the commercial situation of Chinese merchants" and fill Qing coffers with diasporic cash. He was joined by Zhang Zhidong, the governor-general of Guangdong and Guangxi provinces, on a commission to the Philippines, Singapore, the Straits Settlements, Malacca, Penang, Rangoon, Delhi, Batavia, Semarang, Surabaja, and several Australian cities, leaving out only Bangkok and Saigon, and returning to Beijing in spring 1890.[56] These Qing transnational initiatives and consultations show that the Manchu regime was no longer a stranger to the modality of transnational cooperation. Overseas lobbying was in full swing from Southeast Asia to the Caribbean.

Nor was Sino-British transnationalism necessarily a Western initiative on Western terms. On the basis of mutual transnational access, the SSOT's honorary secretary, Joseph Alexander, asked the Qing government "what lines we could best assist them" on in the anti-opium question.[57] Alexander was granted an audience with Zhang Yinhuang, then vice president of the Board of Revenue and soon to be the Qing's peace delegate at the conclusion of the Sino-Japanese war, followed by the president of the Bureau of Control for Railways and Mines during the Hundred Days Reform by Emperor Guangxu in 1898.[58] Dr. John Dudgeon, himself an anti-opium supporter, had requested the meeting on Alexander's behalf. Dr. Blodget of the American Board of Foreign Missions, who claimed forty years' residence in China and was reputedly "the first Protestant Missionary to settle in North China," served as interpreter.[59] In the candid interview, Zhang revealed that he knew of the Royal Commission on Opium concurrently in session Calcutta, that he had personally visited India and discussed the opium trade with the British governor-general, "who appeared embarrassed." Alexander emphasized that SSOT lobbying was willing to respond to Qing directives, urging the Zongli Yamen to issue a strong statement "that opium is like a deadly poison" and "most injurious to mankind." Through the audience, Alexander was put in a position to signal to Zhang the SSOT's support of the terms of Prince Gong's demarche of 1869.[60]

Subentries of the Royal Commission's report strongly denied Prince Gong's anti-opium influence: "Chinese never blame England for introducing opium." Chinese prejudice might have been directed at "foreigners" but not foreigners "as opium introducers," a sentiment described as "non-existent." In blanket terms, any "popular belief that England forced opium on China" was "not credited by the Chinese." As for Qing servants, there was "no official feeling against the English in connexion with opium," and the "erroneous view of the moral and material evils of opium-smoking" was dismissed as some precursor to "fake news." Tellingly, the number of subentries to "public opinion" counted more than six times as many as on the "Anti-Opium Movement," exposing a difficult tension with the commission's official objective to counter the narratives of a chiefly British domestic anti-opium myth.[61]

But counteracting the selectivity of Royal Commission evidence, anti-opium mobilization prior to and during the Royal Commission spread far beyond the British Raj, which helped in keeping a sense of progress. Zhang assured Alexander that Chinese official views had not changed: "Who is there who does not know the great evil of the Opium habit?" Zhang's anti-opium stance flatly contradicted Royal Commission statements that the Chinese government no longer desired to stop the opium trade, whether foreign or internal, caught in fiscal interests. Still, the attention given internationally to Qing policy was dwarfed by the prominence given to British-Chinese transnational lobbying. Whereas London's accusations through Alexander's mediation reached Beijing only to be proven wrong there, Beijing's opposition was oftentimes ignored summarily, not least in the Royal Commission itself.

This explains the pessimism prevailing in transnational Qing-SSOT conversations. Moral convictions aside, the Qing government did not perceive itself "perfectly free to stop the import of Indian Opium if she desires," an argument frequently forwarded in Britain by those unwilling to let British India take an anti-opium initiative. "We did stop it once, and it caused a war," was Zhang's morbid response.[62] A ten-year plan for opium suppression—though Alexander's own brainchild materialized ten years later in diplomacy—received a supportive response from Zhang but did not entirely dispel Chinese skepticism drawn from the First Opium War. "England will never stop the export from India," Zhang was certain; "the Indian Government will never consent to its being stopped."[63] In a separate interview on June 11, 1894, Li Hongzhang remarked "sarcastically that it was absurd to appoint a Commission to enquire whether or not Opium is injurious. . . . Everybody knows that Opium is very injurious."[64] Certainly, an increasing number around the world knew, ever since Prince Gong used those very words.

The Royal Commission's Agenda

The meaning and impact of the Royal Commission on Opium has divided contemporaries and historians. Historians generally agree on the Royal Commission as a landmark event, whether as an attempt to pacify or silence anti-opium "fanatics" or as a hypocritical and self-interested protection of Indian finance. Interpretations of the Royal Commission as a pivotal event usually move between two poles. The first pole presents an evaluation of its political, social, and ideological impact. The second pole seeks to find an inner logic driving the commission inquiries and recover its mental and moral universe. Most accounts of the Royal Commission on Opium lean toward the latter pole.[65]

In fact, an early proposal for a Royal Commission emerged in the anti-opium camp, pressing the government to inquire "what retrenchments and reforms in Indian expenditure could be effected, how Indian resources could best be developed, and what help would be needed from the British Exchequer, in order to carry out the suppression of the Opium Traffic." For the secretary of state for India, this went too far, but anti-opium sentiment forbade an outright refusal of engagement. With the support of Liberal prime minister William Gladstone and 184 versus 105 votes in the House of Commons, the Royal Commission's task was amended to inquire "generally into the whole question of the production and consumption of opium in India."[66] Rather than negotiating the financial means to the objective of prohibition, the features and functions of the opium industry and Indian opium consumption became core objectives. After this less than subtle shift, the commission inquiry could shun the initial question to which degree the opium problem called for a fundamental change of policy. Instead, it could ask whether an opium problem existed at all.

Accordingly, the recruiting commissioner followed a careful selection of official questions and invited testifiers to create a unanimous response to anti-opium policy proposals. The staffing of the commission directly reflected this penchant for institutionalized partiality. As chairman of the commission, Thomas Brassey was joined by two established opponents of the anti-opium cause, Sir Arthur Fanshawe, a former excise revenue officer in India and governor of the Indian Post Office from 1889 to 1906. Sir James Broadwood Lyall, until 1892 the lieutenant governor of the Punjab, joined the board with his uncle, George Lyall, chairman of the East India Company and twice MP for the City of London. Nongovernmental commissioners included the staunch Henry Joseph Wilson, a Liberal, close ally of Joseph Chamberlain before Chamberlain's ascent to president of the Board of Trade in 1880, and the only anti-opium critic. Arthur Pease, a Liberal Unionist and brother of SSOT president Joseph Pease, joined the commission but abstained from overt opposition. The commissioners' team further included Sir Robert Gray Cornish Mowbray, a Conservative who held the seat for Prestwich in the House of Commons from 1886 to 1895, and Sir William Roberts, a professor of medicine at Owens College in Manchester for two decades and an expert on renal disease. The two Indian commissioners were Lakshmeshwar Singh, the loyal maharaja of Darbhanga, and Haridas Viharidas Desai, the diwan of Junagadh. Except for

Arthur Pease, the commission stood disconnected from widespread anti-opium representatives in Asia and Europe from the start.

Like anti-opium activists who sounded out opium "witnesses" as representatives of public opinion and as sources of legitimacy for their ideological agenda, the commission approached an array of opinions within acceptable limits. In contrast to the technique of an anthropological interview of the Powar type, the commissioners couched the survey in the formal setting and rhetorical terms of an interrogation. Few anti-opium interrogations brought in someone with the panache of Man Sukh Lal. Indeed, Lal's assessment that quinine, not opium, figured as the preferred medicine to malaria in the coastal region of Gujarat in western India directly contradicted what the commission wanted to hear, maintaining that opium's effects as a cure were neither popular nor proven.[67]

Revealed by the tone and type of follow-up questions in the protocol of the Royal Commission hearings, it operated like a cross-examination of a trial. Beyond its filtering of "native opinion" by opaque criteria, the deliberate setup of a courtroom arrangement, and the physical and rhetorical projection of power relations, the commission suffered from one great vulnerability: a thematic focus on defending Indian opium consumption without answering the China-centered anti-opium critiques that had proliferated internationally in preceding decades. But had the commission chosen otherwise, historians today would face even more than six hefty volumes of a final report.

What effectively happened was that the commission started mustering evidence to counter anti-opium information, moving into an anti–anti-opium position. SSOT documentation could be cited, if only to "indicate that the habit is alleged to exist in India[,] and the direct connexion of the Government of that country with the production are regarded mainly in connexion with efforts to secure the discontinuance of the exportation of opium from India to China."[68] But tellingly, of the minority of Indian interviewers who had been selected as representative opium consumers, none spoke directly to this aspect, vacillating instead with docility in response to imperial questions, keenly aware of the power hierarchies they were facing. It did not appear to be very convenient to be "brought" before the commission as a "subject."

The decision of the British Court of Directors in the early nineteenth century not to suppress poppy cultivation in British and native territories was once again justified as being demand based. In December 1893, Gujarat in the Bombay Presidency moved into focus as Thomas Duncan Mackenzie, a seasoned British tax official and acting commissioner of customs, salt, opium, and abkari, rationalized its opium policy for the Royal Commission on Opium as a representative discussion of British political practice. However, Mackenzie's characterization of British policy as minimalist, eyeing neither profit nor exports, begged the question of where the oversupply delivered to China came from. In 1893, the British Indian government calculated that 33,758 chests were designated for export and only 3,093 for Indian domestic consumption, a ratio of 12 to 1.[69] But at the Royal Commission itself, the British denial of Chinese demand as at least partially fueled by Indian supplies paid off. With competing debates shut out, most notably anti-opium information, opium consumption rates and effects appeared in an endless variety, conditioned by the physical, nutritional, emotional, and psychological disposition of the consumer. In other words, the opium consumer had long decided what was or was not harmful, while the government had little to do with consumerist choice.

Wherever possible, the government used transnational confirmations of limited Indian opium consumption, showing that the value of transnational information flows could not entirely be streamlined toward an anti-opium purpose. Reverend H. Lorbeer, a missionary of the German Lutheran Church, was based at Ghazipur, one of two headquarters of the government's Opium Department, and summarized twenty-eight years of experience by stating, "I do not consider that the use of opium impedes the progress of Christianity in India. All our converts were made from opium cultivators, and some of them cultivate it still occasionally when they are in pecuniary difficulties."[70] However, from the viewpoint of interviewing him, it was not clear how this statement related to opium consumption. In a further distraction from opium smoking as the existing bone of contention, a handful of witnesses from China and the Straits Settlements were consulted, the Royal Commission predominantly focused on opium eating. But opium eating in the Indian states rarely acquired the psychoactive intensity and moral revulsion of opium smoking in China and in Chinese overseas communities.

Beyond these individual statements in favor of the political status quo of the opium trade generally, the commission's secretary, John A. Baines, understood very well that anti-opium mobilization drew on British as well as Asian strands. When the opium question entered Parliament, it did so "from the standpoint of the great evil that was being caused by the consumption of the drug, not only in China, but in India itself." Indian anti-opium sentiment, he argued, justified the commission's focus on the Raj—which "had not become the subject of special reprobation or inquiry."[71] And in the words of the War Office, India was a dependency, "our hold over which is not based on the general goodwill of those disunited races."[72] But apart from the fact that Britain did not rule China, Baines failed to explain why

India and China, if indeed conjoint in the Asian opium problem and in preceding mobilization, should not be examined together. Ironically, one of the victims of the commission's India focus turned out to be the most prominent trope of decades-long protests: that of Asian victimization through the opium trade.

Faced with multiple existing strands of opposition, the commission itself came under scrutiny as SSOT documentation contextualized government communications in unfavorable ways. The example of Burma once again returned with a vengeance, only to be met with strategic casualness. "Shortly after the Chief Commissioner of that Province had communicated to the Government of India in 1880 the strong views held by himself and local officials of experience as to the injurious effects of the opium habit on the Burman race, those views were adopted by the Anti-Opium Society [the SSOT] in England, and were pressed upon the attention of the Secretary of State for India in the memorial presented to him in 1881," Baines reported. But no conclusions were drawn.

Apart from lip service, first to an Asian opium problem beyond India, and second to consumption patterns above moderate levels and static or decreasing rates, the commission inquiry shunned these dangerous aspects. Its selectivity in the amount of time and detail afforded to controversial questions and, by comparison, its astonishing patience with moderate opium statements made the inquiry tightly focused to a degree that could no longer be called coincidental. Above all, domestic opposition was the easiest to counter. Parliamentary anti-opium agitation at the time of the First Opium War was brushed aside as a "convenient cover for a parliamentary attack upon the general foreign policy of the Government of the day." The conflict from 1856 to 1858, meanwhile, had been "on several occasions quoted as the 'second opium war' by a responsible [i.e., British] statesman as well as by some of the leaders of the movement against the opium traffic" but, Baines claimed, to little avail.[73] Ultimately, the commission did not offer a viable way of making sense of perspectives and perceptions outside the classic imperial perspective of metropolis and periphery. Even if empire had, since the early modern period, constituted a "moral unit," there was no overarching logic that forced policy makers to integrate its formal empire in India and its informal empire in China for the thorny purpose of self-scrutiny.[74]

Having spent much ink and paper on seven heavy volumes of documentation across twenty-five hundred pages, the commission celebrated its conclusions: "Upon every consideration of prudence and statesmanship, it seems clear that in the position of the British Government of India, we cannot deal experimentally with 290 millions of people, in a matter involving interference with the innermost concerns of personal life, without a clear pronouncement of native opinion" in favor of opium control.[75] But the illusion to isolate India's opium consumption as an exemplary case made the Royal Commission the last and ultimately futile governmental attempt to mute anti-opium energies in Asia and around the world. When in 1903 the Louisiana Purchase Exhibition depicted Chinese opium smokers as a feature of that nation, Chinese protests erupted immediately.

The final report of the Royal Commission on Opium of 1895 concluded still optimistically "that the movement in England in favour of active interference on the part of the Imperial Parliament for the suppression of the opium habit in India, has proceeded from an exaggerated impression as to the nature and extent of the evil to be controlled." The critique admitted being focused on British domestic opinion. "The gloomy descriptions presented to British audiences of extensive moral and physical degradation by opium, have not been accepted by the witnesses representing the people of India, nor by those most responsible for the government of the country."[76]

But perhaps predictably, it was in China where the Royal Commission provoked the most bitter outrage. As one of the earliest international opium historians described it in 1934, with the benefit of hindsight: "To anti-opiumists the royal commission's report was a disaster; to the ordinary M.P., bored by a fifty-year-old issue, it promised some relief; but to the Indian government it came almost as a stay of execution. Such triumph was rarely achieved, and the government was quite justified in exulting over the 'vindication of the past action of the Government of India . . . and of the views which have guided us.'"[77] In the long term, the Royal Commission proved less its accuracy than the fierce determination and soon political influence of those ignored by it.[78]

Like the peace settlement of 1858 and 1860, the Royal Commission failed in its central objective to quell the sources of anti-opium opposition and the interpretive grounds of objections to the opium regimes cobbled together from British India to Qing China. Instead, the commission helped raise the international exposure of India's opium regime, without any means to lower its profile afterward, implying an ultimately fatal underappreciation of how international public opinion worked. Expecting the geographically disparate and socially diverse audience of global anti-opium critics and the unknown numbers of their sympathizers to assent to the authority of an official commission report assumed that the global public would react in ways similar to subordinate officials, pliant subjects, or obedient citizens.

Not everyone asked by the commission did in fact give the conservative answers desired and represent existing opium policy as the best possible approach. A minority of dissenters was quietly sidelined. In an appendix of the multivolume Royal Commission report of 1896, correspondence revealed dissenting opinions that were not, however, "considered . . . of special importance as showing the nature of the action which was actually taken by the Government of India," nor did they constitute "material bearing upon the questions discussed," the two criteria for additional documentation in the correspondence.[79] Twelve of nineteen letters included late in the correspondence were either addressed to or authored by the Government of India. A sprawling, pugnacious, and incorrigible global public remained largely aloof to raison d'état.

After the commission in 1896, newspaper reports of India's opium problem continued within India and abroad. That sporadic attempts at censorship and occasional arrest of particularly radical activists did not escalate into a systematic scheme of suppression can be seen as another weakness of the official position.

Looking at the commission from the margins of its operations and through the lacunae it left, the defensive enterprise may have succeeded in sidelining evidence that eroded the political status quo of opium trading across Asia. But crucially, it failed to camouflage the process of sidelining itself.[80] Looking to Southeast Asia's significant entrepôts under British imperial influence in Singapore and the Straits Settlements makes the point. In the Straits Settlements, a crown colony of the British empire since 1867, the memorandum by William Maxwell, the colonial secretary, admitted to a "hastily-prepared resumé of the general results of the answers" obtained on behalf of the Royal Commission. On the social effects of opium, it read: "There is little evidence on this point"; adding with more than a whiff of sarcasm, "it would be curious indeed if, in a community where opium-smoking is so generally practiced and tolerated, the practice of it involved social condemnation or ostracism, or even loss of influence." In a classic play of parliamentary rhetoric, the memo tried to distract from the issue at hand, but judging from the critical public response, it failed.[81]

The Royal Commission was careful enough to stop short of refuting public opinion against the opium trade outright but worked incrementally to marginalize the anthropological validity of anti-opium observations, the social existence of an opium problem, and the political urgency of changing course in any of British imperial opium regimes across Asia. One revealing question posed by the commission to itself read, "Is there among any Asiatic race in your colony a feeling of hostility against England for allowing opium to be exported from India? If so, how does that feeling display itself?" To this, the laconic response stated, "There is absolutely no such feeling in any Asiatic race in the colony," citing "29 witnesses out of 32" as moral support. "Probably very few of the consumers have any kind of information as to the place or manner of the production of opium, or connect England in any way with its distribution."[82]

A "feeling of injury" did reside among "an educated few" who were, however, dismissed for having "perhaps imbibed the special prejudices of a class of European thinkers or writers, and as regards Malays, one witness (Shellabear) speaks of indignation on the part of some at the thought of the use of opium being spread among their race by Chinese influence." The Royal Commission asserted that if a danger for open revolt lay dormant in the current situation, it pointed to a passionate defense of the opium trade: "That a real feeling of hostility would be aroused against England, or the Colonial Government representing England in these parts, if there were any interference with the import of opium is the opinion of several (Haviland, Lister, Meyer, Hüttenbach)." Meanwhile, in Perak, the prospect of rising opium prices, as in the "threatened excise measure" against mixed opium, called *chandu,* was deemed politically unfeasible because Chinese opium traders would mount a "serious rising," one "necessitating resort to firearms to repress it." This scenario was presented as a realistic prognostication and representative of Asian opium dilemmas writ large, as if British opium trading interests played no political role in either the trade or its renegotiation.[83]

Acting from Singapore, colonial secretary Maxwell kept local anti-opium evidence thin. "Public opinion regarding opium in the native states," he declared, "does not differ from that already described as prevailing in the colony." If sustained anti-opium opposition existed among Malays, it fell outside the purview of British political responsibilities.[84] Such was the confidence of proponents of the existing opium regime that even raising the price of the drug through higher import duties in the mining districts— anywhere between $8 and the $21 imposed in the agricultural district of Negri Sembilau—was a presentable proposal that did not need to fear reprisals.[85] In the commission documents, discussions of opium revenue thus stood in an uneasy relationship with the cavalier discussions of medical considerations, especially the treatment of opium addiction. Some of the "medical evidence" mustered by the commission bordered on the anecdotal and ridiculous. Discussing the possibility of opium cure, the Royal Commission considered the experience of a Singaporean doctor "nearly 50 years ago" worth recording who prescribed to an Indian opium consumer "gentle walking exercises morning and evening."[86] Commercial appetite clearly outranked medical analysis.

Beyond the British imperial capacity to create a convenient opium narrative by interweaving social preferentiality of interviewees with interpretive eclecticism, the colonial and international press had some room to go its own ways in transmitting anti-opium information. The *Straits Times* in Singapore reported the Qing dynasty's anti-opium legislation to the SSOT, nonchalantly alongside opium debates in Westminster and opium price fluctuations and Southeast Asian opposition.[87] This helped provide a fuller picture of the opium controversy that the government was addressing through denial.[88] Indeed, the British government knew that prior to the conclusion of the Royal Commission, reports of "anti-opium agitators in Singapore" and a full-fledged "anti-opium party" pointed to a serious lobbying effort poised with determination against colonial opium politics.[89]

The nurtured resilience and strength of Singaporean and Straits Settlements anti-opium opposition both preceded and outlived the Royal Commission, making their marginalization part of the commission's political misjudgment. Chinese anti-opium leaders in Singapore drew on the energy and resources of Singaporean social-reform circles, similar to Hong Kong, and did not self-censor their activities for fear of colonial retribution or out of docile orthodoxy.

In 1890, Singapore's first major anti-opium petition entered the scene of international anti-opium opposition. The petition, which claimed to represent more than eleven hundred residents, sketched the colony's social makeup, "so many of the thousands of Chinese who crowd to these parts of the British possessions to make a livelihood for themselves, as well as to the great advantage of British Commercial interests by their immense industry and enterprise." Bringing together colonial benevolence, political prudence, and moral purpose, the petition urged the government "not to ruin" its subjects, defined as existing and potential opium consumers, "morally, physically, and materially, by affording facilities for carrying on the traffic in this most pernicious drug." Why not instead work toward "the immediate prohibition of the growth of the poppy, and the traffic in opium, in and from any of Her Majesty's dominions, except for strictly medicinal purposes," the petition asked.[90]

In contrast to Hong Kong, where the anti-opium elite had achieved its public renown as a class of commercial compradors and forged transnational partnerships with the women of the WCTU, Singapore's first anti-opium movement forged its own transnational relationships through the circles of medical knowledge exchange. After the 1890s, when anti-opium sentiments in Singapore reached British Parliament via petition, Singaporean anti-opium activists in the 1900s entered the upper echelons of society in the Straits and in Britain, often buttressed by a degree of higher education by Britain's premier universities, like Cambridge or Edinburgh. What Maxwell dismissed as Anglicized colonials was a group not enfeebled but emboldened by its clout in the society of the imperial metropolis.

To be sure, around 1900, the British regime faced greater challenges than anti-opium opposition, such as the influx of revolutionary refugees after the failed Waizhou Revolt of October 1900.[91] But although impelled by crisis, the anti-opium movement in Singapore retained a global versatility of its own. Lim Boon Keng (Lin Wenqing) exemplified the influence held by a rising transnational elite, which evolved independently of any anti-opium impetus.[92] As the first Chinese holder of a Queen's Scholarship in 1887 and a graduate with first-class honors in medicine and surgery from the University of Edinburgh, Lim brought his intellectual brilliance and social clout to an array of social reforms, from the reintroduction of Chinese language classes in Singaporean schools to campaigns against Chinese queues and opium. In 1895, at the age of twenty-six, he was appointed legislative councilor against Governor Sir Charles Mitchell, who had enough foresight to fear Lim's penchant and talent for public mobilization.[93]

Like Lim, his Cambridge-educated colleague in the anti-opium cause, Wu Liande, pioneered scientific knowledge to use policy pressure in high places of negotiation: Chinese Chambers of Commerce, Singapore's Legislative Council, the Qing Court in Peking, British Parliament, and after 1912, the first international opium conferences.[94] Beyond anti-opium leaders, Singapore's and Malaya's experience with local opium consumption gave sufficient reason for a vigorous debate. Building a Singapore-based anti-opium lobby benefited from resourceful Peranakans—that is, Chinese-Indonesian intelligentsia, with their independent periodicals, large-scale donations, and societal respect. Financial and social capital was supplied by the same small number of supporters. Directly counteracting the Royal Commission, Lim tested the public ground in Singapore with fervent anti-opium speeches and, in 1897, the *Straits Chinese Magazine,* a journal with the broad mission "to guide the present chaotic state of public opinion."[95] A flurry of new and revived Chinese-language papers followed, such as the *Thien Nan Shin Pao (Tian nan xin bao)* and the *Jit Shin Pao (Ri Xin Bao),* assembling such diverse interests as Western science and technology and neo-Confucian pamphlets and "linking reformers in Singapore to an increasingly global network of 'progressive' Chinese literati."[96]

Aided by the rising visibility of social-reform lobbying, Lim spearheaded the anti-opium attack, occasionally exchanging the rostrum for the quill. The Royal Commission of 1895 certainly incited his temper: "It is both un-scientific and illogical to surmise that because a group of individuals do not apparently suffer after a prolonged use of opium, the habitual use of the drug is therefore innocuous. Before such a conclusion is justifiable," Lim expressed, "we ought to have before us the percentage of those happy persons who do not suffer any harm from their use of opium, such percentage to be calculated from the total number of consumers."[97]

Lim called for a full-fledged analysis of the combined physiological, psychological, and ethical impact of opium consumption, identifying the average quantity of opium consumption per day, a medical diagnosis of the physical condition, the form and frequency of consumption, the long-term impact on the individual's health and morals, and finally the level of productivity *without* opium consumption. These concerns were not unlike the Japanese colonial preoccupation with the productivity of Taiwan's population and the necessary control of the incapacitating effects of opium, an issue to which we shall return later. Without a scientific understanding of these aspects, Lim argued, opium's harmfulness could never arrive at a reliable estimate. The half medical, half anthropological approach to the opium consumer differed from established religious objections, so prevalent among British domestic anti-opium groups. In Singapore, Lim's lobbying prepared a new epistemic rationale for the kind of opium expertise that would be in international demand in the 1900s and 1910s.[98]

For now, Singapore had to compromise between British and Chinese versions of anti-opium ideology. Lim understood the dilemma well: "Popular imagination certainly puts the responsibility of the introduction of opium on the shoulders of the English. There are millions of Chinese to-day who believe as sincerely as they believe there is a God that some half a century ago the English forced China to allow opium to enter the Empire and thus to corrupt and demoralise her people," echoing once more tropes made famous by Prince Gong. Lim not only pressed for a new interpretation of the opium problem but aimed for a kind of opium analysis that moved on a higher plain of methodological and heuristic superiority: "To look at this problem in its true light, we must divest ourselves of all prejudice whether innate or acquired. . . . A scientific enquiry into the causes and effects of the opium habit is the desideratum of the civilised world."[99]

In a direct counter to colonial reference to an unfulfilled civilizing mission, Singaporean pioneers like Lim himself no longer inhabited a strange place outside the "civilised world."[100] As he pointed out in his pamphlet, it was the duty of the state, whether the state liked it or not, "to diminish the number of opium consumers and . . . to suppress the vice by the establishment of special asylums or hospitals for treatment, and by the gradual restriction of the amount of opium allowed to enter each province."[101]

In return, the duties of colonial subjects included anti-opium education, the early appearance of an institution today considered global commonplace. "Measures for the check of the opium vice should consist more in practical measures of social reform than in distribution of literature and in preaching the evils of smoking," Lim elaborated. "Remove the causes that necessitate the stupefying effect of opium to kill time or relieve the tedium and monotony of an unsocial social life, and it will be found that opium smoking will suddenly die out."[102] Criticizing especially "the Malays in big towns" for "taking to sedentary lives of idleness," he insisted: "If the social gaps are filled up so that social intercourse between friends is ensured and healthy means of recreation are provided, the opium habit will become unpopular," illustrating that "out-door exercise produces manliness of character and induces that athletic habitude opposed to the idle recumbent position required for opium smoking."[103]

Although the ethnic categories drawn between Malay and Chinese lifestyles carried uncanny traces of cultural and ethnic essentialism, they allowed Lim to direct concern to heavy manual labor and its relationship to opium consumption. Chinese coolies who "work too hard, have too long hours and have no comfortable home," Lim argued, "for these reasons . . . take to these narcotics." The local milieu mattered as a crucible of cultural habits. "In these little lodgings of theirs there are no sitting rooms and the only place they have to go are their beds, and they lie down there, and as the habit has become common among others around them, they also take to it."[104] What Singaporean and Malayan society required, then, was a radical renewal of habits and lifestyles, an industrious revolution that would relegate opium consumption to a disdained and asocial pastime.[105] Frances Willard might have agreed, the motto of her autobiography stating, "Nothing makes life dreary but lack of motive."[106] It is one of the ironies of this history that the Royal Commission would prove so self-destructive not because of its penchant to take opium but because of its willingness to supply it to others.

Darker Still: The Royal Commission's Afterlife

The tangents can be telling, too. When in 1940, the Nazi regime commissioned a monograph for its series England Unmasked (England ohne Maske), the history of opium received thorough coverage in its own section. Drawing on the Unitarian anti-imperialist Jabez Thomas Sunderland's *India in Bondage*, published in New York in 1932, the book, titled in English *British Tyranny in India*, became part of what was to be the Royal Commission's last political critique, for the time being.[107] "The British government knows exactly the terrible weakening, the monstrosity of misery, disease and suffering she inflicts on the Indian people," the propaganda roared.[108] An extensive excerpt of the Royal Commission report furthered National Socialist cynicism in its imagined ideological alliance with Indian nationalism. "This astonishing and more than ridiculous report," a critic concluded, "cannot claim that it had not properly understood the effects of opium use on the body and soul. Three years before this report . . . 5,000 medical doctors in England had declared that smoking and eating opium was physically devastating and morally ruinous. In England, the British Government protects its people against any kind of opium trading and consumption except for medical purposes; whereas in India she admits the use of opium not only as a household article but almost as aliment; she [the government] supports and facilitates in every way this unlimited and dangerous use—in India."[109]

This latest echo of anti-opium sentiment was part of a massive propaganda campaign that saw the book translated into English, Italian, Swedish, French, and Slovenian, as well as separate publications of the opium chapter in German, French, English, and Romanian.[110] An almost surreal appropriation of anti-opium rhetoric, it still exemplified what anti-opium activists had been exploiting to their own advantage: there was very little oversight in a movement that knew thematic expansion and ideological radicalization as the only way forward. Anti-opium ideology was malleable enough to bend to dangerous political justifications. Nazi propaganda, in turn, did not remain without effect. Its author, Reinhard Frank, was considered so effective a writer that parts of his work reached the United States under the pseudonym Jeanne d'Arc Dillon La Touche, until detection and exposure.[111]

One year after the end of the Second World War in occupied Germany, when the German Administration for the Education of the People in the Soviet Sector released its more than five-hundred page List of Literature to Be Censored, the Nazi anti-opium book was listed among the one million items of banned books of "fascist or militarist substance, that contain ideas of political expansion, that represent the National Socialist race theory or are in opposition to the Allied Powers." To the Soviet and German authorities, Frank's anti-opium tirade "indicated the criteria for prohibition most conspicuously." His only entries were the first book on *British Tyranny in India* and the separate edition of *Opium in India,* suggesting their prominence, circulation, and contribution to his fame.[112] Overshadowing the challenge of the Royal Commission in its own time, the longest legacy of this affront survived half a century until it met its last, grotesque demise.

CHAPTER FIVE

THE JAPANESE BLUEPRINT AND
ITS AMERICAN DISCOVERY

TWO SHOCKS SHAPED Japan's relationship with opium unlike that of any other Asian country. The reasons lay less in cultural exceptionalism than in active Japanese comparisons of how Asian neighbors coped with the drug, their historical trajectories, and possible lessons to be drawn. Japan's first opium shock emanated from its Western neighbor when the Opium War afflicted the Qing dynasty from 1839 to 1842. Unlike this traumatizing event, the second shock drew on the eventuality of another opium war, conjured up by an official representative of the United States. Conditioned by the recoil from the combination of these two opium shocks, both real and perceived, the Japanese practice of containing opium on the joint initiative of state and society became central to the transnational controversy over opium. Whereas elsewhere across Asia, the opium trade held the upper hand and regulation was just at the cusp of becoming a political program, Japan owned an existing template of opium control, crowned with social and political success. That precedent had consequences beyond Japan as global anti-drug opposition discovered the Japanese experience, a development that induced the key transition from anti-drug discourse to the practical planning of anti-drug politics on an international scale.

A major reason why the Japanese encounter with the opium trade became enmeshed in the mid-nineteenth-century politics of empire was, by international comparison, Japan's unusual sensibility in anticipating paths of world political development as they gained shape. Japanese geopolitical knowledge and finesse in responding to global transformations on its own terms is visible from the earliest days of Japanese-American relations. An almost consequentialist grasp of commercial interdependence spanning the great oceans of the world brought the United States into focus. The relationship with the United States deserves special attention not because American foreign relations equaled global transformations but because the relationship served to recalibrate Japan's wider international relations, especially with Great Britain and China. The two decades following the First Opium War stimulated the first extensive Japanese surveys of North and South America, initially not seen in antagonistic or even competitive terms. *Konyo zushiki* (World atlas) was published by Mitsukuri Shōgo in 1847. *Meriken shinshi* (New account of America), published by Tsurumine Shigenobu (pen-named Kaisei Gyofu) in 1853, depicted a flamboyant George Washington and a heroic war for independence amid the flares of British firepower. America's democratic system of governance attracted attention, too. "In the New Country, there is no distinction of ruler and subject. . . . The officials are not designated from above, but are chosen, according to their ability, by ballot-casting among the people. . . . In these respects, there is a great difference between that country and China."[1]

In 1852, one year before the more threatening "black ships" of Commodore Matthew Perry were sighted, stories of their impending arrival were circulating in advance. "Rumors are rife that the United States of North America will despatch ships to Japan. According to these rumors, an envoy will be sent to Japan . . . and ask that one or two Japanese ports be opened to trade, and that coaling conveniences be provided for steamships en route from California to China." It may be of more than coincidental interest that the scholar who first traced these Japanese responses to the American vision of Japan as a waystation to China in 1939 was Sakamaki Shunzo, known as the founder of Okinawa studies in the United States, who published his findings for the Asiatic Society of Japan under the presidency of George B. Sansom.[2] The American legacies of early contact with Japan were uncovered by scholars personally and professionally committed to a relationship whose past had partly formed them.

Meanwhile, the shogunate in 1853, au courant with global developments, anticipated that the impending American advance would exert consequences beyond U.S.-Japan or U.S.-East Asian relations. Information on parallel British designs of global commerce became available to Japanese officials through Dutch reports known as *Betsudan fusetsugaki*. "It has been decided in London, the capital of England, to cut a canal through the Isthmus of Panama, which links North and South America." Logistical details did not get lost in long-distance communications: "The cut will be made wide and deep, so that large ships can pass through it." The consequences were plainly visible to global minds: "As a result, traffic between American ports, east and west, will be facilitated. . . . The distance between Europe and the eastern seaboard of America on the one hand, and China and India on the other, will be considerably shortened"—to be exact, by reducing one-fifth of required fuel. "Hence, this matter is of great importance to commerce." Thus, technological, logistical, and energy knowledge reached Japan long before the actual sighting of American ships.[3]

Commodore Perry's fabled "opening" of Japan, a mission executed from 1852 to 1854, is commonly celebrated as the foundational chapter of U.S.-Japan relations and has been ably recounted elsewhere.[4] However, a darker encounter arrived in Perry's wake, with another black ship carrying Townsend Harris, the chief delegate for treaty negotiations with Japan. Having served in the Chinese treaty port of Ningbo before, Harris was en route to Japan when he chanced in Aden to meet "a Miss De Quincey" with, as he noted, "a sweet voice" and an "intelligent face," who "sings charmingly." As it turns out, it was Florence de Quincey, second daughter of Thomas de Quincey, the "opium eater" (see Chapter 2), who was about to marry Colonel Baird Smith in India, feted by the British as a hero in the Siege of Delhi during the Sepoy Rebellion of 1857.[5] On a quotidian level of inter-imperial encounters, the British imperial presence, with stratagems from the political to the personal, made itself felt on the same steamship lines watched so warily by Japan.

By the time Harris faced Japanese officials, he had adopted a much more sobering tone. The statement made by the American ambassador at the house of Hotta Masayoshi, the Prince of Bichū, on December 12, 1857, must have lasted several hours, was carefully prepared, and left with little room for improvisation.[6] Documented as Harris's official memorandum, the statement reflected an agenda "of the utmost importance," was explicitly characterized as "coming directly from the President," and matched in length and weight Prince Gong's demarche of 1869.[7] As a monological interpretation of the opium problem and its projected consequences for Japanese foreign relations, Harris's overbearing tenor deserves attention for establishing the contrast to the Japanese perspectives to be explored subsequently. For now, let us turn, by way of international comparison, to the question of American exceptionalism in its commercial relationship with Japan and the place of opium perceptions in it.

For Harris, explaining America's outlook on Asia's international affairs began with the eagerness to distance the United States from the British and European colonial powers. "The United States have no possessions in the east and do not desire to have any, as other countries do. To acquire such possessions is prohibited by the Government of the United States." Many countries had "asked to be admitted into the Union," Harris reported, "but their requests have not been granted." In 1854, he illustrated, the Sandwich Islands had been turned down, in defense of an almost axiomatic principle of American foreign policy. Notwithstanding its treaty tradition, "it is the uniform custom of the United States . . . not to annex any country merely by force of arms." Still, for the Japanese, this American disavowal of colonial aggrandizement did not mean respite from American pressure. Allured by oceanic mobility and the quest for overseas markets, the American advance across the Pacific, even short of colonialism, was relentless. Steamships connected California and Japan, the only temporal obstacle being a passage of eighteen days. For Harris, advancing technology implied historical teleology: "All the world will become as one family." Again, the pressures emanating from a teleological interpretation of commercial interdependence were less than cozy. "Any nation that refuses to hold intercourse with other nations must be excluded from this family," as "no nation has the right to refuse to hold intercourse with others." Harris's warning grew sterner still. "Misfortunes are now threatening Japan in consequence of the state of things in England and other European states. England is not satisfied with the treaty made with Japan by Admiral James Sterling. The English Government," Harris spoke almost as if he represented it, "hopes to hold the same kind of intercourse with Japan as she holds with other nations, and is ready to make war with Japan, as I will now show."[8]

In this deliberately dark vision of war games among the great powers of the day, pressure on Japan's political readiness for commercial partnerships emanated from an international power game. This left space, if not a very comforting one, for the interpretation that the British threat was at least not provoked by supposed Japanese intransigence. "England greatly fears that Russia will disturb her East India possessions," as well as British influence in Manchuria, China, and Southeast Asia. As Britain and France entered an alliance to secure Sakhalin and the Amur, Ezo in the north of Japan with the significant port of Hakodate would inevitably become part of Britain's containment of Russia. Despite its inaccuracies, evoking global military escalation over competing imperial spheres of influence robbed the meaning of oceanic interdependence of its promise of peace. Soon, little would be left of its beautiful capture by Hayashi Shihei: "The waters flowing under Nihonbashi in Edo and the waters in the rivers of China and Holland are one stream without any barriers."[9]

China was a case in point, having issued with the First Opium War the most dramatic warning in Japan's immediate neighborhood of how the encounter with imperialism could go wrong, and its costs. Without knowing it, Harris confirmed earlier Japanese apprehensions about the political fallout that could follow a refusal to engage in commercial intercourse with Britain on an inherently expanding basis of trade and investment. Looking across Asia, so far Asian opposition had proved counterproductive, emboldening British designs on Formosa and French ambitions for Korea. For Japan, Harris emphasized, China's example had clearly laid out the international political consequences of anti-British opposition: "All nations unite in denouncing the unjust conduct of China," leading to multilateral isolation.

And "the cause of the troubles," Harris affirmed, was opium—a social problem traced back to its origins, as he saw it, in international political disagreement. In the 1820s, opium consumption had been limited to Canton; by the 1850s, millions of people had taken to the drug, spending their earnings indiscriminately, up to an estimated $25 million in 1855. "Opium is the one great enemy of China," Harris kept lecturing Hotta. "If it is used it weakens the body and injures it like the most deadly poison; it makes the rich poor and the wise foolish; it unmans all that use it, and by reason of the misery it brings robbers and acts of violence increase." The statement could have been expressed by an anti-opium activist. About one thousand criminals faced execution every year, Harris claimed, for crimes committed in a state of opium intoxication, yet so far, even the harshest possible sentence could not prevent a rise of opium crimes. The Qing emperor's uncle had died of opium consumption. As for the social, political, and economic origin of opium, Harris thought there was no question about it: Opium "comes from India, which is subject to England."

Facing this specter of opium, Harris predicted toward the end of his speech, Japan's options were limited. Britain will profit, not prohibit, even though "the word 'opium' is not used in the treaty between the two countries," he meant the above-mentioned Treaty of Tianjin. The China analogy was also beyond Japan's control, having supposedly lodged in the British mind, a dangerous omen: "The English think the Japanese, too, are fond of opium, and they want to bring it here also." As for the threat of opium, its consequences were ubiquitous, from health risks to social corruption, and therefore expedient as a British weapon: "If a man use opium once he cannot stop it, and it becomes a life-long habit to use opium; hence the English want to introduce it into Japan." The U.S. president, he averred, "thinks that for the Japanese opium is more dangerous than war. The expense of war could be paid in time; but the expense of opium, when once the habit is formed, will only increase with time." In sum, the only guarantee of Japan's continued prosperity was American prohibition in an American-Japanese treaty.[10]

What Harris did not know is that Japanese officials like Hotta Masayoshi hardly needed a history lesson approximating a filibuster of the imperial sort. In Japanese works like the *Kaigai shinwa* by Mineta Fūkō, published in 1849, the First Opium War had been rendered with portentous illustrations of shelled coastlines and harrowing stories of British massacres and mass rape.[11] Additionally, rumors about the First Opium War had seeped into Japan through the foreign community in Nagasaki.[12] But as an international confirmation of national fears, Harris's American appropriation of the First Opium War deepened the historical and political significance of this fateful watershed. Not only China but most of East Asia, it seemed, lived in a postwar period defined by the conflagration from 1839 to 1842.

When in July 1858, Harris and Hotta's successor, Ii Naosuke, signed an opium prohibition clause into the U.S.-Japan Treaty of Amity and Commerce, it determined: "The importation of opium is prohibited, and any American vessel coming to Japan for the purposes of trade, having more than (3) three catties' (four pounds avoirdupois) weight of opium on board, such surplus quantity shall be seized and destroyed by the Japanese authorities."[13] Like its precedent, the U.S.-China treaty of Wangxia in 1844, the 1858 treaty alloyed opium prohibition with a guarantee of American extraterritorial jurisdiction, the first element distancing it from European demands, the second aligning with them. "Americans, committing offenses against Japanese, shall be tried in American Consular Courts," read the 1858 treaty.[14]

But the dynamics of the American entry into the international politics of Asia unraveled differently from what Harris had conveyed to Hotta, with America taking a deliberate distance to British, European, and Russian power play. Instead, he stated later, Lord Elgin of Britain, Baron Jean-Baptiste-Louis Gros of France, and Count Putiatin of Russia were all "surprised at my Diplomatic Success in Japan, and I am gratified in being able to say, that so ample were the provisions of the Treaty made by me, that the Russian, English, French, and Dutch Plenipotentiaries accepted it at once and without alteration of its provisions."[15] It is worth remembering that Elgin and Putiatin were also chiefly involved in negotiating the Treaty of Tianjin and the Peking Convention after the Second Opium War with the Qing, complete with the shared commitment to opium legalization. As for simultaneous inter-imperial cooperation in Japan, Western diplomatic postings that shuffled teams of treaty negotiation across Asia facilitated close cooperation, as when Harris's tenure as the first U.S. consul general in Japan—the highest diplomatic post at the time—coincided with Sir Rutherford Alcock's tenure as British minister to Japan from 1858 to 1864, based in Yokohama.[16]

But in fact the international applause to the supposed American approach to Japan revealed the latter as but one element in a multilateral readjustment of Japan's foreign relations. The Treaty of Amity and Commerce of October 9, 1858, between Japan and France laid the foundations of their own bilateralism.[17] Although rhetorically celebrated, American participation in inter-imperial cooperation in Asia was not solely induced by American initiative. The Russian and Dutch treaties with Japan in 1855 and 1856 had prohibited the importation of opium into Japan several years earlier; the United States and France followed suit in practicing economic abstinence from the drug. Japan's foreign trade benefited from a carefully arranged, multilateral consensus on the prohibition of opium imports. This set of opium prohibitions gave Japanese local law enforcement greater leeway in unilateral action than in many other foreign disputes. Beyond the unexceptional formalization of the American-Japanese commercial relationship, other American-Asian relationships revealed the official American pledge to opium prohibition in trade with China and Japan as far from universal. The 1858 treaty with Japan closely resembled the U.S.-Siam treaty of 1858, concluded by Harris between Aden and his arrival in Japan. In Siam, he had pushed for permission to import opium duty-free into Siam for sale to opium farmers and re-export it duty-free.[18] While the United States split its parallel bilateral relationships with several Asian states in contradictory strands, Western powers including Russia found a common approach with compatible policies vis-à-vis an individual Asian state, such as Japan and China. Not all of the diplomatic intricacies and incoherencies were fully understood by transnational anti-opium observers. American Quaker circles whose British partners supported the SSOT remained lenient in judging Harris's speech to Hotta, describing it "very kindly, but not without menace," and welcoming his view on the "disasters of the opium war in China." American exceptionalism was confirmed by nongovernmental critics who interpreted Harris's move as a "policy . . . to so work upon the sensibilities of the native ministers that they nestled closer to the United States."[19] Seen from Japan, however, both the specter of the Qing's First Opium War and America's legalist entry into Asian inter-imperial politics acquired a very different character and political function.

Japan's Lessons of History

"The Japanese Government was afraid of having an opium war such as China had." Forty-five years after the fact, the words of Andō Tarō, until recently Japan's first consul general in Hawaii, left little doubt about it. On

September 26, 1903, Andō used an interview to explain how Japan's relationship with opium had evolved over time: "The Japanese immediately took measures to prohibit the importation of opium into Nagasaki, which was the only port open at that time, and entirely kept it out."[20] He emphasized China's First Opium War and the subsequent growth of a social opium problem as a historical warning to Japan. Deterred by a replay within its own borders, Japan had implemented a system of tight control in which societal fear of opium matched state interests and in which the opium threat was alarming to the people and officials alike. More than a symbol of foreign aggression, opium was described as inducing societal splintering. This, too, was China's warning. "The Japanese believe that the origin of the trouble and disorder prevailing in China is due to opium." Andō dispelled the new American myth of General Grant's pioneering opium prohibition in U.S.-Japan relations, crediting instead Harris with "a great influence on the Japanese Government in inducing it to prohibit the importation of opium on the opening of the ports to foreign commerce, especially to England." His interviewers, who were American, must have been pleased to hear it, while Andō tactfully put aside the U.S. threat conjured up by Harris.[21]

In an earlier life as a samurai, Andō had defended the Tokugawa in the last stronghold against the Meiji Restoration, the Goryōkaku Castle in Hakodate on Hokkaido. As the Meiji's consul general in Hawaii, the islands annexed in 1898 by U.S. president William McKinley after a U.S.-sponsored coup against the kingdom of Queen Liliʻuokalani, Andō set up the first Japanese NGO there, the Japanese Mutual Aid Association, with Reverend Miyama Kan'ichi, who converted him to Christianity. His wife converted him to temperance and the Blue Ribbon movement.[22] Andō also showed Christian sympathies in Hawaii when he advised Kagahi Sōryū, a Buddhist priest, to let Hawaiians choose Christianity as their religion: "When in Rome do as the Romans do."[23] But Andō's tenure as consul general had its limits; he was criticized in women's folklore for insufficient attention to gambling and prostitution.[24]

Arranged by Reverend Soper of Methodist University in Tokyo, Andō gave his interview not in Hawaii but in the Metropole Hotel in Tokyo. In 1903, Andō's Tokyo interview formed an influential opium assessment gathered by an international team of investigators sent by U.S president Theodore Roosevelt. The aim was to compare all Asian opium regimes that could be reached. In stark contrast to the cross-examinations conducted by the British Royal Commission of 1895, the American-sponsored Philippine Opium Commission from 1903 to 1905 chose a multilateral mode of inquiry.[25] Officially named the Committee Appointed by the Philippine

Commission to Investigate the Use of Opium and the Traffic Therein, the project was tasked to ascertain and record opium governance across East and Southeast Asia: in Japan, Taiwan, Qing China, French Indochina, British Singapore and Burma, and the Dutch East Indies. The findings were then to be compared to local opium conditions in the Philippines and the most suitable policy transfer to be applied. As a multinational exercise in inter-Asian comparison beyond the colonial and imperial powers, including China and Japan, the commission was the first epistemic and political experiment of its kind.

These methods were oriented primarily by the perceived geography of the opium trade at a point of contested crisis, seemingly stretching across Asia writ large. No viable model of opium governance structured opium's political economy between or atop East, Southeast, and South Asia. The United States faced an "opium problem" first in its colony, not at home.[26] Regional mobility facilitated the Asian scope of the inquiry. Manila was less than two thousand miles from Tokyo, compared to almost seven thousand miles between Washington and Tokyo, strongly recommending the practicality of American-Japanese exchanges in policy expertise in an inter-Asian setting. Drawing on this potential, the Philippine Opium Commission became the first major American-Japanese encounter, with a temporary team in the Philippines serving as mediators. Aside from China itself, Meiji Japan emerged from this comparison as offering the most valuable lessons of the opium wars.[27]

In stark contrast to its giant assignment, the Philippine Opium Commission was composed of only a staff of four. Charles Henry Brent, a descendant of English loyalists and Episcopal by spiritual choice, had been a bishop in Boston before taking charge of the well-endowed U.S. Missionary District of the Philippine Island. Brent headed the commission and was instrumental in using it as a springboard for the first multilateral anti-drug summit.[28] Major Edward Champe Carter served as the commission's chairman, was the acting commissioner of public health in Taipei on Japanese Taiwan (Formosa), and was the author of popular works on the U.S. Public Health Service.[29] The third man was Dr. José Albert, a physician educated at the Ateneo Municipal in his native Manila, at the University of Santo Tomas, and the Universidad Central de Madrid. Albert had been a student of Pierre Charles Édouard Potain, the Parisian cardiologist, and Pierre-Constant Budin, the obstetrician and colleague of Potain at the Hôpital de la Charité, not far from Paul Brouardel, whose analysis of opium, morphine, and cocaine consumption pioneered the field of comparative drug research. Albert finished his studies under Jacques-Joseph Grancher in Paris and Robert Michaelis von Olshausen in Berlin before founding the

Colegio Medico-Farmaceutico in Manila.[30] To the transnational missionary leverage of Brent and the public health priorities of Carter he brought a European internationalism in medical and scientific research. Thus, the Philippine Opium Commission's Asian internationalism was directly informed by the biographies of its staff before it even embarked on comparative analysis of Asian governance.

The fourth member of the commission was Professor Carl Jentoft Arnell, a Swedish-born stenographer in the Bureau of Government Laboratories in the Philippines, who also interpreted for the commission from Spanish, Japanese, French, and Dutch, supported by local assistants.[31] Arnell later served as interpreter in the U.S. embassy in Japan for twelve years and made himself a name as "the second white man to complete the course in Oriental languages" at the Imperial University of Tokyo. His obituary flaunted local press coverage of his fifty-three languages from Saratoga to Singapore, "from the Eskimo to the African Hottentots."[32] The commissioners' portfolios implicitly betrayed the absence of preexisting opium officials or experts in any American administration, whether at home or in the Philippines. And despite the piecemeal legalism to select bilateral opium prohibition discussed earlier, the cross-Asian scope of the opium problem went beyond existing diplomatic experience, whether American or otherwise.

Within the commission, Brent's word wielded an influence disproportionate to that of his colleagues and indeed to his own timid temperament, which he kept privately confined to his diaries. In large part, his leverage emerged less from strategizing for personal advantage than from the mode of experimentation that made the commission an open experiment across professions. The commission vacillated between the missionary premium on social ethics, the new social and political priority of public health systems, and scientific fact-finding, be it anthropological interviews on opium consumption or medical assessments of long-term effects. Armed with this combined expertise, a bond for the treasurer of the Philippine Islands, a letter of credit by the Hong Kong and Shanghai Banking Corporation (today's HSBC) on its correspondents in the Orient, stationery supplies, and a hired typewriter, the commission embarked on its compendious inquiry into the opium regimes of Asia.[33]

The commission's openness was less happenstance than strategy and had been a centerpiece of the commission's architect, William Howard Taft. Having just completed his tenure as governor-general of the Philippines—the island group acquired after the swift military victory that ended the Spanish-American War in 1898—Taft counted among the most highly placed U.S. officials in questions of colonial administration and Asian affairs more broadly. This experience helped him become secretary of war from 1904 to 1908 before serving as U.S. president from 1909 and 1913, between Theodore Roosevelt and Woodrow Wilson.

Although later known for facilitating a breakthrough in international cooperation against the opium trade, the commission initially abstained from following a programmed template of opium inquiries. Taft's guidelines for the Philippine Opium Commission refrained from dictating or streamlining the procedure, working methods, or scope in advance. Instead, Taft insisted that the American Philippines administration "has not the slightest desire to influence or control the conclusions of your Committee." Indeed, "any attempt on our part to secure a prejudiced report from you would be met with proper rebuke."[34] Openness and pragmatism gave much leeway for the commission's geographic orientation: "If your investigation shall lead you to suppose that you may obtain information of value in other countries than those mentioned, please let me know, and I will authorize your going to those countries."[35] After all, Taft emphasized, only a "scientific" inquiry produced objective insights, and "all that the Commission desires to know is the truth." No American administrative consultation specific to the opium question on the Philippines should "affect your judgment, formed judicially after an investigation of the facts."[36] In place of imposing expectations in a preemptive manner, the inquiry was characterized from its inception by its responsiveness to the evidence it would find—an almost naïve abrogation of bias that set it methodically far apart from the Royal Commission eight years ago. Whatever evidence would "present itself" to the commissioners would supposedly speak for itself, as if subjectivity could be shed through goodwill alone and neutrality be guaranteed by not believing to have an opinion.

The imprecision of methodical guidelines and the principled commitment to a universalist and apolitical definition of the Asian opium problem allowed, predictably, other influences to steer the commission's work and purpose. The most immediate influence, however, was neglected. The Philippines' status quo regime of the opium administration, left by the Spanish, figured in calculations mostly through its laxity and the inability to reduce consumption rates.[37] The Spanish themselves shared the internationalist and regionalist rather than imperial or colonial scope of opium criticism in the 1910s, when several Spanish observers decried the opium habit on Taiwan, emphasized Japanese prohibition, and condemned the opium wars, while leaving the Spanish opium monopoly in the Philippines to oblivion.[38] Instead of colonial precedent, the greatest influence on the Philippine Opium Commission would emerge out of the personal impressions gathered by the opium commissioners in interviews across Asia, among which Andō's became a forceful example.

Headed to Japan as a first stop, the Asian neighborhood of the American administration in the Philippines came into focus on the itinerary. The American legacy of governmental opium discussions with Japanese officials, through the prism of legalist bilateralism since Harris, had little impact on this opium investigation, determined to study opium conditions in Japan. Even being endowed with the presidential blessings of U.S. president Theodore Roosevelt did not mean that the Philippine Opium Commission, staffed with nongovernmental experts, would follow the governmental line of legalism. If it had, Japan would have been dropped from the list of opium-afflicted countries by reference to treaty prohibitions enacted by previous U.S. administrations. But to the contrary, the Japan focus of the commission distinguished this project from preceding opium communications between Washington and Tokyo, exchanging the established legalist paradigm with fresh scrutiny for opium as a social problem.

On August 17, 1903, the commission left Manila in the Philippines on board the *City of Peking,* transferring in Hong Kong to the *Empress of India* before arriving in Yokohama on August 26 and proceeding on September 4 by train to Tokyo. Forty-five years earlier, Townsend Harris had been received here. Could the commission have followed a more contrasting pattern of informality? Andō's historical account of Japan's social and political aversion to opium was much appreciated and was even documented by the commissioners like a formal statement, much like oral statements in Congress that can become reference points in formalized written processes of political decision making.

In the commissioners' eyes, the credibility of Andō's self-representation derived not only from his own status and experience but equally from other Japan-based observations. Foreign interviewees in Japan corroborated Japanese interviewees independently by identifying similar indications of anti-opium attitudes as a dominant, national, and shared commitment in Japan, an amalgam of ethical thinking across state and society that appeared more unified than in other Asian countries. One of the most authoritative assessments of opium in Japanese society, as judged by the affirmative references in the final commission report, came from a Russian Orthodox bishop. On September 10, 1903, the commission met with Bishop Nicolai, born Nicolai Dmitrievich Kasatkin, in Tokyo.[39]

When the American commissioners explained their objective to "study the opium traffic" to and within Japan, the bearded Russian, then in his late sixties, broke into laughter: "There is none." As for consumption, Nicolai had witnessed "absolutely no indications of the vice among the Japanese."[40] A key role, he argued, fell to Japanese public opinion as the seat of Japanese anti-opium sentiment. When "newspapers told of the occasional conviction of an unfortunate Chinese" caught opium-smoking in Japan, Japanese responded by clinging even more tenaciously to prohibition. Legislation was not a dead letter but "quite successful in its operation."[41] To the commission, all this made eminent sense, and Japan's national anti-opium narrative was wholeheartedly accepted and approved.

Unlike any other representative of Japan's anti-opium stance, Nicolai as the very first interviewee spoke to commissioners with fresh and, as explained earlier, self-consciously open minds. Nicolai's privilege of precedence was further boosted by biographical credentials. Born in Smolensk in 1836, he had reached Hakodate on the northern island of Hokkaido at age twenty-five, on the Russian steamship *Amerika* on July 2, 1861. For ten years, he waited for the ban on Christianity to be lifted. Through article 27 of the Meiji Constitution of 1889, Japanese subjects received freedom of religion.[42] In Japan's changing attitudes toward his own profession, Nicolai first became aware of how revamping the legal landscape of the new Meiji state institutionalized social ideals.

As Nicolai rose as head of the Russian branch of the Greek Orthodox Church in Japan, he was financially backed by the Russia chief negotiator after the Second Opium War, Count Putiatin, with $70,000. The Russian church grew into two hundred branches, and soon boasted 150 Japanese pastors and evangelists who kept all "in the hands of the Japanese."[43] By comparison, Protestant churches claimed 494 Japanese pastors and evangelists and 789 foreign missionaries; the Roman Catholics only 98 Japanese pastors and 229 missionaries. Publicist Alfred Stead, son of William T. Stead, whose own *Pall Mall Gazette* had expressed high hopes for the end of Indian opium cultivation, extolled Nicolai's church as "one of the most striking instances of Japanese religious tolerance."[44] Nicolai, in turn, assumed a prominence of secular as much as religious significance: his long-term residence in Japan and social intimacy with the Japanese made him one of the earliest Russian Japan experts.

For a foreign resident in Japan, Nicolai was on unusually close terms with Japanese daily life and learning, including literary expressions of spirituality. This led him to admire many accomplishments of the Japanese past and present, far beyond their collective anti-opium stance. Nicolai immersed himself in the language and studied the *Kojiki,* the Shinto record of ancient matters, and was tutored by Niijima Jō (alias Joseph Hardy Niijima), a graduate of Amherst College in Massachusetts and founder in 1875 of Dōshisha University in Kyoto.[45]

The wonderment at Japan's anti-opium determination, so easily transferred from Nicolai's reported experience to the commissioners' outlook, was not as idiosyncratic as it might seem. More than Japanophilia, the vision of Japan's social and political landscape in the early Meiji period as beneficially binding together society and state belonged to a historical perspective that had its roots outside the U.S.-Japan relationship. That perspective distanced Japan's anti-opium achievement not merely from U.S. legalism but more generally from a U.S. centrality to either the opium trade or its legalist prohibition. In contrast to twentieth-century observers of U.S. centrality in the globalization of drug control, the Philippine Opium Commission was receptive to the interpretation of America's marginality, although interpretations of the commission necessarily conveying an "American" perspective and pursuing "American" objectives has been tenacious because of its presidential blessings.[46] But there was a gap between the commission's political authorization and its operations. Before turning into a clearinghouse of Asian opium assessments, the commission learned to listen, adopt, and accept the views of others.

That marginality should not be mistaken for active opposition to the idea of American legalist prohibition as politically significant. Rather, transnational perceptions along a different, Russo-Japanese axis came to envisage Japanese superiority in terms that did not require an American reference point. For Nicolai, Japan's superiority was not even his own vision but that of Captain Vasily Mikhailovich Golovnin, who was captured by the Japanese on his failed expedition to the Kuril Islands in 1811. "Generally speaking, the Japanese have more correct ideas than the lower classes in Europe," Golovnin had insisted in his famous and bestselling *Recollections* after his release from Japanese captivity. They drank less than Europeans and Russians, regardless of status and to their credit. Golovnin's respect rose when one of his Japanese guards took a round cup of tea in lieu of a globe to plot "pretty accurately" the position of Japan and Europe. Likewise, other Japanese soldiers spoke eloquently of global geography and mathematics, proving again and again their "extreme readiness" for European knowledge and their "capacious understandings," confirming Father Luigi Froes's *Lettere del Giappone* of 1579.[47] Golovnin was as sure as Nicolai, his later admirer, that Japanese learning superseded European levels of education. The "learned men" of Europe in the early nineteenth century did not "make a nation," but in Japan they did. Here, educated knowledge did not remain the province of a privy elite. Instead, a cultivated curiosity gave Japanese civilization an international edge. Where Europe underperformed, Japan excelled.[48]

So impressive were Golovnin's explanations of Japan's international competitiveness and socially shared openness to a veritable world of knowledge that they motivated Nicolai to migrate to Japan in the first place. Huddling on a lonely hooded cart known in Russian as *kibitka,* Nicolai felt compelled by Golovnin to venture all the way through Siberia to the land that knew more and better.[49] After the Meiji "restoration" of 1868 and its systematic and encompassing quest to reform itself into an internationally recognizable nation-state, attention to Japan's achievements found more social evidence than ever before. Japan's championing of opium control was a perception that fit the progressive self-image of the Meiji era.[50] Against this backdrop, Nicolai mediated an originally Russian view on Japan's superiority to the Philippine Opium Commission. Vice versa, the genealogy of foreign admiration for Japan's societal success found a first American following.

Transferring perceptions of Japan from Nicolai to the commissioners with such immediacy owed much to the intimacy of the personal connection between Bishop Nicolai and Bishop Brent. In their encounter, both of them disregarded their respective Russian and American origins as well as their respective Orthodox and Protestant religious identities. When discussing the opium issue, personal trust raised the professional credibility expected by Brent as the leading commissioner. Nicolai refrained from spiritual competition for human souls, while for Brent, Roman Catholicism meant "no further hope for the nation," but Greek or Russian Orthodox Christianity was met with equanimity.[51]

Beyond the requirements of politesse, Brent described Nicolai as "a fine old man" in his diary. If someone like Nicolai had not "come into contact with the opium habit among the Japanese," Brent recorded for himself, it was "a strong bit of testimony as to the efficacy of the prohibitive law."[52] The Swedish stenographer Arnell agreed. Nicolai was the only interviewee who had "worked exclusively among the Japanese," and if he said "the law is strongly supported by public opinion, as the Japanese have an abhorrence and fear of the vice," it had to be the case.[53] In Brent's diary, Nicolai's individual integrity, discipline, and work ethic were inextricably connected to the accuracy of his testimony.[54] But as reliability of character and accuracy of social representations were treated as two sides of the same coin, the commission's modus operandi digressed far from its professed scientism and "utmost impartiality."[55]

Almost nothing did the commissioners do to curtail or at least track consultations between their interviewees and related contacts. They took no note of the surprise visit of John McKim, a bishop of the Protestant Episcopal Church in Japan, and William Awdry, a bishop of the Church of England in Osaka, to Nicolai days before his interview. Brent's name does not appear to have surfaced in their conversation. In Nicolai's diary, now available in Japanese translation, he noted how his visitors were the first to tell him about the U.S. confrontation with opium consumption in the

Philippines, a habit reportedly introduced by "Qing Chinese immigrants" and taken up by indigenous people.[56]

In a further display of trans-confessional openness, John McKim, interviewed on the same day, testified to Nicolai as "the greatest missionary Japan has known not excepting St. Francis Xavier," recorded by the commission. Other Russian priests, McKim averred, "could not stand the amount of work the good Bishop put upon them" and quit their Japanese service. Nicolai merely stated that they "got homesick and returned." McKim had first met Nicolai at the funeral of U.S. minister Alfred Eliab Buck after his fatal accident at a duck-hunting spree of the Meiji court in early December 1902. Reverend Soper of the Methodist University in Tokyo, the liaison to Andō, and Captain Francis Brinkley, head of the government-sponsored and internationally respected *Japan Mail* in Yokohama, concurred with Nicolai, McKim, and Awdry; whether they were impelled by their sense of friendship is not known.[57]

Beyond the site and moment of the Philippine Opium Commission interviews, numerous Russian intellectuals spoke to Japan as a rare ecumenical confederation of religions, such as Sergei Aleksandrovich Rachinskii of Moscow University, philosopher Vladimir Solovyev, and novelist Fyodor Dostoyevsky, all of whom applauded Nicolai's universalism and aversion to Russian claims to hegemony.[58] Nicolai's own transnationalism had brought him to San Francisco, Chicago, and New York in 1879, in support of Metropolia, the Russian Orthodox Greek Catholic Church of America, followed by London, Berlin, Warsaw, Wilno (Vilnius), St. Petersburg, and Moscow.[59]

What is certain throughout is that the opium interviews and their commentary in the commission report did not posit the anti-opium cause as a proxy for projects of European, Russian, or American superiority, be it the religious mission of proselytizing; the social mission of a civilizational uplift, notably from above; or the political mission of colonialism. A test case may be a civilizing mission that never featured prominently in Nicolai's writings, oral statements, or activities.[60] Strikingly, the judgments by the commission were the product of assumptions, beliefs, and images that were neither uniquely American nor exceptional discoveries by the commission itself. Anti-opium perceptions reached the commission through circulation, but neither the historical provenance of those circulations nor the networks that carried them were scrutinized. Nicolai's debt to Golovnin went as unacknowledged as the leap of faith that corroborated Nicolai's testimony with the network of his personal supporters. That network was not limited to Tokyo or Japan. In 1904, less than a year after Nicolai's interview, the *Missionary Review of the World* in New York and London offered another glowing tribute to Nicolai. The author, T. Gracey of Rochester, drew on the Japanese *Fukuin shimpō*, or Gospel news, and the predecessor of the Dai Nippon as a source. No Russophile, owner Ishikawa Kisaburō let the endorsement cross pages and borders, obscuring the conventional identification of a publishing language with a national point of view. Intertextual transnationalism suffused foreign perceptions of Nicolai, just as Nicolai's own perceptions suffused the Philippine Opium Commission and, through it, a wide international audience.[61]

The commission's own transnationalism, which made it receptive to the transnationalism of others, looks only revolutionary absent a comparative context. Certainly, the commission exhibited an overt extroverted transnationalism by embarking on its Asian opium investigation in the first place. But it also operated in times of peace. By comparison, only one year after the Philippine Opium Commission, Nicolai's transnationalism would have to weather the Russo-Japanese War of 1904 and 1905, when the *Yamato shimbun* charged him with espionage, along with the German personal physician of the Meiji emperor, Erwin Baelz, who had dared treating the ear problems of the Russian minister, Baron Rosen. From the early stage of the war, Nicolai was kept apprised with secret information, thanks to personal contact with the Russian supreme commander, Admiral Evgenyi Ivanovich Alexeyev.[62] The Japanese police were successful in averting arson of Nicolai's church.[63]

Personal references as a culture of social accreditation were the essential working mode of the Philippine Opium Commission, but not its invention. They predated the commission in Nicolai's transnational socialization. A certain Russian captain Yakimoff wrote a letter of reference for the peripatetic British clergyman Henry Lansdell to consult the Russian bishop with an Orthodox spirit and a Japanese soul.[64] Once again, interviewees acting as liaisons brought their own circles of sociability into the orbit of the Philippine Opium Commission, tilting the balance of opium testimonies. One circle of recommendation comprised scholars at Meiji Gakuin University, whose colonial mobility between Japan and colonial Taiwan offered a natural transnational bridge to Americans brought to Japan through colonial mobility via the Philippines.

On the Japanese side, Ibuka Kajinosuki was one of them, perceived as "a Japanese gentleman well informed and speaking English fluently, who had just returned from Formosa." Before anyone else, Ibuka drew the commissioners' attention to the Japanese colony of Taiwan and its efficient enforcement of control legislation and decreasing opium use, according to Japanese colonial statistics. Ibuka explained how harsh punitive measures were successful: he had "no record that any opium habitué," whether imprisoned or free, "has been permanently injured by being deprived of opium."[65] As to public opinion in Taiwan, "there is a strong feeling among the Chinese, particularly among those of the better class, that it would be wiser to apply to Formosa the law in force in Japan." Colonial adaptation, according to this representation, was proceeding rather well.[66]

As a member of the YMCA World's Committee, president of the Japan Christian Educational Association, chairman of the Christian University Promotion Committee, and holder of an honorary degree from Princeton, Ibuka himself gave another opium interview to the commission.[67] Like Nicolai, Ibuka's transnationalism did not merely respond to American initiative, nor was it confined to the commissioners as interlocutors. In fall 1906, Ibuka and William Imbrie, a Meiji Gakuin colleague and commission interviewee, refuted rumors of "Japan Turning Moslem."[68]

So flexible was the transnational sociability appropriated by the commissioners that it extended beyond the formal documented interviews, bringing Brent in contact with older and earlier circles of social reform in the vicinity of the anti-opium cause. Not included in the commission report was Bishop Brent's visit to the Women's English Academy (*Joshi eigaku juku*), which brought him into the circle of its founder, Tsuda Umeko. On the morning of September 25, 1903, Brent gave a speech at the school so "admirably conducted," as his diary states.[69] Without apparently knowing it, Brent followed in the footsteps of Pandita Ramabai, whom Tsuda had invited to lecture on her return journey from the United States to India in 1891. Beyond the parallels of Ramabai's and Brent's approaches to Tsuda, Tsuda herself had used U.S. publicity circles to reach Anglophone readers with the first transnational account on the status of Japanese women in 1891.[70] The lifetime of the ties between U.S. publicity, social reform for Asian women, and the anti-opium movement extended for decades. In the 1910s, Fujita Taki, a student of the Women's English Academy, took a class in international law at Bryn Mawr, taught by Charles Ghequiere Fenwick. This sparked her engagement with "international problems," defined by Fenwick along League of Nations lines: "protecting women and children; the prevention of white slavery; the prevention of the opium trade."[71] Decades later, Fujita would lobby for Japan's membership in the United Nations.

JAPANESE OFFICIALS CONSTITUTED the second group of interviewees, all of whom conveyed their nation's opium control as "prohibitive and effective." Among them was Kumagai Kiichirō, born in 1866 and a law graduate from Tokyo Imperial University. Kumagai served as counselor of Hokkaido in the Ministry of Agricultural and Commerce, at the Ministry of the Army, at the Ministry of the Interior, and as the chief of civil administration of Sakhalin. To the Philippine Opium Commission, he was known only as "K. Kumagai, Chief Official in charge of Formosan Affairs, Department of Home Affairs."[72] His verdict on Japan's relationship to opium could not have been more unequivocal in confirming Japan's success in prohibition, to the point that the commission defended its findings: "This is not an *ex parte* assertion; among foreigners resident in Japan, as well as among the Japanese themselves, there is but the one verdict. . . . Neither in formal interviews nor in any of the frequent conversations on the subject which the various members of the Committee held with people of all classes was a dissenting opinion heard."[73] And how could the commissioners believe otherwise, absent contradicting testimony?

"So rigid are the provisions of the law that it is sometimes, especially in interior towns, almost impossible to secure opium or its alkaloids in cases of medical necessity," the report read. Meanwhile, the old theme of Japanese education and intellectualism reappeared forcefully: "Not that the Japanese are ignorant of the medicinal qualities of the drug, for they are abreast with the foremost in their scientific knowledge, and the medical profession of Japan is worthy of admiration as is that of America or England," the report stated. It was seemingly unaware of pioneering Tokugawa doctors like Sugita Gempaku, who had insisted on Western medical knowledge as more accurate than that of the Chinese sages.[74] But with the Meiji era maturing into its energetic thirties, the political will of the Japanese state impressed. "The government is determined to keep the opium habit strictly confined to what it deems to be its legitimate use," the report explained in reference to Japan's burgeoning pharmaceutical industry, which would soon find itself in the crosshairs of international politicization.[75]

Some other sources disputed this rosy picture. In 1896, Reverend David S. Spencer claimed in a Methodist Episcopal paper that Yokohama saw the import of 3,500 koku (140,000 gallons) of opium in 1893, 5,500 koku (220,000 gallons) in 1894, and 14,000 koku (560,000 gallons) in 1895.[76] The claim was as scandalous as it was undocumented. By comparison, the United States imported as much as 615,957 pounds of crude opium in 1893, rising to 716,881 pounds in 1894 and dropping to 358,455 in 1895 before peaking at 1,072,914 in 1897.[77] These numbers documented exclusively legal imports, while the total margin of smuggling remains unidentifiable until smuggling records are found.[78] But crucially, for the Philippine Opium Commission, external statistics did not compete with the qualitative information gained in firsthand and face-to-face interviews.

Undeterred, the commission continued in its documentation of a Japan where state and society intertwined. Like Nicolai, the commissioners could only conclude that Japan fared very well in international comparison and as a sociopolitical entity enjoyed superiority over their own country—that is, the United States. "The law, then, is not an injunction superimposed on the people by the will of despotic authorities, nor is it the fruits of a victory of the majority over the minority, as in the case of some of our American states where a prohibition liquor law is found on the statute books," the report enthused, "but it is crystallized public opinion." In Japan, "the people not merely obey the law, but they are proud of it; they would not have altered it if they could. It is the law of the government, but it is the law of the people also."[79] What to an authoritarian audience would have been reduced to conservative law abidance here became an expansive celebration of Japan as a sociopolitical consensus that served society as well as the state. In inter-Asian comparison, "the single-mindedness" of anti-opium "carries with it the force of concentration, a force that is lacking in countries where opium is reckoned with as a source of revenue."[80]

Given the perceived context of Japanese society as a principal reason for the success of anti-opium sentiment opium control, the commission took a special interest in Japan's national characterization, with the usual pitfalls of generalization: "Added to the fear of the effects of opium," the commission reflected, "there is that powerful moral lever which society holds in its hands of ostracizing those who disregard its conception of propriety. An opium user in Japan would be socially as a leper."[81] In this, Meiji Japan was not alone, as the commission argued by comparing it to Burma, where the term "opium-smoker" paralleled "liar" in Anglo-Saxon countries.[82]

More than a national achievement, Japan's perceived advantage enabled the commission to draw the starkest contrast between divergent Asian encounters with opium. "China's curse has been Japan's warning, and a warning heeded." The depth of Japanese feeling and the national impact of China's warning seemed to authenticate anti-opium sentiment on a universal scale. "No surer testimony to the reality of the evil effects of opium can be found," the commission was persuaded, "than the horror with which China's next-door neighbor views it." Simultaneously, the commission became so enamored with Japan's national anti-opium experience that Japanese national development, quite apart from specific anti-opium arguments, became a subject of its own, rendered in a literary style that was at odds with the technical task at hand. "In the days of the Tokugawa dynasty, when the gates of Japan were barred to the world, there was small opportunity for good, let alone bad, commodities to gain entrance into the land. But when the bars were let down and foreign products flowed in with a rush, the spear-point was lowered against opium and its alkaloids."[83] As the Meiji urged for change nationally, the commission took Meiji change as a primary reason to urge an international rethinking of opium's place in international society.[84]

OCCURRING eight years after the Japanese colonization of Taiwan, the commission grasped the opportunity to interview some of the first Japanese administrators of Taiwan. Gotō Shimpei, then vice governor of Formosa, was among them, along with T. Iwai, director of the Bureau of Monopolies, and Mr. Kato, director of the Bureau of Sanitation. Reverend Terada, the pastor of the Protestant Episcopal Church in Taipei, was introduced as "intimately associated with the Social Life of the Natives," having observed them since the "Japanese Occupation." Colonization implicated imperial perceptions of race. Gotō explained that once the Chinese "acquired the habit, it is impossible or difficult for them to give it up."[85] Japanese residents in Taiwan therefore served as a social example to the Chinese, Gotō averred. "Only two Japanese have violated the opium law thus far. . . . There are many Chinese who, seeing the good physical condition of the Japanese who do not use opium, desire to imitate them; they appreciate the fact that it is injurious to them." Unsurprisingly, from a Japanese colonial perspective, Japan's superiority did not only manifest itself in civilizational achievement or political achievement but also embodied a social and ethical standard, consciously placed above the Chinese.[86]

Japanese domestic opium control as a social and political priority, however, contrasted with the Taiwanese opium issue, categorized as a colonial problem. After thorny debates, the Japanese authorities judged it unfeasible to implement a regime of opium prohibition in a social setting of preexisting Taiwanese consumption. In its place, they introduced a Japanese-controlled opium monopoly, dispensed by 105 Japanese physicians throughout Taiwan until 1898. Thereafter, as Gotō explained to the Philippine Opium Commission, colonial toughness gave way to a milder engagement. The Japanese licensing system, coupled with anti-opium education through pamphlets and ten opium hospitals across Taiwan, replaced surveillance by opium inspectors, whose expenses burdened the budget. Japanese colonial statistics supplied in abundance to the Philippine Opium Commission showed an overall decrease of Taiwan's registered opium smokers, from 169,000 in 1900 to 143,492 in 1903. Reverend Terada reaffirmed in his interview that Japanese colonial education assimilated Chinese youth to "Japanese ideas and ideals, among which the idea most deeply inculcated is the perniciousness and disgrace of the opium vice, for which they are taught to have an abhorrence."[87] To its delight, the commission learned that "in Formosa the merry Japanese boys are teaching the placid Chinese lads to play tennis, football, polo, vaulting, etc., with a view—the Japanese teachers say—of improving them physically and also of developing in them a love of sports which will prevent them from wishing to spend their leisure indoors smoking opium."[88] Just as Japanese anti-opium opposition signaled the society's overall quality in international comparison, the colonial anti-opium agenda aimed at society's improvement from without.

Correlating Japanese assessments of Taiwan's opium status with a separate, internal Japanese assessment helps balance the findings of each. In September 1903, when the Philippine Opium Commission began its inquiries in Tokyo, the Japanese colonial government appointed the first officers to conduct a comprehensive census across Taiwan.[89] The census results did not become available until October 1, 1905, by which time the commission report was already in print, having been submitted to the civil governor on March 28, 1904.[90] Beyond the positivism of the Washington-sponsored Philippine Opium Commission and the Tokyo-sponsored Taiwan census, Japanese official opium information exceeded what was communicated to the Americans.

The Taiwan census offered richer historical background, pointing to Chinese immigration to Taiwan as the perceived origin of opium consumption. Historically, too, opium control took the highest priority in the Japanese project of colonization as a social process. Preventing the spread of opium presented a social problem so urgent that Japanese plenipotentiaries discussed it at the conclusion of the treaty of Shimonoseki after the Sino-Japanese War in 1895: "A pledge was given by our representative which attracted the watchful eyes of the world." Over time, Japanese colonial officials hoped, the Japanese anti-opium imprint on Taiwan would distinguish itself in health and sobriety from a China besotted with opium. In the Japanese view, opium had been "China's greatest bane" and became "as a natural consequence" Taiwan's, but fortunately, Japanese control was built on a promise of colonial progress.[91]

Information between Japan and the United States did not just flow but must be appreciated against the impediments of transfer. When the Russo-Japanese War and its budget squeeze had delayed the domestic application of Tokyo's Population Census Law of 1902, Japanese documentary priorities shifted from population statistics to industrial statistics. In Korea, Japan's other experiment in imperial administration, the March First Uprising, prevented the census from covering the entire Japanese empire.[92] But the policy discussions and information exchange of which Japanese opium reports were a part made use of an existing Japanese-American level of interco-lonial interest. Taiwan had come under Japanese control in 1895, the Phil-ippines following under American control in 1898. In that year, Wash-ington learned of Tokyo's interest in having Washington "hold and govern the islands in the interest of peace, commerce and good government."[93] The Philippine Opium Commission's respect for Japanese opium information as the oldest and the most accurate across Asia was certainly welcome, even if based on incomplete data.[94] In Taiwan alone, Tokyo managed to control the conditions of efficient information governance, enabling both piecemeal communication to the Philippine Opium Commission and more extensive colonial documentation to serve as a counterpoint.

Meanwhile, fully cognizant of an intercolonial neighborhood, official Japanese interpretations of the opium regime on Taiwan preferred a heroic rendering of its colonial technocracy.[95] Colonial suppression, the asserting of state, and the crackdown on "brigands and outlaws . . . overrunning the land" became firm elements in the inventory of colonial self-praise.[96] As opium control confirmed the rule of law as an essential condition of ad-vanced colonial governance, its application became another jewel in the na-tional crown.

Japan's Taiwan census also offered an alternative conceptualization of the conditions of opium consumption itself. Unlike most British, French, Dutch, and even American assessments, the Taiwan census appropriated a global comparative perspective to posit the relative but not innate inferi-ority of the Chinese race. Appropriating a global comparative perspective, the census expressed the belief that "the eating and smoking of opium is a vicious habit almost peculiar to the Chinese race; for although there are some eaters and smokers" in the Ottoman Empire, Persia, and British India, "most are found in places inhabited by the Chinese or where crowds of Chinese labourers live together," a thinly veiled swipe at so-called coolies. But locally in Taiwan, the census knew better: "Wherever mixed races are found, some smokers are found among other races than the Chinese."[97]

Contingent explanations of ethnic characteristics impelling opium use were supplemented by social and anthropological analysis. The Taiwan census distinguished among children of wealthy families who contracted the habit by "sportively handling the smoking apparatus in imitation of their parents," the temporary quest for a pain reliever among adults turning permanent, the different quest to "seeking relief from trouble arising from failure in business or family misfortunes," parental pressure "to preserve a young widow in chastity," and the contrary "indulgence in brothels, grog-shops, '&c.'"[98] To the Japanese, the most disturbing use was sedating crying babies with opium. Taiwanese parents generally seem to have been apprehensive about the health hazard of "blowing smoke," a point when the census lost its patience: "What people are there who are wholly without some evil habit? But what is more destructive to the spirit of a people and more wasteful of national resources than the habit of smoking opium? The habit once contracted makes its victim a confirmed eater or smoker, popularly known as 'smoky devil,' or 'smoking ghost,' irredeemable for life."[99]

Opium assessments like this revealed that social decline was a specter haunting Taiwan as a colonial setting, similar to that of the Qing in a semi-colonial setting. In both cases, opium undermined the productivity of the people, a key concern of most colonial labor regimes. In this sense, Japanese colonial opium control fit other colonial reforms, be it the desired decrease of female infanticide, bound feet, or the increase of women in the labor market.[100] The Taiwan census itself assisted in political control, with the *hokō* system becoming the backbone of surveillance and colonial infrastructure alike.[101]

That these opium assessments and the inferences they allowed about Japanese colonial motivations were missed by the Philippine Opium Commission did not mean that Japanese officials withheld that information. In fact, the referenced exchange at Shimonoseki between Li and Itō attracted international public opinion. Although the *Tientsin and Peking Times,* which ran an anti-opium supplement later, bemoaned that the two statesmen did not "much elucidate a very old problem," the historic significance of this rhetorical duel between China's and Japan's anti-opium capacities was recognized. The exchange was "significant of the attitude of the two countries towards the much disputed traffic," a small testament to two decades of anti-opium mobilization. Opium, that "very old problem," was "being brought into new prominence just now," the same paper remarked in 1895. "To say nothing of China, up to date Japan has evidently not been much impressed by the late Opium Commission," referring to Britain's Royal Commission.[102] While this statement underestimated Chinese knowledge of the Royal Commission, the observation of Tokyo's aloofness was not far off the mark. The silence of Japanese official records toward the Royal Commission mirrored Japanese dismissals of useful precedents in the U.S. Philippine administration for its Taiwan census. Japanese imperialism was not as inevitably derivative as its lateness appears to suggest.[103]

In fact, uneven Japanese information flows set Japanese and American opium assessments further apart than the Philippine Opium Commission realized. In U.S. eyes, Japanese-American affinity in opium control made the Taiwanese experience a suitable analogy. Mutual rhetoric in commission interviews was friendly and welcoming, while that behavior was also in each party's interest. The commission craved maximum information.

In turn, its interviewees benefited from learning about U.S. anti-opium ambitions and objectives. What both Japanese and American colonial administrations shared was a commitment to "scientific" ethnographic inquiry for analyzing opium consumption among populations little known.

When, after the conclusion of the Philippine Opium Commission, the Taiwan census of 1905 did reach a U.S. audience, the American Geographical Society in New York admired it for its "enormous amount on many topics" but was "especially noteworthy as a study of census methods in a land whose conditions are, in some respects, exceptional."[104] Readers of Josiah Strong's *Social Progress* caught glimpses of the first Taiwanese population figures in 1905, with their never-ending compilations of global statistics, from population figures and per capita debt to comparative sea power and the scores of U.S. social-reform movements.[105] In June 1896, the new Taiwanese model of Japanese opium governance drew endorsements from as far as the Representative Board of the Anti-Opium Societies in Britain, the same institution monitoring simultaneous anti-opium activism in India.[106]

Letting Japanese-American intercolonial relations segue into British anti-opium perceptions raises the comparative question of how the Philippine Opium Commission related to its great rival, the Royal Commission of 1895. There were interviewees who sided with the Royal Commission and whose encounter with the Philippine Opium Commission is telling. On January 10, 1904, Frederic Kersey Jennings—prosecuting agent for the opium and spirit farms of Singapore, Malacca, and Johor—referenced the Royal Commission sympathetically. "In my experience," he told the Philippine Opium Commission, "the habit of opium smoking in a moderate degree after the day's labor, by a Chinese, especially in malarial districts, appears to be not only harmless but in some ways beneficial." He added, apparently attempting to forestall American criticism: "I base my opinion on the report of the Royal Commission." The Philippine Opium Commission was predictably provoked: "What is the character of the benefit of which you speak?" Jennings responded vaguely: "The effect on the working-man is refreshing." The next question moved to morphine use.[107] At the close of Jennings's interview, the commission wished to know, "Is Chinese sentiment against the use of opium?" Jennings's response was suspiciously absolute: "There is no public sentiment about it."[108] However, the commission's summary of interviews in the Straits Settlements disregarded Jennings's assessment, perhaps wary of the impartiality of a retired chief inspector of police who continued to live in the tropical climate on a government pension.

Other commission interviewees contradicted Jennings's denial of an anti-opium problem in the Straits Settlements. Dr. F. B. West, a doctor of Malay and Tamils for seventeen years, affirmed that "there is a constant agitation going on, . . . a strong sentiment among the Chinese, as it affects them seriously," describing as "alarming" the increase of opium use: "To them the question is a live one. They have a right to be disturbed."[109] But while those interviewed covered a broad spectrum of opium opinion, the commission's final verdict on its British royal rival voiced a definitive stance: The British conclusions of 1895 were "chiefly a study of the Indian problem" and "did not close (on the contrary, it only opened) investigation regarding a subject in which history, observation, and the progress of scientific methods and knowledge all have a part to play."[110] While political interests had guided the Royal Commission, the Philippine Opium Commission prized scientific inquiry as the analytic antipode.

American criticism sharpened by scrutinizing British inquiry methods. Not only did "the drift" of the Royal Commission report speak "the official mind of Great Britain in the Orient," but its defense of opium as "not necessarily injurious to Orientals" was too compatible with a defense of governmental opium revenues to remain socially legitimate, the American commission reasoned. While the legacy of American legalism through prohibition treaties was silently shoved aside, British legalism was confronted: "As carefully drawn laws protecting trade interests, they are above criticism, barring their failure to quench the practice of smuggling. They do not pretend to be laws for the protection of a people against a vice, but rather commercial regulations guarding a branch of commerce," the Philippine Opium Commission judged.[111]

Japan, gradually emerging as the virtuous opposite of Britain, kept orienting the opium attitudes of other countries. Even as the missionary incentives and objectives loom large in the historiography of a commission headed by an American bishop, the religious difference by no means diminishes Asian anti-opium achievement in Japan and elsewhere. "It is worthy of more than passing attention that Japan, which is a non-christian [*sic*] country, is the only country visited by the Committee where the opium question is dealt with in its purely moral and social aspect."[112] Where the moral, social, and financial aspects of opium policy in a particular country were paramount, the particularity of religion shrank as a factor in its own right. So did nationality. Burmese Buddhist anti-opium opposition and its historical depth were noted without dismissals.[113] British activity, including the missionary presence, was cast in a negative light. "Buddhism was once so strong a force as to keep the Burmese from the use of opium; but this force became weakened by contact with English influence."[114] Thus, Asian examples of anti-opium attitudes, exemplified by Japan and Burma, gained higher marks than Anglo-Saxon ambiguity vis-à-vis prohibition.

Further southeast in Java, too, a colonial army physician, A. H. Vortsmann of Soekaboemi, stated "that the people of the west" of the island, "being the most religious, are at the same time the least contaminated by the vice," read by the commission as a sign of opium's presence as a commercial imperialist import rather than a culturally or socially homegrown entity. Indeed, espousing an American cross-confessional hope, the commission envisioned Filipino anti-opium opposition as following the example of "Mohammedan Malays in the Straits Settlements or among the Buddhist Burmese," distinguished from a more "permissive" control system for the Chinese in the Philippines. Only some Filipinos had formally converted to Christianity, and among them, disappointingly, "no religious sentiment regarding opium prevails of a sufficiently definite character . . . to protect them with a similar armor."[115]

Neither race nor religion nor nationality helped in determining the qualitative hierarchies of opium governance. With Japan entering the top ranks of Asian opium regimes, British colonial opium governance fell lower with the example of Singapore. There, Lim Boon Keng, an early anti-opium pioneer, echoed the reverence for Japan expressed by Nicolai and other interviewees. "Our views on the subject," Lim Boon Keng in Singapore emphasized, "are based on the study of the recent history of India, the Straits, Japan and China." Transnational perceptions across Asia confirmed the bifurcation between British fiscal interests and popular welfare. "The Government of Japan," Lim expressed, "forms however a notable exception." Lim analogized Taiwan and Borneo as Asian precedents for prohibiting opium imports.[116] Borneo entered the picture because Lim, as the husband of Margaret Wong Tuan Keng, was the son-in-law of Wong Nai Siong (Huang Naishang), the head of the *Siang Pau* newspaper and a supporter of Kang Youwei, the towering pioneer of late Qing's reform, and Sun Yat-sen, modern China's founding father. When Wong sought shelter for Chinese Christian refugees from Fuzhou Province after the Boxer Rebellion of 1900, Sibu, or New Fuzhou (*Xinfuzhou*), in Sarawak seemed more attractive than Malaya, Sumatra, or the Dutch East Indies.[117] Simultaneously, Lim advocated the expulsion of "all those Chinese who will not apply to the government hospitals for getting rid of the opium habit." After a grace period of "say six months," the "order of banishment should be applied against them," Lim suggested. U.S. exclusion laws against Chinese immigrants were not far from his mind, as he knew the American Philippines' administration was considering the Chinese Exclusion Act.[118]

As Lim discussed his father-in-law's experiment with opium control with Major Carter, he framed it in universalist terms. "Wherever a new settlement is established, prohibition can be put into effect," with Japanese Taiwan serving again as an inter-Asian example. The commission noted, "It seems very significant that three different persons"—namely Lim, Wong, and the governor of Sarawak, "White Rajah" James Brooke—"should have the same idea to occur to them."[119] To Dr. West, this cascade of comparisons was among many analogies connecting British Singapore and Japanese Taiwan. On the latter, West testified: "I have visited that colony two or three times. The prohibition of opium in that colony is absolute." Along those lines, Singapore had "just organized a colony for Chinese," and "there is no fence around it either."[120]

When Dr. West spoke about government institutions for opium treatment, Major Carter of the commission drew the inter-Asian parallels himself: "Your idea, then, is the same as that of the Japanese. That is the system they employ in Formosa. The Island is not very large, but they have twelve hospitals where opium-smokers are received for treatment."[121] In China, a certain Ms. Fearon, a medical missionary and former first secretary of the Anti-Opium League in Suzhou, confirmed the Formosan system as "an effective way of dealing with the opium problem."[122] The fascination with Japanese opium control in Taiwan made for a conspicuous reference point throughout Asia.

Intercolonial lessons crisscrossed Asian settings as the Philippine Opium Commission toured Asian opium regimes, with the American Philippines and British Singapore looking intently on Japanese Taiwan's opium control as a forerunner. As Lim Boon Keng in Singapore put it to close the triangle: "The system of control best adapted to the Philippine Islands is that so successfully carried out by the Japanese government in Formosa." Himself of Chinese descent, Lim supported mandatory medical treatment for addicted Chinese. Both opium smoking and the more "pernicious" hypodermic injection had made the drug an "absolute necessity of life," affecting the "moral state" of consumers. It was not immediate or permanent depravity but the variation of mental and emotional states that upset the balance of social relations, "for the unfortunate victim under the influence of the drug is not the same person as when he is suffering from the pangs of deprivation."[123] And it was mostly a him, not a her.

A woman named Ms. Blackstone, an active member of the Woman's Christian Temperance Union, which had created the gigantic Polyglot Petition, was interviewed together with Dr. West on her own request—"simply to enter my protest"—and offered liberally her views on female opium consumption in Singapore's private and public settings and its connection with the gambling culture.[124] She, too, applauded the idea of "a crusade among the school children against the vice," emphasizing, "it is not original with me. That is what the Japanese are doing in Formosa."[125] In Hong Kong, too, "the laws of Formosa were spoken of as being the most efficacious known to the Chinese."[126]

Attention to the Philippine Opium Commission moved beyond private into public reception. In Singapore, the *Straits Times,* a generally conservative paper, reported on December 11, 1903, its own interview with José Albert, the medical expert on the commission team: "Asked if he was against the opium trade," Albert answered that "the question must be faced in a statesmanlike spirit. Theories were all very well, but when they came to legislation they had to deal with hard facts." The Singaporean journalist pressed him further to express the "opinions" of his findings in Japan, Formosa, Shanghai, Hong Kong, and Saigon, but Albert "smiled and put off the question: "It is rather premature to express an opinion." He went on to say that in Singapore he had "seen the Government regulations," and according to the article "even sought to pump the interviewer, but of course that was not in the contract."[127]

In the commission report, he was less diplomatic: "The Committee finds nothing" in the Straits Settlements opium legislation "commending it as apt to check or prevent the extension of the opium habit."[128] The tension, even contradiction, between the subjective opium perceptions and scientific inquiry remained unresolved. Summing up, the report stated, "The Philippine Committee feels that in however small a degree, yet at least some measure it has made a contribution to what is one of the gravest, if not the gravest, moral problems of the Orient."[129] Opium opinions were rife, "formed by every-day experience or by personal prepossessions," but "facts established by scientific methods were few and far between." What remained was the focal point on Japan's prohibition and Japanese Taiwan's control, confirmed as it was by a multiplicity of Asian observers across a spectrum of opinion on who, how severely, and to what effect opium consumers suffered.[130]

The fact that the Philippine Opium Commission could hardly cope with the vastness of preexisting Asian opium information, from perceptions to assessments and suggestions, was also part of the Philippines' own opium debate, the setting where we first see political consequences of the commission's Asian information-gathering. In July 1903, ten thousand Chinese signed a petition to support Bishop Brent and Homer Stuntz of the Episcopal Church and oppose an opium bill by Bernard Moses, a professor of history at the University of California, educated in Michigan and Heidelberg. The bill envisioned to grant opium contracts to the highest Chinese bidder, in the best tradition of the opium farm system in the French, British, and Dutch colonies of Southeast Asia. Stuntz, however, used opium supply statistics from India, Java, Taiwan, and other countries, showing increasing sales under an opium farm. The petition reached the eyes and ears of President Theodore Roosevelt, and the opium farm was rejected.[131]

As a result of this massive comparison of Asian opium problems and possible solutions, a new, restrictive opium monopoly on the American Philippines decreed to limit all opium sales to salaried officials "whose incomes shall in no way be influenced by the sales they make." Monopoly revenues should meet exclusively the running costs, "to demonstrate that this method aims solely at control, repression, and abolition of the use of opium and the traffic therein, and is not a revenue method."[132] Throughout, the administrative distance to British India was thinly veiled. On March 3, 1905, these proposals became law. Total prohibition was scheduled to start on March 1, 1908.[133] Further recommendations proscribed the import, purchase, or other introduction of opium into the islands for other than medical purposes after a transition period of three years, designed to force opium habitués to prepare psychologically and physically to "disaccustom" themselves.[134] Opium licensees during the transition period had to be male and older than twenty-one, and all members of the population were to be warned against opium consumption through anti-opium education and legislation. Finally, the government pledged to "aid in caring for and curing those who manifest a desire to give up the habit, and . . . to punish, and if necessary, to remove from the islands, incorrigible offenders."[135] This commitment not only to a Philippine model of prohibition but to an explicit rejection of the opium trade as a source of state revenues concluded the U.S. apprenticeship in studying older Asian opium regimes and reforms.

But above all, the inquiries showed that opium use in the Philippines "does not constitute so grave a social calamity in the Philippines as it does in the neighboring territories."[136] To widen the international rather than local impact of the commission, then, it was key that the Philippine Opium Commission would publish its findings, not only to override the Royal Commission but also to stay connected to the rising international debate over a political solution to a specifically Asian opium problem. With an interpretive alternative to the Royal Commission, Britain edged closer than ever to becoming the opium villain of Asia. For Tagore, the publication of *Letters from John Chinaman* in 1901, although penned by G. Lowes Dickinson, signaled the onset of a pan-Asian turn against British rule and civilization, a turn that drew its discontent from China's victimization, as perceived by neighboring Asians.[137] Inter-Asian, anti-imperialist, and regional comparisons bound Asia together not by value, culture, or religion but through the shared burden of a social problem.

As the American inquiry presented Asia's colonial and national models of the opium problem side by side, the commission report unraveled its informational value at a time when controversy mounted. Although "a molehill" of some five hundred pages beside "the mountain submitted by the Royal Commission," which stretched across twenty-five hundred pages, the leaner American report exerted more international opinion than its weightier imperial predecessor.[138] Its success consisted not only of giving Americans antidrug ambitions but of conveying a plethora of Asian anti-opium views to an international audience, laying the basis for the international public politics of narcotic drugs.

Despite their disparities in approach, operation, and conclusions, the British- and American-sponsored investigations did share at least one objective: to forge international public opinion in their favor. In the Royal Commission report, one among the almost two hundred subentries argued that the "belief that England forced opium on China does not exist among the Chinese," and that "American missionaries" were the "only people who hold this view."[139]

But through scrutiny, protest, and reportage, public opinion and the press upheld steady pressure on the questions of state responsibility, popular support, and the referenceable role of the law. When the report appeared in 1905, transnational, nongovernmental sources of Asian opium assessment found their views largely validated in the light of international publicity. But as with all transnational initiatives of this scale, the issue arising was how to harness fresh informational leverage. Brent, Albert, and Carter hoped to use this report as a "starting point of a new investigation" in non-Asian countries, if possible along scientific lines.[140] With so many interviewees pointing to a convergence of opium assessments across the Asian region, the moment was pregnant with public expectations of a diplomatic, multilateral breakthrough.

CHAPTER SIX

ACTIVISTS INTO DIPLOMATS

Toward the International Opium Commission

I N 1905, the same year that the Philippine Opium Commission published its report, a confrontation over territory rather than opium brought the Qing and Britain face to face for negotiations in Calcutta. Their subject was Tibet, their response to the crisis induced by Britain's Younghusband mission of 1903, an intervention aimed at ousting a presumed Russian presence in Lhasa. Crucially, the Sino-British contest over Tibet, initially a classic issue of geopolitical rivalry, produced an only loosely related opium exchange between Qing and British diplomats. The Calcutta track, initially envisioned by the Qing as a meeting to obtain British recognition of Tibet as its own commercial and territorial priority, was repurposed as a channel for communicating mutual progress in anti-opium lobbying. As a consequence, preparations were made for the first British-Chinese opium accord, based on the information conveyed in Calcutta.

To prevent a permanent British occupation of Tibet, the Qing sent one of its most able diplomats, the young Tang Shaoyi, as special commissioner for Tibetan affairs.[1] Tang's education at Hartford Public High School in Connecticut and at Columbia University (frequently misidentified as Yale) made him a transnational Chinese equally versed in Anglophone and Sinophone circles.[2] His American years were followed by a swift diplomatic career as a protégé of Yuan Shikai in Korea, where he rose as consul general in Seoul from 1896 to 1898. In 1901, Tang became the chief magistrate and superintendent of customs (*daotai*) in Tianjin.[3] Tang's internationalist orientation was more than posturing. He regularly read the *Times* in Beijing. When a stalemate threatened to derail the Tibetan talks, Tang cited to his own government Wellington's replacement of Castlereagh, Richelieu's substituting for Talleyrand at the Congress of Vienna, and the Russian government pulling out Butzow from the Ili negotiations as international precedents for recalling him.[4] As one of Qing's foremost foreign-policy experts, Tang was indispensable in Calcutta, the stronghold that symbolized so evocatively British commercial power and imperial prestige.[5]

When in April 1906 the Peking Adhesion Convention brought the welcome compromise of British recognition of Qing special status among foreign powers, in return for Qing noninterference in British-Tibetan relations, much of the credit went to Tang. For the first time, the Qing obtained official suzerainty over a region equally coveted by British expansionists.[6] In the process, Tang illustrated a diplomat's skill by forging private ties with his British colleagues. He actively engaged their personal interests, feeding Lord Kitchener's connoisseurship with an abundance of porcelain and other artifacts.[7] He also elicited the likelihood of a Liberal victory at the elections, which materialized in December 1905.[8] Within this far-flung probing, Tang—together with his assistant, Liang Shiyi—inquired about the Indian opium regime with Sir Edward Baker, the finance secretary of the Indian administration. As long as railway receipts compensated for the deficit of lost opium revenues, Baker welcomed Indian crop diversification by cultivating rubber, cotton, and rice, moving the Indian exchequer further away from its reliance on opium cultivation and export.

But for the Qing, the legacy of the opium wars made these revelations historically counterintuitive if not perplexing. Baker even signaled his personal unofficial sympathy for a British Indian scheme of opium prohibition. Tang immediately seized on this information after his return to the Qing capital as junior vice president of the Board of Foreign Affairs.[9] The opportunity of a Qing-British opium rapprochement in 1905 would never return. In fact, the president of the National Opium Prohibition Union of China argued by the 1910s that questions of Tibetan administration as a perennial quid pro quo now restricted Chinese anti-opium pressure, rather than bolstering it.

Tang was well prepared to engage in the surprising Calcutta exchange. In around 1900, he rid himself of opium addiction, like so many young nationalists of his generation. His uncle, Tang Tingshu, had been leading the China Merchants' Steam Navigation Company, where he reputedly owned one-fourth of its capital, and worked for Jardine, Matheson & Co.[10] Despite Jardine's extensive opium trading, the elder Tang had entered the SSOT as a member, translating its pamphlets for Chinese distribution.[11] The nov-

elty of unofficial opium talks at the official Tibet negotiations, however, reflected not only Tang's acumen but the growing potential of anti-opium
discussions to entangle unexpectedly with distinct international agendas.
In intangible ways, decades of anti-opium lobbying had made the opium
problem a presence on political minds, a subject ever more likely to be
picked up at unrelated occasions, not quite like the weather, but increasingly so.

In addition to the Tibet exchange, a second occasion for a closer Qing-
British understanding arose shortly later among one of Yuan Shikai's sworn
enemies, the Manchu prince Zaize, head of the Plain Blue Banner and Qing
minister of finance under Prince Qing. Zaize, known in English as Duke
Zaize, was head of the Qing Imperial Mission of 1905 and 1906 to study
constitutionalism in Japan, Europe, and America, the Qing's multilateral
investigative commission in the style of Japan's Iwakura Embassy of 1871.
In England, he learned firsthand how well organized the British domestic
anti-opium movement was. Upon his return to Beijing, Zaize told John
Jordan, the British minister in China, "that he was deeply impressed by conversations . . . with Members of the British House of Commons." Zaize
was "surprised to find that the prospective loss of revenue was regarded
with comparative equanimity," reporting these new perceptions dutifully,
like Tang. "If England could sacrifice her revenue, and China failed to follow
her example, she would," he said, "stand discredited before the world."
Jordan knew as well that it was "in India" where Tang "gained the conviction that the question could be brought within the sphere of practical
politics."[12]

A third condition facilitating Qing preparation for a fundamental rethinking of the rules governing the opium trade stemmed from the internal
efforts of Qing officials to rally around reform causes beyond the anti-opium
agenda. Like Zaize's engagement in constitutional reform, late Qing official networks revealed a transnational leverage through exchanges with
nongovernmental institutions and individuals overseas. Illustrating the
point, Duan Fang, another member of the Qing Imperial Mission and
governor-general of Hunan, was assassinated by Chinese revolutionaries in
November 1911. Late Qing reformers gained an international edge across
a sprawling if belated front of initiatives of which the anti-opium agenda
was one element that survived the fall of the dynasty in 1911.

To press for the abolition of the Qing examination system for the civil
service, Duan Fang joined hands in an "epoch-making memorial" with Yuan
Shikai, governor-general of Zhili; Zhang Zhidong, governor-general of
Hebei and Hunan; and Zhou Fu, who has "always shown himself a pru-
dent, honest, progressive, and careful administrator," in the admiring words

of the American minister in Beijing, William Rockhill. Zhou's foreign co-operation was not limited to the opium problem or to Western diplomats. Simultaneously, he studied the Japanese salt monopoly on Taiwan as a model for his own province of Manchuria and hoped to recruit a Japanese financial adviser for Yuan Shikai.[13] Zhou also advocated mobilizing and unifying the force of public opinion (*gonglun*) for the purpose of political centralization and for "dissolving the borders" between erstwhile Manchu conquerors and the Han ethnic majority.[14]

This multiplication of interprovincial, national, transnational, and international lobbying for social and political reform by Qing officials was unprecedented, explaining the excitement among foreign observers. A second team of memorialists for the abolition of the examination system brought in Cen Chunxuan, the governor-general of Liangguang, before Zhou Fu and Zhao Erxun took over in 1906.[15] Zhao later became one of the anti-opium heroes regularly cited by John Newell Jordan, the British minister in Beijing, for having "done more than any other man to rid his country of opium," partly due to "the knowledge that British eyes were watching and British observers reporting on the progress of the opium campaign in every corner" of Sichuan province.[16]

The abolition of the examination system for civil servants was driven by a Qing concern for the future of the political elite. Outdated and ineffective seemed to be a kind of civil service recruitment that produced a "vast army of civil mandarins" that descended into opium addiction, as Zhao, Zhou, Cen, and Zhang Zhidong in Wuchang criticized in charges of systemic corruption.[17] In line with the renewed attention to public opinion as a political force, their memorial to the Qing emperor attracted considerable attention in the press, where opium addiction appeared not only as an official curse but as a primary social impediment to national progress: "China can never become strong and stand shoulder to shoulder with the Powers of the world unless she can get rid of the habit of opium-smoking by her subjects, about one-quarter of whom have been reduced to skeletons and look half dead."[18]

Meanwhile in London, the Society of Friends announced the same petition in its periodical Anti-Opium Committee's Meeting for Suffering, taking special note of the petitioners' pressure on their own government in Beijing to approach London.[19] The appeal "of four of China's leading Viceroys—men who rule over eight of China's provinces with more than 179,000,000 of people," was celebrated for its pressure on the Qing Foreign Ministry. Yuan Shikai, whose autocratic ambitions would discredit him in the eyes of most foreigners after the fall of the dynasty, was still held up as an example of Chinese recognition of Japanese opium control on Taiwan, and his instructions for provincial prohibition were received by the governors-general.[20]

Owing to Zhao's mediation, Zhou Fu as governor-general in Nanjing granted a full hour for an interview to the delegation of the Anti-Opium League in May 1906, coinciding with Yuan Shikai's short-lived anti-opium proclamations. Joseph Alexander Gundry, a key figure to ensure Quaker financial support for the anti-opium cause in Asia and a later member of the Opium Traffic Committee of the League of Nations Union, was among those invited for an interview with Zhou and read it as most fortuitous divine providence, not only when Zhou bade him farewell: "You are a good man and working in a good cause; may Heaven bless you."[21] Meanwhile, Zhao liaised with J. L. Rodgers, the American consul general, and Rui Cheng, the governor-general of Huguang, who would five years later narrowly escape the revolutionaries. Rui Cheng facilitated cooperation between the Anti-Opium League and Zhou. Personal reasons made Zhou particularly receptive to the anti-opium plight, as he had, as one report put it, "just lost his eldest son by what may be termed opium-dropsy and was a bear robbed of its whelps."[22] The league officers' introduction to Zhou on May 25, 1906, was "presented in Mandarin, readily understood," as the annual report of the league proudly pointed out. Perhaps it was Guy Achison, superintendent of *lijin* in the Suzhou district and one of the Anti-Opium League's interpreters, considered "among the leading sinologues of the empire," who assisted on the occasion, but we do not know for certain.[23] The interview yielded revolutionary results of its own. Zhou proposed an anti-opium memorial signed by missionaries of all nationalities, which he would submit on their behalf to the Qing emperor for a new anti-opium edict from the very top.[24]

In its international reach, these memorials played a crucial role in bolstering the transnational credentials of key Qing officials. Zhao's American credentials, for example, grew for his strong backing of the currency reform plan, devised in consultation with Jeremiah Jenks of Cornell University, who in turn advised the governments of China, Mexico, Nicaragua, and Germany.[25] In later years, when this circle of reformist, high-placed officials had dissolved after the brutal success of the nationalist Xinhai Revolution, Zhao spearheaded arms purchases from the United States and Japan before being executed by the revolutionaries.[26]

Opening up these new lines of communication through memorial projects raised Qing-Anglophone transnationalism in the anti-opium cause to new levels of political influence within established practices of the dynastic system. Information flowed through this new channel more reliably than through regular diplomatic communications, as illustrated by the hiatus of opium communications through the British Legation in Beijing from September 1904 to July 1906.[27] Based at the Union Presbyterian Synod in Nanjing, the Anti-Opium League became an interface of Chinese and American anti-opium interests.

The league's president, Hampden Coit DuBose, had long craved political anti-opium influence, but for years, he had lacked access to Qing governors. A brief retrospective illustrates DuBose's transnational legacy of anti-opium lobbying and the transformations of the Anti-Opium League. In a lecture before the Shanghai Missionary Association in Union Church Hall on November 6, 1900, DuBose addressed the causes of the Boxer Rebellion of 1900, directly challenging the ideology of free trade imperialism: "What are the wares brought to these shores by the merchant? Does he seek only to help a poor heathen people?"[28] But whatever spiritual or material import was concerned, Chinese alienation, Prince Gong's erstwhile prediction, could not be so easily undone. "Alas! Poison is sold in great chests and the Westerner rejoices in seeing the poverty and suffering, ruin and degradation his hand has wrought. In health or wealth opium touches one hundred millions of the Chinese. For this the Chinese hate the foreigner with an intense hatred."[29]

Transnational observers of Chinese public and private sentiment saw this hatred exacerbated by social evidence of opium's familial, psychological, and emotional harm. One of the most diverse collections of medical anti-opium opinion, made available in Chinese and referenced in DuBose's Shanghai speech, was *Opinions of over 100 Physicians on the Use of Opium* of 1899. Several of the silk merchants in Nanjing proposed to issue it in a new edition of ten thousand and "scatter it through the empire."[30] New prefaces were "found most denunciatory of England, describing side by side in all their horrors the slave-trade of the 18th century and the opium traffic of the 19th," an analogy no longer used by British anti-opium activists alone. DuBose was persuaded by representatives of Nanjing millionaires that their anti-opium agitation was justified and not overly radical. In Chinese representations made to DuBose, social unrest in China was directly caused by opium. This echoed the Philippine Opium Commission's interviews in Shanghai on November 7, 1903, when six "substantial Chinese merchants . . . all advocated government regulation on opium," while prioritizing control over prohibition. "None of them belonged to the anti opium league [*sic*], but all were strong in feeling that some steps should be taken to mend matters."[31]

As Chinese anti-opium voices sought and received endorsement from American anti-opium NGOs, those NGOs in turn attracted support from American diplomats posted in China. In its survey questions regarding opium consumption and opium revenue in China, the Anti-Opium League mustered dozens of testimonies by American consuls that flatly contradicted the Royal Commission, published as "The Report of the American Consuls on Opium in China" in the *Shanghai Mercury* as well as in the *Chinese Recorder.*[32] Much of it echoed arguments previously forwarded by the first Qing diplomats in Europe, like Guo Songtao's identification of opium as comprising the historical, physical, and moral roots of "the West's threat to China" and the "cause of this great and painful wound."[33] The American consul's report included the same contacts used in the Anti-Opium League's lobbying campaign, among them Edwin H. Conger, the American minister in Beijing, and David J. Hill, temporary secretary of state in lieu of John Hay, known for his involvement in the Open Door policy proposals. The letter introduced DuBose, who himself carried the letter to Washington. Still, the Anti-Opium League remained dissatisfied with American anti-opium support and craved opium statistics, which the Qing Foreign Ministry, the reorganized Waiwubu, was unable to furnish in time.[34]

These efforts tied seamlessly into the perspectives just carved out by the Philippine Opium Commission. Already in late January 1905, DuBose requested the commission report from the Bureau of Insular Affairs at the War Department in Washington through John Tyler Morgan, a former general in the Confederate Army during the American Civil War and a senator from Alabama from 1877 to 1907, who served as his liaison. On January 31, 1905, three days after the request, Morgan forwarded the report to DuBose, several months ahead of its publication. This enabled the Anti-Opium League to start early preparing for its mass distribution: an edition of ten thousand, generously supported by the *North China Herald*'s printing office. The Anti-Opium League's abridged edition, titled *Opium in the Orient: Report of the Philippine Commission,* ran across twenty-four pages and publicized the main conclusions, without the preceding testimonies.[35] This shorter version, with its benefits of lighter shipping and reduced printing costs, was more suited to widespread, nongovernmental distribution, as proven by its presence in libraries around the world. Simultaneously, officials less sympathetically disposed toward the report requested it at this early stage, like Matthew Nathan, governor of Hong Kong from 1904 to 1907, and Sir Cecil Clementi, the Hong Kong delegate at the upcoming International Opium Commission, who requested the report from the American Philippine administration.[36]

But to reach key figures of Qing foreign policy, the Anti-Opium League needed intermediaries with some measure of political leverage as a proven source of persuading the dowager empress, who had taken over the reins of power in the conservative backlash against the Guangxu reforms. In spring

1906, three officers of the Anti-Opium League's Executive Committee contacted two governors in Suzhou, reporting that "the old said, 'Foreigners
by treaty right sell opium; I can do nothing.' The new: 'I am in entire sympathy with the movement and will do all in my power to advance the cause.'
The next month he sent his cheque for $200."[37] Persistently, DuBose worked
with rather than against Manchu officials that other Westerns despised so
much. Zhou Fu, the governor-general in Nanjing, proposed that DuBose
and other missionaries should first sign a memorial to be presented by the
governor-general to the throne. After extensive circulation of the draft memorial to China-based missionaries, members of the Anti-Opium League,
and others, the governor-general followed suit.

The Western response to Zhou's proposal to the Anti-Opium League was
nothing less than exuberant. A memorial signed by 1,333 missionaries from
seven countries was sent to Nanjing on August 13, 1906. Tang Shaoyi, the
top diplomat in the Tibet talks in Calcutta, made sure that the Waiwubu
paid sufficient attention and communicated the ministry's "great pleasure"
back to the Anti-Opium League. Again, the Anti-Opium League relished in
the endorsement by the most relevant Qing organ, celebrating laurels that
only the SSOT had received before. Tang, too, was feted in the headlines as
the intellectual creator of the anti-opium petition. DuBose announced that
"the two great capitals, London and Peking were happily joined in philanthropic union." After consultations between the Qing government and Zhou
for the Commission of Reforms that led to the legendary Anti-Opium Edict
of September 1906, Emperor Guangxu appropriated the missionary petition straight for Qing imperial legislation: "The edict was in the very letter
of the Memorial."[38] For the first time in the global anti-opium campaign,
the gap between transnational lobbying and state legislation had closed.

The landmark achievement of the imperial edict is worth quoting: "Since
the restrictions against the use of opium were removed, the poison of the
drug has practically permeated the whole of China. The opium smoker
wastes time and neglects work, ruins his health, and impoverishes his family,
and the poverty and weakness which for the past few decades have been
daily increasing amongst us are undoubtedly attributable to this cause,"
echoing all major tropes of anti-opium ideology. "To speak of this arouses
our indignation, and, at a moment when we are striving to strengthen the
Empire, it behooves us to admonish the people, that all may realize the necessity of freeing themselves from these coils, and thus pass from sickness
into health. It is hereby commanded that within a period of ten years the
evils arising from foreign and native opium be equally and completely erad-
icated." The Qing's Grand Council (*junjichu*) was ordered to "frame such
measures as may be suitable and necessary for strictly forbidding the con-

sumption of the drug and the cultivation of the poppy, and let them submit their proposals for our approval."[39]

It would be misleading, therefore, to construe the first Qing edict on opium control of September 1, 1906, as another Chinese response to the West. Nor was it "Chinese" legislative innovation from within the confines of the state. Rather, the transnationalism of preparatory lobbying matched the transnationalism of post-legislation effects. The edict became integrated into Qing public diplomacy, with an explicit order to send it to Washington and elsewhere: "Let this be published abroad for the information of all."[40] The U.S. consular reports almost broke into song. "China Abolishes Opium," titles ran, celebrating in a renewed fervor of legalism the impending abolition of poppy cultivation, the limitation of opium use for medical purposes, and the observation that this imperial anti-opium edict "was the direct result of the report of the Chinese commission appointed to visit this country and Europe, and the edict is signed by the heads of both civil and military affairs." But even for U.S. diplomats, it was not the legalist precedent of the 1844 Treaty of Wangxia and its opium prohibition between China and the United States that merited late praise. Rather, Chinese antiopium initiatives since Lin Zexu received recognition. "This is not the first attempt of China to free herself from the effects of the opium trade. The first effort was made in 1839. That result led to a war with Great Britain, which profited by the export of opium to China, and as a result of the war the edict was recalled and China had to pay an indemnity of about $6,000,000. The Chinese commission which visited England last year found public sentiment far different from what it was three-quarters of a century ago."[41] The SSOT, American diplomatic observers, and Qing officials were beginning to close a circle of anti-opium cooperation.

British recognition of Qing anti-opium progress returned to the aforementioned abolition of the civil servants' examination system as a crucible for teams of Qing political reform. Jordan, Britain's top-ranking diplomat in Beijing, reported to Edward Grey, the foreign minister, of Tang Shaoyi's first announcement of the imperial opium edict: "To Western minds all this sounds like an attempt to make people virtuous by Act of Parliament, and without showing any lack of appreciation of the efforts of the statesmen who are trying to cope with what is undoubtedly a great and growing evil." He remained uncertain "whether the proposed remedies are of a practicable nature." The abolition of the examination system, foot binding, and opium use "effected some far-reaching changes," Jordan acknowledged. "But to sweep away in a decade habits which have been the growth of at least a century and which have gained a firm hold upon 8,000,000 of the adult population of the Empire is a task which has, I imagine, been rarely attempted with success in the course of history." At the same time, Jordan's focus on Waiwubu remained on state actors, anonymizing transnational influences on policy making left behind by the documentation of the Anti-Opium League and connected private actors. "The attempt, it must be remembered, is to be made at a time when the Central Government has largely lost the power to impose its will upon the provinces. The authors of the movement are, however, confident of success, and China will deserve and doubtless receive much sympathy in any serious effort she may make to stamp out the evil."[42] To Britain, the "essential" and so far unfulfilled condition was "that the Chinese Government should give proof of their bona fides in the matter."[43]

They did not need to wait long. The imperial opium edict ordered the provincial establishment of anti-opium societies, knowing full well that this type of organizational unit would be recognizable to British observers accustomed to the SSOT and its partners. The institutionalization of anti-opium sentiment, in turn, would help convince Whitehall of China's willingness and ability to enact opium prohibition, a central bone of contention for the Foreign Office before Grey. Lack of British trust based on the Qing's lackluster law enforcement and Chinese popular disregard of law abidance had prevented a diplomatic accord for years. But on the basis of the edict, and for the first time in the history of British-Chinese relations, an agreement was reached that phased out the opium trade from British India to China on a ten-year plan. Concluded in 1907, the Sino-British agreement decreased British Indian opium imports and Chinese domestic opium supplies, each by an annual rate of 10 percent until 1917.

The 1907 agreement was not without its ironies, considering the overwhelming emphasis of anti-opium lobbying on foreign supplies of opium as the cause of China's woes. The accord, however, split political responsibility for opium's presence into equal halves, namely British Indian opium imports and Qing domestic opium cultivation. Since the 1880s, domestic opium supplies had grown to rival the foreign product, approximating import substitution. Chinese poppy cultivation made farmers' livelihoods dependent on local demand. This accrued considerable costs to Chinese poppy farmers, some of whom would resort to armed resistance against poppy eradication following 1907.[44] As a political program, Chinese poppy cultivation had historical roots of its own, although it has since been carefully eclipsed by the nationalist memory of universal revulsion against opium that is itself the product of anti-opium mobilization. But in June 1894, the young Sun Yat-sen, claimed today as a founding father both of the Republic of China on Taiwan and the People's Republic of China, had proposed domestic opium cultivation to Li Hongzhang, albeit in vain. Sun had argued that "in the future, when opium cultivation has become widespread, it will surely preempt the profits from Indian opium. . . . Once we have preempted the profits from Indian opium, the British will voluntarily stop importing it, and then we can stop planting it. If at that time we issue a decree prohibiting the consumption of opium, we can end this scourge of more than a century in a short time. So promoting the planting of poppies is actually the beginning of banning opium."[45] By 1907, this economic strategy had obviously paid off. With the central supply route from British India to China under attack, the beginning of the end of opium trading was in sight.

WHAT ENABLED this diplomatic breakthrough was not merely a change of political attitudes but the synchronicity of massive overlapping lobbying campaigns that reached into the very heart of decision-making circles in London, notably parliament and the Foreign Office. It is worth remembering that the principle of British-Chinese reciprocity of opium suppression hailed back to Tang Shaoyi's proposal, presented by Zeng Zixe and Xie Daren to Alexander of the SSOT in 1891.[46] More fully than any British or Chinese official source, the annual report of the Anti-Opium League published in the *North China Herald* the complex backdoor lobbying that broke through the existing legitimacy of the opium trade, thereby facilitating the bilateral agreement. Qing legislation became a cause for celebration in the international public sphere. "Orders were issued to the Grand Council of state to prepare regulations for its prohibition."[47] Jordan received his "sympathetic action" and, for seeking "to deliver this nation from the thralldom of a mighty curse," had put "the British Government . . . itself in the foreground of the Anti-Opium movement," the League argued.[48]

Even without foresight, the Anti-Opium League was well placed to offer the first narratives of anti-opium success, with a lobbying record that stretched back more than ten years. In December 1896, a preliminary branch in Suzhou near Shanghai had convened the first meeting for an integrated China-based anti-opium lobby, while a Provisional Executive Committee took charge of the Anti-Opium League's first major publication. Edited by William Hector Park, the chief surgeon at the Suzhou Hospital, the survey was titled *Opinions of over 100 Physicians on the Use of Opium in China*.[49] "Based on the questions asked by the Royal Opium Commission," the revisionist assessment combined the "scientific" method of the Philippine Opium Commission interviews with the wealth of missionary information-gathering in China to bring Chinese opium consumption, the Royal Commission's blind spot, center stage.[50] DuBose developed the

American-Chinese aspect of the international opium problem far beyond the American Philippine aspect of the colonial opium problem, an important basis for American-sponsored sinocentrism of the first antidrug summit in 1909.[51] In Washington, President William McKinley, Theodore Roosevelt's predecessor, and Secretary of War Elihu Root paid serious attention to DuBose's prohibitionist proposals for the Philippines.[52]

Despite its title, *Opinions of over 100 Physicians* included Chinese anti-opium fighters of different professions. Named only as Li, general manager of the Suzhou Salt Gabelle, a vital source of Qing imperial revenues, Li in his preface urged London to assume its responsibility to act in concert with the Zongli Yamen.[53] "The woe that comes to China through opium," Li explained, "was not only recognized by the government but every one that uses it is aware of its hurtfulness." In accordance with opium's damage to both the state and the people, as argued by Prince Gong, Chinese anti-opium opposition had to combine the political and social dimensions of the problem. "When both rules and people are of one mind it could easily be accomplished."[54] It almost sounded as if Nicolai's judgment of Japan was coming close to realization in China.

In summer 1906, the Anti-Opium League contacted Senator John Tyler Morgan of Alabama, who had furnished DuBose with an advance copy of the Philippine Opium Commission report. Morgan was asked to help coordinate a meeting with Alexander of the SSOT, initially at the summer resort of the Anti-Opium League in northern China. When in September 1906 Rockhill, the American minister in China, offered to "do all in his power to render aid" for a meeting between Alexander and DuBose, the place was relocated to Beijing. DuBose had his traveling expenses covered, "nearly doubly met by the gift of the Treasury of $56 gold from three gentlemen in South Carolina—cotton manufacturers—and by Mr. Alexander" of the SSOT, "turning over $32 silver given to him personally to visit Peking."[55] Rockhill, by "forwarding letters to the High Mandarins and in zealously promoting the Anti-Opium cause," also secured an appointment under "special instructions" for Alexander at the Waiwubu. Tang, then its vice president, remained vocal in his support for an explicitly international anti-opium front: "We need at this time help from everyone in every way."[56] In return, Tang asked the delegation of the Anti-Opium League to "keep him informed" of anti-opium movements "in the West and in this country, hoping explicitly that this transnational cooperation would spur local anti-opium mobilization, "that there would be begun through all the villages and hamlets a preaching crusade against opium, so as to reach the unlearned populace." Tang requested the dispatch of medical doctors to open anti-opium refuges: "The Christians need to help the smokers."[57]

To the Anti-Opium League, there was "one distinguished feature of this opium reformation which delivers twenty-five millions from the annual consumption of 100.000,000 pounds avoirdupois, and that is, the humanitarian provision for the unfortunate habitués of the pipe and the splendid display" of national benevolence.[58] The multiplication of opium refuges made for a "splendid display." Two years later, T. Gracey, who had compiled Bishop Nicolai's biographical sketch, helped by heaping praise on the opium refuges in Shaanxi, Chengdu, Sichuan, Hong Kong, Guangdong, Hebei, and "even" Manchuria.[59] Behind these social relief organizations, the institutional form of an anti-opium society indicated the novelty of Chinese society caught up in one of its most historic, symbolic, and visceral social reforms: "The Chinese Anti-Opium Societies" in Suzhou and "their network of branches throughout all the provinces," the League acknowledged, "are now at their zenith of influence."[60] The imperial edict's strategy had worked out.

As DuBose reported in a private letter, copied to the Society of Friends, his Waiwubu interview was first "long delayed" before translating the anti-opium pressure of Nanjing consultations straight into Qing legislation, namely the Opium Regulations of November 22, 1906, authored by Tang. The regulations specified that in the case of noncompliance with the imperial order to cease poppy cultivation, the Qing would threaten with land confiscation. Rewards beckoned for those willing to suppress poppy cultivation ahead of the imperial schedule. Second, Tang's regulations required smokers to register themselves and their consumption rates. The third demand required smokers under the age of sixty to reduce their amount of opium consumption by 20 percent each year, with public denunciation of their names following noncompliance after a generous ten years. The fourth demand ordered the closing of opium dens within six months and the sale of pipes within a year. The fifth prohibited the opening of new opium shops. The sixth prohibited morphine and offered free distribution of anti-opium remedies, followed by the seventh demand: an explicit call on the state to form anti-opium societies, with official support guaranteed. In contrast to disparate attempts to organize local anti-opium societies in the tradition of landed-gentry associations, such as Guo Songtao's *Zunxinghui,* the Respectful Action Society of 1879, the newly decreed anti-opium societies constituted a state-led campaign of mass mobilization.[61] The eighth demand ordered Qing officials under the age of sixty to cease opium consumption within six months and those above the age limit to stop opium consumption within half that time. The ninth announced the intention to cooperate with the British minister and signaled that even in the absence of British support, domestic opium suppression would continue. The tenth and final demand ordered the governors-general of all the provinces to proclaim and enforce the imperial prohibition.[62]

The Anti-Opium League hailed the prohibitions as the "Ten Anti-Opium Commandments" and did not fail to celebrate a second edict, which gave imperial sanction to Tang's legislation. Opium prohibition was "now the law of the land."[63] To assist in the Qing's enforcement of its own rule of law, the Anti-Opium League offered its best skills: the distribution of anti-opium publicity. It immediately ordered the reproduction of Tang's Opium Regulations, printing within the first year three thousand copies in Chinese; ten thousand in English; thirty thousand for the supplement of the *Nanfangbao* paper; a semiannual published report; and copies of the correspondence the league had received from the four governors-general. After this printing frenzy, the Anti-Opium League's message was sobering: "Our Treasury is empty."[64]

To prevent the financial breakdown of an overstretched publicity campaign, the league continued in its annual report in the *North China Herald,* "it is only necessary to mention the fact and at every city where foreigners reside some friend of the cause will be appointed to collect and forward monies to Dr. W. H. Park," in Suzhou, the editor of the *Opinions of Over One Hundred Physicians,* who did not shy away from writing an anti-opium memorial to the Qing emperor himself and served as an adviser to the Society of Friends, the Quakers.[65] A "worthy example" for fund-raising was Reverend J. D. Adams, an "anti-opium lecturer" and chairman of the Anti-Opium League's Annual Meeting in 1907, whose private correspondence with DuBose was transmitted to the Society of Friends.[66]

Contrary to the classic dichotomy between international influences on the late Qing as cultural imperialism in disguise and nationalist rebellion as a counter, the transnational anti-opium campaign after 1906 merged into the nationalist renewal of Chinese society that remained compatible with a Qing Manchu regime and Western sympathies—a combination that few other movements of the 1900s shared. "The national rise of the patriotic spirit has for its focus the abolition of opium," the Anti-Opium League announced. As Manchu officials decreed policies in the interest of public opinion and popular health, and imperialist drug peddlers could claim to have changed their ways, both appeared absolved from past misdeeds.

Qing officials like Duan Fang supported the publicity swirl, which exceeded the public response to the abolition of the examinations system as recently as 1905. "The Government has planked its efforts at reformation on its power to break the cruel yoke of the 'worm evil,'" Du Hai, the governor-general explained, "and there is no question of the ultimate success of the movement."[67] For the Anti-Opium League, this confluence of transnational policy pressures and their combined effect allowed a reenvisioning of the late Qing society and its state, more than once criticized to be impervious to change and caught in the past: "Here we have a despotic government and a democratic people uniting to save the most ancient of nations."[68]

The Anti-Opium League did not stop with the grand gesture of upgrading the late Qing empire in foreign eyes. Readers' expectations were directed to the details of Qing law enforcement. "The first step in gradual emancipation is the closing of the dens," a demand that exposed the league's naïve or hyperbolic expectation that within months all—that is, "several hundred thousand"—opium smoking establishments across the Qing would be closed. But international trust, the principle that had led to the Anglo-Chinese agreement of 1907, seemed more essential than ever. The closing of opium dens proved "that the Government and the people are in earnest: the smoking is reduced thirty three per cent, and China's young men are saved from becoming victims of the habit."[69] Chinese sincerity, even in the eye of the foreign beholder, remained a guarantee for political success.

According to the new opium licensing system, purchasers of liquid opium in stores were now assigned to groups of ten for mutual security and subject to police search. The legal demand, as per Tang's Opium Regulations, was argued to prove "that the Chinese Mandarinate is suited to the Chinese people."[70] Even Imperial Maritime Customs, the primary institution of British informal empire, assisted enforcement of prohibition, leaving no opium-smoking staff after July 1.[71] Meanwhile, liaisons between the Anti-Opium League and Qing officials extended beyond Tang and Zhou. When DuBose used his stay in Beijing to pen another anti-opium statement, the American legation assisted to transmit it to Yuan Shikai, who forwarded it to the Qing Grand Council on November 11, 1906.[72] This access supplemented the provincial governor's connection to the Guangxu emperor and Tang's connection to the Waiwubu.

Unilateral pressure proved significantly inferior to the multinational flexibility of lobbying. Tang's attempt in October 1906 to convince Sir Robert Hart at Maritime Customs to raise the opium duty to an exorbitant 150 taels was similarly rejected as unlikely to inspire other governments to embark on an opium control course.[73] Tang's direct appeal to William W. Rockhill, the American minister in Beijing, in January 1907 for a unilateral U.S. anti-opium initiative against Britain was rejected by the American government as an imbalance of American and Chinese obligations. Rockhill insisted on distinguishing between the formal American renunciation of the opium trade of 1844 and its enforcement.[74] He did, however, recognize Tang as a key figure on the transnational front. In October 1906, Tang's first contact with DuBose materialized, after a month of waiting, through Rockhill's mediation: "Yes, I am deeply interested as an anti-opium advocator and grasp firmly the hands of those who have the same feeling."[75]

As in earlier cycles of anti-opium mobilization, teams of opposition proliferated. The coalition between the Anti-Opium League and two Chinese governors-general spawned three anti-opium resolutions at the Centenary Missionary Conference in Shanghai on April 25, 1907.[76] Alexander was stuck in Nanjing, "detained here by indisposition."[77] The resolutions were forwarded by the Medical Association and by Arnold Foster, "whose review of the British Opium Commission Report gave him undying fame." For almost a year, the Society of Friends had hoped Foster would act as liaison and spokesman for a "united expression of opinion," to convey to Qing officials "the willingness of Britain to withdraw from the trade."[78] Although Foster's response was positive, he simply saw no need, absent "clear signs of slackness on their part."[79] In late December 1906, he first met Alexander and took "charge of the memorial to be presented" in Shanghai. The opium question "is in excellent hands," Alexander noted in his journal on December 24, 1906, only minutes before five o'clock, when the Russian mail office in Hankou (Alexander's preferred trans-Siberian service to keep the Society of Friends in London apprised) closed.[80]

Third and most importantly, the Centenary Conference took up another set of anti-opium resolutions by the International Opium Commission, the new name confusingly given to the Philippine Opium Commission. Written by Bishop Brent and presented by Bishop Graves—the chairman of the conference's Executive Committee—this anti-opium pact aimed at international antidrug legislation, moving to a multilateral level with Qing legislation just in place and the Anglo-Chinese agreement still to be signed off in December 1907. In Alexander's own report, the timing is described in detail. On May 12, 1907, "on the closing afternoon," the participants of the Centenary Missionary Conference, breaking with Puritan abstinence from work on Sunday, adopted a resolution urging that the subject of international opium control be brought before the Second Peace Conference in The Hague in the Netherlands, to open a month later, on June 15, 1907. "Only adopted in a very attenuated sitting, by 33 votes to 28 (or 27)," with "great pressure at the close" of the conference, the resolution passed with "just enough time" for the final vote, ironically, "on the observance of Peace Sunday [on militarism]." Alexander himself did not "think the subject at all relevant," preferring to anti-trafficking as a peace-building measure an international anti-opium accord in its own right.[81]

Despite Alexander's personal reluctance, the proposal did reach the Hague Peace Conference, and three times no less. The anti-opium resolution of the Centenary Missionary Conference in Shanghai was cabled to The Hague, London, and Washington—the telegrams costing about $300—and also by mail to Tokyo, as DuBose reported separately. At the suggestion of the Anti-Opium League, Zhou Fu wired the Chinese representatives in The Hague, who worked under the direction of John W. Foster, former secretary of state under president Benjamin Harrison from 1892 to 1893 and now in Qing service, where he was welcome because of his advisory role in the peace negotiations of Shimonoseki and his opposition to the U.S.-Chinese exclusion laws. At the Peace Conference in The Hague, Foster's grandson, John Foster Dulles, had his diplomatic debut as his grandfather's secretary-clerk, at age nineteen still a junior at Princeton University and a far cry from his later post as President Eisenhower's secretary of state from 1953 to 1959.[82]

It is important to recognize that transnational channels of political pressure were used by Qing officials in reverse direction. Zhou Fu, just before his transfer to Guangdong, pushed DuBose by "urging action in response to the action of Great Britain," Alexander noted in his invaluable journal letter on his Asian anti-opium tours. Zhou "had learned of this privately" through Dr. Park from Suzhou, one of the organizers of a massive medical anti-opium petition at the time. A deputation of the Canton Anti-Opium Societies contacted Alexander as well as Zhou, with a photograph that seems unfortunately lost. Thus, the consolidation of anti-opium policies across the Qing empire was not in any immediate conflict with the presence of transnational mediators and interested anti-opium parties.

Distant observers testified to the global lateral effect of the late Qing's radical turn against opium. A certain Dr. Grave from a Quaker family in Baltimore learned to rethink his China perceptions through these transnational exchanges, grasping that China's new militarism in fact strengthened the anti-opium cause. "Young China is determined to defend herself against European aggression, and the example of Japan has shown her that this is impossible whilst the opium habit prevails, hence a powerful reinforcement of anti-opium sentiment." To himself, Alexander noted that the resulting dilemmas for foreigners were a price that had to be paid for an anti-opium breakthrough: "This makes it very difficult at once to oppose the opium habit and militarism, at least in public, it may be that our work for the latter will have to be in private conversation. I trust we shall be given the needful wisdom and guidance day by day."[83] These circles of transnational lobbying also extended to Dr. Ho Kai, an early revolutionary coconspirator of Sun Yat-sen. Ho Kai explained to Alexander that great armies will lead to a Chinese civil war, a prediction that preoccupied Alexander after his departure.[84] Five years later, the dynasty would fall in the Xinhai Revolution.

WHILE CHINA braced for the revolution, British parliamentary pressure creaked under radical legal opium reform. Although typologically democratic and not by imperial decree, anti-opium lobbying in Britain did not differ radically in substance or in timing. Merely five years after the Nanjing interview of May 30, 1906, the house of Commons passed the anti-opium resolution, which condemned the opium trade to China as "morally indefensible," repeating the 1891 motion but also demanding the government to bring it to a "speedy close." As in the transnational engineering that produced the Nanjing memorial, it took external yet intrusive lobbying to change the terms of the debate rather than going roundabout in circles, as it had for so many decades before. By May 1906, British parliament boasted no less than 250 members of the Society for the Suppression of the Opium Trade. It is no surprise that the anti-opium motion passed without division. Parliament aided in the victory of an anti-opium movement that stretched farther back in time and across space than most supporters realized.[85]

Before the 1910s, civil anti-opium movements originating in China, England, the United States, and the Netherlands had suffered from a lack of representativeness and authority. China before 1911 was still an imperial polity. Political reform had to legitimize itself by coiling up the channels of an elaborate bureaucracy. Empire-wide anti-opium advances had to be sanctioned by the emperor himself, a top-down approach that prevented earlier amalgamations of nongovernmental anti-opium forces from China and abroad. Delay through state bureaucracies, however, also affected political systems other than the Qing. Until the 1906 parliamentary motion in London, few anti-opium movements had seen political evidence of their effective pressure.[86] American activists had opposed the trade for decades, but despite presidential endorsement of the Philippine Opium Commission's report in March 1906, they had to wait until 1908, when Theodore Roosevelt officially asked Congress to support "the high aim of this international project, placing, as it does, considerations of human welfare above all others, . . . a fine example of what is best in modern civilization and international good will and cooperation." He hastened to add that "such an undertaking can not but appeal most strongly to the American people."[87] The Dutch government had censored and incarcerated outspoken opium activist J. F. Scheltema before his American escape.[88]

In June 1906, a few weeks after both Parliament's anti-opium motion and Zhou's audience in Nanjing, the British Foreign Office first raised the possibility of fundamental change in its opium policy with China.[89] Favorable conditions appeared when the department received word of the rigorous opium prohibition for officials in June 1906, authored by Yuan Shikai, Tang's superior, patron, and personal friend. The communication reached Parliament circuitously, thanks to the monitoring of the *North China Herald* by Benjamin Broomhall, author of several book-length opium treatises; founder of the Christian Union for the Severance of the British Empire with the Opium Traffic; and brother-in-law of Hudson Taylor, founder of the China Inland Mission, through marriage with Taylor's sister Amelia.[90] Broomhall in turn had sent the *North China Herald*'s headlines to Sir Henry Cotton, a sympathizer of Indian nationalists and Liberal MP since the 1906 election victory.[91]

Cotton, despite his aggressive support of the Tibetan intervention, which put him politically at loggerheads with Tang, was as committed as his Chinese foe to the anti-opium cause and eager to keep the Foreign Office fully informed of any Chinese anti-opium initiative. On May 25, 1906, the *North China Herald* reported how Yuan had "put a stop to the opium-smoking habit" of officials and literati under the age of forty. With echoes of admiration for Meiji Japan and the Qing's own 1898 reforms for national renovation, Yuan announced, "When promulgating these instructions to the masses they are to be told about the flourishing condition of the men and youths of Japan as compared with the effete and emaciated state of the great portion of the people of this Empire who are opium-smokers."[92] His reasoning resonated with the Philippine Opium Commission's stark contrast between Japanese youth education and social discipline with the sluggishness of China under the spell of opium. Yuan interpreted Japan's anti-opium success as proof that social anti-opium norms could be cultivated by a strong-willed state. In the eyes of an authoritarian, Japan turned into a model of authoritarianism.

The Foreign Office's response to Yuan's reformist zeal had much praise for the determination of the governor-general of Zhili, "the creator of the new Army of China," as Sir Edward Grey, Britain's foreign secretary, noted with his characteristically red ink.[93] Two months after the Nanjing meeting, on July 2, 1906, Sir Edward Grey received the first signals of an impending Qing initiative against opium, through a telegram from Lancelot Carnegie, secretary at the British legation in Beijing and later Britain's ambassador in Portugal. Tang had informed him privately of Qing preparations for restricting opium use and intentions to approach the British government for negotiations.[94] On July 20 at the Waiwubu, Carnegie and Tang consulted over the Qing's planned anti-opium rapprochement. Tang assured "that legislation would not be directed especially against foreign opium, but against all opium." Still, the final regulations opened with a ban on the foreign drug. The correspondence was widely circulated among officials across Britain's Asian empire.[95]

Carnegie's response was that London would meet Beijing "half-way," referring to the expectation that the Chinese government "were really in earnest," an expectation doubted by the British since the period between the two opium wars (1842–1856), when the Qing's insufficient enforcement had frequently been derided as a sign of China's "insincerity." Tang referenced "several officials" in "India" to inquire about intentions to supplant poppy with hemp and rice. Carnegie did not immediately support Baker's assumptions, remarking that "it appeared from what he [Tang] said that India was voluntarily suffering a loss in order to supply the Chinese with opium, which I could hardly believe," but reaffirmed that on the British-Chinese level, Britain "would help China if she evinced a firm determination to restrict not only the consumption of opium, but also its cultivation, which was yearly increasing in many provinces." In response, Tang confirmed that Qing financial considerations (4 million to 5 million taels) had been taken into account, along with the "possible measures for checking not only the consumption, but also the cultivation of the drug."[96]

Simultaneous, overlapping, and effective as these anti-opium initiatives were, in and of themselves they defied synthesis. The British Foreign Office's recognition of Yuan Shikai's anti-opium policy, the American recognition of Zhou Fu's anti-opium potential, and finally Zhou Fu's recognition of Alexander's anti-opium mobilization on behalf of the SSOT could each be treated as a separate story. But lobbying networks behind the initiatives knew of the causalities, influences, and achievements of persuasion. Transnational anti-opium lobbyists read the overwhelming political response to their clamor as a confirmation that they could craft policies of opium control that captured the anti-opium sentiments of opium societies.

In this spirit, Duan Fang, as governor-general of Hunan, took several initiatives of his own. He liaised closely with an anti-opiumist named Adams and with Joseph Alexander. With the help of an interpreter who had served in the Qing diplomatic service in the United States, Duan Fang used these personal meetings to emphasize Qing enforcement of opium den closures and anti-opium mobilization among Qing officials. With the referral of the British consul, the viceroy granted a meeting to Alexander and a certain Mr. Meizs of the Christian Disciples of Christ on Monday, April 22, 1907, in Nanjing. During the audience, Duan Fang disclosed that twenty-five *daotais* (officials) were meeting at that very moment. The signal beyond political information did not escape Alexander: Duan conveyed the most recent anti-opium news. Meanwhile, Duan asked in return about opium remedies from Malaya and requested research reports from Hong Kong, which Alexander would obtain during his visit to Shanghai through Ho Kai. Finally, Duan bequeathed to Alexander and Meizs two portraits of himself and "a rubbing of a hieroglyphic stone he had procured at Cairo, in his recent journey round the world."[97]

Duan Fang also asked DuBose "to send a second telegram" to Alexander Ivanovich de Nelidoff, president of the Hague Peace Conference, "urging the appointment" of an international commission against the opium trade. Although, as DuBose reported, "the confidence expressed in this request could not fail to be appreciated," Sir Edward Grey—a figure very sympathetic to a bilateral Anglo-Chinese agreement, replied by telegram that "the question was without the scope of the Peace Conference."[98] Like Alexander and Grey, the American response on July 3, 1907, judged that "the subject belongs to a class of limited administrative questions included in the Hague" agenda, announcing at the same time Washington's intention to press for multilateral cooperation against the opium trade, but discreetly separate from other political issues of international law.

Against this background of Chinese mobilization and its international recognition, the U.S. priority of multilateralism to include "all the nations, including China, that have territorial domain or interests in the Far East" revealed a capacious integration of transnational and nongovernmental as well as diplomatic participants in anti-opium mobilization so far.[99] Like the Philippine Opium Commission, Washington aimed to make political use of the transnational exchanges of lobbying contacts, agendas, and synergies that straddled the analytic distinction between governmental and nongovernmental forms of political influence. The first drug-control summit in human history did not distinguish clearly between government officials and their nongovernmental lobbyists, perceived more neutrally as experts.

Behind this effervescence of transnational cooperation between Chinese and foreign transnationals, a vital advantage of this new momentum was British and international acknowledgment, unprecedented so far, that anti-opium expressions reflected "China's sincerity." In this controversial issue, trust gradually accumulated since the Calcutta talks on Tibet underpinned and stabilized the Sino-British accord until its expiration in 1917. To be sure, British and Chinese expectations never fully coalesced. Each side perceived the other party's commitment so extraordinary that the contribution of the other side dwarfed one's own sacrifice. During those ten fateful years, pessimists on each side suspected the agreement to fail and falter. What could seem to Beijing a counterintuitive, even unrealistic bet on British imperialist reform was mirrored by deep-seated British suspicion that China was a regime and society unwilling and unable to deliver on most fronts of social and political change. Whether Britain's imperial pursuit of profit maximization was to blame or the Qing regime's difficulties in keeping provinces under law and order, each prejudice kept participants enthralled—until 1917 proved pessimists on both sides wrong. To London's surprise, Beijing not only managed to keep the deadline but even increased annual suppression rates.[100] Like Great Britain, China had fulfilled its obligations under the agreement, maintaining an equal measure of political progress and diplomatic reliability. But as Chinese responsibilities were fulfilled, British India's responsibilities rose, prefiguring the battles of legitimacy raging through the League of Nations in Geneva in later years.

The International Opium Commission and the Inauguration of Global Drug Control

When Great Britain, Germany, France, Holland, Japan, and China accepted the American invitation for the International Opium Commission (IOC), nongovernmental organizations such as the Anti-Opium League perceived these developments as more than an initiative among states. The league knew, thanks to Zhou Fu, of broad Qing support for the 1907 agreement. More importantly, it welcomed the cosmopolitan perception that the opium trade as a shared problem would "bind both the Orient and the Occident to the extirpation of this evil."[101] On the pages of the *North China Herald* and other major newspapers, international public expectations were fed advance information on French colonial preparations for Asian prohibition as well as German denials of any involvement in the drug trade through Qingdao. Like the Philippine Opium Commission before, the Anti-Opium League sought international comparisons that confirmed political anti-opium positions as feasible, as when it received word of the "deep sympathy" with "the noble efforts of your League in the meritorious campaign against the opium curse" by Wilhelm II of Prussia.[102] Britain, the Anti-Opium League reported, had been "induced to undertake the suppression of opium in the Straits and in Ceylon."[103] Japan, as readers of the Philippine Opium Commission's long or short report knew, pointed "to Formosa as an example for the nations," while "America in espousing the question of China's freedom is the philanthropic leader in world-wide reform." The multiplicity and synchronicity of international support against opium, then, stimulated the thought that "a new era" had begun, "crystallizing in the Anti-Opium movement," speaking to the potential of the world to tackle "moral problems of the human race."[104] Thus, nongovernmental observers were awake to the historical significance of the International Opium Commission, contributing to the summit's international prominence before it even opened.

Prior to the IOC's opening in February 1909, the agenda widened from international opium to international drug control. "The use of morphia has received the earnest attention of the Executive Committee" of the Anti-Opium League. "Since a duty of Tls. 3 per ounce was imposed by the Imperial Customs the smuggling of this drug has been wholesale." The league exposed morphine manufacture in China's treaty ports. In protest, the league lobbied Senator John T. Morgan concerning morphine, "with the request that he forward the same to the State Department," with Washington assenting.[105] Encouraged by the Anti-Opium League, Duan Fang pressed for analogous anti-morphine legislation, together with the governor-general of Jiangsu, who had not come in contact with the organization.[106] When in January 1908 DuBose contacted George Ernest Morrison—the former *Times* correspondent in Beijing, who would attend the IOC in an advisory capacity approved by the British and Chinese delegations—the anti-opium lobbyist thanked the journalist for "the power of your cablegrams on opium" and pointed to the power of public opinion to move governments to press Washington, London, and Tokyo toward "execution" of antidrug treaties, now including both opium and morphine. From transnational lobbying to political enforcement, international pressure subjected state action to the scrutiny of a sensitized public sphere.[107]

Preparations from the Centenary Missionary Conference and the plea by the Anti-Opium League at the Second Hague Conference to address opium control had merged nongovernmental coalitions of anti-opium lobby groups, which supplemented the international rapprochement of governments. Always ideologically related, the Anti-Opium League of DuBose and the International Reform Bureau of Wilbur Fisk Crafts became institutional kin.[108] Crafts spoke in Shanghai as the representative of "Washington in the interests of Anti-Opium," while Alexander acted as the representative of the British Anti-Opium Societies.[109] Crafts, born in 1850, eight years after the end of the First Opium War and eight years before the Treaty of Tianjin, aspired to be "a sort of unofficial diplomat-at-large, seeking not the advantage of one nation but of all, through the promotion of those moral and social reforms which history proclaims are the real question of life or death to nations." The tension between acting as an officially "American" delegate and the disavowal of national interests did not pose a dilemma to him. As illustrated by the thirty-three books on international social reform that he had published by 1902, he perceived the American advantage in addressing international problems to be impartiality, contrasting with British complicity.[110]

Crafts's access to Japanese dignitaries ranged from Prime Ministers Itō Hirobumi and Ōkuma Shigenobu to Hayashi Tadasu, the architect of the Anglo-Japanese alliance of 1902; Yuan Shikai, governor-general of Zhili Province in China; Liang Zhendong (Liang Pixu), first secretary to the two Qing princes Chun; and Zaizhen and Tang Shaoyi, Yuan's top adviser and confidant since their days in Korea.[111] The International Reform Bureau's link to Tang Shaoyi was strengthened through the Bureau's Asia delegate, Edward Thwing, a missionary long based in Hawaii. At the IOC, Thwing was designated the International Reform Bureau's special secretary of China. Wu Tingfang, the Chinese minister in Washington, endorsed Thwing's mission to the IOC as the representative of the Anti-Opium League, the audience of a "special meeting" at the Chinese United Societies Hall in Honolulu, learned on October 25, 1908.[112] Bishop Brent, formerly of the Philippine Opium Commission and now propelled into the chairmanship of the International Opium Commission, described the idea in bold terms: "No country will ever again be able to pursue an avowedly selfish policy regarding colonies. Our aspiration and ideal will set a new political standard to nations."[113] Homer Stuntz, the Episcopal bishop who had cooperated with Brent and Crafts to take down proposals for a Philippine opium farm, described the position almost verbatim: "America ought to be an example to the nations about."[114] In the world of public international relations, the example of Japan ceded some space to a new American assertiveness, disproportionate to the length of its actual experience with opium control.

From February 1 to 26, 1909, the IOC convened in Shanghai's Palace Hotel, today known as the Swatch Art Peace Hotel (Heping Fangdian). Situated at a corner of Nanking Road and the Bund, the venue bordered on the promenade unrivaled across Asia as an architectural testament to Western privilege, gracing like a tiara the International Settlement, the crowning achievement of Western extraterritorial superiority. No other borough in China came closer to the social, legal, and cultural features of a European colony. The diplomatic quarter in Beijing certainly could not compete with its pride.[115] Three years later, Sun Yat-sen, as China's first provisional president of the newly proclaimed republic, would celebrate the victory of the Nationalist revolution here. Beyond the symbolism of Western architecture, investment capital, and clientele, the hotel offered itself to scores of journalists and their photographs, whose documentation was widely shared, up until the centennial of 2009.[116]

Like China's first elevators carrying Palace Hotel guests to their rooms, firmly supported by 188′ × 325′ concrete rafts, which kept the building from sinking into Shanghai's alluvial soil, expectations at the IOC ran high in the penultimate year of the Qing dynasty.[117] Optimism emerged especially in a *longue durée*. Since the First Opium War, perceptions of the trade and the definition of political responsibilities for it had shifted dramatically. Two generations after Lin Zexu, the opium commissioner of indelible tragedy, the International Opium Commission of 1909 forwarded a new anti-opium ideology, carrying a global, political anti-opium consensus.[118] Continuities of kin highlight the substantial change between the two poles of political contestation around 1840 and 1909. Lin's grandson, Lin Bingzhang, rose as a Chinese paragon of the antidrug fight, much acclaimed by anti-opium parties in China, the United States, and elsewhere as president of the Anti-Opium Society in Fujian Province.[119] In a parallel Indian lineage, the anti-opium trajectory was illustrated by Indian tycoon Dwarkanath Tagore, who ensured in 1841 proper compensation for the opium burnt by Lin Zexu and the property of British Indian opium trading companies, including his own Carr, Tagore and Company. Dwarkanath's grandson Rabindranath Tagore would be perceived to condemn the "death traffic" in opium twice: in Bengali in 1881 and then in the 1920s, when Indian anti-opium activists protested the official representation of the British Indian opium delegation at the League of Nations in Geneva.[120]

Although the United States showed greater transnational and diplomatic determination than European and Asian parties to the IOC, an exclusive focus on American ambitions and achievements obscures the political value of China's newfound centrality in the global fight against the drug and international recognition of that centrality in symbolic, economic, and political respects.[121] The attraction of public opinion played a key role in translating this centrality into reputational leverage in negotiations of China's international obligations after 1909. Duan Fang, governor-general of the Liangjiang provinces that were west and south of the Yangzi River, today's Jiangsu, Jiangxi, and Anhui provinces, had been appointed the Qing's chief delegate to the IOC. Duan Fang, tasked to give the opening statement, addressed first the criteria of China's observable credibility and sincerity in its poppy eradication program since 1907: "Up to the present progress has been made in reducing the area under cultivation of the poppy plant in the various provinces."[122] Previously the aim of anti-opium critics, now it was the Qing government's policy goal "to eradicate a poison and a bane to mankind." The universal recognition of opium's social, emotional, and mental harmfulness had moved IOC participants "to put aside all prejudices of nationality and race, and be guided solely by that world-wide philanthropy and enlightenment which have brought about this International Conference."[123] The IOC served as one among numerous settings where Duan upgraded the Qing for international public opinion, as the following year at China's first nationwide exposition, the Nanyang

Exposition for Encouraging Industry (*nanyang quanye hui*) in Nanjing, meant to coincide with the "Festival of Empire" Exhibition in the Crystal Palace of London.[124] Like Duan, Tang Guoan, a Yale-educated Chinese delegate and advocate of Chinese overseas education, explained public opinion as a force of social validation. "Public opinion is now at a high pitch. The determination of the people is risen to a high degree. It is a well known fact that such intensity is difficult to maintain over an extended period. The public mind cannot be centered for a long period of time upon a single reform."[125]

IOC delegates committed to the anti-opium cause invoked public opinion publicly as a moral check to opium policies. Dozens of telegrams by NGOs congratulated the IOC even before it had officially been opened. The visibility and alertness of public opinion intensified the need for international cooperation. Between January 31 and February 17, telegrams from the Commercial Association, the Association for the Investigation of Opium Suppression of the Local Government Bureau, the Anti-Opium Society, and educational societies in Suzhou; two anti-opium societies and two charitable institutions in Quanzhou; the central Anti-Opium Association in Canton; seventy-four branch associations in Guangdong; nine anti-opium associations, twelve philanthropic associations, and the Girls' School of the Methodist Mission in Fuzhou; the Anti-Opium Society of Chuanshi; representatives of the Anti-Opium Society in two districts of Fujian Province; all presidents and members of the Anti-Opium Society in Zhangzhou, Quanzhou, Xiamen, and South Fujian, as well as from the Advisory Bureau in Shansi, were received.[126] Expressions of support by foreign professional bodies included the exchange with the Shanghai Missionary Association; the president of the S. L. Baldwin School of Theology, W. A. Main; the representative of the World's Woman's Christian Temperance Union in Shanghai; the Young Men's Christian Association in Tokyo; and the Belgian consul general in Shanghai.[127] Here, multilateralism appeared to comprise the governmental and nongovernmental dimensions of global support, extending the range of stakeholders beyond the limited domain of diplomacy.

Just as NGOs validated governmental progress, the IOC took special care to highlight Qing anti-opium commitment through explicit recognition of anti-opium progress. The first IOC resolution read in full: "That the International Opium Commission recognises the unswerving sincerity of the Government of China in their efforts to eradicate the production and consumption of Opium throughout the Empire; the increasing body of public opinion among their own subjects by which these efforts are being supported; and the real, though unequal, progress already made in a task which is one of the greatest magnitude."[128] Subsequent resolutions urged each delegation "to take measures for the gradual suppression of the practice of Opium smoking in its own territories and possessions" and the restriction of opium use to medical purposes only. Both the medical harmfulness of opium and the illegitimacy of unchecked international consumption had been officially accepted by all powers. China's foreign settlements were included in the seventh of its resolutions, thereby affecting the legal sphere of extraterritoriality, one of the core privileges of imperialism in China. The closing of opium dens in extraterritorial settlements constituted the first move toward a rollback of the Western imperial prerogative to decide all rights and privileges autonomously, without pressure to bow to Qing preferences.

Adding to the public international influence of anti-opium lobbyists, the very composition of the IOC was rife with political uncertainty. As most administrations around the world lacked opium officials that could be sent to the IOC, the majority of delegations were composed of perceived opium experts. The Qing and Britain sent some diplomats to strengthen domestic lines of political accountability as well as representational clout at the IOC, thereby forcing their delegates to represent a state. European delegates from Southeast Asia—Singapore and British Malaya, Hong Kong, French Indochina, the Dutch East Indies, and Siam—coped with a record of opium monopolies that they knew would not sit well with an international IOC mandate of opium suppression. The Canadian delegate, William Lyon Mackenzie King, later known as the tenth prime minister of Canada, joined the British delegation after having pressed for the first anti-opium legislation at home.[129]

The political change they all faced, now that they had accepted the U.S. invitation, could not be reduced to mere lip service to an anti-opium ideology and conciliating public opinion.[130] Public opinion had already stimulated legislative precedents that forced several Asian opium regimes into trajectories of opium control that created inconvenient comparisons to averse regimes. When on May 4, 1907, British parliament ordered the Hong Kong government to close down all opium dens in the colony, it did so because it recognized "that it is essential in dealing with the opium question in Hong Kong, that they must act up to the standard set by the Chinese Government."[131] Beyond British perceptions alone, as subsequent years would prove, the Qing regime had turned from an international symbol of political inefficiency into a progressive power. Although only a few years away from its fatal demise, the Qing's own opium prohibition forced the British empire to follow suit, despite its supreme commercial clout and military might.

The depth of British rethinking, as well as the scope of political change that it necessitated, distanced itself from Palmerston's skepticism of Qing prohibition as mere hypothesis. Hong Kong, the British colony secured as spoils of the First Opium War, lay officially outside the trade from British India to China. Despite this seemingly extraneous disposition, obligations emanated from the "standard set by the Chinese Government." Reputational comparisons created political interdependence between polities hitherto in enjoyment of autonomous opium politics. Similarly, Ceylon and the Straits Settlements were drawn into the British prohibitionist turn. In 1908, William Lyon Mackenzie King, then Canada's deputy minister of labor, pleaded for analogous opium prohibition in Canada in a letter to Rodolphe Lemieux; Lemieux forwarded the Canadian proposal to Sir Edward Grey, the foreign secretary in London. King referenced not only British India, Hong Kong, Ceylon, the Straits Settlements, and the international expectations their opium regimes faced but also Japan, whose prohibition was described as "prohibitive and effective." This wording stemmed from the Philippine Opium Commission, whose own publicity had evoked a growing international consensus of public opinion before such a consensus existed as a political fact.[132]

Thus, the anti-opium momentum that became visible at the IOC in 1909 saw an early potential in Asia for international policy diffusion, among colonies and imperial spheres commonly considered in blissful isolation from one another. But the policy choice of one state carried an immediate impact on that of another when compared side by side by external, public observers. Mackenzie King was cognizant that policy diffusion reacted to the transnational production of state reputation. "Other instances of legislative enactments to suppress the opium evil, and protect individuals from the baneful effects of this drug, might be given, if further examples were necessary," King wrote. "What is more important, however, than the example of other countries, is the good name of our own."[133]

The very argument that opium control could become a powerful criterion for a state's reputation was borrowed from elsewhere. Back in British Columbia, Peter Hing of the Wa-Ying Yat-Po, the Chinese Daily Newspaper Publishing Company, and concurrent secretary of the Anti-Opium League in British Columbia, had pressed Mackenzie King to take an "interest in the social condition of the Chinese" in the province, pointing to the perception that "opium is a social evil in this world," which the Anti-Opium League shared with the Moral Reform Association of Canada.[134] Mackenzie King adopted the perception of these demands, their language, and their political implications without major amendments. "In enacting legislation to this end," he wrote, "the Parliament of Canada will not only effect one of the most necessary of moral reforms so far as the Dominion is concerned, but will assist in a world movement which has of its object the freeing of a people from a bondage which is worse than slavery."[135]

King helped publicize the change of British imperial attitudes. Formerly, British imperial reservations had denied Qing imperial prohibition to exert any kind of pressure on Britain. As the *Times of India* of May 8, 1908 summarized one version of the commonplace critique: "Edicts emanating from the Chinese Government have not always fulfilled their purpose," conditions under which "sacrificing a large portion of Indian revenue to meet the wishes of China in respect to the opium traffic" were regarded as "Quixotic." But King insisted that China's new prohibitionist advance left "no margin of doubt" that it was "thoroughly in earnest. . . . It is this fact that has caused opinion at home to veer round." The consequences of this unprecedented anti-opium development, the *Times of India* argued, warranted equally radical policy change on the British side: "It would be little short of a scandal if after all the sympathy expressed for a people struggling to free themselves from the habit, the indiscriminate sale of opium were to be permitted in British settlements." A glimpse into the original article beyond King's excerpts made the point even clearer. British imperial prohibition, it argued, "shows very clearly the change that has been wrought in public opinion on this subject. The credit is mainly due to the Chinese themselves."[136]

International recognition of China's anti-opium progress, the international imperatives it issued, and public expectations for the IOC, however, did not ease the political task of finding common ground among IOC participants, a motley and incoherent group of nongovernmental and official representatives, observers, and advisers. Brent's perception of his own role as chairman was not without private apprehension. "I was unanimously elected Chairman on the nomination of Japan and Great Britain," regarding it "an honor which I am far from courting, and which I shall be glad to see passed to someone else."[137] Brent, a personality ironically not given to public relations, saw the IOC as "full of interest though of course full of anxiety," adding with audible caution: "My colleagues are excellent men, much better posted in the broad question than I myself." He referred to the transnational more than diplomatic delegate Hamilton Wright, a medical doctor thoroughly versed in international law, and Charles Tenney, Chinese secretary to the American legation in Beijing. In the absence of opium officials in either the American Philippine administration or at home, this trio constituted the American delegation.[138]

As public opinion raised the stakes of the IOC within international society, a belief in the potential of timely decision making to enact global ethical change raised the stakes through historical time. Brent trusted "that our deliberations will issue in some wise resolutions and recommendations and that eventually there will be an International Conference to arrange a Convention as definite as that of the Brussels Conference which acted upon the slave trade."[139] Specific policy templates undergirded the analogy between slave trading and opium trading. The American proposal to enact the right of search on ships suspected of carrying opium and the investigation of unlawfully flying a foreign flag, although rejected by British opposition, built on the parallel agreement of July 2, 1890, at the Anti-Slavery Conference in Brussels.[140]

Historical expectations and public sensitivities, both strategically cultivated, did provoke the first international displays of governmental self-defense in drug-control politics. The Japanese delegation was a case in point. Along with Miyaoka Tsunejirō as chief commissioner and Dr. Takagi Tomoe (T. Takaki)—a former student at the Koch Institute in Germany, director of the medical school in Taiwan, and chief of the Sanitary Bureau of the Government of Taiwan—it also included Dr. Tahara Yoshizumi, director of the Imperial Hygienic Laboratory in Tokyo, and used information-sharing as a display of sincerity. The Japanese government operated three chemical laboratories, in Tokyo, Osaka, and Yokohama, with opium manufacturing for medical use confined to Tokyo. Dr. Tahara was therefore introduced as "the only man who is responsible for the production of opium for medicinal purposes in Japan."[141]

The Dutch delegation served as another example of the immediate impact of antidrug criticism on state reputation at the IOC. A. A. de Jongh, inspector-in-chief and head of the Opium Régies in the Dutch Indies and chief commissioner of the Dutch delegation, "being proud of the Java Régie system, and also deeply convinced of its useful effect in other regards," recommended the Netherlands monopoly system as a model to be adopted by China in the last session.[142] The Americans and the British employed similar tropes, employing policy interdependence, so amply displayed in the terms of the Anglo-Chinese Agreement of 1907, as a way to minimize reputational exposure. "Before 1909, treaties had been signed and agreements had been made between individual nations looking to a satisfactory adjustment of the needs of the situation existing at a given time in relation to the nations involved; but not concerted action by all of the nations had yet been taken when the International Opium Commission, recognizing the presence of a world problem, in 1909, endeavored to take a step forward in its solution."[143]

For the Qing, the Philippine Opium Commission served as a welcome precedent for IOC discussions, substituting for the more explosive British-

Chinese history of opium encounters, which China pledged not to reopen. Instead, the positivism of a Philippine Opium Commission pledge offered an uncontroversial opportunity to nudge opium-trading European powers further along a path already chosen. "The manner in which the Governments of the countries concerned have set about to stop the consumption of opium in their colonies and dependencies such as Taiwan, Annam, the Philippine Islands, Java, etc., has been to undertake the monopoly of the sale of opium therein, a procedure which China alone has not yet put into actual force."[144] Apart from the two Hague Peace Conferences, China gained the opportunity to engage for the first time as an equal member of multilateral diplomacy, outside postwar negotiations of a peace or diplomatic apologies for Chinese massacres forced from abroad, the two most depressing modalities of public Qing foreign relations since the opium wars.

The Chinese challenge was much appreciated by Brent, as he confided to a friend: "The inside history . . . will make interesting reading some day."[145] Further details can be gleaned from the private correspondence of George Ernest Morrison, the *Times* correspondent turned unofficial IOC delegate, who revealed some of the internal dynamics in response to the possibility of a Chinese opium monopoly. "Things are not going well at the Conference," Morrison reported from Shanghai to the British minister Jordan in Beijing, misnaming the nonbinding commission as a binding conference, like many contemporary commentators. "A very aggressive American Hamilton Wright who is wholly ignorant of conditions in China has formulated a resolution which will be submitted to the Conference recommending . . . that the Regie or Government Monopoly System is the best for dealing with opium restriction." Accordingly, "the Powers should consent to such alteration in the existing Treaties with China as will permit China to establish this monopoly," Morrison argued. "The Revenue derived therefrom is to be wholly devoted to combating the evil until *the Powers are satisfied* that China has done so when she may devote the Revenues so obtained to other purposes of General Revenue. This Resolution seems to me to be wholly mischievous and I will oppose it bald headed. Dr Wright showed me his resolution, 15 in all, and I communicated them" to Sir Cecil Clementi, the head of the British delegation; James Bennett Brunyate, the acting financial secretary to the Government of India; and Alexander Hosie, former opium commissioner in China, "who will be well prepared to discuss them."[146]

Sparing Duan Fang and the Qing for proposing the opium monopoly in opening statements, Morrison focused his criticism on the Americans. Brent's private correspondence reveals—beyond the general difficulty for a Chairman "to rule over thirty-five Commissioners representing thirteen Powers!"—that the focus on the American proposal was sufficiently serious to warrant counteraction.[147] On February 18, Wright's resolution was dropped "under joint pressure" of Morrison and H. P. Fletcher. Morrison described Fletcher, another unofficial attendant of the IOC, as "a close friend of mine," knowing already that he would be replacing Rockhill as the new American chargé d'affaires in Beijing. Fletcher, in turn, had seen Jameson, "a leading American merchant," who was not registered in the IOC but aligned with Brent.

Brent urged attendees to distinguish between European colonial experiences with opium monopolies and their applicability to Qing China, refuting the former's universality. "The "Regie" undoubtedly is the best system considered abstractly, but like all fine instruments it needs a skilled hand to use it. China could not control a Government monopoly. It would be simply an opportunity for graft," the sinophile argued.[148] "A calm review at this distance leaves me fairly well satisfied with the work of the Commission, considering that Great Britain angrily refused to discuss the ten year agreement with China in the sessions of the assembly." As to the Waiwubu, it "was weak, very weak." Even if Qing officials refrained from referencing the opium wars, other IOC participants were obliged to include their psychological effect and historical legacy. "The Chinese fear the British, who are discerning enough to recognize the fact and behave accordingly." The fault for China's diplomatic inferiority, particularly in a uniquely new setting of multilateralism under formally equal conditions, lay elsewhere. "I admit that China as a nation is exasperating to deal with, but the European countries have done nothing but rob her under the shelter of treaties and agreements." Reflecting the standpoint of the Philippine Opium Commission, which criticized European opium regimes to elevate the Japanese example, Brent was privately unequivocal: "England has not been the least offender."[149]

By embedding international public scrutiny in the world of international politics, the IOC expelled existing models of opium administration from the range of legitimate choices. Off the table were opium monopolies. If run by Beijing, it "would be most injurious to China," as it would be "perpetuating the use of opium not checking it," Morrison wrote to Charles Tenney, the third American delegate. "It is deplorable that China should be given assistance and encouragement to perpetuate the opium evil as it would be perpetuated if she were permitted to establish an Opium Right."[150] Meanwhile, Morrison used his connection to Tenney for correcting other influences, as when he suspected Tenney's superior Hamilton Wright to have fallen prey to statistical misinformation on the opium regime of the Dutch East Indies. "The Java figures seem to me very significant and quite inconsistent with the pious declaration that the object of the system is to check the consumption of opium." In a warning against false intercolonial lessons as a result of doctored opium reports, Morrison pointed out that "Dr. Wright" had been hoodwinked by the Dutch promotion of the Javanese opium system "as being the ideal one for introduction into China."[151]

Morrison's own intervention against a Chinese opium monopoly enjoyed significant support among American diplomats in China. "Rockhill I may add disapproves of the resolutions put forward by the American delegates at the Opium Commission especially those recommending a revision of the existing treaties forbidding China to establish a Government Opium Monopoly." Diplomatic criticism, however, mistook results of transnational lobbying for political posturing, underestimating the positions taken as products of external forces rather than simply stances taken freely. Rockhill approved "the British attitude and considers that it would be false kindness to give China unrestricted liberty to deal with the Opium evil for her first act would be to establish a monopoly and create new revenue which would mean perpetuation of the evil which she set herself to eradicate. Fear of 'losing face' before the world is the best incentive to China's continuing her efforts to suppress opium."[152]

International public opinion came to function as an audience before which states could lose face. To Brent, this confirmed its role as a core criterion for establishing the international legitimacy of international drug control. The IOC showed how the previous antidrug discourse impinged on the diplomatic boundaries in which imperial and colonial states could legitimately pursue economic practices. While the production of international public opinion in response to the opium trade became the profession of anti-opium lobbyists and their organizations, Brent soon realized that public anti-opium opinion did not sustain itself. "The press does not seem to have grasped the significance of the Opium Commission. In the first place we were greatly limited by the inherent character of the commission." Affording a rare perspective on the paradigms of the IOC, Brent reflected, "My idea was a Conference with plenipotentiary power, but England preferred the milder scheme. A commission can do nothing except recommend. Then men fail to realize that Great Britain held the key in her hand, but chose the role of passive resistance rather than that of constructive leadership."[153]

International legal obligations were essential to the institutionalization of a coordinated system across borders. "From the first I urged upon the Commission unanimous action. I knew that England would not give heed to a majority vote but that unanimity among thirteen nations would compel her into line even if she were inclined to hold back. Consequently no resolution was put to the vote which did not carry *nem. con.*"[154] The main priorities, however, had been accomplished: "Smoking is condemned as pernicious and something to be suppressed—compare this with the Royal Commission's attitude." As to the security aspect, smuggling was to be checked at the port of export, not entry—"a new point in international law."[155] The IOC opted to agree on non-binding resolutions, a strategy insufficiently appreciated by public opinion, always more eager for results than accepting of political compromise. But the international legal level was not dropped by the IOC, merely postponed.

China's subordination was never total; the long list of imperial entitlements manifested itself in spheres of influence that gave unquestioned economic dominance to the technologically, militarily, and legally superior foreigners. Western political administration, however domineering, remained confined to control of the political economy, without ambitions to supplant China's political system—a task too unwieldy for the imperial powers of the day.[156] Short of colonization, Shanghai symbolized the focal point both of the opium trade and hopes for its abolition, which looked with pride on the 1907 agreement as a first bilateral step between Britain and China. It was, above all, in China that opium had become a surrogate and synecdoche of Western imperialism.

Beyond the IOC but coinciding with its prospects, political and economic measures to rein in the drug threat pointed to deeper currents of social alarm over public health. The narrowly political search for the lowest common denominator for a mutually agreeable legal framework remained limited in its participatory integration and its effects. But in fields outside, antidrug alarm unraveled almost uninhibited. Parallel to simultaneous struggles against plagues and other epidemic damages to human health, the fight against opium and other addictive drugs was driven by the fear that the physical and mental prosperity of societies was under threat in numerous settings around the world. "Addiction" was not limited to the borders of any one state, whether national or colonial, whether European, American, or Asian. The drug problem and its intrinsic globality spurred a social and epistemic widening of observers in the field of science.

In France, a simultaneous surge of research in narcotic addiction and treatment arose, while policy relevance and legislation set in with a delay in the 1910s.[157] In Britain, following the SSOT, the British branch of the WCTU reported these public drug fears in France in a British publication. The same piece noted how the antidrug agenda seemed to pull together disparate a circle of medical experts, including the French Republic's foremost expert on venereal disease, Jean Alfred Fournier, who famously clashed with Professor Petersen from the Russian delegation at the Health Congress in 1899. Other opium critics were Édouard Adolphe Drumont, editor of the *Libre Parole,* anti-Semite, and notorious self-declared enemy of Alfred

Dreyfus; former prime minister Jules Simon; journalist-celebrity Emile de Girardin; the "Premier Père Blanc canadien" and missionary in Uganda, John Forbes; and Aimé Humbert, the first general secretary of the International Federation of State Regulation of Vice.[158] In Switzerland, too, Carl Hartwich, a professor of pharmacognosy at the Polytechnic Institute in Zurich, wrote the first scientific comparison of opium-consumption patterns. Despite knowledge of large-scale opium consumption and traffic affecting French Indochina, British Malaya, the American Philippines, several Pacific islands, North America, and Peru in the 1890s and despite the Swiss professor's support for the anti-opium movement in the Dutch East Indies, the study did not envision a political strategy for reducing opium use.[159] Where international public opinion and scientific research fell short, an exogenous influence impelled the codification of the drug-control agenda into international law: the anarchy of the First World War.

CHAPTER SEVEN

THE DRUGS OF WAR

Germany, Japan, and the Morphine Threat

THE BEGINNINGS WERE innocent enough. At the Universal Exhibition in Paris in 1856, Francesco della Sudda—director of the Central, Civil, and Military Pharmacy of the Ottoman Empire, known in Turkish as Fayk Bey—and his son, Giorgio della Sudda, promoted opium vigorously as the best of its kind.[1] Likewise, in global comparative evaluations of opium quality, the Levant emerged as a preferred source in German market assessments, with the drug from Smyrna ahead of its competitor from Constantinople. Both outrivaled a long list of candidates on the global market: Thebaian and Alexandrian opium from Egypt and the varieties from Persia, East India, and Greece. The Ottoman government's opium monopoly, introduced in 1830 and dissolved in 1850, turned Constantinople and Smyrna into the "central stockyards" of Europe's own drug trade in the second half of the nineteenth century.[2]

The perceived commercial certainty of a high-quality supply raised European enthusiasm for opium from the Ottoman domain to new heights. The Ottoman Empire's agricultural plenitude, so vividly captured by French historian, Middle East scholar, and later Romanian citizen Jean-Henri-Abdolonyme Ubicini, evoked a productive base connecting the markets of Europe, Asia, and Africa. It held commercial opium fantasies in thrall and boasted with copious quantities of rice, corn, and, in no particular order except that of the connoisseur, "yellow seed, madder root, valonia, oils, different kinds of wool, coal, tobacco, dried fruit, perfumes, and rose oil."[3]

Among these, the Ottoman poppy had been known in Europe since the sixteenth century, when Pierre Belon proposed cultivation in France, Germany, and Italy. By the 1870s, the *Medical Times and Register* in Philadelphia effused about "the practical monopoly which Turkey and Egypt hold of the European and American opium markets."[4] Had western European societies developed a culture of opium consumption, the Ottoman product could have become a staple of daily life, like the Ottoman tulips that now grace the inventory of Dutch national culture.[5]

But instead of entering European consumption in functions similar to Middle Eastern "politesse and Muslim hospitality," the drug became most attractive to European pharmaceutical scientists and their discreet research behind closed doors.[6] A leading German handbook for pharmacists from the early 1870s stated that "the production of opium in Germany and England has not yet moved beyond an experimental stage, although prepared opium reaches up to 18% morphine."[7] In Britain and the United States, opium-based medicines like laudanum and meconium had been in circulation since the 1870s. Chemical handbooks known as pharmacopoeia circulated across western and southeastern Europe, Scandinavia, the United States, and Japan.[8] From botany and race theory, scales and categories of scientific taxonomy entered the drug industry. From raw material extraction to industrial output, the world of narcotic drug industries was thoroughly, even aggressively, competitive. In continental Europe, Levantine opium was consistently ranked as the highest among commercial grades, superseding four other varieties. As a result of European scientific appreciation and appropriation, German pharmaceutical research, among the most advanced for much of the nineteenth century, harnessed opium supplies to numerous new purposes. As research and development spurred opiate production, raw opium supplies fueled new structures of investment for opiate distribution and sale around the world. Crucially, the long genesis of the German drug industry made it vulnerable to the sudden scandal in the First World War when, in East Asia, morphine trafficking moved into the global headlines, triggering its political suppression at the Paris Peace Conference of 1919.

In September 1881, a report on agriculture in the Smyrna region of the Ottoman Empire insisted that from a trade perspective, "no crop in Anatolia is as important as opium," an analysis commissioned by the Foreign Ministry of France.[9] Like the Germans, the French eyed with fascination the opium flourishing in the Ottoman hinterland, especially the *incemal* variety concentrated in the provinces of Sivas, Ankara, Mamuret-ül Aziz, and Salonica. Disappointing by comparison were the opium samples from Persia, East India, Greece, Italy, southern France, and French colonial Algiers, which had all been scrutinized. None of them yielded a morphine content above 10 percent, slightly more than half of that produced by the Anatolian variety.[10] Governments were not the only candidates embarking on a global opium quest. Growing numbers of experimental poppy cultivators tried their luck in Melbourne, Australia; Württemberg, Germany; England; and Illinois. Japan did not miss the global appeal of opium's scientific value. In 1896, Nitanosa Otozō, of later fame as an opium king, was an ambitious man at age twenty-one, when he petitioned Japan's Home Ministry for a license to grow opium. The government granted his request.[11] Inherently, ratings of opium quality elsewhere were dampened by climatic fluctuations that exposed poppy agriculture to systemic risk.

But the most systematic progress in scientific applications of opium research appeared across the Ottoman-German connection. To reach German pharmaceutical factories, opium traveled from Constantinople and Smyrna via London, Rotterdam, and Hamburg. British and Dutch transshipment points were supplemented by opium supplies from the south. A second line of supplies ran from Smyrna via Trieste, the only free port and maritime access of the Austro-Hungarian empire. Deliveries arrived in the shape of "opium cakes" or "opium loaves," each covered with a layer of docks and sorrel seeds to prevent them from sticking together in tight packaging aimed to maximize the volume of each shipment. Each cake contained between 7 and 15 percent morphine.[12]

In a western European context of intermittent warfare and almost ceaseless national vigilance, even pharmaceutical production was not separate from foreign policy. The nexus between opium supplies and warfare emerged first in the pharmaceutical handbook by Hermann Hager, who argued for the strategic role of opium as medical painkillers for troops. "Since opium," if stored properly, "does not perish for several years," Hager reasoned, "it would be a reasonable demand, considering the eventuality of war, that pharmacists always be obliged to keep bulk opium stocks."[13] Medical criticism from the last German-French war necessitated new legal guarantees for replenished national opium stocks to prevent another "total dearth of opium," as experienced in 1870. During the Franco-Prussian War, German pharmacists and agricultural experts from Württemberg in the South to Silesia in the North experimented with opium cultivation, which proved equivalent in morphine content and harvest output to the older, Ottoman competitor.[14] Hager even suspected that "the French had bought up the best opium" in the "war that they wanted," correlating a nation's military strength and the availability of opium. The provision of opiate painkillers, a "cardinal medicine" like arsenic, would have "brought many a brave soldier home," Hager lamented with a view on the human cost of opium shortages. "Opium is always needed and most of all in wartime."[15] Hager could have further referenced the American Civil War as the crucible of American morphine addiction to bolster his argument.[16] Forty years later, when the First World War not so much knocked at the doors of Europe than knocked them down, Hager's advice was validated by the military's record demand for opiates. Here, the functionality of opium in national security became the reverse of the Qing experience: not a foreign drug threatening one's own security but one's own drug strengthening the physical condition of those tasked with national defense.

The joint exigencies of scientific progress and industrial competence gave an unprecedented boost to Germany's pharmaceutical industry after the Franco-Prussian War (1870–1871). Julius Jobst, a leading German pharmacist, sought a different kind of advice from Ottoman experts. Thanks to English translations of his work, Jobst's reputation reached Italy, Austria-Hungary, France, the United States, and Canada, engaged in stiff competition in opium production with Australian John W. Hood and American George W. Kennedy in a virtual race of pharmaceutical productivity.[17] Jobst's research on bark from Dutch Java and Bolivian seeds made him the leading German manufacturer of quinine. Quinine and morphine manufacturing occurred within the same pioneering companies. This success benefited the Vereinigte Fabriken (United Factories) and the Zimmer company until its absorption by the pharmaceutical giant Boehringer, soon a leading producer of morphine.[18]

Until the 1900s, East Asia's eclipse from the connections of western European research and development in narcotic drugs owed more to European than to Asian isolationism. Homer of the eighth century BCE, Pliny the Elder of the first century AD, and Greco-Roman antiquity dominated European scientific perceptions of opium's historical significance. By contrast, the opium wars remained obscure or entirely absent. Asia became linked to European morphine interests only through the IOC of 1909. In Shanghai, the German government had understood that the intermediate trade in opium included and implicated the German commerce in East Asia. Great Britain, France, and Germany acted as Europe's transshipment centers for opium, like British Straits Settlements and Hong Kong in Asia.[19] In China, Germany functioned less as an outsider than as an inferior player. It shared neither the considerable ambition of Britain and France in extracting rights and privileges from the Chinese government, nor did it enjoy the clout the United States won through transnational connections to the Chinese government. Given German inferiority, however, German consular correspondence from across Asia shows that its information-gathering in international opium politics and its understanding of the multi-imperial tussle over opium control was broadly on a par with British, French, American, and Chinese documentation.

To appreciate the global fallout with German drug production, it is necessary not only to outline the scientific rise of its pharmaceutical industry but also to position German opium policy amid a variety of global political arenas. Not expecting to escape from the pressures of international drug control, Germany's lower political stakes brought their own benefits in the immediate aftermath of the IOC of 1909. In its lone colony of Qingdao, opium imports had already been banned by the time the Qing government asserted opium control in neighboring territories. In the long term, Qingdao would gain far greater fame as a production center for Tsingtao beer, not opium. In the international politics of opium, it became a German listening post more than an active trading hub.

Germany's relative distance to the politics of opium trading allowed for cool-headed observation and early adjustment to the Chinese and transnational anti-opium momentum around the IOC of 1909. In 1910, reports from the German general consulate in Simla, responsible for British India and Ceylon, explained to the government at home that American-Chinese amity had synchronized their respective anti-opium positions for the IOC. Encouraged by their successful efforts to curb opium use in specific territories in 1909, the Chinese government had redoubled its efforts to implement opium control in the interior and the closing of opium dens in international settlements, earning wide acclaim. Concerning possible inter-imperial tensions, German consular officers identified the emerging fault lines of conflict succinctly. On the one hand, the U.S.-Chinese coalition, rooted in transnational anti-opium lobbying and on full display at the IOC of 1909, pushed IOC recommendations further into binding commitments under international law. This coalition was increasingly pitted against a British Indian press apparatus as a key pressure group of British colonial policy, countering "interfering philanthropists at home and elsewhere." Specifically in India, German diplomats learned to understand that the loss of opium revenues would plunge European, not only British, financial interests into turmoil.[20] It did not dawn on them, however, that the consequences for German business could ever move into the center of a global controversy.

While in its naval rivalry with Britain, German political ambitions confirmed deep-seated tensions, German engagement with the international opium problem in the 1900s and 1910s did not limit itself to anti-British opposition, sharing in China the position of a colonizer. In urging for colonial legal adjustments to the new imperative of drug control, German concerns even saw value in China's reassertion of foreign policy control. Accordingly, in March 1910, the German government decreed the suppression of opium consumption in each and every territory. Diplomatic posts across the German colonial empire received the same telegram ordering enforcement in October.[21] Checks that colonial legislation abided with the so far non-binding demands of the International Opium Commission ranged globally from Qingdao in China to Buea in Cameroon and Windhuk in German Southwest Africa. Consultations with international positions vis-à-vis the impending International Opium Conference in The Hague were reported to Chancellor Bethmann Hollweg, among others, from Tehran, where the German minister was on close terms with the Persian Foreign Ministry and informed of Persia's opium economy as the main reason for its diplomatic caution at the forthcoming International Opium Conference in The Hague. In Ottoman Pera, the German embassy was on equally intimate terms with the Turkish government, receiving confidential information about Turkey's reasons for abstaining from the Hague negotiations. Beyond Middle Eastern affinities, German legislation revealed a global colonial perspective, including the implementation of opium control in territories as far as German New Guinea, where the main opium house was shut down.[22]

Both political change in drug control and social change in anti-opium mobilization caught the attention of German observers. Among the European empires, the interdependence of opium problems overseas raised the desirability of mutual policy adaptation, resulting in a kind of European closing of ranks through external cooperation outside Europe. The Dutch Anti-Opium Bond of 1890 started a new round of recruitment and mobilization in late 1910. Under the guidance of Baron Schimmelpenninck van der Oye van Hoevelaken and treasurer Jonkheer Wittert van Hooglandt, the Anti-Opium Bond was heartened by the work of the IOC.

Until 1917, cooperation and information exchange between Germany, Britain, the United States, and Japan permeated all stages of drug production, from the global search for the most suitable raw opium to the sale of opium-based pharmaceuticals. When the British Imperial Institute recommended Indian opium, favoring it over the Turkish variety for the production of morphine and codeine because of its higher percentage of narcotine, the leading journal of Germany's chemical industrialists routinely reported the recommendation, despite its obvious competition to Germany's favored opium source and the even more apparent benefits to India as a potential supplier not only of opium but of the more concentrated and more lethal morphine.[23]

In a global posture of active engagement, then, the German government watched, listened, and documented scientific, commercial, political, and social changes as they contextualized the drug business in unforeseen ways.[24]

As the web of mutual anti-opium adaptations grew denser, attributing the order and direction of inter-imperial support became analytically more difficult and politically less meaningful. The Germans appeared sympathetic to Dutch anti-opium mobilization, the Dutch were openly supportive of China's anti-opium campaign, the Chinese relied ever more trustingly on American partners, and the Americans praised Germany for its anti-opium stance at the IOC.

By THE TURN of the twentieth century, the aspiration of the Kaiserreich's pharmaceutical industry acquired new significance as both a colonial and a European domestic competitor. In 1898, German cocaine, produced from the conversion of the alkaloid of coca leaves, was patented. South American coca leaves dropped proportionately in international scientific evaluations. Dutch coca producers started shipping coca leaves to Germany for processing. In Darmstadt, Merck Company did not take long to overtake Dutch cocaine manufacturers in the Dutch East Indies. When the Dutch secured the largest market share for cocaine through the new *Nederlandsche Cocainefabriek* in Amsterdam in March 1900, the German Merck Company shifted part of its manufacturing to newly acquired plantations in Java in the Dutch East Indies.[25]

No pharmaceutical company other than Merck ran its plantations in the Asian colony of another nation while operating manufacturing plants in the United States, from Midland, Michigan, to Rahway, New Jersey. Up until the First World War, Merck's preeminence in morphine, codeine, and cocaine production was boosted by products developed alongside, such as hydroquinone—an X-ray and photographic chemical reaching 75 percent of its market—and phenol, required for synthetic pharmaceuticals. At the height of the war in 1917, Merck's recapitalization jumped from $250,000 to $1 million; its sales reached more than $8 million in 1917 and 1918, with employees numbering around seven hundred. The company's exports to Allies continued even in wartime.[26]

The First World War did not entirely erase the internationalist orientation of industrial interests that crossed combatant lines. The front-matter advertisement of German standard journals for pharmacists, such as the *Pharmaceutische Rundschau,* praised products of U.S. pharmaceutical companies, such as Kola from Western tropical Africa, made from coca and manufactured by Parke, Davis & Company, alongside broadsides from the U.S. branch of the German-based Merck Company in New York. Today's more famous Coca-Cola reached consumers for the first time in 1886, advertised among others as a cure against morphine addiction.[27] Meanwhile,

Japan knew of the Dutch-German competition for the cocaine industry in the Dutch East Indies and decided to enter that market. Japan purchased coca leave supplies that were not sent off to Amsterdam for shipment to Japanese cocaine refineries in Tokyo.[28] The Japanese pharmaceutical industry itself emanated from a combination of German and American pharmaceutical cooperation and commercial partnerships with German morphine manufacturers up until the First World War. Japan's premier pharmacist was Hoshi Hajime, who graduated in politic science from Columbia University in 1901 and founded the Hoshi Pharmaceutical Company in 1911. As with German companies, quinine and morphine production went hand in hand, both of which Hoshi pioneered in Japan in both production and sale. In the memory of Japanese-German relations, Hoshi is today known and praised for his efforts to bail out the Relief Society of German Academia (Notgemeinschaft der Deutschen Wissenschaft) from its financial straits in the 1920s with generous donations, benefiting scholarship holders like Fritz Haber, Max Planck, and the discoverer of nuclear fission, Otto Hahn, who was famously devastated when he learned in English internment of the American atomic bombs on Japan.[29]

Like its German competitors, Hoshi Pharmaceutical Company drew on overseas bases to build its pharmaceutical empire, as in the purchase of 30,000 cho (73,519 acres) of land in Turmayo in Peru and 500 cho (1,225 acres) in Peru's Pumpayacu, which pointed to the diversifying quest for pharmaceutical production, market expansion, and the continuing internationalization of research and development. Neither the old concept of colonial resource extraction nor a relationship across an early Global South fit the phenomenon of Japanese overseas expansion in South America. Hoshi's agent in Peru used his business trip to Latin America to recruit to Japan Peruvian and Japanese personnel, in the latter case a Stanford graduate who had settled in Peru at around 1910 and turned himself into a premier expert of Peru's cinchona supplies.[30] From the viewpoint of these Japanese pioneers, their quest for pharmaceutical supremacy was no less global than those of their competitors. When German pharmacists were told in their handbooks that "Persian opium rarely reaches Europe," part of the reason (which they were not told) was that the Persian product went east, to Qing China and Meiji Japan.[31]

As in Germany, where Merck's advanced technology for cocaine production from Java had begun displacing Peruvian coca leaves from the market, in Japan, Hoshi's morphine production replaced the dwindling of British Indian opium supplies after 1913 with a search for Ottoman and Persian opium, with a morphine content, he observed, close to 12 percent. Hoshi proposed to the opium monopoly on Taiwan to switch supplies for Japanese morphine production from Indian to Middle Eastern sources. Despite the logistical risks of long-distance opium shipments, Hoshi made a case for the switch as a cost-saving measure, as domestic morphine production offset the costs of Middle Eastern imports.[32] If Hoshi could be criticized for some aspect of the scheme, it was in how the more addictive morphine as a replacement for Indian opium on Taiwan could possibly align with gradual suppression of drug consumption on Taiwan. Japan's commercial outlook on the narcotic drug business did not lack in globality.

In a Japanese domestic context, there was nothing unsavory about Hoshi's launch into Japan's first morphine production in the early 1910s, facilitated by a divergence between Japan's opium prohibition and the legality of semi-refined morphine. It helped that Hoshi could count on the support of his sponsor, a former student of Robert Koch and, since 1910, director of the Colonial Office, Gotō Shimpei. This connection had enabled Hoshi to acquire surplus stocks of raw opium from the government monopoly in Japan's colony of Taiwan, acquired after the Sino-Japanese War in 1895. That opium monopoly, which stood in stark contrast to Japan's domestic opium ban, was Gotō Shimpei's brainchild.[33] With Hoshi's savvy for morphine production and distribution on a mass scale, Gotō's erstwhile promise of opium suppression as the ultimate goal of the monopoly system on Japanese Taiwan dropped from an indeterminate promise to an implausible idea. Consolidating the young Japanese colonial empire after 1895 was directly linked to the global reach and potential of its research and industry.

But even if German attention to its own global role as a producer of drug manufacturing was captured, this presented only one half of the global political economy of drugs. The other half, especially in the absence of political frameworks of regulation, was the possibility of supplies to trigger demand not only overseas but at home. As it turned out, this dynamic was by no means limited to China or societies with a Chinese immigration population but structurally similar to western European societies. At the IOC and in its immediate aftermath, the German government, the U.S. government, and international public statements largely concurred that, in official words, "an opium question does not exist in Germany; consequently, there is no incentive to submit trade and industry to the restrictions." At the IOC, the German consul general in Guangdong proudly recalled, "The Americans even congratulated us on our circumspect legislation. Hamilton Wright said verbatim: 'We congratulate our German, Austrian and Italian colleagues" that the opium question in their own countries that their prudence of their governments and the discipline of their peoples cause no concerns whatsoever."[34]

After the outbreak of the First World War in 1914, that blissful absence itself disappeared. The Reich chancellor's justification for the first proposal to draft a rule for the trade of opium and other narcotics explained: "For a considerable time now the trade in morphia and other narcotics" has brought to the fore "inadequacies . . . during the war and springing from the war." Those inadequacies of drug control had amounted to an urgent public health crisis. The number of people who underwent medical treatment with morphine and other painkillers had dramatically increased. As a consequence, popular addiction was conceived by the state as a critical case of criminal conduct in wartime. To acquire narcotic drugs by force, German addicts stimulated a budding underground economy of drug trafficking. In turn, the profitability of the trade led traffickers to circumvent legal requirements for production and distribution. By 1917, the government knew that morphine and other narcotic drugs were available "at any time and in any preferred amount, without major difficulties," according to the government surveillance of the German drug problem.[35]

So far was the Prussian state removed from its proverbial sternness that as late as September 1917, the minister of the interior still defended the legitimacy of a profitable morphine trade by "particularly trustworthy" wholesale traders with legal permits.[36] A policy so flexible was not unlike the British Indian opium statements after 1860. Law-abiding German pharmaceutical companies were officially recognized and defended for catering on a minimal basis to legitimate medical demand. Implicitly, German manufacturers were not to be held responsible for the product diverted overseas and were unlikely to distribute drugs for profit. Trust ran deep and oversight remained shallow as the German Imperial Health Office asked the pharmaceutical industry to estimate the value of domestic morphine and alkaloid production without demanding figures from the companies themselves. What the office felt uncomfortable to document officially the Merck Company from Darmstadt willingly confirmed in private discretion or, as the president of the Imperial Health Office acknowledged in a handwritten note on the margins, "in confidence."[37]

The intimacy of shared interests between German state power and the pharmaceutical industry made it likely that British political moves in narcotic drug control would be interpreted symmetrically in Berlin, that is, as a shared interest of the British state and British drug producers. Out of this extrapolation arose the German suspicion that the British proposal to control morphine and cocaine directly aimed at crippling the German pharmaceutical establishment. Analytically, however, the German government's resistance to the international "limitation" of morphine and cocaine production cannot be divorced from its pharmaceutical supremacy with its managerial elite, its access to the highest echelons of power, and its scientific reputation shielded by the state.[38] For which other reason would the government invite representative heads of all pharmaceutical companies repeatedly for consultations, uniformly labeled "Secret," to brace against the anticipated pressures of the Hague Opium Conferences?

German regulations for the sale of morphine and cocaine outside German "territory on the European continent" did not suffer from domestic restriction to pharmacy stores as customers. Even domestically, the wholesale trade allowed for legal sales to state-owned research and educational institutions, as well as any commercial druggist, apothecary, and ill-defined "technical merchants." In German dependencies around the world, the regulation of narcotics sales differed by sociology and ethnic makeup, from Jiaozhou (Kiachow) to German East Africa, from German New Guinea to Samoa, where the legal regime was run by the commissar of the Chinese in Apia. From East Africa to Asia Pacific settings, German drug laws rather neglected morphine and cocaine and focused unmistakably on opium, as if it were a drug of the colonized.[39]

Despite the mix of legal laxity, commercial clout, and political defensiveness, Dr. Rößler, one of the most influential advisers in China policy for the German government, then based at the consulate in Copenhagen, urged that a German exit from the Hague Opium Conferences was not in the cards, even in the face of the British taking aim at German morphine and cocaine. Tellingly, it was not to Britain that Germany should concede but to the new Republic of China in the East, proclaimed in 1912. "China depends in this question on the assistance of the powers and values most highly their cooperation. Great Britain's attitude of rejecting the opium question had caused very ill feelings there for a long time. After England [*sic*] has recently, by taking great sacrifices, aimed at a rapprochement with China, Germany cannot afford to take a position of rejection, based on mere limitations to its chemical industry, and earn the odium of having brought the conference to collapse." Alienating China carried a high price for all imperial powers: "We would, in such a case, be chastised by the opposing side of indirectly favoring morphine trafficking." Directly acknowledging the emphasis of anti-opium protesters on public opinion as a key force, Rößler confirmed: "The opium question [including morphine] engages the public opinion of China to such a degree that we have to fear damage to our general, commercial interests."[40]

In the German political response to international drug politics prior to the first World War, the China-centrism of the international campaign and its almost futurist outlook played a greater role in informing German colonial policy change than criticism of existing opium governance by Britain.

Some, like the governor of Hong Kong, speculated in November 1915 that "an increase in smuggling from Europe to China is to be anticipated" in wartime, causing "the nuisance" of dumping Hong Kong's own opium prices.[41] But apart from this limited financial concern—and in many ways a traditional one in transshipment ports like Hong Kong—neither the German government nor its pharmaceuticals nor, for that matter, the economists engaged with the structural transformation of worldwide commodity trading anticipated how fundamentally and abruptly the war would change the terms of the international debate and the direction of global political scrutiny. Since Britain (including British India) had found itself on the international pillory of public opinion for its opium trade to China in the 1890s, no country had fended off anti-opium criticism successfully by inaction or ignorance.

Although the three Hague Opium Conferences between 1911 and 1915 got deadlocked by a reluctance to ratify the International Opium Convention of 1912, for Chinese observers the "war on opium," once started, was irreversible.[42] The weight of international public opinion was not wholly conditioned by the degree to which it pervaded political motivations. Its success hinged on its external reception by states as a major factor of their international political legitimacy. In an ironic circularity, the respect paid to international public opinion multiplied its power of persuasion.

Failing to rein in the smuggling of German morphine to Asia would cost German diplomacy dearly. Berlin's approach, centered on securing pharmaceutical privilege, underestimated the warning, first communicated by the London Foreign Office in January 1911 and enhanced by Washington in March, that the First Opium Conference in The Hague would condition British participation on morphine and cocaine control alongside opium control. Convening in the Hall of the Knights (Ridderzaal) at The Hague on December 1, 1911, the First Opium Conference extended the IOC's humanitarian and scientific priorities of drug use as social harm into an international legal demand for political responsibility. Morphine and cocaine, it is true, were far more devastating to minds and souls than opium—dark auspices for German pharmaceutical industrialists.[43] To the German government and its council of leading pharmacists, the legacy of The Hague Opium Conferences was nothing other than the beginning of an international encirclement of Germany's hitherto preeminent champions of pharmaceutical science and production. In this light, expanding the mandate of "opium control" to "drug control" smacked of British insincerity. Regardless of whether or not German accusations of British competition under the camouflage of antidrug politics were a correct psychological reading of the British official mind, the resistance expressed articulated the importance

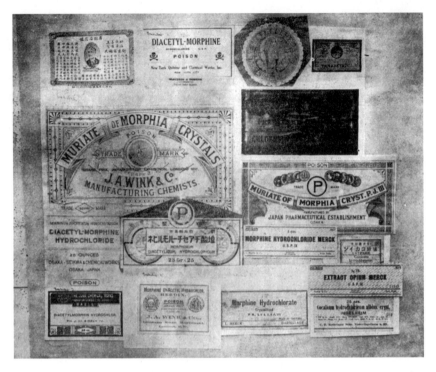

FIGURE 7.1. Contraband morphine, heroin, and cocaine of German, Swiss, and Japanese origin.

Source: The War Against Opium, International Anti-Opium Association (Peking: Tientsin Press, 1922). Harvard Law Library, Harvard University.

that the German state placed in its morphine industry. International drug control was decried as a thinly veiled attempt to distract from Britain's imperial opium business in Asia by finding an agenda that could substitute the opprobrium of international public opinion that Britain had endured since at least the 1870s.

Berlin may have overestimated the degree to which Britain was inspired by European competition instead of Asian concerns over drug use in general, publicly debated especially in the aftermath of the Philippine Opium Commission. Meanwhile, Britain's own morphine producers were unlikely to be spared in a global crackdown through international law, undermining the German suspicion of "drug control" as an exclusively anti-German diplomatic conspiracy. What Berlin underestimated, with serious consequences not only for Germany but for the shape of global drug control after war's end, was the potential of wartime economic anarchy to take advantage of the absence of workable, legal, political, or territorial control. Drug production and distribution did not stop at the borders of the state in the way that laws and their enforcement did at the time. Trade and smuggling, in particular, were inherently more transnational than governance. Drug trafficking held western Europe and East Asia trade together, even in wartime. With the start of the First World War on July 28, 1914, efforts to enforce multinational ratification of the International Opium Convention were cut short. But the war allowed drug trafficking to continue and even rise to unprecedented heights. Revolution and war may well be the seedbeds of transnational crime. Albeit further removed from the gaze of the state, German narcotic drugs created dilemmas not merely within Germany and among Germans but equally in Asia, particularly in northern China. Yet the consequences of the German failure to rein in morphine trafficking would nonetheless be fatal to Chinese public health.

Exposing the global market of narcotic drugs involved international transitions of political responsibility. The transition from German to Japanese morphine became known publicly and attained political sensitivity only when its global political economy had matured. When international opposition against Japanese drug trafficking arose, it exposed to international public opinion Japan's "opium system" (*ahen seido*), morphine trafficking as an offshoot across its colonial empire, and its spheres of influence in East and northeast Asia between 1915 and 1918. Edward Grey at the British Foreign Office was already convinced by 1911, not quite correctly, that "by all accounts Japan is one of the countries from which morphia is conveyed in large quantities, in spite of the preventive efforts of the Chinese Government, into China."[44]

Rather than treating international public opinion as an amorphous, anonymous, and indeterminate phenomenon, it can be analyzed as the product of journalistic initiatives that harnessed antidrug information to recast the very sources of international political legitimacy, with states coming under scrutiny for trading practices routinized for decades.

A far-flung network of journalistic informants emerged to expose the geographic scale, global political economy, and social consequences of the Japanese opium system. One of them was Wu Liande, who had spearheaded the anti-opium movement in Singapore, served as a Chinese delegate to the Hague Opium Conferences, and worked for the establishment of the Chinese National Medical Association in 1915. While working to contain the bubonic plague in Manchuria in 1914, Wu had started communicating with William Collins, his British delegate at The Hague, although Collins occasionally misspelled his name as "Wu-hai-The." Wu produced evidence of ostensible anti-opium remedies that contained, ironically, a high dosage of morphine. Thanks to Wu's correspondence from Harbin, Max Müller learned of the urgency of this new drug crisis in China's Northeast. Müller in turn lobbied Lord Robert Cecil to supply Collins with supporting diplomatic information by John Jordan, the British minister in Beijing. Collins, for his part, read "with great interest the despatches from Sir John Jordan *re* morphine smuggling in China." Alarmingly, Wu argued that "China has been flooded with smuggled morphine, which comes mainly by way of Japan . . . He asked me to find out if it was true that this morphine from Japan came largely from Great Britain."[45] As in previous attacks on the opium trade, it was again individuals active in NGOs accomplishing transnational information-gathering that forced governments to reconsider their practices and policies.

Between the pressures of The Hague and the social crisis triggered by East Asian trafficking, information flows moved almost more rapidly than the drug itself. While Wu conveyed to Collins the unraveling emergency, Bishop Brent, the head of the IOC in 1909 and president of the First Hague Opium Conference, wrote to Collins from Manila in the Philippines. Brent indicated that the Southeast Asian dimension exacerbated Wu's East Asian observations. "He complained that Sandakan, the chief town in British North Borneo, was a great centre for contraband trade in opium in the Far East and in the Philippine Islands." To verify, Collins consulted British Board of Trade figures, only to discover that morphine exports from the United Kingdom to Japan had "increased enormously between 1911 and 1914," using once more, as in the case of the opium trade, Hong Kong for transshipment. In 1911, morphine exports amounted officially to 17,200 ounces.[46]

William Harcourt, the British secretary of state for the colonies, kept a close eye on opium trafficking between Hong Kong, Ceylon, the Malay Archipelago, and 288 square miles of Weihaiwei, leased to the British from 1898 to 1930. He conceded to Collins that "he had no power to interfere in North Borneo," citing, wrongly, the restrictions of the Opium Convention, although they had not yet come into force.[47] Harcourt understood that "most, if not all, the trade in morphine and cocaine was, before the war, in German hands." Collins's information pointed to a more embarrassing source: "In 1913, 252,110 ounces (118,794*l.* value) were, in fact, exported from the United Kingdom to Japan (including Formosa, &c.). I added that it was difficult to believe that this amount could be absorbed by the necessities of 'medical purposes.'" For unknown reasons, he never received a reply.

In 1915, Collins further conveyed this information to Theodore Taylor, one of the lobbyists of the British-Chinese opium agreement of 1907, which spelled the beginning of the end for the British Indian opium trade to China.

Taylor brought the controversy before Parliament in 1915, in response to learning that "the enormous increase had continued in 1914 when the export of British-made morphine to Japan reached the figure of 352,130 ounces (value 143,975*l*.)!" As for the indefatigable Collins himself, he went public in April 1915 with the observation that "China is being drenched with morphia at the present time." By then, it was more than moral objections that scandalized the discovery that Britain should directly aid the Japanese empire, including Taiwan, in perpetrating the traffic in China. Before international ratification of the International Opium Convention of 1912, The Hague framework was already beginning to stick. "It is incredible that anything approaching that amount of morphine should possibly be devoted to legitimate medical purposes."[48]

Despite the British policy precedent of the Anglo-Chinese agreement of 1907, British drug diplomacy at The Hague as the first international experiment of its kind did not endow the government with a unique position of strength. Rather, Whitehall found itself almost immediately caught between attacks on new drug trades, especially in morphine—attacks that were launched domestically on the parliamentary floor and abroad in Beijing. Pressure in Westminster provoked a defensive rhetoric in 1915, the year of the last Hague Opium Conference: "His Majesty's Government are of opinion that it would not be desirable to put the Opium Convention into force pending the deposit of ratifications by all the signatory Powers." Playing for time helped in figuring out an estimated 800,000 ounces of British morphine and morphine salts, worth almost £400,000, delivered to Japan, Formosa (Taiwan), and the Japanese leased territories in China between 1912 and 1915 alone.[49]

Collins understood this predicament. Cocaine, he analyzed, had been chiefly an export article of Germany and the United Kingdom, which had acted as the primary suppliers for East Asia. Manufacturers in Edinburgh and London topped the list. In confidence, Collins had learned by an unnamed informer that "one of the partners in the chief Edinburgh manufacturing company had resigned rather than be a party to so demoralising a trade, but I cannot vouch for this." Even in the face of British complicity, key figures like Collins sided with the international antidrug lobby, rather than with British nationals—a fact that further undermined German conspiracy theories of "British" self-interest. Collins's position was tenable because it enjoyed the support of Müller and others, proving "the wisdom of the consistent policy of Great Britain at The Hague Conference, which maintained that it would be idle to deal with opium (raw, prepared, or medicinal) alone and not include morphine, cocaine, and other drugs liable to similar abuse within the terms of the convention." As in the preceding case of anti-opium politics, the political economy of international drugs became subject to political interpretation that further consolidated the focus on controlling supply rather than demand. As one of the best-informed British delegates of the Hague conferences, Collins agreed "that control at the source is even more important, and more likely to be successful than control of consumption or even of distribution." His hope was that Britain, Russia, Japan, and France might pull along with the United States, the Netherlands, and China with the ratification of the Opium Convention and "in stopping the Far East illicit trade in morphine, since Germany's export trade," by 1916, "is presumably cut off." Here, British perceptions of wartime conditions almost saved Germany massive international criticism, while London knew next to nothing about Merck's continuing wartime gains. However, British benevolence had little to do with it. Yet unbeknownst even to Collins, journalistic plotting ran on a schedule and chose targets of its own.[50]

Despite Collins's centrality, he was not the only node amid the circulation of vital and immediately policy-related antidrug information. This dynamic laid the pattern for League of Nations politics based on antidrug informers. But the publicized antidrug pressures from which Germany was spared fully affected Japan. Between 1915 and 1918, newspapers based in Shanghai but circulated across Asia, Europe, and North America launched an anonymous exposure of the opium system. Morphine trafficking, the focus of the exposure, was immersed in a global political economy of drug production, distribution, and consumption that stretched from Germany and Britain via Russia and India to Japan, Taiwan, Korea, Manchuria, and North China. In structural terms, the opium system combined numerous forms of Japanese superiority, including Japan's attempt to assert hegemony over Indian coastal trade and the eastern end of the Siberian Railway. By the early 1910s, before the First World War, the Siberian mail service opened up as an alternative land route to China and Japan. As journalistic intelligence had discovered, the price for Siberian morphine deliveries was "arranged telegraphically, . . . the mail train being used because of the certainty of its arrival at due date."[51] Japanese formal governance in Taiwan and Korea and Japan's informal empire in Northeast China backed these operations through control, especially of customs.

But confronted with the attack, the Japanese cabinet switched into self-defense for the first time, ordering the abolition of the entire drug-trafficking system. The cabinet did not spare words: Japanese citizens engaged in drug trafficking were chastised for "illegitimate actions" and for becoming the "focal point of foreign and Chinese criticism," as it summarized after a highly alarmed meeting on January 18, 1919.[52] In the past months, extensive English news articles that indicted Japanese sponsoring of global morphine trafficking had passed from translator clerks at the Japanese Foreign Ministry all the way to Hara Kei himself, famously the first commoner to be appointed prime minister and famed figurehead of "Taishō democracy" in the 1910s and early 1920s.[53] In the view of his cabinet, the international press attacks warranted the most comprehensive political countermeasures regarding the drug, seeking to abolish all of Japan's monopolies throughout the empire. Japan's historical record of successful prohibition at home had made domestic anti-opium movements unlikely. Foreign criticism of Japanese drug-smuggling cases jeopardized the young nation's good name on the international scene.[54]

The reasons why Japan could not easily avoid international accusation had to do with the genesis of morphine's political economy, which may be best understood in comparison with that of opium. As a derivative of opium, morphine moved through its own political economy, set apart from opium by the degree of pharmaceutical and industrial expertise required. The political economy of the opium trade had been circumscribed by its Asian dimension. Compared to the morphine trade, the opium trade had a measure of transparency—the main supply line ran indisputably from British India to China. This feature of opium's international political economy had increased the relevance of bilateral agreement, like the 1907 agreement. By contrast, morphine production originated by and large in Britain and Germany, whereas the Japanese pharmaceutical industry offered transshipment and processing points, especially Kobe.

It was only outside Japan's domestic polity, outside even its formal empire, that the drug operations of Japanese big business incited sudden international outrage. The affront took its origins in Korea, Manchuria, and particularly Northeast China. From Osaka to unnamed Korean destinations, Dalny (Dalian), and Shanghai, the global structure of morphine trafficking seemed to satisfy Japanese interests in its informal empire on the Asian continent. Straightforward denial of governmental responsibility appeared unfeasible to mitigate Japan's public relations disaster. As the morphine scandal over Japanese trafficking unraveled and spun out of control, the confrontation between investigators and investigated was uneven in several respects. While the press revelations named the Japanese government explicitly as the primary culprit, the prosecution and, crucially, their investigators remained in the shadows of anonymity, hidden behind carefully guarded correspondents. In the eyes of readers, other journalists in Asia and elsewhere, and the wider public, this imbalance between attacker and attacked did nothing to diminish the clout of the indictment. On the contrary, the fact that an anonymous party launched an avalanche of attacks on the

Japanese government foreclosed the suspicion of vested interests and helped sympathizers of the scoop to cast it as the international voice of the public interest.

To the investigators who gained insight and assayed the inner workings of morphine's global political economy, it appeared implausible that a systematic flood of morphine could elude Tokyo's cognizance. Ignoring or denying the agency of Chinese or Korean intermediaries and collaborators, the article maintained that the morphine traffic was firmly and "exclusively in the hands of the Japanese and is carried on with the full approval of the Japanese Government."[55] Japanese sovereignty in a given territory and the centralized coordination of transportation and postal systems were "essential" to running the morphine industry. The combination of infrastructure control and territorial expansion made Manchuria a suitable setting for sustained drug operations, with Shandong and Fujian as potentially following in its wake.

Once the outlines of morphine's political economy had surfaced, it took only the shortcut of politicization to blame Tokyo for coordinating this public health disaster for Chinese addicts.[56] Unlike international perceptions of Chinese opium smokers abroad in last third of the nineteenth century, Chinese morphine consumers were not seen as racially inferior perpetrators, driven by strange appetites to self-destruction, but appeared to be hapless victims of a Japanese poisoning plot. In the scandal over Japanese morphine trafficking during the First World War, reckless profit seeking clashed frontally with rising concerns over Chinese popular welfare. This vision, produced by antidrug publicity, began acting like a simulacrum of China's first war against opium.[57]

Unknown to the Japanese government, those who aided the exposure of the Japanese morphine scheme included diplomats, doctors, chemical experts, customs officials, missionaries, and at least one spy from numerous countries: Canada, Britain, Singapore, China, and Japan. Those who found themselves on the pillory of international newspapers included Japanese and German shipping companies. Almost one hundred steamers of the Bremen-based *Norddeutscher Lloyd* (North German Lloyd) plied this route, surpassed only by the China Japan Trading Company.[58] In Yokohama, Kobe, Osaka, and Nagasaki, the China Japan Trading Company operated under American aegis, but the information was suppressed in press reportage.[59] The court of international public opinion also confronted postal authorities, petty traffickers, the Bank of Japan, and the Japanese government itself. On the generating and the receiving end of the morphine scandal, the key players recognized that the problem at hand required them to think and act beyond national or imperial dimensions. This had also been true of the global anti-opium campaign, but in the case of morphine, the campaign of mobilization directly confronted European and Japanese governments with the lack of industrial oversight. While the genealogy from anti-opium mobilization to anti-morphine mobilization spoke to continuity, the shifting focus of political controversy now subjected the world's industrial powers to unprecedented scrutiny.

Protestors took first offense with the impression of a massive, unregulated oversupply of the drug. This observation took its origin in investigations of the rampant spread of consumption. Oversupply of the drug market triggered the search for the sources, whether near or far, of drug overproduction and the places of primary agency. The surplus of morphine suggested an abusive excess of power at those sources. More seriously, the overwhelming scope of drug supplies seemed increasingly to rule out the possibility that merely the forces of the market were at free play. As in the case of early anti-opium opposition, suspicion about morphine trafficking as the planned calculation of a drug plot arose not solely from rational motives. The sheer desperation over staggering masses whose health fell prey to morphine addiction made the identification of culprits a moral as much as a political endeavor.

On the end of Chinese consumers, the spreading presence of morphine enhanced the suspicion that its massive oversupply was part of Tokyo's imperial calculus. Behind the addictive features and destructive effects of the drug seemed to lurk a cold craving for revenues, satisfied by the vicious spiral of ever-increasing demand as it permeated Chinese society. Traced back to the sites of morphine production and the routes of its distribution, the morphine scourge involved considerable segments of the administrative infrastructure of Japan's informal empire: the big business of pharmaceutical giants within Japan, Japanese customs authorities and postal services in China, and petty peddlers from Manchuria in the North to the foreign entrepôt enclaves along the China coast.[60]

By deciding to back out of the narcotics business, Tokyo's sudden condemnation of morphine trafficking reflected more than the urgency that often follows the realization of political neglect. Questions of the government's imperial omniscience aside, the documentation of cabinet discussions reveal that Tokyo knew more about drug operations on the Asian continent than it intimated. Still, governmental and nongovernmental initiatives were sufficiently intertwined to warrant the official term "opium system." Despite Tokyo's professed innocence as to why Japanese drug operations flourished—a self-defense that prevailed even behind closed cabinet doors—rolling back the opium system lay very much within, not beyond, the capacity of the imperial state.

That Tokyo took active political responsibility for the conduct of its subjects within the imperial frontier was surprising for two reasons: it contradicted the prior policy of toleration, and it regarded less radical alternative solutions to the problem unfeasible. Reprimanding Japanese subjects abroad would have been easier in political terms and cheaper in financial terms. The cabinet broke with precedent by treating existing political responses as an unsatisfying measure for preventing imperialist deviance. What set anti-morphine mobilization apart was that international press criticism caught Japanese colonial planning at the cusp of an empire-wide scheme for narcotic self-sufficiency, from Taiwan to Korea, North China, Manchuria, Mongolia, and even the Pacific Islands.[61] On the face of it, the First World War did indeed contribute to the collapse of several empires of "the West" and to the stabilization of another empire in "the East." Whereas German, Austro-Hungarian, Ottoman, and Russian imperial ambitions and achievements were rendered null and void, Taishō Japan found its territorial interests firmly fixed on the map. Japan's military record marked an unbroken chain of success since 1895, from the Sino-Japanese and Russo-Japanese Wars to the shared victory of the entente of the First World War, and seemed to confirm Japan's further claim to Asia's championship.

Neither in territorial nor in ideological terms did Japan's imperial expansion show any obvious signs of weakness.[62] The Japanese opium system, for its part, was immersed in and dependent on a series of successful Japanese expansions: the official administration of Taiwanese, Korean, and Manchurian territory; a near-hegemonic position in Northeast China's fractured political economy; and the steady growth of control over the gateways of China's infrastructure. First among them were the customs apparatus, the postal system, and the shipping and railway services, which tied drug production in Japan and Taiwan to the bulk of drug consumers in Manchuria and the China coast. The combination of Japanese strength and vulnerability, then, pointed to a new element of information warfare in the global mobilization against narcotic drugs. As part of this contest, policy makers became, with growing frequency, objects of antidrug mobilization before they transformed themselves into subjects of global antidrug politics.

The long, sustained, and powerful impact of publicists and journalists on raising the stakes of the international political debate over narcotic drugs was not entirely exceptional. As early as 1850, Thomas Carlyle used the pages of his *Latter-Day Pamphlets* for a description of the incipient rise of journalistic influence in international relations: "I hear persons extensively and well-acquainted among our foreign embassies at this date declare that a well-selected *Times* reporter, or 'own correspondent,' ordered to reside in foreign capitals and keep his eyes open, and (though sparingly) his pen going, would in reality be much more effective; and surely we see well he would come a good deal cheaper."[63] More than sixty years later, the war correspondent of the *London Daily Chronicle,* George H. Perris, took stock of the global interdependence of information flows: "All foreign correspondents of leading journals have peculiar sources of information; many of them have considerable influence in the countries where they reside. It was at that time the pride of the *Times* to maintain something as nearly as possible approaching the status of a diplomatic service. [Henri Opper] De Blowitz in Paris and Dr. Morrison in Peking were only two of the notable names in this hierarchy."[64] George Ernest Morrison—former *Times* correspondent in Beijing and recently made political adviser to China's president, Yuan Shikai—had built up an extensive network of correspondents that not only conveyed "information" but played the role of accreditation. Privately disclosing to the German minister in Beijing, for instance, plans for British-Chinese opium inspections was not simply a service of friendship or diplomatic banter; rather it lent credence to Beijing's efforts to clear seven provinces of opium.[65]

Manchuria emerged as the most critical area of Japanese morphine smuggling. In perhaps the earliest anticipation of today's concept of "trafficking," which links drug trafficking and human trafficking, international press criticism forwarded the accusation that Japan fundamentally disrespected the human dignity of Asian peoples abroad. Articles indicted Japanese-induced prostitution from Australia and South America to India, Siam, and the Straits of China and Siberia. Morphine trafficking in China and to a lesser extent Korea seemed to enjoy even greater support and to involve higher returns.[66] It is worth emphasizing, however, that "Japan bashing" in the 1910s was mainly driven by politicization of unstoppable drug movements, rather than by altruistic outrage over the public presence of morphine as such. Sporadic and unsystematic reports of transnational morphine trafficking had surfaced in several papers before. First glimpses of European morphine imports to Hong Kong in the early 1890s created headlines but fell short of a scandal. The same political and international irrelevance haunted scattered reports of morphine on the China coast. Likewise, anecdotal evidence of morphine poisoning was reported across continents but remained nevertheless inconsequential. At age twenty-three, Miss Helen Tombs of Melbourne did not take morphine "as directed" in July 1884, with lethal consequences. Parisian stamp collector and morphinist Aubert, who murdered *philathéliste* Julien Émile Delahaeff over some precious little piece of paper in 1896, could not be tried in court without a morphine injection.[67] The elaborate medical exposition on drug addiction published in 1906 by Paul Brouardel, a pioneer of public health and forensic medicine and president of L'association fran-çaise pour l'avancement des sciences, raised further public attention.[68] Two years later, morphine addiction in China was reported to foreigners for "doing more harm than opium," yet the complaint remained, for the time being, a mere lament.[69]

In September 1912, correspondents like Morrison had identified two heartlands crisscrossed by the drug: Shandong Province in China, "now being opened" just after China had been "closed to opium," and Fujian, the home province of Lin Zexu, now seemingly submerged by morphine from Japanese Taiwan. While the Asian leg of deliveries appeared to be a deliberate scheme of Japanese imperialism, German and Austrian pharma-ceutical production was still known as the recent monopoly holder of the market. Mannheim and Ingelheim were named as headquarters of the Böhringer firm and the origin of East Asia's excessive supplies. Foreign firms in Japan, like Karl Rohde, typologically an institutional inheritance of the age of European imperialism, shared the blame for directing morphine im-ports from Hamburg, Berlin, and Vienna.[70]

By the same token, China became once more molded into the image of a drug victim, now not only in Asia but in the world. The mental maps of anti-drug publicists globalized through their transfer to the League of Na-tions. Morphine trafficking into China evoked a dark reminiscence of the opium wars, at a time when the fledgling republic had just emerged victo-rious from its battle against opium, with 1917 as the celebrated end of the Indian-Chinese opium trade. The narrative strategy behind the image of a drugged China thus ran counter to the perceived course of historical devel-opment, adding insult to injury.

To ensure expeditious transmission, Japanese post offices had issued ad-vance permit forms for dealers that specified the quantity to be delivered. The duty of the tariff rate of 10.20 yen per pound represented the proceeds for the Bank of Japan, with return receipts to make the transaction official. Tokyo, in a clear show of its perceived dependence on Chinese and inter-national respect and goodwill, claimed to respect Beijing's import ban and that it "would scorn to lend official support to the movement of contra-band."[71] Such a scenario would, in other words, equate Japan's paramount influence in the drug traffic with Japanese control over it.

Despite his criticism of German morphine output and the Japanese use of its Northeast Asian informal empire as an entryway for morphine into China, Morrison did not hesitate to point to British participation along-side the German role. It amounted to 1¾ tons of a total 6¼ tons of East-bound morphine in 1913, with a final profit of £840,000 to Japanese traders in China. The remaining 4½ tons originated at a firm of British manufacturing chemists of Glasgow, Edinburgh, and the industrial district of Battersea in South London. The morphine that reached their own commercial agents in Japan was processed in English and Scottish factories and based on opium from Smyrna, with up to a 12 percent morphine content, and muriate of morphine, with an average 75 percent morphine content.

The Edinburgh connection had first acquired notoriety at the Mission Conference in 1910, when, upon criticism of certain chemists, "some of the Elders present were observed to change countenance."[72] As with German participation, the British role in morphine traffic affected production centers and shipping strategies alike. Morrison was eager to convince Edward Manico Gull, then acting editor of the *North China Herald* and the *British Chamber of Commerce Journal* in Shanghai, correspondent of the *Manchester Guardian* in China, and contributor to the *New York Evening Post* and *Chicago Daily News,* that it would be "worth your while making an enquiry into the smuggling of opium into Shanghai on British steamers." To uncover the illicit dimension of morphine trafficking, Morrison pointed Gull to the recent interception of one ton of morphine by the well-paid Inspectorate General of Customs, whose chief secretary, Cecil Arthur Verner Bowra, served as a source of information for Morrison's scoop.[73]

What made Japanese morphine supplies an affront to Morrison and his like-minded informers—and what made Morrison's exposure of it an affront to the Japanese government—was, at this stage, less the assault on Chinese popular health than the violation of China's legislative sovereignty. The distinction between illicit smuggling and Japanese sponsoring was, however, not watertight, nor did it need to be when the appeal aimed at raising public alarm. In reaction to China's raise of the duty on morphine in 1903, smuggling was suspected to have shot up. Against China's Morphia Import Prohibition Law of January 1, 1909, except for "qualified foreign medical practitioners and foreign chemists and civil and military hospitals," the traffic remained in full swing. Prodded by the scoop's emphasis on Tokyo's knowledge of and responsibility for the drug trafficking by Japanese citizens abroad, the arbitrariness of Japanese expansionism, particularly in its abusive aspects, became more questionable than ever before. The confusion that had failed to rationalize the logic behind drug trafficking as a coherent "opium system" until the scoops during the First World War was now dispersed at a stroke. Indeed, there was little difference between the term "opium system" (*ahen seido*) as the Japanese government discussed it behind closed doors and the observations made by Morrison and his informers, their ignorance of the term aside.

In addition to Edinburgh, Whiffen and Sons from Battersea had installed an agent in Osaka, who in turn had at least two chief clients, Shionogi of Doshomachi, Osaka, and "a prominent bookselling firm in Tokyo," at his disposal. Although Morrison knew these details, he preferred to leave firms and their clients unnamed, reassuring Gull as much as himself: "There is nothing in the article I think that can give any offence to anyone."[74] Maximizing the effect of public exposure while minimizing Morrison's own and his informants' vulnerability was one of the more shrewd techniques of transnational intelligence and investigative journalism. Morrison confided to Gull: "I have headed the morphia letter 'From a Correspondent' since the information came from Japan."

But that information was not publicly available. It was acquired by means of industrial espionage, through an employee of the Suzuki or Mogi firm, both of which were principally "engaged in the traffic."[75] It was only due to the intervention of Owen Mortimer Green, Gull's predecessor at the *North China Daily News* and *Herald* and *Times* correspondent in Shanghai, followed by the China posting of the *London Observer,* that the final article refrained from identifying the Japanese firms, forestalling a legal imbroglio.[76] Morrison revealed his chutzpah not only in the use of informants in Japan but equally in the careful simulation of the hidden investigator, writing from behind the scenes: "I thought first in order to mislead people as to the origin of the letter, of saying that it was from a correspondent in Japan," his letter whispered to Gull. "If you thought this could be done with propriety it would be perhaps wise to give it such a heading. Of course I am particularly anxious that my name should not appear in connection with it in any way."[77] Spreading the scientific details of Japan's pharmaceutical production of morphine to medical audiences through the *Lancet,* Morrison was sure, "would attract widespread attention. Only good can be done by their publication."[78]

The geographical and moral reach of Morrison's antidrug propaganda was as far-flung as the intelligence network that made it possible. His second anonymous attack on Japanese drug trafficking opened with an innocuous reference to the first exposure of 1915, where "a correspondent explained in some detail the large proportions to which had attained Japan's morphia traffic with China."[79] Drawing an unmistakable parallel to the British legacy of opium trading after two victorious opium wars (1839–1842 and 1856–1860), this exposure was titled "The Japanese Opium Trade with China: A Scandal Calling for Instant and Drastic Repression." That the substance of the article referred to the exacerbating state of the morphine problem rather the much older "opium problem" mattered. Much more essential was to catch the attention of readers in civic circles and ministries near and far. On the receiving end of news communication, it speaks to the stature of the *North China Herald* and all information printed in it, as well as to the careful attention of news readers, that they took notice of the attack, although it was not a lead article. Clearly, this episode bespoke a hitherto neglected realm of a very high international sensitivity to the expanding, political, and economic function of weekly news.

"Your admirable article . . . caused quite a sensation down here," wrote *Times* correspondent Green from Shanghai, having again censored out the names of Japanese drug firms. Nevertheless, "all the local Japanese merchants are much exercised over the article." Missionaries, too, "want to know who it was who wrote the article, so that they may get further information, which they propose to lay before that very much-enduring body, the Peace Conference." This anticipated the achievement of the Paris Peace Conference to oblige all signatories to ratify the International Opium Convention of 1912. Green played his part in guarding Morrison's identity: "I told them that I could not possibly disclose the writer's identity without his consent."[80]

The deadlock, or at least dead end, of international negotiations for the ratification of the International Opium Convention did little to dampen international public expectations that the world had moved closer to its freedom from drugs than ever before. It may have been part of the continuing crusade against narcotic drugs—whose Chinese dimension was called a "war on opium"—to claim the inevitability of that destination.[81] These assessments, however, emphasized that the IOC had limited the opportunities of states with a stake in the Asian opium trade to pull out altogether from drug-control negotiations. As the IOC raised anti-opium expectations in East Asia and via the Southeast Asian colonies in European metropoles, the binding force of IOC recommendations had come within political reach. While many of these hopes were expressed in the international public sphere and did not equate a radical political rethinking (if such rethinking indeed exists), overestimating the change of the times was not necessarily self-defeating. The exposure of Japanese drug trafficking was one of the earliest examples of investigative journalism fashioning the very content of international moral imperatives. In its public constituents, international legitimacy was at its most malleable.

The political success of targeted projects to win international public opinion for usually undefined interests, waged by warriors against drugs, cannot be dismissed as mere hysteria by either the attackers or the attacked. Not all antidrug journalism bore fruit. The drugged Kaiser was a story that surfaced in American newspapers, supposedly leaked by the Kaiser's own chauffeur in a spa, but carried no political consequences whatsoever—in the twenty-first century, it might be different.[82] The Kaiser did not die from an overdose. Germany, historically complicit in the negligence to prevent what international legal scholars today would call transnational harm, escaped the odium and international scrutiny that haunted Japanese drug production from 1915 to the Tokyo War Crimes Tribunal after the Second World War. In Asia, Germany did not suffer Chinese reprisals over the morphine exposures, as initially feared. Why? First, Japanese morphine trafficking excelled over the dispersal of German supplies. Second, Germany's defeat in the First World War deprived it of all colonies and territories, including Qingdao, which was ceded to Japan. As for Chinese popular sentiment, a colonial empire that no longer existed was hard to criticize, and Japan began to virtually monopolize the odium of Chinese public opinion, not least for its wily acquisition of Shandong.

What the First World War did introduce was a mass phenomenon in western Europe, which European writers of the nineteenth century conceived only possible in Asia. Wartime tensions emanating from prior antiopium mobilization and the addition of new journalistic networks into the drug-control campaign played a significant role in raising drug control as a global political priority for the Paris Peace Conference. The phenomena of "morphinism" and "cocainism" took the analogous forms of consumption, characterized by an individual's loss of willpower, self-control, and consequent resort to semi-legal or illegal purchases.[83] To provoke drug panics, patterns of narcotic drug consumption appeared to know no bounds: drug consumption showed an inherent force to compel emulation. In the physical and psychological distress of war, morphine and cocaine became expressions of societies that had lost their balance.

As the domino effect of large-scale drug trafficking under the aegis of the state became explicit, Japan followed Britain as the worst drug offenders. Weak international oversight opened global commercial loopholes in the now intercontinental political economy of narcotic drugs. Unless the states embraced a moral deterrent of global control, the global marketplace of drugs would never regulate itself. When the League of Nations as the first actor in charge of global governance made its appearance in the Paris negotiations, its function was less the fulfillment of idealistic dreams than a pragmatic response to the perceived need for centralized international decision making.

CHAPTER EIGHT

TOWARD INTERNATIONAL ACCOUNTABILITY FOR TRANSNATIONAL HARM

THREE MONTHS after the First World War had opened its throat to devour millions of lives on the lethal battlefields of Europe, a close observer struck a decidedly optimistic note. Intellectually alert and politically well-connected, Sir William Job Collins descended from the Huguenot Garnault family and was by training an eye surgeon and by conviction a Liberal MP for West St. Pancras. At his death, he was praised for his gifts in law, medicine, politics, university administration, and municipal government. During the First World War, Collins served as Red Cross commissioner in France, which may have inspired his postwar lobbying for motorized ambulances in Britain.[1]

In October 1914, Collins envisioned the historical function of world wars as part of a global, if rocked, trajectory toward a higher plane of humanity in international affairs, in terms not unlike Aristotelian catharsis, in which the witnessing of tragedy ultimately results in the redeeming purification of a ravaged soul: "One of the first objects attained in 1815 at the Congress of Vienna, after the close of the Napoleonic wars, was the abolition of the Slave trade," Collins stated, extending the historical precedent into a historical prescription. "If as a result of the Great War there be secured, as now seems probable, close supervision of opium-production and of the narcotic drug trade, it will be felt by many that the last hundred years will have registered another step in the progress of humanity, also that another and not the least important of their victories will have been added to those forces which won the Great War."[2] This chapter investigates the transnational forces of global span that anticipated the Paris Peace Conference's tackling of global drug control, and tracks the decision from the earliest expectations to fulfillment through the response by international society.

Although the First World War presented numerous ruptures in the life of international society—especially across the Atlantic world, in many ways the center of gravity for the emerging architecture of global governance. But international cooperation in drug control had preceded the outbreak of war, receiving its initial momentum from the IOC, addressing ratification of the International Opium Convention in the Hague Opium Conferences and experiencing its first failed attempts to ratify the convention. More than a prelude, these early years of drug-control diplomacy brought Collins into transnational and international focus as one of the very few civilians respected for his expertise in the politics of opium. A member of the British delegation to the International Opium Conferences in The Hague from 1911 to 1914, his antidrug initiatives extended to the well-honed field of antidrug publicity in the *British Medical Journal* and elsewhere. In public as in private, however, Collins's anti-opium lobbying defied loyalty to British officialdom despite his seconding to The Hague.

While the brush of globalism was conspicuous in his engagement against drug trading, Collins's explanation of the First World War and its "deeper origin" remained tightly focused on Europe, with blame falling on the European obsession with science, materialism, the secular state, and hunger for power, each at the expense of intelligent sentiment, disinterested virtue, and Christian compassion.[3] But acting like an internationalist counterpoint to his historical and philosophical efforts, Collins's largely private anti-opium diplomacy strove to establish China as the center of global antidrug politics and the magnet of global public attention.

The disjuncture between British policy at The Hague and Collins's individual lobbying did not lead to his dismissal from the Hague delegation. Instead, the British delegation acknowledged that the international legitimacy of government-sponsored drug trading had changed its premises, terms, and objectives over the last two decades. Indeed, the 1895 verdict of the Royal Commission on opium consumption never made a powerful international comeback during the entirety of the League of Nations era. By contrast, the anti-opium position of the Sino-British Agreement of 1907 continued to hold sway in The Hague in 1912 and beyond, with its bilateralism now augmented on a platform of multilateralism. As a clear signal, British pro-opium interests were excluded from having any voice at The Hague. Britain's international anti-opium alignment did, however, incite brief domestic controversy. Questions in Parliament attacked the fact "that there is absolutely no representative of British commerce among the delegates."[4] Despite such protests, London refused to appoint a defender of British drug-trading interests and cautiously limited its reservations to the demand for equal distribution of international antidrug obligations, arguing for a proportionate distribution of sacrificed trade interests among the participating powers "for the sake of international morality," partly chagrined that "there are many outside Powers on which no such obligation would rest." Fairness prescribed that the altruism of one should not be exploited by another. "Drastic measures" should discourage drug revenues in general, not merely among the powers already inclined to drug control, among which Britain now counted itself.[5]

The sources of Collins's anticipation of a global breakthrough in the politics of drug control as "probable" lay elsewhere, in the world of transnational, British, Chinese, and American lobbying far from Europe. Alternative avenues of political lobbying, populated by non-diplomatic experts, activated new pressure groups explicitly in preparation for the end of the war and for peace negotiations. Beyond nationality, place of residence, or profession, a coterie of Britons, Chinese, and Americans convened in Beijing's British legation in June 1918. Collins was but one member assisting in the grand collective task of including international drug control in the Paris Peace Treaties. The group's efforts aimed at the global ratification of the International Opium Convention of 1912, under which "the Contracting Powers shall not allow the import and export of raw opium except by duly authorized persons"—in other words, by licensed opium dealers that had the approval of the importing country's government.[6] This constituted a major departure from the Treaty of Tianjin and its groundwork for an opium tariff. In the eyes of the Anglo-American and Chinese anti-opium community that gathered in Beijing, the effective enforcement of international opium control after the Third Opium Conference in 1915 seemed to depend on two possibilities: to expand both the international basis of political cooperation in opium control and to connect it to a locally based but globally active basis of social support. After the war had interrupted the momentum of the Third Opium Conference in The Hague, Britain and Germany were locked in a state of mutual suspicion, more reluctant than ever to adjust domestic legislation to the calls of an international convention.

The global coordination of opium control regimes was embedded in the expanding institutionalization of global obligations, from readjusted imperial administration through the Mandates system to the installation of international public health agendas in the global politics of the League of Nations. After the scandal over Japanese morphine trafficking from 1915 to 1918, much of the global, solely forward-looking grandeur of international cooperation had given way to the practical need to close international legal loopholes of evaded compliance or even violation of the non-binding requirements that existed. Never before had supervision of drug supplies appeared with such urgency and the reduction of excessive shipments to legitimate medical and scientific needs in the receiving country more essential.[7] Governments played for time to shield and shift vested interests, proven both by Britain's reluctance to desist from the opium trade before 1906 and Japan's tolerance of morphine trading until the First World War. In each case, transnational information-sharing and an early version of investigative journalism had brought about political, legislative change. Collins and his Beijing friends therefore engaged in an unprecedented project of institutionalized antidrug lobbying: the plan to create an NGO that served as a clearinghouse of drug information across East Asia.

The aforementioned analogy between the African slave trade and the Asian opium trade was already prominent and no longer limited to Anglophone circles of communication. Historical legacies endowed global drug control with symbolic value, almost as if the humanitarian progress of the global past, once properly grasped, could be stretched into the future and be pinned down. First, the idea gained currency against the fear, expressed frequently since Prince Gong if not Lin Zexu, that the drug trade had disturbed, if not derailed, the political, economic, social, and ethical interactions between China, European colonial powers, and the United States. This historical misprision had had its costs: the "opium curse" cast millions of Chinese into addiction, estimated at fifteen million around 1890.[8] Simultaneously, the political privileges that facilitated the participation of Western powers and Japan in the infamous trade were perceived as manifestations of the yoke of imperialism weighing China down. This view originated in the nationalist ambience of the young Chinese Republic after 1911 but spread to international anti-opium activists through whom international attention was directed, from Chinese demand to Western supply, as the guilty stimulus. The end of the First World War, precisely because of its unexpected corrosion of existing international norms, the global magnitude of its human toll, and its epistemic incommensurability, offered a transformational moment unlike any other international conflict since the opium wars. More than a cosmopolitan hope at war's end, drug control was seen as a necessity dictated by history itself.

In Beijing, the upsurge of anti-opium activism during the First World War brought together Sir Francis Aglen, Robert Hart's successor at the Chinese Imperial Maritime Customs, who lamented, aligned with Chinese perceptions of opium as a national curse: "The opium trade . . . was so infinitely

injurious to her [China's] good name and prejudicial of her future," he pronounced at a private dinner in the British embassy. He, too, characterized
future prospects for global drug control as not only an issue related to China
but one of China's own priorities: "At the Peace Conference will she have
a hearing?"[9] Sir John Jordan, the British minister to China, agreed that the
opium problem was pressing. An ardent supporter since his lobbying for
the 1907 agreement to phase out Indian opium exports to China alongside
Chinese domestic opium cultivation, Jordan was joined by Australian
George Ernest Morrison, adviser to the Chinese president, Yuan Shikai;
Putnam Weale, his American colleague; American minister Paul Reinsch;
H. B. Woodhead, editor of the *Peking and Tientsin Times*; E. G. Hillier of
the Chamber of Commerce; and others. They had all seen the enormous
energy with which the Chinese government enforced the virtual elimina-
tion of poppy cultivation until 1917.

Like the new Nationalist government of China, they saw opium eradication as a ticket for China to join the family of modern nations. This idea
was rooted in the very first years of the Chinese Republic. Worse than the
symbolic proof of the state's inability to enforce the rule of law, the temporary resurgence of opium cultivation in the revolutionary turmoil of 1912
had provoked Foreign Secretary Sir Edward Grey to make recognition of
the Republic conditional on its adherence to the 1907 agreement, reaffirmed
in 1911. Opium suppression became the British litmus test for the Chinese
nation-state, despite Sir Edward Grey's prioritization of safeguarding British
treaty rights and interests as a matter of established principle.[10] Jordan remained unimpressed by such high-level political gambling. He reassured
Grey of his trust in the sincerity and likely success of Chinese opium suppression and proved, in the end, to be right. The ball was back in Britain's,
or rather British India's, backyard, and soon recognition was officially extended to the Republic of China.[11] China's "good name" was bound up with
its future legal position in international affairs. In a striking conflux of political forces, local social control over opium farmers became a measure of
China's international legitimacy. By consequence, China's chances to advance in the ranks of international society were significantly raised, and
both Chinese and Western internationalists dedicated to the anti-opium
cause, like those in Beijing, saw a unique opportunity in the approaching
peace settlement.[12]

To foreign Beijing residents like Jordan, Chinese and Japanese governmental involvement in the opium business quenched hopes for a stable settlement of the international opium problem. The bad news in 1918 about
the Chinese government's purchase and sale of 1,577 chests of Indian surplus opium to foreign merchants aroused bitter protests by increasingly

distrustful governments and audiences in China, England, and America. Even once uncovered, the safe transport of the valuable yet forbidden freight from the Shanghai combine to Beijing was uncertain. To avoid further scandals and to mellow anti-opium sentiment at home and abroad, the Chinese government decided to sacrifice stocks worth $37,000,000, and burnt the surplus opium in the presence of the public and the press at the site of Maritime Customs in Shanghai.[13] American minister Paul Reinsch, another dinner guest, was equally relieved and strongly supported President Xu Shichang's determination to rely on missionary reports as an additional source of information on illicit opium cultivation for provincial governments.[14] Jordan congratulated President Xu on this noble move: "We have removed finally the stigma attaching in the popular mind to our connection with this traffic. . . . By keeping our own hands clean in the future we can continue to exercise pressure to prevent the exploitation of China by other countries."[15]

Further north, in Korea and Manchuria, opium cultivation and smuggling once again reached scandalous proportions in the first quarter of 1919.[16] The Japanese concession in Tianjin, the suspected transshipment center for Japan in North China, was closed to Americans.[17] Not only did Britain find out in 1917 that its legal morphine exports to Japan had been illegally transferred to China, but it learned that Japanese smugglers chose the United States as a convenient transit country for drugs destined for China.[18] Sir Francis Aglen, as director of the Imperial Maritime Customs, came in embarrassing proximity with the drug because somebody had attempted to smuggle opium worth $16,000 in his luggage on his return from Hong Kong to Shanghai.[19] Maritime Customs confiscated as much as twenty-one tons of opium and four hundredweights in 1919 alone.[20]

In contrast to the American uproar about Chinese corruption, Washington seemed surprisingly unimpressed by these precariously ingenious Japanese methods of curtailment. In the words of the American ambassador in London, the U.S. government showed reluctance to support the case of opium to be transmitted to the Peace Conference and did "not feel that the question of suppressing the illegal trade in opium and other habit-forming drugs is one to come before the Peace Conference—which should deal only with questions growing out of the war and related subjects."[21] Two weeks later, a similarly noncommittal letter from the American ambassador read that "while the United States government is in hearty sympathy with the idea of the suppression of the illegal trade in opium, it nevertheless hesitates to agree in advance as to whether this is a matter which may be incorporated in the Peace Treaty until such time as the subject is actually brought to the consideration of the Conference."[22]

FIGURE 8.1. President Xu Shichang, supporter of the IAOA, orders the destruction of opium worth $37,000,000.

Source: The War Against Opium, International Anti-Opium Association (Peking: Tientsin Press, 1922). Harvard Law Library, Harvard University.

FIGURE 8.2. Opium burning at the Xiannongtan (Temple of Agriculture), Beijing, January 1921.

Source: The War Against Opium, International Anti-Opium Association (Peking: Tientsin Press, 1922). Harvard Law Library, Harvard University.

FIGURE 8.3. Opium cases ordered to be destroyed by President Xu.

Source: The War Against Opium, International Anti-Opium Association (Peking: Tientsin Press, 1922). Harvard Law Library, Harvard University.

FIGURE 8.4. Morphine smuggled in sulfate blocks of soda; cylinders confiscated by the Maritime Customs Tianjin, November 1921.

Source: The War Against Opium, International Anti-Opium Association (Peking: Tientsin Press, 1922). Harvard Law Library, Harvard University.

STATEMENT showing the REVENUE derived from OPIUM, the AREA under POPPY and the OUTTURN during the period 1910-11 to 1916-17.

	Revenue Opium (net)	"Excise" (gross)	Total	"Excise" Opium quantity manufac-tured	Provision opium quantity manufac-tured	Area of culti-vation	Output in maunds of 87 lbs.
	Rs	Rs	Rs	Accts	Chests	Acres	maunds
1910-11	9,41.29.574	155.56.205	10.96.85.779	8.611	15000	362.868	44.926
1911-12	7,84.77.394	1.57.46.775	9.42.24.169	9.126	14000	200.672	31.473
1912-13	6.78.72.944	1.78.24.021	8.56.96.965	9.947	7000	178.263	26.813
1913-14	91.86.578	1.93.71.719	2.85 58.297	8.307	12000	144.561	24.292
1914-15	1.37.71.945	1.94.98.845	3.32.70.788	8.943	10000	164.911	28.293
1915-16	1.15.37.341	2.05.45.065	3.20 82.806	8.391	12000	167.155	27.001
1916-17	3.37.14.162.	2.11.46.200	5.48.60.362	8.732	12000	204.186	32.124

It is not possible here to give complete statistics, of any period later than 1916-17, but the above statement will give some idea of the extent of the trade done in India itself, with the countries of the Far East, and with other countries. The closing of the China market certainly affected the Indian opium trade, but no statistics are available to show to what extent. The fluctuations indicated by the following figures are worthy of notice.

Year.	Acreage under cultivation.	Opium revenue.
1910-11	362,868	£7,521,962
1913-14	144,561	£1,624,878
1916-17	204,186	£3,160,005

These figures prove that the acreage under poppy cultivation, and the revenue derived from opium were at one time greatly re-duced. They now appear, however, to be again on the increase.

THE FOLLOWING FIGURES SPEAK FOR THEMSELVES :—

	Excise	Opium	Total Revenue.
1907-8	£6,214,210	£5,244,986	£88,670,329
1908-9	£6,389,628	£5,844,788	£86,074,624
1909-10	£6,537,854	£6,534,683	£91,130,269
1910-11	7,030,314	7,521,962	97,470,114
1911-12	7,609,753	6,961,278	100,580,799
1912-13	8,277,919	5,124,592,	106,254,327
1913-14	8,894,300	1,624,878	105,220,777
1914-15	8,856,881	1,572,218	101,534,375
1915-16	8,632,209	1,912,514	104,704,041
1916-17	9,215,899	3,160,005	118,799,968

FIGURE 8.5. Opium revenue statement for British India by the IAOA, 1910–1917.

Source: The War Against Opium, International Anti-Opium Association (Peking: Tientsin Press, 1922). Harvard Law Library, Harvard University.

FIGURE 8.6. Opium balls destroyed by President Xu.

Source: The War Against Opium, International Anti-Opium Association (Peking: Tientsin Press, 1922). Harvard Law Library, Harvard University. International Anti-Opium Association, *The War Against Opium* [Peking: Tientsin Press, 1922], pp. 108–109

FIGURE 8.7. Opium burning at Changde, Hunan, 1920.

Source: The War Against Opium, International Anti-Opium Association (Peking: Tientsin Press, 1922). Harvard Law Library, Harvard University.

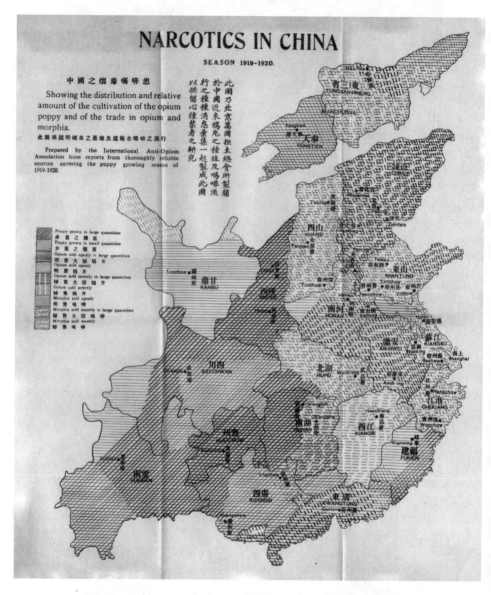

FIGURE 8.8. Recrudescence of poppy cultivation, the opium trade, and the morphine trade, 1920.

Source: The War Against Opium, International Anti-Opium Association (Peking: Tientsin Press, 1922). Harvard Law Library, Harvard University.

Enraged by the nonchalance of the American government and the rough-and-tumble of Chinese opium politics, a recently widowed American lady rushed to Beijing. Elizabeth Washburn Wright, the widow of Hamilton Wright, Collins's American colleague at the Hague Opium Conferences, was feared internationally for her scrutiny and talent in exposing vested opium interests, her uncompromising outspokenness, and her long experience in the field. These credentials would later bestow upon her the honor of the first American woman with plenipotentiary powers as an assessor of the Opium Committee of the League of Nations. Back at the dinner table in Beijing's British legation, the Australian adviser to the Chinese president, George Ernest Morrison, himself an opponent of the opium trade, fell victim to one of her attacks on the sorry state of current opium control (and its proponents): "She spoke with vehemence, suggesting mental unbalance, rating us all for . . . apathetic and indifferen[ce] when we ought to insist upon the continuance of China's moral regeneration. . . . She gave me a real dressing down."[23] Indeed, Beijing was not the best place to recover from the loss of her beloved husband or from the trials and tribulations of anti-opium work. Frustration rose further when reports on Japanese-smuggled Indian opium, British morphine, and heroin reached the capital. London reported on a simultaneous increase of opium smuggling within wartime Europe, encouraged by shortages in licit supply and the lifting of import and export restrictions.[24] But Wright's scorn did not last for much longer than the dinner, and soon she would channel her fervor against the real opium gangsters and join hands with Morrison, Jordan, Reinsch, and many others to establish one of the most crucial nongovernmental organizations for opium control, which would serve as the lifeline of local information for the peacemakers in Paris and later the league officials in Geneva.

Within the coterie, three prominent Chinese approached Morrison, preventing it from turning into an ordinary Anglo-American club. Morrison's three visitors had been educated in England. Wu Laishi, former Queen's Scholar of Singapore and editor of the *Peking Daily News,* and Wu Liande had received degrees in medicine from Cambridge and had attended the 1909 IOC as well as the First Hague Opium Conference in 1912.[25] Diao Minqian (commonly known as Min-chi'en Tuk Zung Tyau), founder and editor of the *Peking Leader* and later professor of international law at Tsing Hua College, had earned his LL.D. in London.

Compared to previous Chinese anti-opium activists, the two Wus and Diao transcended the moral dimension of the debate that denounced opium as a social vice, an economic threat, and an imperialist evil. They searched pragmatically for political solutions to the problem of disparate national anti-opium campaigns and found a solution set apart in space and time—in

Paris at the upcoming peace conference, expected for 1919. One of the "big powers" had to be approached as soon as possible, preferably Britain. To this end, the three decided to send a cable to Theodore Taylor, an influential anti-opium activist, and Sir William Collins, then in London. The choice was deliberate and wise. The Taylor connection enlisted support of the British public, whose anti-opium sentiment had not ceased since the successful attack on the British opium trade in 1906. Memories of the fateful motion that dismissed the trade "morally indefensible" were still fresh among anti-opiumists. The Sino-British agreement of 1907 and the phasing out of Chinese opium cultivation and the Indo-Chinese trade built largely on the success of a public opinion hostile to opium. But the sentiment did not confine itself to British society; it proliferated with amazing speed into the international arena. Only six years later, the chairman of the Opium Conference in The Hague would announce: "In approaching our task, we have the consciousness that any legislative action which may ultimately result from the work of the Conference will have behind it a public opinion that is worldwide. Without this, an international agreement or legislative effort would be, if not futile, at any rate of minor value. Sentiment without formal expression lacks that precision and definiteness which human nature looks to as a support. On the other hand, mere superimposed law is impotent."[26]

Based on this ethical consensus, the interdependence of national control programs became a core lesson of the first decade of international anti-opium politics. British reluctance to sacrifice trade interests if it could not make sure that other parties did not lose even more had been evident to close observers of the Sino-British agreement of 1907 as well as the delayed ratification of the International Opium Convention of 1912. Returning to an old Qing blueprint, so frequently ignored by Britain, the Wus and Diao urged this time, through Collins and Taylor, to pursue a multilateral control system to forestall the Chinese opium cultivation by banning both opium trading and cultivation in international law. Synchronous control of domestic and foreign sources of supply should build on the 1907 agreement and globalize its principle of reciprocity for international society writ large.

Diverting British criticism from increasing Chinese cultivation (reports of which dotted the headlines in London and Washington) was perhaps a tactical but also a necessary step if the international community was ever to be convinced of opium trading, not Chinese craving, as "a world problem." In the view of British critics, the domestic anti-opium movements of the Qing dynasty had failed, excessively focused on demand.[27] In Western discussions of opium consumption outside Asia, Chinese laborers, so-called coolies, in Southeast Asia, Latin America, and the major cities along the

North American coasts were depicted as the racially inferior sponsors of a vice that constituted a danger to white populations in the West. By contrast, the Asian opium problem and its concern with colonial trade and supply was the pitiable but racially determined flip side of the Chinese "vice." During the 1910s, the majority of states came to adopt the Chinese view of supply-focused opium critiques with greater acceptance.[28] Transnational anti-opium activists with medical expert knowledge, like the Wus and Diao, became central figures in the gradual infusion of Chinese perceptions of the opium problem into the international arena. This was another aspect of the dynamic characteristic for the "internationalization" of Republican China, one that illustrates that the export of Chinese ideas and images of world politics served increasingly to balance the prevalence of Western ideas and images of China.[29] China's increasing political influence and the dispersion of its opium perceptions went hand in hand.

Cosmopolitan anti-opium crusaders like Elizabeth Washburn Wright were aware of their privileged position at stages like Beijing, where transnational flows of ideas, ideals, and interests intersected and conflicted. As Collins's analogy with the abolition of slavery had suggested, the anti-opium movement was a latecomer in transnational reformism. Now it was ready to dog the drug wherever it went, and Wright, Collins, Reinsch, the Wus, Diao, and many more friends realized that what they needed was an institutionalized initiative. Hence was born in Beijing in 1918 the International Anti-Opium Association (IAOA), known in Chinese as *wanguo jinyan hui,* representing the joint product of the British, Chinese, and American anti-opium community and an expression of the intellectual and social exchange of anti-opium information and opinion across national and imperial borders.[30] Much to the chagrin of its precursor, the SSOT, which had partnered with Cantonese anti-opium organizations at a very early stage, the IAOA took much of the credit for the anti-opium lobbying just prior to the Paris Peace Conference. The SSOT, while advertising copies of the IAOA's *The War Against Opium* at three shillings unbound and four shillings bound from Marshall Brothers, one of the social reform printers in London's Paternoster Row, deplored its own marginalization. "Yet it was our Society, assisted most sympathetically by several other bands of earnest workers, which for 43 years (1874 to 1917) carried all the practical parliamentary and international work to the triumphant success of the abolition of the Indian opium trade with China. We don't mind being ignored or forgotten, . but the omission is certainly odd." But contrary to the IAOA, the SSOT did not have a physical presence in the Chinese capital, lacked China-based American support, and did not prevent its supporters from offering their services elsewhere. William Collins's own information-sharing had contributed to the international exposure of Japanese morphine trafficking, crowned by his comprehensive *The War against Opium*.[31] With this unsurpassed survey of the IAOA's knowledge and agenda, the IAOA's own paradigmatic focus on China's drug situation displaced the distant China watchers of the SSOT. These preparations would soon make it into the Asian brain of the League of Nations.

The IAOA was committed to exposing opium transactions in East Asia and designed to provide governments and international organizations with local information that was otherwise difficult to obtain. Transnational connectivity and political influence were two distinguishing characteristics. High-ranking benefactors included the president of China, Xu Shichang, and his predecessor, Li Yuanhong; Premier Jin Yunpeng and his predecessor, Qian Nengxun; and several cabinet members, who formed an advisory board. International cooperation with diplomats was facilitated by involving Jordan, Aglen, Morrison, and many other dinner guests from the British legation. Medical expertise was provided by Sir William Collins and Wu Liande, and public attention was guaranteed by the unmistakable presence of Elizabeth Washburn Wright.

The variety of professions and interests represented in the IAOA ensured that the organization had access to an invisible body of expert knowledge, which served as the intellectual tool set for a "scientific" and hopefully less biased evaluation of opium exposures. Thanks to Reuter's correspondent in Beijing, Major A. E. Wearne, and the initiator of the anti-opium supplement in the *Peking and Tientsin Times*, H. B. Woodhead, an international press apparatus channeled the findings of the IAOA to shape public opinion and to shift political perceptions of the opium problem in China and abroad. The IAOA in Beijing subsumed the activities of a host of urban or provincial anti-opium societies that covered the major Chinese cities from 1918 onward, as if the places most stigmatized by opium could be rehabilitated by the installation of an anti-opium organization. Due to the efforts of Wu Liande, a main base was of course Shanghai, but Tianjin, Kaifeng, Changsha, Hankou, Suzhou, Yancheng, Taiyuan, Jinan, and Guangzhou followed suit until about two hundred sub-branches existed in 1920. For all of them, the IAOA served as the center and umbrella, with the most elaborate network of informants across continents.[32] It paved the way for league work in "delimiting, and to a degree managing, the shifting boundaries between state power and international authority" and, we might add, local representation and legitimacy.[33]

The rising initiative and influence of the IAOA reached London through Jordan, who asked Earl Curzon of Kedleston—viceroy of India until 1905, then lord president of the council, and soon foreign secretary—on April 14, 1919, "to be supplied with copies of all the laws and bye-laws etcetera at present in force in the British empire controlling the manufacture, sale, import and export of opium, morphia and other narcotics."[34] Jordan drew the attention of the foreign office to the endeavor of the IAOA to organize public opinion in China against the drug traffic and thus helped to turn the IAOA into an intermediary organ between the local opium conditions within and beyond China's borders, in Beijing and Whitehall. The IAOA further proposed an "International Opium and Narcotics Ordinance which, if adopted and enforced would, whilst in no way interfering with the legitimate use and trade in of these drugs, render the illicit trade in and the clandestine shipment to China of such drugs impossible."[35] This ordinance should be submitted "to the Chinese Government, Foreign Commercial Attaches and or Representatives of Treaty Powers and the league of nations with a view to obtaining their support and acceptance of same and where possible its adoption and immediate enforcement."

In London, Sir William Collins, who had been toying with the idea of bringing the opium problem to the peace conference since 1917,[36] made sure that a telegram the IAOA sent to Lloyd George was not ignored.[37] It asked the British prime minister "to impress upon the League of Nations the importance of restriction of the cultivation of opium throughout the world to actual medical requirements." This choice of words mirrored the originally American idea of restriction to "legitimate medical requirements," later incorporated into international official vocabulary by the League of Nations. Since the major offensive by over one hundred medical experts from the United States, Canada, England, Scotland, Ireland, China, and even Germany, opium addiction, an interpretive concept devised by anti-opium activists, forfeited its political defense.[38]

Given the pioneering impetus of the IAOA, it reinvented itself as the main source of information and consultation for the League's Opium Advisory Committee after 1921. Lord Curzon transmitted the request to the colonial office, receiving in return a catalog of drug-control legislation, now introduced in Jamaica, British Honduras, British Guiana, Bahamas, Trinidad, Barbados, Grenada, Leeward Islands, Gibraltar, Malta, Cyprus, Bermuda, Falkland Islands, Fiji, Western Pacific (New Hebrides, Gilbert, Ellice, and Solomon Islands), South Africa High Commission, Nyasaland, Sierra Leone, Gambia, the Gold Coast, Nigeria, Kenya, Uganda, Zanzibar, Tanganyika, Ceylon, Hong Kong, Mauritius, Seychelles, the Straits Settlements, Weihaiwei, and Saint Helena. Legislation in the Malay States was still in process.[39] The ties between foreign diplomats and missionaries in China; the Chinese government and medical experts; and journalists,

Western governments, and later the League of Nations would ensure something rare in the history of international public opinion: enduring international attention to the Chinese perception of and role in the international
opium problem. Quick access to governmental and nongovernmental information on opium conditions in China marked the investigations of the
IAOA and added to its international authority. Western governments were
overwhelmed by the influx of IAOA data on opium cultivation and
smuggling, which seemed to be more accurate and reliable than the governmental data they had previously relied on. As a result of the IAOA
reports, the opium problem, centered on East and Southeast Asian borders but with an outreach that connected Great Britain and Australia,
Manchuria and Singapore, Persia and California, New York and Marseilles,
and drew them into the same frightfully elusive net of illicit cross-border
flows, unfolded before the eyes of great and small powers in the East
and West.

Little surprise, then, that the Chinese, the principal "victims" of the opium
trade according to the nationalist view of history, were no less eager to
champion the opium cause in Paris. The American minister to China, Paul
Reinsch, had heard from President Xu of the intention of the Chinese government to bring opium control to the attention of the peace conference.[40]
At the same time, Yan Huiqing, who had met William Collins and Hamilton Wright as the Chinese representative to two opium conferences, suggested to U.S. Secretary of State Robert Lansing that all signatories to the
peace treaties would automatically be obliged to ratify the International
Opium Convention.[41]

The Americans did not waver and reengaged actively in the negotiations for opium control at the Peace Conference. In the early summer of
1918, the State Department sent notes to the American ambassadors in
Tokyo, London, Paris, and The Hague, admonishing the signatories of the
International Opium Convention to comply with the stringency of measures despite wartime exigencies.[42] In American and British eyes, Germany,
Austria, Hungary, and Turkey were the new troublemakers, also in the
area of opium control, whose refusal to enforce the convention gave a bad
example of resistance against new international norms, thus weakening
the ethical standing and political effectiveness of the international opium-
control regime. Yan Huiqing was perhaps least surprised about this move.
As early as January 1915, a German diplomat had in private expressed
his relief about the impending interruption of international cooperation
against opium through the war, when Germany depended on Turkish supplies for narcotics and revenue more than ever before.[43] London suspected
Germany and Turkey of having deliberately delayed ratification of the In-

ternational Opium Convention—a fear that fueled its ambition for inclusion of opium control in the Peace Treaties considerably.[44]

When London presented its proposal for the enforcement of the International Opium Convention by signing the peace treaty, Washington reacted with outright jealousy. After all, it argued, the international opium-control movement since 1909 had been dominated by Americans. The IAOA had been established upon the initiative of at least one American, Elizabeth Washburn Wright. However, British members of the IAOA had chosen to communicate their petitions to London, thus enabling their home government to steal the thunder from their American cousin across the sea. After a short period of confrontation on the grounds that the peace conference was not in charge of any questions beyond those arising out of the war, Washington changed its mind and cabled to the American peace mission in Paris that "it would . . . seem unfortunate for any other country to receive the sole credit for bringing this matter to the attention of the Peace Conference."[45]

The Anglo-American sense of rivalry illustrates the prestige that was associated with leadership in international opium control. Both sides claimed to be creators of the grand idea to use the Paris Peace Conference as an instrument to enforce international opium control. Their struggle for the better proposal mirrored their self-understanding as pioneers of truly global peacemaking. The British and American proposals for an opium clause in the peace treaties crossed in the post.[46] The fact that the actors at the time did not notice this irony of historical agency helped avoid delays through contestation and sped up implementation.

Within half a year, officials and civil activists in China changed Sino-Western opium relations from a clash over excess opium stocks in Shanghai to the shared objective of opium control at the Paris Peace Conference. The IAOA evinced that the anti-opium movement constituted a politically valid, professional, and persistent opposition movement, one that communicated priorities and pressure between internationalist Republican China and the China-oriented international community. In early 1919, even Japanese prime minister Hara Kei paid lip service to multilateral action against the drug trade in order to strengthen Japan's position on racial equality negotiations. Contrary to the Chinese preparation for negotiating the opium problem in Paris, Japan decided surprisingly late to place racial equality at the top of its agenda but also to cooperate in the emerging opium-control regime in the Council of Five, entrusted with discussing the opium question at the Paris Peace Conference.[47] Sir John Jordan in Beijing was convinced that Hara Kei's commitment to repair the damage of Japan's international reputation after the smuggling scandals in North Asia sprang from a sincere anti-opium stance.[48] This is not, however, the place to engage in a psychological debate over political motivations. The scandal became indicative of the pressures for global adherence to the International Opium Convention of 1912, the specific risks of reputational shipwreck, and the steps necessary for post-scandal rehabilitation.

China could have claimed to be the "oldest" pioneer of the anti-opium movement. However, in response to Japanese determination to make territorial gains, Chinese diplomats concentrated their own demands to have Shandong, previously under German control, restored to China. This focus turned out to be a diplomatic blind alley because of previous British-Japanese mutual guarantees. Also, China, unlike Japan, had not been accepted in the Council of Five. Beyond the immediate diplomatic repercussions, this exclusion had wider implications. China's cost-benefit calculation that 300,000 military laborers from China could literally "earn" their country's equal position in international society did not tally. Even John Jordan considered the offer "hardly practicable," and the British War Office "considered it not feasible, as any such step would involve China taking her place on the side of the Allies against the central powers, and this had for political reasons been considered an impossibility."[49] No wonder that the Chinese delegation reacted with disappointment, anger, and ultimate withdrawal. The contested transfer of German Shandong to Japanese tutelage was the last straw that appeared to annul Chinese wartime efforts for peace claims, such as Wang Zhengting's hopes for the Chinese labor forces on European fronts. "Although China was much divided internally, she was still recognized as a member of the family of nations."[50] The Allied powers feared that China could use the international setting for the pursuit of solely national interests. Wang and his colleagues had overestimated Western recognition and decided to reduce the range of Chinese claims to maximize Chinese leverage for the restoration of Shandong. Alongside other "problems which had to be straightened out with other countries," including customs autonomy, foreign courts, and other concessions—in short, the unequal treaties that had "robbed China of many of her sovereign rights"—opium did not fall "within the competence of the Peace Conference," Wang knew, "but at such an international gathering we considered that it was the right place to bring these problems before the nations of the world." After all, since Prince Gong, protest and publicity had achieved much of what diplomatic restraint had left unresolved. "A dossier was prepared, entitled The Case of China, and presented to the Conference," Wang reported. "We knew there would be not action taken by it but the way would be prepared for China to take diplomatic actions looking for the revision of the unequal treaties. So we concentrated our attention on our main problem, namely to get Japan out of the Shantung peninsula."[51]

The lobbying that led to the global illegalization of opium trafficking bypassed the Chinese delegation at the Paris Peace Treaties. Opium control had been a Chinese foreign policy priority before the war, yet against all expectations, Chinese delegates did not spearhead the effort in Paris and consequently ignored its success. Since European and American delegates seemed similarly distracted by geopolitical issues arising out of the war, civil activists and organizations from Asia, Europe, and America combined their transnational leverage to gain governmental attention for the anti-opium cause. But China's social concerns, so ably communicated by the IAOA, were disconnected from its foreign diplomatic posture, which clung to the territorial re-negotiation of a peninsula whose fate had already been sealed by secret arrangements between Britain and Japan. For the Chinese delegation, opium control was off the table. But not for others. The Council of Five, including the United States, the British empire, France, Italy, and Japan, did discuss the opium problem in the room of the French minister for foreign affairs, Stéphen Pichon, at the Quai d'Orsay in Paris, and muddled through Italian intricacies concerning the limited time period for compulsory ratification and Japanese attempts to dodge the same. As Japanese delegate Baron Makino put it, "there might be technical difficulties, since it was proposed that legislative action should be begun within three months."[52]

A brief comparison of the league's covenant drafts illustrates how intricate the negotiations for inclusion of opium control in Paris must have been. The first versions did not yet include any references to the International Opium Convention. It took severe negotiations among the Council of Five until on April 28 they agreed on the final formulation of Article 13. They "will entrust the League with the general supervision over the execution of agreements with regard to . . . the traffic in opium and other dangerous drugs."[53] Article 295 of the Versailles Treaty, by which all signatories of the Opium Convention agreed to bring it into force, was settled. Italy's claim on time limits trumped Japanese reluctance and urged the signatories "to enact the necessary legislation without delay and in any case within a period of twelve months." Furthermore, all "newcomers" in international opium control, that is, all signatories to the Versailles Treaty, automatically became subject to the Opium Convention.[54] In a difficult birth, the institutional foundation for an internationally monitored drug-control regime, which continues to the present day under the aegis of the United Nations, had been laid. Historical ironies started piling up when China initially refused to sign the Treaty of Versailles because of the Shandong dispute, although the document included the deathblow to the greatest evil of imperialism.

Friends and members of the IAOA, however, were emphatic about the successful inclusion and binding force of the opium clause in all the Paris Peace Treaties. Two weeks before the first battle of Ypres, Collins and his British delegation colleague, Max Müller, had submitted their final report to the Third International Opium Conference at The Hague. Having served in this capacity, Collins knew the competitive struggle for opium control and national or imperial reputation between China, France, Germany, Great Britain, Japan, the Netherlands, Persia, Portugal, Siam, Switzerland, Turkey, and the United States, to name the principal participants.[55]

The league consensus on international drug control, however, was not without its international pitfalls. American non-membership combined with the Chinese trauma over Shandong. Elizabeth Washburn Wright, who attended the Peace Conference, foresaw Japanese postwar opium smuggling through the German treaty port of Qingdao, provoking anti-Japanese sentiment in the United States. Although opium control was part of the league settlement, so was China's sidelined position. For the moment, the country with the highest stakes in global opium control lacked the standing to celebrate this multilateral breakthrough, achieved by transnational lobbyists between Beijing and Paris, but not by Beijing and not in Paris. The Sino-Japanese antagonism revolved to the United States, where Henry Cabot Lodge warned in the prominent Senate debate on the peace treaty against Japanese aggression in China and denounced the Japanese infusion of opium as an instrument of imperialist penetration. Lodge was responsible for the insertion of the testimony of W. E. Macklin into the record of the debate, with the pithy if explosive formula "Shantung and Opium."[56]

Japan did not withdraw into isolationism despite the rebuff of the racial equality proposal, a predicament shared on a different level with the inter-ethnic conflict in Australia, New Zealand, Great Britain, and Serbia. Likewise, China did not withdraw into isolationism because of the loss of Shandong. International opium control brought Japan and China together again at the emerging opium-control regime under the League of Nations.[57] The settlement of global opium control in 1919 was, we might argue, an unprecedented success for Chinese society as the oldest "victim" of trade, consumption, and production, but less so for the Chinese state. The benefit of the supply-oriented perceptions of the opium problem and the nature of mutually binding institutional arrangements favored China arguably more than any other member of the league's opium bodies.

In the resolution of the first session of the League Assembly on December 15, 1920, the specific duties concerning the traffic in opium, formerly placed upon the Netherlands government by the Opium Convention of 1912, were transferred to the League of Nations. At the same time, the establishment of the future Advisory Committee in the Traffic of Opium and Other Dangerous Drugs (often abbreviated as Opium Advisory Committee) was decided. Let us appreciate the historical announcement in its entirety: "That in order to secure the fullest possible co-operation between the various countries in regard to the matter, and to assist and advise the Council in dealing with any questions that may arise, an Advisory Committee be appointed by the Council which shall include representatives of the countries chiefly concerned, in particular Holland, Great Britain, France, India, Japan, China, Siam, Portugal, and shall, subject to the general directions of the Council, meet at such times as may be found desirable. . . . That the Advisory Committee shall, three months before the beginning of every session of the Assembly, present to the Council for submission to the Assembly, a report on all matters regarding the execution of agreements with regard to the traffic in opium and other dangerous drugs."[58]

Wellington Koo, a Columbia University graduate; confidant of U.S. President Woodrow Wilson; later China's ambassador in Paris, London, and Washington; and the most promising diplomat at the Peace Conference urged the league to follow with concrete action. The league appreciated Koo's advice and proposed three assessors to the Opium Advisory Committee: Sir John Jordan, Henri Brenier, and Elizabeth Washburn Wright. A deadline for the first report of the committee to the council was set for June 1, 1921.[59] Since 1921, the cooperation between China and the League of Nations has been surprisingly successful in the enforcement of an international opium-control regime.

Despite successful American lobbying for the inclusion of the opium clause into the Covenant of the League of Nations, the Opium Advisory Committee was not officially recognized by the United States until 1923. The American mistrust toward the league, however, did not prevent substantial involvement of American "assessors" to various league committees. Elizabeth Washburn Wright took advantage of this position and rose to become one of the most influential and indispensable figures on the committee. She helped link policies in Geneva to those in Washington, London, and Beijing, a multilateral principle of interdependent obligations since the Anglo-Chinese agreement of 1907. Her early involvement in international opium-control politics brought several advantages. Governmental circles in America, England, Geneva, and China derived their information on the illicit cultivation and trafficking from Wright and the IAOA. Due to her expertise in the field, the American press appreciated her criticism of Chinese, league, and American policies and used her views to lobby for continuing support in public opinion. It is no exaggeration to state that for the first time in human history, drug control was now an official institutionalized concern of global governance, raising the interdependence among national and imperial drug regimes and drug consuming societies in Asia, Europe, and the Americas through voluminous flows of information, observation, and criticism. At this stage, Wellington Koo was well aware that the league was more than a platform for diplomatic representation. Its institutional machinery was still working out its structures and open to Chinese efforts concerning the opium traffic bodies. The Opium Advisory Committee served as an auxiliary body and supervised the enforcement of all resolutions, conventions, and agreements against opium and other dangerous drugs until the transfer to the United Nations toward the end of the Second World War.

Unlike the historiography and public memory of the "humiliation" of defeated claims at Paris, the peace settlement inaugurated procedures for incremental change of international norms of political conduct. Like most peace settlements, it did not solve all war-related problems at the stroke of a pen, despite astonishing efforts to do so. The Washington Conference in 1921 revised the Shandong question in China's favor. Later, Chinese league officials and lobbyists learned to exploit the victory it had not achieved.

In their autobiographies, Chinese diplomats chose to write more pessimistically than they had acted at the time. Was it the later "loss of China" that turned their diplomatic service for the Republican government in a pessimistic light? Was it the never-ending search for "complete recognition" (whatever that may imply), the final exit from the "century of humiliation"? In any case, the overemphasis on Chinese failures on the international stage has tended to cloud critical historical evaluation. An example of this larger trend is the testimony of Wunsz King (Jin Wensi), a Columbia graduate, a later Chinese delegate to the Washington Conference, and a longtime ambassador to Belgium, who recorded in laconic manner "two major successes" in Chinese diplomatic history: Shandong and the pursuit of tariff autonomy. China "was less fortunate in all other matters."[60]

Other contemporaries came to different conclusions when they reflected on China's record in 1919 and beyond. Alston, Jordan's successor as British minister in Beijing, took to the opposite view, writing to Earl Curzon in 1920 of China refusing "to be bullied into the Treaty of Versailles," earning in response "the rising tide of international esteem": "Though the momentary political victory at that time went to Japan, the moral victory remained with China, and has since culminated in her obtaining one of the temporary seats on the Council of the League of Nations."[61]

Chief among the newly formed pressure groups remained the IAOA, now composed of medical doctors, missionaries, journalists, and diplomats.

Although the IAOA also included British and American members, it acquired, transmitted, and internationalized the Chinese view on the opium trade as an evil outgrowth of the imperialist age that belonged to the past. The Chinese perception that treated the drug problem as supply based, not demand based, would keep its explanatory dominance for much of twentieth-century debates of global drug control's obstacles and objectives. The IAOA hoped to add with global drug control "another step in the progress of humanity," in the spirit of the Congress of Vienna, when the abolition of slavery marked the ethical quality of a postwar international order. More pragmatic considerations, notably the fear of German industry as a potential drug purchaser and producer, helped convince Britain and America to include the international opium problem in the negotiations at the Quai d'Orsay and formulate the opium clause as binding international law to all signatories of the Peace Treaties. This, in turn, provided the basis for the opium committee of the League of Nations, to which the IAOA was the most important advisory body in Asia.

The nongovernmental augmentation of anti-opium politics became part and parcel of the global control regime after 1919. The rapid conflux of new political forces, connecting a small nongovernmental organization in Beijing to the high politics in Paris and later Geneva, showed the limitations of formal diplomatic channels. It introduced a new social dimension to Republican China's cooperation with international organizations, one that remains unacknowledged in much of Chinese and Western historiography and memory. In sum, the IAOA laid the epistemic foundations and the social infrastructure of league advice, an information regime in Beijing that undergirded the League of Nations' opium bodies. The IAOA as an NGO was born as an organ of political lobbying, with its necessarily partisan mechanisms of social, political, and ideological inclusion and exclusion. Despite the visibility of this partial perspective, the institution became a virtually unchallenged think tank for Geneva. The internal coherence of this transnational information network largely bypassed international criticism. IAOA autonomy pointed beyond the organization itself. Its information gathering, compilation, distribution, and reception showed the great extent to which the League of Nations relied on generative processes of legitimacy beyond its own control.

In many ways, this conundrum has obscured the transnational origins of literally international drug control for a long time. Countless causes of some invented ideological grandeur and desperate political purpose have transnational corollaries. Nationalist revolutions, once seen as a mythical founding of a people taking shape as a purer form of collectivity than before, are now known for their recruitment of exiles; expansive social integration; and strategic blindness toward some transnational imports, such as money, but not others, such as religion or language. Fights on the humanitarian front in the postwar period have their transnational pioneers, their NGOs, and occasionally the governments that can help secure the long-term survival of those causes. But even by comparison, the movement against the opium trade and its local and national sub-movements blurred the analytic borders we commonly draw around a historical legacy of personal, national, imperial, or regional vintage. Would Prince Gong, the erstwhile protester of 1869, have recognized the questions debated by the League of Nations' opium bodies in the early 1920s? Would Soonderbai Powar be delighted or abhorred to comment on the professionalized bureaucracy of Geneva's opium information? Would Chinese nationalists in the 1930s and 1940s have signed the Opium Agreement of 1907 with British officials if it had never preexisted and the wording was the same?

Even history does not hold all the answers. What the story told here can teach us today is that while national legacies of grand reckonings remain, curated and polished by the state, the tracks of transnational legacies of mobilization easily disappear over time. For conveying an agenda from one society to another, transnationalism is essential, but without an enlarged collective identity attached to it, the transmission remains less conspicuous than the parts it once connected. The traces of border-crossing mobilization against the opium trade is one example of this oblivion, having almost vanished, like yesterday's footprints in the desert sand, spirited away by a nightly wind. The next morning, nothing is left except the fact that they once existed.

Transnational mobilization could and did cross borders of personal identity, walls of individual perspective, mountains of institutional loyalty, and even continental boundedness in ways that neither contemporaries nor historians fully grasp. An expansive look at the growth of protest, its proliferation, and its effective communication to audiences near and far revealed it at once as both intimate and universalist, planned and improvised, appearing in new places and times unexpectedly, as in the revival of a Marathi protest after four decades in serene Switzerland. Restoring these dynamics of political problematization helps give us a sense of the power not only of stubbornness but of a stubborn commitment to social change. Stagnation can be inexorable, transformation equally so. Global drug control came into existence through voices of persuasion that could never know for sure if their words would come to political fruition. Theirs was the persuasion by the weak.

CONCLUSION

"THE WORLD campaign against opium," a journal article announced in July 1922—was not it over yet? Three years before, the Paris Peace Conference had concluded the First World War and begun the painful process of pressing the formerly unruly belligerents into the massive straightjacket of five peace treaties: of Versailles, Saint-Germain-en-Laye, Neuilly-sur-Seine, Trianon, and Sèvres. One year after Paris, the first guardian of international drug control in human history—the League of Nations—saw the light of day, uncertain how long that day would last. Mandates, resources, narratives, goals, leadership, membership, resistance, and timing would all become subject to tense negotiations that continue to this day at the United Nations Commission on Narcotic Drugs.

The article of 1922 did not project a utopian vision of a world without drugs. It did not propose a grand diplomatic feat, nor did it present a desperate cry of political contestation. Its author invoked instead an international political cause already in existence. Unlike today's commentary on drug control, where questions of political responsibility usually take center stage, this article called for assessing the social damage of drugs in the recent history of humankind. "We in China," the article in the *Asiatic Review* averred, "are even more concerned than are Western peoples. We have suffered more than they have from the demoralization caused by the drug evil."[1] Some readers of the *Asiatic Review* will have been familiar with the historical, political, ideological, social, and economic background of this argument, having been exposed to antidrug sentiment and politics for several decades. To readers in the early twenty-first century, particularly outside Asia, the argument may appear more cryptic. Why take tally of which society, nation, or culture suffered more under drugs? What motivated this competitive self-pity, and what endowed it with political purpose?

The Republic of China's legation in London was where the author of the above piece served as the second in line. Zhu Zhaoxin could have limited the above communication to family, to his own superiors, or to colleagues serving other states—to those whom he knew or those empowered to make political decisions. But an open editorial seemed to suit best his intentions. "The world knows, or ought to know, that China has made unparalleled sacrifices to suppress a traffic against which all that is best and wisest in the country has protested with energy, and acted, when opportunity offered, with determination." In a gesture characteristic of engineers of public opinion, who represent and shape it at the same time, Zhu stuck close to his agenda. "I have appealed, through the Press, to the people, with the object of rousing public opinion against the use of opium." International public opinion was identified and addressed as a key element in global drug politics, the factor that defined its scope, orientation, and priorities. "The world is beginning to grasp that this problem is a world problem—not a Chinese problem, not a Far-Eastern problem. . . . I am glad . . . to think that opinion is setting steadily in this direction."[2] As preceding chapters have illustrated, Zhu shared this perception with thousands around the world.

A British journal founded in 1885, the *Asiatic Review* opened its pages to views at variance with existing practices of British imperial rule and the cultural dominance that secured narratives and discourses in its interest. Intellectual luminaries contributed alongside Zhu, among them Abdullah Yusuf Ali, the Indian-born Qur'an translator; Romesh Chunder Dutt, the astute critic of British Indian tax policy, land policy, and wealth distribution as causes for India's famine disasters; Syud Hossain, who served as one of three Indian delegates to the Paris Peace Conference; Sarojini Naidu, staunch fighter for the rights of the Indian nation and of Indian women; Samuel Satthianadhan, known for having married India's first woman novelist writing in English, Krupabai Satthianadhan; and India's first woman lawyer, Cornelia Sorabji. Overall, however, there were fewer prominent China connections in the 1920s, with the exception of Kavalam Madhava Panikkar, who became independent India's ambassador to China, after being commissioned to the UN General Assembly in 1947. As a former French chief of staff put it aptly: "When the old freedom fighters were fighting against occidental European countries, they were supported all over the world by the powerful trumpets of our press system and consequently, by our own occidental public opinions."[3]

The journal and its openness to representatives of new Asian intellectual critiques and political discourses, many of them tackling key junctures of Asian-European relations, partly explain why Zhu addressed international public opinion here. But the persisting idea that appealing to international public opinion would make any difference in legitimating norms and practices of governance—the opium trade was the business of the powerful, after all—may require some further reflection. Whereas empires have traditionally been seen as the producers, engines, and beneficiaries of international law—its norms and its legitimate practices—this book has shown that some transnational forces could bypass the dynamics of imperial legitimation. Coalitions of perception, mobilization, and imagined consensus brought into being international norms that curtailed the political, economic, and social practices that empires and later nation-states could legitimately pursue. During the oft-cited age of imperialism, a level of political contestation emerged that lay atop the imperial great powers as well as the "imperialized," a domain of transnational political engagement that was produced, manipulated, exploited, and recognized by both.

Zhu's life as a writer was filled with far more ambitious interventions. As peace dawned after the First World War, Zhu used his position as consul general in San Francisco to identify the Republic of China, its new status, and its old marketplace as a field for international development and foreign investment: "We have driven the Huns out of business in China. . . . This is the chance for Americans to expand your trade in the Far East for the replacement of the Huns."[4] Elsewhere, he analyzed the mental map of the League of Nations in Geneva to one of the core problems of China's international relations, that of the "unequal treaties."[5] The sum of these interventions aimed to prepare the international scene for China "to take her place among the nations of the world as a dominant factor."[6]

Short of national resistance, writing and rioting became the most militant weapons of imperial criticism, beyond the prominent causes of Asian, African, and Middle Eastern nationalism. Voicing social and political concerns in appeals to international public opinion was driven by more than a Liberal belief that public opinion did in fact exist and played a role in keeping governance, domestic as well as imperial, in check. Antidrug publicity, in particular, addressed an increasingly widespread frustration that China's most severe social problems, although caused and perpetrated by foreigners, did not receive nearly sufficient attention. Protesting against Western, international negligence, then, became virtually identical with political action. Since the 1870s, when Prince Gong elaborated on the grounds of anti-opium opposition, international public opinion increasingly became a point of discursive and political reference, manifested by the wake of a burgeoning, transnational print and newspaper industry in China, Japan, the European colonies of Asia, the United States, and elsewhere.

The movements against drugs and the politics of control had raised their own stakes, nearly inevitably, by recourse to public opinion as its driving force. Just as public opinion had justified this ideological, social, and political change of course—reversing existing ideological positions on consumption and supply, standard and deviant behavior, and legitimate and illegitimate policies—so public opinion remained a pillar once a global regime had emerged. But every form of predominance carries its own liabilities. Here, international public opinion further enhanced the perception of states and societies that they had to insist on the chosen course—an insistence that would last across most of the twentieth century, with the exception of a few global outliers of liberalization, like the Netherlands. Speaking on real and imagined platforms of international publicity restricted rather than augmented the room for policy adjustments.

None of the participants in the global anti-drug cause could legitimately claim the lion's share of what was called "the world campaign against opium." National histories place holds on the universal human past that involved many more players, actors, and influences than those of the nation. National history is thus by definition reductionist, although its pride forbids saying so. Globally, there is not less difference than one might expect in the ways that nations monopolize, or perhaps colonize, the past with a claim to exclusivity. The interpretation forwarded by one nation cannot and must not be contested by anyone else. National histories are non-negotiable, and at times the transnational appendices to those national histories share the same traits. But for a reflective and balanced understanding of the past, little of the ready-made fare served on a daily basis by nation-states withstands analytic and archival scrutiny.

The opium wars were no exception to this manner of relating to the human past. Curiously, however, the opium wars have not become a fixed point of numerous national identities but almost exclusively of China's. The point here is not to identify who suffered more—a fruitless exercise, as each claim to victimhood defies, by definition, any comparison and poses as unique—but to state that ideas do not necessarily remain fixed in the places where they were conceived. Political ideas, in particular, are territory that can be claimed by states, because states remain powerful entities to occupy the human past. The "world campaign against opium" carried many of the accoutrements to be expected from postwar political movements. But the world of the late nineteenth and early twentieth centuries was in political, ideological, and social respects more deeply integrated than we assume. Historical research offers the opportunity to discharge the mutual repulsion of conflicting narratives—much like to magnets with a negative charge—and re-envision the force field of historical influence that has given shape to the boundaries of acceptable cross-border conduct by states and businesses around the world.

Historical amnesias, then, have pertinent rationales. Like historical knowledge, they are products of collective memory across generations. Despite the prevailing cliché that the Chinese were alone in opposing a hostile world intent on poisoning them, there were many others who joined, assisted, and proclaimed their fight. This book has presented anti-opium mobilization as fault lines of loyalty beyond national affiliation. It illustrated how one agenda—the campaign against drug trading—could produce personal alliances, coalitions of interest, and communities of partnership in terms other than those of national, ethnic, or social belonging. In the century following the opium wars, narcotic drugs have changed position in the conjoint life of societies and states. Once in full enjoyment of the blessings of international law, government-sponsored drug trading was ousted from the legitimate repertoire of state conduct and transnational economic intercourse. Since the League of Nations, drug-trading governments risk pariah status. At the end of Asia's Second World War, when the Tokyo War Crimes Tribunal deliberated how to assess Japanese drug trafficking to China in wartime, the verdict was implacable. Overwhelmingly indicted by Chinese anti-opium information from wartime propaganda organs, drug trafficking received the strongest condemnation available to international society. It became a war crime.

This is not the place to debate the War on Drugs in its multiple versions, regions, and contradictions around the world. It is poignantly criticized today as a political practice. It has multiplied rather than reduced social violence in regions ridden by drug cartels. It has failed to take into account the financial and social long-term costs of mass incarceration and of penalizing consumer choice in liberal societies. But neither criticism can be transposed to global conditions between the 1860s and the 1920s. What did resonate was the scale and depth of damage that opium could inflict on Asian societies, against their will.

Anti-drug opposition challenged an imperial practice rather than empires or imperialism per se. Vice versa, in governmental responses to local and transnational protest, drug control came to serve as a way to restore their own tarnished reputation and thereby reassert empire's raison d'être. On the political level, economic interdependence and newly perceived opium emergencies pressed for intercolonial cooperation toward mutually agreeable systems of opium control to counteract the unlimited trading and consumption of the drug.[7] Anti-opium ideology was taken seriously, even literally, but neither to endorse nor to deconstruct it. As suggested in these pages, we need to rethink the ways in which this ideology was produced by social forces, reached the world of politics, and gave rise to new hierarchies: the upgrades and downgrades of political ethics and popular legitimacy between states and societies in Asia, Europe, and North America.[8] It is not about a moral argument regarding the qualities or pitfalls of radical, moderate, or virtually absent "anti-foreignism" among Asian anti-opium activists, a supposition anticipating the telos of nationalist independence as the default mode and defining characteristic of Asian-Western interactions prior to decolonization.[9] Short of independence and open revolt against imperialist institutions, there were causes worth fighting for, some of which—as this book hoped to show—introduced new norms of conduct into international society before empires had come to an end.

NOTES

ACKNOWLEDGMENTS

INDEX

NOTES

Abbreviations

CBYS, XF   Gugong bowuyuan (Palace Museum), *Qingdai chouban yiwu shimo* (The Qing Dynasty's management of barbarian affairs from the origins to the end) (Beiping: n.p., 1929–30); Xianfeng

COROP   Great Britain, Foreign Office, Further Correspondence Respecting Opium, F.O. 415

ECCP   Arthur W. Hummel, Eminent Chinese of the Ch'ing Period, 2 vols. (Washington, DC: U.S. Government Printing Office, 1943–44)

FRUS   US Department of State, Papers Relating to the Foreign Relations of the United States (Washington, DC: U.S. Government Printing Office, 1864–)

GEMP   George Ernest Morrison Papers, Mitchell Library, State Library of New South Wales, Sydney

GSPK   Geheimes Staatsarchiv Preußischer Kulturbesitz, Berlin

IAOA   International Anti-Opium Association

JFMA   Japanese Ministry of Foreign Affairs

KKS   K'euen Keae Shay

POC   Philippine Opium Commission

PROT   Great Britain, *Papers Relating to the Opium Trade, 1842–1856* (London: Harrison and Sons, 1857)

SOFL   Society of Friends Library, London

SSOT   Society for the Suppression of the Opium Trade

TOT   Great Britain, Foreign Office, The Opium Trade (Wilmington, DE: Scholarly Resources, 1974)

UKNA   National Archives of the United Kingdom, Kew
UNOG   United Nations Office at Geneva
WCTU   Woman's Christian Temperance Union

Introduction

1. Syamal K. Chatterjee, *Legal Aspects of International Drug Control* (The Hague: Martinus Nijhoff, 1981), 35–68.
2. Maia Ramnath, *Haj to Utopia: How the Ghadar Movement Charted Global Radicalism and Attempted to Overthrow the British Empire* (University of California Press: Berkeley, 2011); Ilham Khuri-Makdisi, *The Eastern Mediterranean and the Making of Global Radicalism, 1860–1914* (Berkeley: University of California Press, 2010).
3. Georg Jellinek, *Die sozialethische Bedeutung von Recht, Unrecht und Strafe* (Hildesheim: Olms, 1878; Berlin: Häring, 1908), 77; Jellinek, *Die Erklärung der Menschen- und Bürgerrechte. Ein Beitrag zur modernen Verfassungsgeschichte* (Leipzig: Duncker und Humblot, 1895); Martti Koskenniemi, *The Gentle Civilizer of Nations: The Rise and Fall of International Law, 1870–1960* (Cambridge: Cambridge University Press, 2001), 198–208.
4. Charlotte Walker-Said and John D. Kelly, eds., *Corporate Social Responsibility? Human Rights in the New Global Economy* (Chicago: University of Chicago Press, 2015).
5. Ian Clark, *International Legitimacy and World Society* (Oxford: Oxford University Press, 2007). The global characteristics of transnational activism are still better understood in the postwar period: Maureen R. Berman and Joseph E. Johnson, eds., *Unofficial Diplomats* (New York: Columbia University Press, 1977); Margaret E. Keck and Kathryn Sikkink, *Activists beyond Borders: Advocacy Networks in International Politics* (Ithaca: Cornell University Press, 1998).
6. Matteo D'Alfonso and Maria Laura Lanzillo, *Gouverner la peur: réflexions politiques et visions de l'autre de l'époque moderne à l'ère globale* (Hildesheim: Georg Olms, 2010).
7. Peter Andreas and Ethan Nadelmann, *Policing the Globe: Criminalization and Crime Control in International Relations* (Oxford: Oxford University Press, 2006).
8. Christopher Leslie Brown, *Moral Capital: Foundations of British Abolitionism* (Chapel Hill: University of North Carolina Press, 2006); Sidney Tarrow, *The New Transnational Activism* (Cambridge: Cambridge University Press, 2005); Deen K. Chatterjee, *The Ethics of Assistance: Morality and the Distant Needy* (Cambridge: Cambridge University Press, 2004).
9. Great Britain, Parliamentary Papers, *East India (Opium): Return of an Article on Opium by dr. Watt* (London: Eyre and Spottiswoode, 1891), 27.
10. On the international leitmotif of over-exercised power: Ernest May, Richard Rosecrance, and Zara Steiner, "Theory and International History," in *History and Neorealism* (Cambridge: Cambridge University Press, 2010), 3.

11. This distinguishes the global assessment of anti-opium pressure from existing assessments on an imperial scale, most prominently Paul C. Winther, *Anglo-European Science and the Rhetoric of Empire: Malaria, Opium, and British Rule in India, 1756–1895* (Lanham: Lexington, 2003).

12. Howard Padwa, *Social Poison: The Culture and Politics of Opiate Control in Britain and France, 1821–1926* (Baltimore: Johns Hopkins University Press, 2012), 48.

13. Moses Hess, "Die eine und die ganze Freiheit," in *Philosophische und sozialistische Schriften 1837–1850* (Berlin: Akademie-Verlag, 1961; Vaduz: Topos, 1980), 227–228.

14. Dong Wang, *China's Unequal Treaties: Narrating National History* (Lanham: Lexington, 2005); Jianlang Wang, *Unequal Treaties and China*, 2 vols. (Honolulu: Silkroad Press, 2015–2016). Orig. Wang Jianlang, *Zhongguo feichu bupindeng tiaoyue de licheng* (The Record of Abolishing the Unequal Treaties in China) (Nanchang: Jiangxi renmin chubanshe, 2000).

15. Jonathan D. Spence, "Opium," in *Chinese Roundabout: Essays in History and Culture* (New York: Norton, 1992), 238; United Nations Office on Drugs and Crime (UNODC), Policy Analysis and Research Branch, *A Century of International Drug Control*, 37.

16. UNODC, *Century of International Drug Control*, 24–25.

17. Pierre Hauck and Sven Peterke, ed., *International Law and Transnational Organised Crime* (Oxford: Oxford University Press, 2016).

18. Despite criticism especially on methodology and conclusions, we still have no more comprehensive overview than Carl Trocki, *Opium, Empire and the Global Political Economy* (London: Routledge, 1999).

19. Kathleen L. Lodwick, *Crusaders against Opium: Protestant Missionaries in China, 1874–1917* (Lexington: University Press of Kentucky, 1996); Ian R. Tyrrell, *Reforming the World: The Creation of America's Moral Empire* (Princeton: Princeton University Press, 2010).

20. David Edward Owen, *British Opium Policy in China and India* (New Haven, CT: Yale University Press, 1934); S. H. Bailey, *The Anti-Drug Campaign: An Experiment in International Control* (London: S. King, 1935); Charles Clarkson Stelle, *Americans and the China Opium Trade in the Nineteenth Century* (New York: Arno Press, 1981); Arnold H. Taylor, *American Diplomacy and the Narcotics Traffic, 1900–1939* (Durham, NC: Duke University Press, 1969); William O. Walker III, *Opium and Foreign Policy: The Anglo-American Search for Order in Asia, 1912–1954* (Chapel Hill: University of North Carolina Press, 1991); David F. Musto, *The American Disease: Origins of Narcotic Control* (Oxford: Oxford University Press, 1999); William B. McAllister, *Drug Diplomacy in the Twentieth Century: An International History* (London: Routledge, 2000).

21. For ideological foundations: Heinz Gollwitzer, *Die Gelbe Gefahr: Geschichte eines Schlagworts. Studien zum imperialistischen Denken* (Göttingen: Vandenhoeck und Ruprecht, 1962). For an underappreciated case study: Sebastian Conrad, *Globale Arbeitsmärkte und die 'Gelbe Gefahr'. 'Kulis', Migration und die Politik der Differenz* (Essen: Klartext, 2010).

22. On this theme: Diana L. Ahmad, *The Opium Debate and Chinese Exclusion Laws in the Nineteenth-Century American West* (Reno: University of Nevada Press, 2007).

23. "How China is dealing with opium-intemperance," caption under a photograph of a public ceremony of burning opium pipes in Hankou," in Clarence Poe, *Where Half the World Is Waking Up: The Old and the New in Japan, China, the Philippines, and India, Reported with Especial Reference to American Conditions* (New York: Doubleday, Page, 1911), 106; *Qingmo minchu de jinyan yundong he wanguo jinyan hui* (Shanghai: Shanghai kexue jishu wenxian chuban she, 1996); Yongming Zhou, *Anti-drug Crusades in Twentieth-Century China: Nationalism, History, and State Building* (Lanham: Rowman and Littlefield, 1999).

24. On the historiography on the sources of change, the now classic references are Ssu-yü Teng and John King Fairbank, ed., *China's Response to the West* (Cambridge, MA: Harvard University Press, 1959), and its counter: Paul A. Cohen, *Discovering History in China* (New York: Columbia University Press, 1984).

25. For a recent example: "10 People Sentenced to Death for Drug Crimes in Southern China," *South China Morning Post,* December 17, 2017, http://www.scmp.com/news/china/society/article/2124673/10-people-sentenced-death-drug-crimes-southern-china.

26. Frank Dikötter, Lars Laamann, and Zhou Xun, *Narcotic Culture: A History of Drugs in China* (London: Hurst, 2004). Note also the review by Timothy Brook, *Bulletin of the School of Oriental and African Studies* 69, no. 2 (June 2006): 338–339. John F. Richards, "Opium and the British Indian Empire: The Royal Commission of 1895," *Modern Asian Studies* 36, no. 2 (May 2002): 375–420; Paul Gootenberg, *Andean Cocaine: The Making of a Global Drug* (Chapel Hill: University of North Carolina Press, 2009); Isaac Campos, *Home Grown: Marijuana and the Origins of Mexico's War on Drugs* (Chapel Hill: University of North Carolina Press, 2012); Phil Withington and Angela McShane, eds., *Cultures of Intoxication* (Oxford: Oxford University Press, 2014); James H. Mills and Patricia Barton, eds., *Drugs and Empires: Essays in Modern Imperialism and Intoxication, c. 1500 to c. 1930* (London: Palgrave Macmillan, 2007).

27. *War on Drugs: Report of the Global Commission on Drug Policy* (Rio de Janeiro: Global Commission on Drug Policy, 2011).

28. Yangwen Zheng, *The Social Life of Opium in China* (Cambridge: Cambridge University Press, 2005). For anti-opium controversies over consumption: Keith McMahon, *The Fall of the God of Money: Opium Smoking in Nineteenth-Century China* (Lanham: Rowman and Littlefield, 2002).

29. Seymour Drescher and Pieter C. Emmer, eds., *Who Abolished Slavery? Slave Revolts and Abolitionism: A Debate with João Pedro Marques* (New York: Berghahn, 2010); Susan Bayly, "Imagining 'Greater India': French and Indian Visions of Colonialism in the Indic Mode," *Modern Asian Studies* 38, no. 3 (July 2004): 703–744; Prasenjit Duara, "Nationalism in East Asia," *History Compass* 4, no. 3 (May 2006): 407–427; Cemil Aydin, *The Politics of Anti-Westernism in Asia: Visions of World Order in Pan-Islamic and Pan-Asian Thought* (New York: Columbia University Press, 2007); Petra Pakkanen, *Au-*

gust Myhrberg and North-European Philhellenism: Building the Myth of a Hero (Athens: Suomen Ateenan-instituutin säätiö [Foundation of the Finnish Institute at Athens], 2006); Émile Malakis, "French Travellers in Greece (1770–1820): An Early Phase of French Philhellenism" (thesis, University of Philadelphia, 1925); Suzanne L. Marchand, *Down from Olympus: Archaeology and Philhellenism in Germany, 1750–1970* (Princeton, NJ: Princeton University Press, 1996).

30. Maurizio Isabella, *Risorgimento in Exile: Italian Émigrés and the Liberal International in the post-Napoleonic Era* (Oxford: Oxford University Press, 2009); Christopher A. Bayly and Eugenio F. Biagini, eds., *Giuseppe Mazzini and the Globalization of Democratic Nationalism, 1830–1920* (Oxford: Oxford University Press, 2008).

31. Edward R. Slack Jr., *Opium, State, and Society: China's Narco-Economy and the Guomindang, 1924–1937* (Honolulu: University of Hawai'i Press, 2001).

32. "Centennial anniv. of int'l anti-drug meeting commemorated," accessed September 19, 2016, http://v.cctv.com/html/media/ChinaToday/2009/02/China Today_300_20090227_2.shtml; Cao Li, "UN Warns of Drug Menace at Shanghai Conference," *China Daily,* February 27, 2009, http://www.chinadaily .com.cn/china/2009–02/27/content_7519871.htm; Embassy of the People's Republic of China in the State of Israel, "Foreign Ministry Spokesperson Jiang Yu's Regular Press Conference on February 19, 2009," http://www.chinaembassy.org .il/eng/fyrth/t538341.htm; Permanent Mission of the People's Republic of China to the United Nations and Other International Organizations in Vienna, "Statement by the Chinese Delegation at the High-level Segment of the 52nd Session of Commission on Narcotic Drugs" (Vienna International Centre, March 12, 2009); "Century of War on Drugs Has Brought Problem 'Under Control' but Fight Goes On—UN," *UN Daily News,* DH/5347, February 26, 2009, 5–6; "'Positive Balance Sheet' from Century of Drug Control," accessed March 10, 2009, https://www.unodc.org/unodc/en/press/releases/2009/February/2009-02.26.html.

33. M. Cherif Bassiouni, "The International Narcotics Control System: A Proposal," *St. John's Law Review* 46, no. 4, 713–763, here 715, 718.

34. Reportage reached up to the website of China's Ministry of Public Security: http://www.mps.gov.cn/n16/n80209/n397794/1261852.html, http://big5.ynjd .gov.cn:81/pubnews/doc/read/gnxw/768548863.236183500/index.asp (accessed November 25, 2008).

35. Permanent Mission of the People's Republic of China to the United Nations and Other International Organizations in Vienna, "Shanghai Declaration," accessed September 8, 2016, http://www.fmprc.gov.cn/ce/cgvienna/eng/xw/t553678.htm.

36. Timed to be published together with the centennial: Su Zhiliang; Liu Xiaohong, *Quanqiu jindu de kaiduan: 1909 nian Shanghai wanguo jinyan hui* (The origins of global drug control: The International Opium Commission in Shanghai 1909) (Shanghai: Shanghai sanlian shudian, 2009) and Su Zhiliang, *Shanghai jindu shi* (The history of drug control in Shanghai) (Shanghai: Shanghai sanlian shudian, 2009). For the political framework today: Hong Lu, Terance D. Miethe, and Bin Liang, *China's Drug Practices and Policies: Regulating Controlled Substances in a Global Context* (London: Routledge, 2009), 77–188.

37. Nancy Rosenblum, "Memory, Law and Repair," in *Breaking the Cycles of Hatred: Memory, Law, and Repair,* ed. Martha Minow (Princeton: Princeton University Press, 2002), 4.

1. Thunders before the Storm

1. Christian Le Marec, "Histoire de l'opium medicinal. Du pivot aux alcaloïdes de l'opium," *Douleurs* 5, no. 2 (2004): 83–98, here 86.

2. Richard Harvey Brown, "The Opium Trade and Opium Policies in India, China, Britain and the United States: Historical Comparisons and Theoretical Interpretations," *Asian Journal of Social Science* 30, no. 3 (2002): 623–656, here 628.

3. Richard J. Grace, *Opium and Empire: The Lives and Careers of William Jardine and James Matheson* (Montreal: McGill-Queen's University Press, 2014).

4. "The Production, Consumption, and Export of Opium as Affecting the Protected States of India," in Royal Commission on Opium, *Final Report of the Royal Commission on Opium,* vol. 6 (London: HMSO, 1895), 28. On British concerns over French control in the Portuguese colonies: M. N. Pearson, "Goa in the Early Nineteenth Century—Some British Accounts," in *Medieval Deccan History: Commemoration Volume in Honour of Purshottam P. M. Joshi,* ed. A. Rā Kulkarnī et al. (Bombay: Popular Praksahan Pvt., 1996), 229–236, esp. 235.

5. Man-houng Lin, *China Upside Down: Currency, Society, and Ideologies, 1808–1856* (Cambridge, MA: Harvard University Asia Center, 2007).

6. David Anthony Bello, *Opium and the Limits of Empire: Drug Prohibition in the Chinese Interior, 1729–1850* (Cambridge, MA: Harvard University Asia Center, 2005).

7. On the sea as social space: Sunil S. Amrith, *Crossing the Bay of Bengal* (Cambridge, MA: Harvard University Press, 2015).

8. Ronald D. Renard, "The Making of a Problem: Narcotics in Mainland Southeast Asia," in *Development or Domestication? Indigenous Peoples of Southeast Asia,* ed. Don McCaskill and Ken Kampe (Chiang Mai: Silkworm Books, 1997), 307–328, here 310; Renard, *Mainstreaming Alternative Development in Thailand, Lao PDR and Myanmar: A Process of Learning* (Vienna: UNODC, 2010), 22.

9. Chris Baker, "Ayutthaya Rising: From Land or Sea?" *Journal of Southeast Asian Studies* 34, no. 1 (February 2003): 41–62, here 48.

10. Bhawan Ruangsilp, *Dutch East India Company Merchants at the Court of Ayutthaya: Dutch Perceptions of the Thai Kingdom, c. 1604–1765* (Leiden: Brill, 2007), 50, 185–186, 190, 232n42.

11. James Windle, "How the East Influenced Drug Prohibition," *International History Review* 35, no. 5 (2013): 1185–1199.

12. Thanapol Limapichart, "The Prescription of Good Books: The Formation of the Discourse and Cultural Authority of Literature in Modern Thailand (1860s–1950) (PhD diss., University of Wisconsin-Madison, 2008), 30.

13. Renard, "Making of a Problem," 309–310.

14. Thant Myint-U, *The Making of Modern Burma* (Cambridge: Cambridge University Press, 2001), 50.

15. Renard, "Making of a Problem," 310; Sugata Bose, *A Hundred Horizons: The Indian Ocean in the Age of Global Empire* (Cambridge, MA: Harvard University Press, 2006), 54.

16. W. H. Coates, *The Old "Country Trade" of the East Indies* (London: Imray, Laurie, Norie and Wilson, 1911), 68; Christopher Bayly, *Imperial Meridian: The British Empire and the World 1780–1830* (London: Longman, 1989), 73–74.

17. Bayly, *Imperial Meridian*, 224.

18. Coates, *Old "Country Trade,"* 64, 54.

19. Ibid., 68–69.

20. Ibid., 52.

21. Ibid., 33.

22. A first step may be Koizumi Tatsuya, *Ahen to Honkon, 1845–1943* (Opium and Hong Kong, 1845–1943) (Tokyo: Tokyo daigaku shuppankai, 2016).

23. "Section IV: The Export of Indian Opium to China and the Straits," in Royal Commission on Opium, *Vol. VI. Final Report of the Royal Commission on Opium. Part I. The Report* (London: Her Majesty's Stationery Office, 1895), 48; Eric Tagliacozzo, *Secret Trades, Porous Borders: Smuggling and States along a Southeast Asian Frontier, 1865–1915* (New Haven, CT: Yale University Press, 2005).

24. Pamela Crossley, *The Wobbling Pivot. China Since 1800: An Interpretive History* (Malden, MA: Blackwell, 2010), xiii.

25. Agricole Joseph François Xavier Pierre Esprit Simon Paul Antoine Marquis de Fortia d'Urban, *La Chine et l'Angleterre: ou Histoire de la declaration de guerre faite par la Reine d'Angleterre à L'Empereur de la Chine* (Paris: Chez l'auteur, 1840), 171.

26. Ibid., 172–173.

27. Louis Rousselet, *India and Its Native Princes* (London: Chapman and Hall, 1875), 556.

28. Chantal Descours-Gatin, *Quand l'opium finançait la colonisation en Indochine: l'élaboration de la régie générale de l'opium, 1860 à 1914* (Paris: L'Harmattan, 1992); Philippe Le Failler, *Monopole et prohibition de l'opium en Indochine: le pilori des chimères* (Paris: Harmattan, 2001); James R. Rush, *Opium to Java: Revenue Farming and Chinese Enterprise in Colonial Indonesia, 1860–1910* (Ithaca, NY: Cornell University Press, 1990); M. Emdad-ul Haq, *Drugs in South Asia: From the Opium Trade to the Present Day* (Houndmills: St. Martin's Press, 2000).

29. A. Hischmann, *Die Opiumfrage und ihre internationale Regelung* (Tübingen: H. Laupp, 1912), 14–17; Carl A. Trocki, *Opium, Empire, and the Global Political Economy: A Study of the Asian Opium Trade, 1750–1950* (London: Routledge, 1999); Thongchai Winichakul, *Siam Mapped: A History of the Geo-body of a Nation* (Honolulu: University of Hawai'i Press, 1997), 101–121; Niels Petersson, *Imperialismus und Modernisierung: Siam, China und die europäischen Mächte 1895–1914* (Munich: Oldenbourg, 2000), 91–135; Stefan Hell, *Siam and the League of Nations: Modernisation, Sovereignty and Multilateral Diplomacy, 1920–1940* (Bangkok: River Books, 2010).

30. Bello, *Opium and the Limits of Empire.*

31. Richard Platt, *Smuggling in the British Isles: A History* (Stroud: Tempus, 2011).
32. Viscount Palmerston to Rear-Admiral Elliot and Captain Elliot, February 26, 1841, in "Memorandum respecting Opium, communicated Sir H. Pottinger to Commissioners Keying and Elepoo, and Governor-General Newkeen," in Great Britain, *Papers Relating to the Opium Trade in China: 1842–1856* (London: Harrison and Sons, 1857), 2. On Britain's commercial reputation: Glenn Melancon, *Britain's China Policy and the Opium Crisis: Balancing Drugs, Violence, and National Honour, 1833–1840* (Ashgate: Aldershot and Burlington, 2003). On press criticism of Palmerston during the Second Opium War (1856–1860): Nicholas A. Joukovsky, "Peacock and His 'Pet Politician': An Unpublished Latin Squib on the Coalition against Palmerston," *Modern Language Review* 91, no. 4 (October 1996): 833–839.
33. Julia Lovell, introduction to the English edition of *The Qing Empire and the Opium War,* by Haijian Mao (Cambridge: Cambridge University Press, 2005), xix.
34. Mao, *The Qing Empire,* 12.
35. On Xu Naiji: Lin Man-houng, "Late Qing Perceptions of Native Opium," *Harvard Journal of Asiatic Studies* 64, no. 1 (June 2004): 120–121.
36. The most succinct and balanced analysis available is Peter C. Perdue, "The First Opium War: The Anglo-Chinese War of 1839–1842," https://ocw.mit .edu/ans7870/21f/21f.027/opium_wars_01/ow1_essay02.html, https://ocw .mit.edu/ans7870/21f/21f.027/opium_wars_01/ow1_essay03.html.
37. Arthur Waley, *The Opium War through Chinese Eyes* (London: George Allen and Unwin, 1958), 44–45.
38. Haijian Mao, *Tianchao de bengkui* (The collapse of the celestial empire) (Beijing: Sanlian shudian, 2005), translated as Haijian Mao, *The Qing Empire and the Opium War: The Collapse of the Heavenly Dynasty* (Cambridge: Cambridge University Press, 2016).
39. In addition to Mao, on British stratagems: Julia Lovell, *The Opium War: Drugs, Dreams and the Making of China* (Basingstoke: Picador, 2011).
40. Peter D. Lowes, *The Genesis of International Narcotics Control,* 38.
41. Waley, *Opium War through Chinese Eyes,* 51.
42. Jürgen Osterhammel, "Semi-colonialism and Informal Empire in Twentieth-Century China: Towards a Framework of Analysis," in *Imperialism and After: Continuities and Discontinuities,* ed. Wolfgang J. Mommsen and Jürgen Osterhammel (London: Allen and Unwin, 1986), 290–314.
43. Court, "Opium Trade," 5. The author may have been identical with the eponymous Lieutenant-Colonel of the Bengal Cavalry, proficient "in two of the native languages." "Asiatic Intelligence," *Asiatic Journal and Monthly Register for British and Foreign India, China, and Australasia* 38 (May–August 1842), 39. He also translated *Sher Ali called Afsos. The Araish-i-Mahfil; or, the Ornament of the Assembly* (n.p., 1871) and *Mir Hasan. The Nasi-Benazir . . . of Mir Hasan* (n.p. 1889), and authored *An Exposition of the Relations of the British Government with the Sultaun and State of Palembang* (London: Black, Kingsbury, Parbury and Allen, 1821). "List of Civil Servants in the Presidency of Fort William, Corrected up to the 19th July 1859," 46, appendix of *Quar-*

terly Army List of Her Majesty's British and Indian Forces of the Bengal Establishment, exhibiting the Rank, Standing, and Various Services of Every Officer in the Army . . . (Calcutta: P. M. Cranenburgh, Military Orphan Press/R. C. Lepage and Co., British Library, 1859).

44. Viscount Palmerston to Rear-Admiral Elliot and Captain Elliot, February 26, 1841, in "Memorandum respecting Opium, communicated Sir H. Pottinger to Commissioners Keying and Elepoo, and Governor-General Newkeen," in Great Britain, *Papers Relating to the Opium Trade in China. 1842–1856,* 2.

45. Ibid.

46. Pottinger to Parker, 10 April 1843, *PROT,* 5.

47. Pottinger to Earl of Aberdeen, 25 July 1843, *PROT,* 7.

48. M. H. Court, "The Opium Trade," *Times,* 16 December 1842, 5.

49. Ibid., 5.

50. Bob Dye, *Merchant Prince of the Sandalwood Mountains: Afong and the Chinese in Hawai'i* (Honolulu: University of Hawai'i Press, 1997), 46.

51. Davis to Earl of Aberdeen, 17 March 1846, *PROT,* 25, also FO 682/1977, UKNA.

52. Viscount Palmerston to Rear-Admiral Elliot and Captain Elliot (26 February, 1841), *PROT,* 1. Also included in "State Paper No. 2221", in Great Britain, House of Commons, *Accounts and Papers 1857,* sess. 2, vol. 19 (n.p.).

53. Ibid.

54. Footnote, *PROT,* 2.

55. Palmerston to Elliot and Elliot, 26 February 1841, *PROT,* 1.

56. "Reply by the Imperial Commissioners to Memorandum on Opium," *PROT,* 3.

57. Franklin Bakhala, *Indian Opium and Sino-Indian Trade Relations, 1801–1858* (PhD thesis, London University, 1985), 68. For Jardine Matheson coverage: MS JM/A7 and Papers of Richard Bourke, 6th Earl of Mayo. MS Add. 7490, Cambridge University Library, Department of Manuscripts and University Archives.

58. Pottinger to Parker, 10 April 1843, *PROT,* 4. Pottinger to Earl of Aberdeen, 25 July 1843, *PROT,* 8.

59. "Commissioner Keying's reply to Memorandum of June 30, 1843," *PROT,* 7; Fang Chao-ying, "Ch'i-ying (Kiying)," in *Eminent Chinese of the Ch'ing Period,* ed. Arthur W. Hummel (Washington, DC: Government Printing Office, 1943), 130–134.

60. "Commissioner Keying and his Colleagues to Sir H. Pottinger," 24 August 1843, *PROT,* 11.

61. Ibid., 12.

62. Davis to Earl of Aberdeen, 1 May 1845, *PROT,* 21.

63. Davis to Earl of Aberdeen, 24 June 1844, *PROT,* 16.

64. Pottinger to Earl of Aberdeen, 10 April 1844, *PROT,* 14; Lay to Pottinger, 1 April 1844, 10 April 1844, *PROT,* 14.

65. Davis to Earl of Aberdeen, 17 March 1846, *PROT,* 25.

66. Davis to Earl of Aberdeen, 23 August 1844, *PROT,* 20.

67. Keying to Davis, 13 March 1846, *PROT,* 27; Bowring to Earl of Malmesbury, 5 February 1853, *PROT,* 27, 32.

68. Davis to Palmerston, 15 May 1847, *PROT,* 28. For British international legal attitudes globally: Antony Anghie, *Imperialism, Sovereignty, and the Making of International Law* (Cambridge: Cambridge University Press, 2007), 32–114.

69. Pottinger to Commissioner Keying and his colleagues, 30 October 1843, *PROT,* 13.

70. Keying to Davis, 19 August 1844, *PROT,* 21.

71. Keying and his colleagues to Sir H. Pottinger, 24 August 1843, *PROT,* 12.

72. Pottinger to Commissioner Keying and his Colleagues, 30 August 1843, *PROT,* 13.

73. A. E. Moule, "The Use of Opium and Its Bearing on the Spread of Christianity in China," *Records of the General Conference of the Protestant Missionaries of China, Held at Shanghai, May 10–24, 1877* (Shanghai: Presbyterian Mission Press, 1878), 358.

74. Jonathan Spence, *God's Chinese Son: The Taiping Heavenly Kingdom of Hong Xiuquan* (New York: Norton, 1996), xxvi.

75. Bowring to Earl of Clarendon, 8 January 1856, *PROT,* 38; Ching Him Felix Wong, "The Images of the Taiping Heavenly Kingdom as Shown in the Publications in France, Germany, and Italy during the Second Half of the Nineteenth Century," *Journal of Chinese Studies* 55 (July 2012): 139–174.

76. Stephen R. Platt, *Autumn in the Heavenly Kingdom: China, the West, and the Epic Story of the Taiping Civil War* (New York: Vintage, 2012), 156.

77. Alcock to Bowring, 29 January 1853, *PROT,* 33.

78. This was according to the secretary of the British legation. William Frederick Mayers, *"The Peking Gazette": Translation of the Peking Gazette for 1874* (Shanghai: North China Herald, 1875), iii, cited in Natascha Vittinghoff, *Die Anfänge des Journalismus in China (1860–1911)* (Wiesbaden: Harrassowitz, 2002), 56. See also Barbara Mittler, *A Newspaper for China* (Cambridge, MA: Harvard University Asia Center, 2004), 173–244.

79. "Peking's Venerable Newspaper," *New York Times,* 6 June 1885, quoting the *Pall Mall Gazette;* "The Pekin Gazette," *Wanganui Chronicle* 333, no. 11152 (December 1890): 2; "Rashness in Chinese Journalism," *Pittsburgh Gazette Times,* 3 September 1911, 2/4.

80. Bowring to Earl of Malmesbury, 10 February 1853, *PROT,* 33; "Abstract of a Memorial Advocating the Legalization of Opium, published in Pekin, in the 'Gazette' of January 4, 1853," *PROT,* 34.

81. John K. Fairbank, "The Legalization of the Opium Trade before the Treaties of 1858," *Chinese Social and Political Science Review* 17 (1933–34): 227–228. This was Fairbank's first academic publication.

82. Alcock to Bowring, 29 January 1853, *PROT,* 33; "Abstract of a Memorial," 35.

83. "Großbritannnien," *Neue Münchener Zeitung,* 1 January 1853, 888–889.

84. "Abstract of a Memorial," 35; Sihe Qi, ed., *Dierci yapian zhanzheng* (The Second Opium War), vol. 1 (Shanghai: Renmin chubanshe, 1978), 404.

85. "Abstract of a Memorial," 35.

86. Ibid.

87. Fairbank, "Legalization," 228–229.

88. On Qing military operations at the request of Zhejiang, the failed notice of the Taiping threat to Hangzhou, and He Guiqing's focus on Suzhou: Xiucheng Li, *Taiping Rebel: The Deposition of Li Hsiu-ch'eng* (Cambridge: Cambridge University Press, 1977), 231n48.

89. James T. K. Wu, "The Impact of the Taiping Rebellion upon the Manchu Fiscal System," *Pacific Historical Review* 19, no. 3 (August 1950): 265–275; Joseph Edkins, *The Revenue and Taxation of the Chinese Empire* (Shanghai: Presbyterian Mission Press, 1903), was the earliest non-Asian study of the Qing taxation system in its entirety.

90. Fairbank, "Legalization," 230–231.

91. Inoue Hirosama, *Shindai ahen seisaku shi no kenkyū* (Studies of the history of Qing opium policy) (Kyoto: Kyoto University Press, 2004).

92. Fairbank, "Legalization," 236–239; Guy Boulais, *Manuel du Code Chinois* (Shanghai: Imprimerie de la Mission Catholique, 1924), 431, sec. 940.

93. *Treaty of Friendship and Commerce between Great Britain and Siam, signed April 18, 1855, ratified April 5, 1856* (Bangkok: n.p., 1856); Niels Petersson, *Imperialismus und Modernisierung: Siam, China und die europäischen Mächte 1895–1914* (Munich: Oldenbourg, 2000).

94. Antony Anghie defines it as a voluntary capitulation treaty: Antony Anghie, *Imperialism, Sovereignty, and the Making of International Law* (Cambridge: Cambridge University Press, 2007), 85–86. For Siam's joint concessions of territory and commercial rights to Britain and France and the Bowring Treaty as an international precedent: Swan Sik Ko, *Nationality and International Law in Asian Perspective* (The Hague: Martinus Nijhoff, 1990), 467; Hellmuth Hecker, *Das Staatsangehörigkeitsrecht von Bangladesh, Burma, Sri Lanka (Ceylon), Thailand und der Malediven* (Frankfurt: Metzner, 1975), 146.

95. For defenses of Bowring: Jardine, Matheson & Co. to Woodgate, 12 December 1855, *PROT,* 64–66; Dent & Co. to Bowring, 28 December 1855, *PROT,* 70–71; Lindsay & Co. to Bowring, 7 January 1856, *PROT,* 73–76; Bowring to Clarendon, 8 January 1956, *PROT,* 36 (Siam), 41 (Southeast Asia).

96. "Memorial to the Right Hon. The Earl of Clarendon," *PROT,* 79.

97. Hobson to Bowring, 6 November 1855, *PROT,* 42–47; "Chinese Tract entitled "A Discourse to Awaken a Stupified Age to Life,'" *PROT,* 47–49.

98. Sinclair, 14 August 1856, enclosed in Bowring, 15 September 1856, UKNA, FO 17/250; Fairbank, "Legalization," 240.

99. Fairbank, "Legalization," 240.

100. *North China Herald,* 25 October 1856 and 1 November 1856.

101. For the treaty ratification: Hevia, *English Lessons,* 115–116.

102. Robertson to Bowring, 17 April 1857, UKNA, FO 17/310; Fairbank, "Legalization," 242. For the emergence of this rank: Bingxian Xu, *Qingdai zhixian zhizhang zhi yanjiu* (A study of the powers of the county magistrate in the Qing dynasty) (Taipei: n.p., 1971).

103. Thomas Francis Wade, 8 May 1857, enclosed in Bowring, 8 May 1857), UKNA, FO 17/268; Fairbank, "Legalization," 245. On Wade: James C. Cooley, *T. F. Wade in China: Pioneer in Global Diplomacy, 1842–1884* (Leiden: Brill, 1981). N. G. D. Malmqvist, *Bernhard Karlgren: Portrait of a*

Scholar (Lanham, MD: Lehigh University Press/Rowman and Littlefield, 2011), 197–199 reevaluates the Wade-Giles system.

104. Fairbank, "Legalization," 242.
105. Ibid., 244.
106. Meadows, 11 April 1857, UKNA, FO 17/310; Fairbank, "Legalization," 245.
107. Ye to Hale, 3 May 1857, UKNA, FO 17/269; Fairbank, "Legalization," 246.
108. Bowring, 19 May 1857, UKNA, FO 17/269.
109. Bowring, 7 July 1857), UKNA, FO 17/271; Fairbank, "Legalization," 249.
110. Fairbank, "Legalization," 248.
111. Hale, 12 June 1857, UKNA, FO 17/271.
112. Shi Daotai, 27 November 1857, UKNA, FO 17/273.
113. Meadows, 11 April 1857, UKNA, FO 17/310; Fairbank, "Legalization," 250.
114. Fairbank, "Legalization," 254.
115. Palmerston on 3 March 1857, cited in J. Y. Wong, *Deadly Dreams: Opium, Imperialism, and the Arrow War (1856–1860) in China* (New York: Cambridge University Press, 1998), 457.
116. Bowring to Clarendon, 7 July 1857, UKNA, FO 17/271.
117. Ye to Bowring, 30 June 1856, UKNA, FO 682/1989/9; Cassel, *Grounds of Judgment,* 54; Tieya Wang, "International Law in China: Historical and Contemporary Perspectives," in Edward Macwhinney, *Judicial Settlement of Disputes: Jurisdiction and Justiciability* (Recueil des Cours 221) (Dordrecht: Kluwer/Académie de droit international de la Haye, 1990), 195–370, here 239.
118. He Guiqing, memorial of 15 April 1858, Gugong bowuyuan [Palace Museum], *Qingdai chouban yiwu shimo* (The Qing Dynasty's management of barbarian affairs from the origins to the end) (Beiping: n.p., 1929–30), Xianfeng, 20 quan; 4b, 2–8a, 5 (hereafter *CBYS, XF*). Earl Swisher, *China's Management of the American Barbarians* (New Haven, CT: Far Eastern Association, 1951), 413. The imputation that He "deliberately contravened instructions from Beijing in order to get revenue to fight the Taipings" awaits concrete evidence. Wong, *Deadly Dreams,* 415. For the emperor's subsequent moderation: 43, n. 111.
119. Prince Gong, Memorial of 24 January, 1861, *CBYS, XF,* 72 quan, 3a, 5–7b, 4; Swisher, *China's Management of the American Barbarians,* 694.
120. Frederick Wells Williams, *The Life and Letters of Samuel Wells Williams* (New York: Putnam, 1889), 259; *New York Times,* 14 July 1858, 20 October 1858, 20 November 1858. William B. Reed and John Elliott Ward, both U.S. ministers to China, had ordered W. A. P. Martin to pen the *New York Times* articles. Ralph R. Covell, "The Life and Thought of W. A. P. Martin: Agent and Interpreter of Sino-American Contact in the Nineteenth and Early Twentieth Century" (PhD thesis, University of Denver, 1975), 173, 188; "The Chinese Treaties," *Daily Alta California,* 22 December 1858.
121. Williams, *Life and Letters,* 277.

122. Muraviev confronted British general William Fenwick Williams and the Ottoman Mehemet Vasif Pasha on September 29, 1855. "Plan of the Fortress of Kars with the surrounding country from Russian Staff Map of 1829, etc.," UKNA, MR 1/195/4, 7, 10.

123. On Muraviev and Ignatiev between 1858 and 1860: Nikolai Pavlovitch Ignatiev, *The Russo-Chinese Crisis: N. P. Ignatiev's Mission to Peking, 1859–1860*, trans. John L. Evans (Newtonville, MA: Oriental Research Partners, 1987); Platt, *Autumn in the Heavenly Kingdom*, 171; Mary Clabaugh Wright, *The Last Stand of Chinese Conservatism: The T'ung-chih Restoration, 1862–1874* (Stanford: Stanford University Press, 1957), 34–36; George Cyril Allen and Audrey G. Donnithorne, eds., *Western Enterprise in Far Eastern Economic Development* (London: Allen and Unwin, 1954), 21–24.

124. "The Journal of S. Wells Williams," *Journal of the North China Branch of the Royal Asiatic Society* 42 (1911): 51; David Edward Owen, *British Opium Policy in China and India* (New Haven, CT: Yale University Press, 1934), 224; Susanna Soojung Lim, *China and Japan in the Russian Imagination, 1685–1922: To the Ends of the Orient* (Abingdon: Routledge, 2013), 76–108 explains the role of Russian travelogues on China.

125. Prince Gong, Memorial of 24 January 1861, *CBYS, XF,* 72 quan, 3a, 5–7b, 4; Swisher, *China's Management of the American Barbarians*, 694.

126. "The Journal of S. Wells Williams," 93–94.

127. Covell, "Life and Thought of W. A. P. Martin," 176.

128. Samuel Wells Williams, "The Toleration Clause in the Treaties," *Chinese Recorder* 11 (May–June 1880): 227; Covell, "Life and Thought of W. A. P. Martin," 177.

129. Prince Gong, Memorial of 24 January 1861, *CBYS, XF,* 72 quan, 3a, 5–7b, 4; Swisher, *China's Management of the American Barbarians*, 694.

130. "The Journal of S. Wells Williams," 96.

131. Ibid.

132. Elgin to Reed, 19 October 1858, *Correspondence Relative to the Earl of Elgin's Special Missions to China and Japan, 1857–1859* (London: Harrison and Sons, 1859), 399.

133. Covell, "Life and Thought of W. A. P. Martin," 187.

134. I borrow from Sebastian Mallaby, "The Reluctant Imperialist: Terrorism, Failed States, and the Case of American Empire," *Foreign Affairs* (March–April 2002): 2–7.

135. Owen, *British Opium Policy in China and India*, 227.

136. *Correspondence Relative to the Earl of Elgin's Special Missions*, 459.

137. *London Times*, 22 October 1880; *The Times*, 22 October 1880, cited in Owen, *British Opium Policy in China and India*, 226; "Mr. George Batten's paper read before the Society of Arts on the 24th March 1891," in Royal Commission on Opium, *First Report of the Royal Commission on Opium, with Minutes of Evidence and Appendices* (London: HMSO, 1894), Appendix I, 137.

138. "Report on the Revision of the Tariff," in *Correspondence relative to the Earl of Elgin's Special Missions*, 401.

139. Memorial of 9 October 1858, *CBYS, XF,* 31 quan; 18a, 9–19b, 1; Swisher, *China's Management of the American Barbarians,* 523–524; Edict of 13 Oct. 1858, *CBYS, XF,* 31 quan, 21b, 6–22b, 9; Swisher, 524–525. By August 1859, He Guiqing's memorials on Shanghai's opium duties, amounting to 7,000 taels, did no longer provoke the emperor's reprimands. Memorial of 1 August 1859, *CBYS, XF* 41 quan, 5a, 9–7b, 10, and the Edict on the same day, *CBYS, XF* 41 quan, 9a, 7–10a, 2. Swisher, *China's Management of the American Barbarians,* 609–610.

140. Report on the Revision of the Tariff," in *Correspondence Relative to the Earl of Elgin's Special Missions,* 401.

141. Martin, *Cycle of Cathay,* 184. On Martin's services: Williams, *Life and Letters,* 274–275.

142. Covell, "Life and Thought of W. A. P. Martin," 129–130.

143. Williams, *Life and Letters,* 260–261; Exodus 20:13.

144. Reed to Elgin, 13 September 1858, *Correspondence Relative to the Earl of Elgin,* 394.

145. By 1877, the Treaty of Wangxia had become merely one among several "instruments, no longer in vigour, but historically interesting," according to William Frederick Mayers, the Chinese secretary of the British Legation in Beijing and treaties specialist in the 1870s. William Frederick Mayers, ed., *Treaties between the Empire of China and Foreign Powers* (Shanghai: North-China Herald, 1906), iv.

146. Reed to Elgin, 13 September 1858, *Correspondence Relative to the Earl of Elgin,* 394.

147. Ibid., 395. Repeated in the report to Washington on Article 14. "Lord Elgin's half-expressed reluctance to comply with his instructions was very creditable to him, believing as I do that he feels a strong repugnance to this infamous traffic, and the connection of his government with it." Reed to Cass, 30 June 1858, 356–357, here 357.

148. Mayers, ed., *Treaties between the Empire of China and foreign Powers,* 28. For the final version of import prohibitions, see paragraph 5: Mayers, *Treaties,* 29.

149. For the charge that Britain deliberately withheld the opium legalization from the French: Wong, *Deadly Dreams,* 275. This ignores the evolution of the British agenda even within British consultations and the fact that other items on the agenda were not forwarded to the French either. Owen, *British Opium Policy in China and India,* 219.

150. Horatio N. Lay, *Note on the Opium Question, and Brief Survey of Our Relations with China* (London: Rickerby, Walbrook, 1893), 12.

151. Régine Thiriez, "Les Palais européens du Yuanmingyuan à travers la photographie: 1860–1940," *Arts asiatiques* 45 (1990): 90–96; Haiyan Lee, "The Ruins of Yuanmingyuan, or How to Enjoy a National Wound," *Modern China* 35, no. 2 (March 2009): 155–190; Daocheng Wang, ed., *Yuanmingyuan chongjian da zhengbian* (The dispute over the reconstruction of the Yuanmingyuan) (Hangzhou: Zhejiang guji chubanshe, 2007).

152. Demetrius C. Boulger, *The Life of Gordon* (London: T. Fisher Unwin, 1906), 46. For a multi-archival account: Ines Eben von Racknitz, *Die Plün-*

derung des Yuanming yuan. Imperiale Beutenahme im britisch-französischen Chinafeldzug von 1860 (Stuttgart: Franz Steiner, 2012). For French debates and justifications, Erik Ringmar, *Liberal Barbarism and the European Destruction of the Palace of the Emperor of China* (Basingstoke: Palgrave Macmillan, 2013).

153. "The Journal of S. Wells Williams," 97; Theodore Walrond, ed., *Letters and Journals of James, Eighth Earl of Elgin* (London: John Murray, 1872), 282.

2. The Porosity of International Law

1. Vera Schwarcz, *Place and Memory in the Singing Crane Garden* (Philadelphia: University of Pennsylvania Press, 2008), 71–73; Tony Yung-Yuan Teng, "Prince Kung and the Survival of the Ch'ing Rule, 1858–1898" (PhD diss., University of Wisconsin–Madison, 1972); Jason Holloman Parker, "The Rise and Decline of I-hsin, Prince Kung, 1858–1865: A Study of the Interaction of Politics and Ideology in Late Imperial China" (PhD diss., Princeton University, 1979). On his portraits: Elizabeth Chang, *Britain's Chinese Eye: Literature, Empire, and Aesthetics in Nineteenth-Century Britain* (Stanford: Stanford University Press, 2010), 147–150, 173. For the imperial politics of princes: Evelyn Rawski, *The Last Emperors: A Social History of Qing Imperial Institutions* (Berkeley: University of California Press, 1998), 96–126.

2. Gugong bowuyuan [Palace Museum], *Qingdai chouban yiwu shimo* (The Qing Dynasty's management of barbarian affairs from the origins to the end) (Beiping: n.p., 1929–30); Xianfeng, 71 quan (hereafter *CBYS, XF*), *Negotiated Power in Late Imperial China: The Zongli Yamen and the Politics of Reform*, trans. Jennifer Rudolph (Ithaca, NY: East Asia Program, Cornell University, 2008), 59; S. M. Meng, *The Tsungli Yamen: Its Organization and Functions* (Cambridge, MA: East Asian Research Center, Harvard University, 1970); Rune Svarverud, *International Law as World Order in Late Imperial China Translation, Reception and Discourse, 1847–1911* (Leiden: Brill, 2007), 69–162; Immanuel Chung-yueh Hsü, *China's Entrance into the Family of Nations: The Diplomatic Phase, 1858–1880* (Cambridge, MA: Harvard University Press, 1960), 180–198; Pär Cassel, *Grounds of Judgment: Extraterritoriality and Imperial Power in Nineteenth-Century China and Japan* (Oxford: Oxford University Press, 2012).

3. Weigui Fang, "*Yi, Yang, Xi, Wai* and Other Terms: The Transition from 'Barbarian' to 'Foreigner' in Nineteenth-Century China," in *New Terms for New Ideas: Western Knowledge and Lexical Change in Late Imperial China*, ed. Michael Lackner et al. (Leiden: Brill, 2001), 95–124, esp. 117; Masataka Banno, *China and the West, 1858–1861: The Origins of the Tsungli Yamen* (Cambridge, MA: Harvard University Press, 1964); Henri Cordier, "Thomas Francis Wade," *T'oung Pao* 6, no. 4 (1895): 407–412; James L. Hevia, "An Imperial Nomad and the Great Game: Thomas Francis Wade in China," *Late Imperial China* 16, no. 2 (December 1995): 1–22.

4. William Frederick Mayers, ed., *Treaties between the Empire of China and Foreign Powers, together with Regulations for the Conduct of Foreign Trade, etc.* (Shanghai: North-China Herald, 1906), 12.

5. Ibid., 86.

6. Britain refused to ratify the Supplementary Convention to the Treaty of Commerce and Navigation with China in 1869 and elsewhere, note esp. Art. II and VI. Ibid., 37.

7. Knight Biggerstaff, "The Secret Correspondence of 1867–1868: Views of Leading Chinese Statesmen Regarding the Further Opening of China to Western Influence," *Journal of Modern History* 22 (1950): 124–125.

8. I follow the most complete version of the protest available. J. Spencer Hill, *The Indo-Chinese Opium Trade* (London: Henry Frowde, 1884), 23.

9. Ibid., 25.

10. Ibid., 23.

11. Ibid.

12. Ibid., 23–24.

13. Akira Iriye, "Public Opinion and Foreign Policy: The Case of Late Ch'ing China," in *Approaches to Modern Chinese History*, ed. Albert Feuerwerker et al. (Berkeley: University of California Press, 1967), 216–238.

14. Karl Polanyi, *The Great Transformation: The Politics and Economics of Our Time* (Boston: Beacon Press, 2001), 46.

15. *British Documents on Foreign Affairs: Reports and Papers from the Foreign Office Confidential Print. Part I, From the Mid-Nineteenth Century to the First World War. Series E, Asia, 1860–1914*, vol. 21: *Treaty Revision and Sino-Japanese Dispute over Taiwan, 1868–1876* (Frederick, MD: University Publications of America, 1989), 115–116.

16. Lucien Bianco, "The Responses of Opium Growers to Eradication Campaigns and the Poppy Tax, 1907–1949," in *Opium Regimes: China, Britain, and Japan, 1839–1952*, ed. Timothy Brook and Bob Tadashi Wakabayashi (Berkeley: University of California Press, 2000), 292–319.

17. Hill, *Indo-Chinese Opium Trade*, 24.

18. Frederic Wakeman Jr., "The Civil Society and Public Sphere Debate: Western Reflections on Chinese Political Culture," *Modern China* 19, no. 2 (April 1993): 108–138; William T. Rowe, "The Problem of 'Civil Society' in Late Imperial China," *Modern China* 19, no. 2 (April 1993): 139–157; Mary Backus Rankin, "Some Observations on a Chinese Public Sphere," *Modern China* 19, no. 2 (April 1993): 158–182; Philip C. C. Huang, "'Public Sphere'/'Civil Society' in China?" *Modern China* 19, no. 2 (April 1993): 216–240. Compare Mary Kaldor, *Global Civil Society: An Answer to War* (Cambridge: Polity, 2003).

19. Hill, *Indo-Chinese Opium Trade*, 24.

20. Ibid.; Owen, *British Opium Policy in China and India*, 245.

21. R. K. Newman, "India and the Anglo-Chinese Opium Agreements, 1907–14," *Modern Asian Studies* 23, no. 3 (1989): 525–560.

22. Hill, *Indo-Chinese Opium Trade*, 24–25.

23. Ibid., 25–26.

24. Alcock to Clarendon, 19 May 1869, in *Correspondence Respecting the revision of the Treaty of Tien-tsin* (London: Harrison and Sons, 1871), 396–397.

25. Natascha Vittinghoff, "Readers, Publishers and Officials in the Context for a Public Voice and the Rise of the Modern Press in Late Qing China (1860–1880), *T'oung Pao*, 2nd ser., 87, Fasc. 4/5 (2001), 393–455, here 404.

26. John V. Crangle, "Joseph Whitwell Pease and the Quaker Role in the Campaign to Suppress the Opium Trade in the British Empire," *Quaker History* 68 (Fall 1979): 63–64; Virginia Berridge and Griffith Edwards, *Opium and the People: Opiate Use in Nineteenth-Century England* (New Haven, CT: Yale University Press, 1987); B. Johnson, "Righteousness before Revenue: The Forgotten Crusade Against the Indo-Chinese Opium Trade," *Journal of Drug Issues* 5 (1975): 304–326. For French-British comparisons: Howard Padwa, *Social Poison: The Culture and Politics of Opiate Control in Britain and France, 1821–1926* (Baltimore: Johns Hopkins University Press, 2012), 48; Guo Songtao, *Yang zhi shuwu quan ji*, 12:3 (Guangxu 18 nian [1892]).

27. Hill, *Indo-Chinese Opium Trade*, 23.

28. For China's impact on the non-Asian world: William C. Kirby, Mechthild Leutner, and Klaus Mühlhahn, eds., *Global Conjectures: China in Transnational Perspective* (Münster: Lit, 2006); Jonathan Spence, "Opium," in *Chinese Roundabout: Essays in History and Culture* (New York: Norton, 1992), 228–258.

29. Joseph G. Alexander, ed., *Interviews with Chinese Statesmen with Regard to the Opium Traffic* (London: Society for the Suppression of the Opium Trade, 1894).

30. Ssu-yü Teng and John K. Fairbank, eds., *China's Response to the West: A Documentary Survey, 1839–1923* (Cambridge, MA: Harvard University Press, 1979), 2.

31. "Opium Trade in the East: Its Character and Effects," *National Magazine* 6 (1855): 40–47; Major-General R. Alexander, *The Rise and Progress of British Opium Smuggling* (London: Judd and Glass, 1856). Among the earlier sparks: A. S. Thelwall, *Iniquities of the Opium Trade with China* (London: W. H. Allen, 1839); *Compendium of Facts Relating to the Opium Trade* (n.p., 1840).

32. "The Anti-Opium Association," *Examiner*, 11 December 1858, 786–787; "Oratorical Opium," *Punch, or the London Charivari*, 1 December 1860, 211.

33. "China," *Straits Times Overland Journal*, 7 December 1869.

34. Westel Woodbury Willoughby, *Foreign Rights and Interests in China*, vol. 2 (Baltimore: Johns Hopkins Press, 1927), 1094.

35. Sabyasachi Bhattacharya, *The Financial Foundations of the British Raj: Ideas and Interests in the Reconstruction of Indian Public Finance, 1858–1872* (Hyderabad: Orient Longman 2005 [1st ed. Indian Institute of Advanced Study, 1971]), 19.

36. "Missionary Conference," *North China Herald*, 16 May 1890, 602–603; Hosea Ballou Morse, *The International Relations of the Chinese Empire, II: The Period of Submission, 1861–1893* (London: Longmans, Green, 1918), 220.

37. Rev. Eric Lewis, *Black Opium: An account of a 'morally indefensible' trade in this horrible drug,' with an appeal to the Churches in Great and Greater Britain to unite in one great concerted effort, calling upon our country to pay the price of a God-honouring ending* (London: Marshall Brothers, [1910]), 46; Westel W. Willoughby, *Opium as an International Problem: The Geneva Conferences* (Baltimore: Johns Hopkins Press, 1925), 13.

38. William D. Rubinstein, Michael A. Jolles, and Hilary L. Rubinstein, eds., *The Palgrave Dictionary of Anglo-Jewish History* (Basingstoke: Palgrave Macmillan, 2011), 487.

39. *Food Journal* 4 (May 1873): 149.

40. See the assessment of M. Carné, quoted in Theodore Christlieb, *The Indo-Chinese Opium Trade and Its Effect* (London: James Nisbet, 1879), 54–55; Samuel S. Mander, *Our Opium Trade with China* (London: Simpkin, Marshall, 1877), 8; *Parliamentary Debates*, 29 April 1881, 1459.

41. Samuel Wells Williams, *The Middle Kingdom: A Survey of the Geography, Government, Literature, Social Life, Arts, and History of the Chinese Empire and Its Inhabitants*, vol. 2 (London: W. H. Allen, 1883), 388.

42. G. de Contades, "La Jeanne d'Arc de Thomas De Quincey," *Revue des deux mondes* 115 (February 1893); A. Barine, "L'Opium—Thomas De Quincey," *Revue des deux mondes* 138 (1896); Thomas de Quincey, *The Confessions of an English Opium-Eater* (New York: Macmillan, 1900), xxxiii.

43. *Use of Opium and Traffic Therein: Message from the President of the United States* (Washington, DC: Government Printing Office, 1906), 59th Congr. 1st session, 15; Charles Richet, "Les poisons de l'intelligence," *Revue des deux mondes* 20 (March–April 1877); Richet, *Physiology and Histology of the Cerebral Convolutions: Also, Poisons of the Intellect* (New York: Wm. Wood, 1879); J. Bouquet, "Cannabis," in United Nations Office on Drugs and Crime, *Bulletin on Narcotics* 1 (1951): 5.

44. F. A. Flückiger, "Pharmacognostische Umschau in der Pariser Ausstellung und den Londoner Sammlungen," *Archiv der Pharmazie*, January 1879, 15–16. The official catalog with 122 pages was Chine. Douanes impériales maritimes, *Catalogue spécial de la collection exposée au palais du Champ-de-Mars, Exposition universelle, Paris, 1878* (Shanghai: Bureau des Statistiques de la direction générale des douanes, 1878). Flückiger, *Pharmacographia: A History of the Principal Drugs of Vegetable Origin, Met with in Great Britain and British India* (London: Macmillan, 1874).

45. Frederick Storrs Turner, *British Opium Policy and Its Results to India and China* (London: Sampson Low, Marston, Searle and Rivington, 1876), vi, 59.

46. Ibid., iii–v.

47. Ibid., iii–v, 188.

48. *Friend of China* 1 (March 1875): 25; *Contemporary Review* 27 (December 1875–May 1876): 454.

49. "What We Are Doing in China," *London and China Telegraph*, 26 February 1877, 12. For the British-Chinese correspondence: Great Britain, *China*

No. 3 (1877): Further Correspondence Respecting the Attack on the Indian Expedition to Western China, and the Murder of Mr. Margary (London: HMSO, 1877), 27–59.

50. Turner, *British Opium Policy,* 124.

51. *Church Missionary Intelligencer and Record* 1, New Series (1876), 519; *London Quarterly Review* 46 (April–July 1876): 389.

52. John Dudgeon, "Testimony of Dr. Dudgeon," *Friend of China* 1, 2 (April 1875): 59; Dudgeon, "The Opium Traffic from a Medical Point of View," *Friend of China* 2 (1876): 12–17; Dudgeon, "Opium in Relation to Population," *Edinburgh Medical Journal* (September 1877): 239; Dudgeon, *Review of the Customs Opium Smoking Returns* (Shanghai: American Presbyterian Mission Press, 1882); "Obituary: John Dudgeon," *British Medical Journal,* 16 March 1901, 679; Jean-Claude Martzloff, "Li Shanlan (1811–1882) and Chinese Traditional Mathematics," *Mathematical Intelligencer* 14, no. 4 (1992): 32–37, here 35; Hao Ping, *Beijing daxue chuang banshi shikao yuan* (Beijing: Beijing daxue chubanshe, 1998), translated as Hao Ping, *Peking University and the Origins of Higher Education in China* (Los Angeles: Bridge21, 2013), although the Tongwenguan was *not* the direct predecessor of Peking University.

53. *London and China Telegraph,* 25 January 1875, 81; Hilary J. Beattie, "Protestant Missions and Opium in China," *Harvard Papers on China,* 22A (1964), 112–113.

54. Also W. K. Baron van Dedem, "De Opium-Kwestie (Vergadering van 3 November 1876)," *Verslagen der Algemeene Vergaderingen,* 103–184.

55. Mander, *Our Opium Trade with China,* 18.

56. Lewis Appleton, *Memoirs of Henry Richard, the Apostle of Peace* (London: Trübner, 1889), 33, 183.

57. *Parliamentary Debates* 4 (1876): 550–552; Mander, *Our Opium Trade with China,* 67.

58. *Penn Monthly* 8 (January–December 1877): 227.

59. Christlieb, *Indo-British Opium Trade and Its Effect,* 71; Benjamin Broomhall, *The Truth about Opium-Smoking* (London: Hodder and Stoughton, 1882).

60. *China's Millions* 67, no. 6 (January 1881): 58; *Evangelical Magazine and Missionary Chronicle* 12, New Series (1882), 518; Griffith John, *China: Her Claims and Call* (London: Hodder and Stoughton, 1882), 48; Broomhall, *Truth about Opium-Smoking,* 68; *Parliamentary Debates,* 29 April 1881, 1465.

61. John Willis Clark, *Endowments of the University of Cambridge* (Cambridge: Cambridge University Press, 1904), 386–387.

62. "Advertisement," in Hill, *Indo-Chinese Opium Trade,* n.p.

63. Hill, *Indo-Chinese Opium Trade,* 24; William Alexander Parsons Martin, *A Cycle of Cathay* (New York: Fleming H. Revell, 1900), 89.

64. Joshua Rowntree, *The Imperial Drug Trade: A Re-statement of the Opium Question, in the Light of Recent Evidence and New Developments in the East* (London: Methuen, 1906), 96.

65. David P. Ekvall, *Outposts, or Tibetan Border Sketches* (New York: Alliance Press, 1907), 85; Shoun Hino and Toshihiro Wada, eds., *Three Mountains and Seven Rivers: Prof. Musashi Tachikawa's Felicitation Volume* (New Delhi: Narendra Prakash Jain/Motilal Banarsidass, 2004), 610.

66. Ralph Wardlaw Thompson, *Griffith John: The Story of Fifty Years in China* (London: Religious Tract Society, 1906), 287; Hubert Howe Bancroft, *The New Pacific* (New York: Bancroft, 1915), 127.

67. Man-houng Lin, "Late Qing Perceptions of Native Opium," *Harvard Journal of Asiatic Studies* 64, no. 1 (June 2004): 117–144.

68. *Reply of the K'euen Keae Shay* (London: Anglo-Oriental Society for the Suppression of the Opium Trade, 1877), 2 (republished as *Reply of the K'euen Keae Shay* [London: Dyer Brothers, n.d. (after 1881)]); Beattie, "Protestant Missions and Opium in China," 113.

69. *Reply of the K'euen Keae Shay,* 12.

70. Broomhall, *Truth about Opium-Smoking.*

71. H. H. Kane, *Opium-Smoking in American and China* (New York: G. Putnam's Sons, 1882), *Opium-Smoking,* x; *Friend of China* 3, no. 1 (August 1877): 2–3; *Our National Responsibility for the Opium Trade* (London: Anglo-Oriental Society for the Suppression of the Opium Trade, 1880).

72. "The Opium Traffic in China," *Methodist Quarterly Review* 46 (1884): 421.

73. Published in full as "Li Hung-Chang on the Opium Trade," *China's Millions, 1880* 67, no. 6 (January 1881): 112. The China Inland Mission editor appears to have confused the publication dates in this journal. Several documents in the January issue date from May 1881. Li's letter was republished in Joseph G. Alexander, "Mr. Alexander's Interviews with Chinese Statesmen," *Friend of China* 15 (December 1894): 97. Also Jinxiang Wang, *Zhongguo jindu jianshi* (A short history of drugs in China) (Beijing: Xuexi chubanshe, 1996), 52–54.

74. "The Opium Trade: An Appeal by the Society of Friends in Great Britain to Their Fellow Countrymen," *China's Millions, 1880* 67, no. 6 (January 1881): 38.

75. Crangle, "Joseph Whitwell Pease and the Quaker Role."

76. Joseph Pease, "India and China—The Opium Trade—Observations," *Parliamentary Debates* 260 (April 1881): § 1465.

77. Ibid.

78. *Japan Weekly Mail,* 21 May 1881, 572.

79. Handwritten note, London, March 1882, in Anglo-Indian, *The Opium Question Solved* (London: S. W. Partridge, 1882), 24. Originally Turner, *British Opium Policy and Its Results to India and China* (London: S. Low, Marston, Searle and Rivington, 1876).

80. *Parliamentary Debates,* 3rd ser., April 3, 1883, 1335–1336. For the antiopium initiatives of the Zongli Yamen: David Edward Owen, *British Opium Policy in China and India* (New Haven, CT: Yale University Press, 1934), 268–269. For Alcock's original statement: *Parliamentary Debates,* 3rd ser., April 3, 1883, 1337–1338; James Forbes B. Tinling, *The Poppy-Plague and England's Crime* (London: Elliot Stock, 1876), 134–135; Rowntree, *Imperial Drug Trade,* 99; Willoughby, *Foreign Rights and Interests in China,* vol. 2, 1094;

Mary Clabaugh Wright, *The Last Stand of Chinese Conservatism: The T'ung-chih Restoration, 1862–1874* (Stanford: Stanford University Press, 1957), 290–292.

81. Charles Reginald Haines, *A Vindication of England's Policy with Regard to the Opium Trade* (London: W. H. Allen, 1884), 102.

82. Cucheval-Clarigny, "La déclin de la puissance Chinoise," *Revue des deux mondes* 54 (September 1884): 412. The article reviewed Demetrius Charles de Kavanagh Boulger, *History of China* (London: W. H. Allen, 1881–1884), L'abbé Castaing, *Vie de Mgr Faurie, member de la société des missions étrangères, vicaire apostolique du Kouy-Techeou (Chine)* (Paris: V. Lecoffre, 1884 [1st ed.: Bordeaux: B. Dabadie, 1873]). Augustus Raymond Margary, *The Journey of A.-R. Margary from Shanghae to Bhamo, and back to Manwyne. From his journals and letters* (London, Macmillan, 1876).

83. Philippe Athanase Cucheval-Clarigny, *Histoire de la presse en Angleterre et aux États-unis* (Paris: Amyot, 1857); Cucheval-Clarigny, *The Election of Mr. Lincoln: A Narrative of the Contest in 1860 for the Presidency of the United States,* trans. Sir Willoughby Jones (London: James Ridgway/Trübner, 1861) (compiled from articles originally published in the *Revue des deux mondes*); Cucheval-Clarigny, *L'instruction publique en France: Observations sur la situation de l'instruction publique en France et sur les moyens de l'améliorer* (Paris: Hachette, 1883).

84. Paul M. Kennedy, *The Rise and Fall of the Great Powers: Economic Change and Military Conflict from 1500 to 2000* (New York: Vintage, 1989); Dambisa Moyo, *Winner Take All: China's Race for Resources and What It Means for the World* (New York: Basic Books, 2012); Ivan Tselichtchev, *China versus the West: The Global Power Shift of the 21st Century* (Indianapolis: Wiley, 2012).

85. *Literatur-Blatt für orientalische Philologie* 2 (October 1884–September 1885): 157.

86. "The Opium Traffic in China," *Methodist Quarterly Review* 46 (1884): 421.

87. *Japan Weekly Mail,* 22 June 1889, 602–603.

88. Testimony of Sir T. F. Wade, *First Report of the Royal Commission on Opium,* 94.

89. Herbert Allen Giles, *A Chinese Biographical Dictionary,* vol. 1 (Shanghai: Kelly and Walsh, 1898), 392.

90. Morse, *International Relations of the Chinese Empire,* 236, quoting Robert Hart, *'These from the Land of Sinim': Essays on the Chinese Question* (London: Chapman and Hall, 1901), 68; Martin, *Cycle of Cathay,* 449; and *North-China Herald,* 25 January 1872.

91. David Scott, *China and the International System, 1840–1949: Power, Presence, and Perceptions in a Century of Humiliation* (New York: State University of New York Press, 2009); Zheng Wang, *Never Forget National Humiliation: Historical Memory in Chinese Politics and Foreign Relations* (New York: Columbia University Press, 2012).

92. A far from exhaustive chronological cascade of references to the opium clause: Leone Levi, *Annals of British Legislation* (London: Smith, Elder, 1861), 91;

Theodore Walrond, ed., *Letters and Journals of James, Eighth Earl of Elgin* (London: John Murray, 1872), 278–279; "Taxation on Opium in the Foreign Settlements of China," *London and China Telegraph*, 24 May 1875, 9; *Friend of China* 3, no. 3 (October 1877): 25; Hill, *Indo-Chinese Opium Trade*, 21–22; Carl Hartwich, *Das Opium als Genussmittel* (Zurich: Zürcher und Furrer, 1898), 29; Mayers, ed., *Treaties between the Empire of China and Foreign Powers*, 28; Morse, *Trade and Administration of the Chinese Empire*, 338–340, including a brief account of the negotiations toward a legalization consensus; *Supplement to the American Journal of International Law*, vol. 3, *Official Documents* (Cambridge University Press, 1909), 262; J. F. Scheltema, "The Opium Question," *American Journal of Sociology* 16 (1910): 215; Chin Chu, *The Tariff Problem in China* (New York: Faculty of Political Science, Columbia University, 1916), 36; Tyler Dennett, *Americans in Eastern Asia: A Critical Study of the Policy of the United States with Reference to China, Japan and Korea in the 19th Century* (New York: Macmillan, 1922), 322–326; International Anti-Opium Association, Peking, *The War Against Opium* (Tientsin: Tientsin Press, 1922), 12–13.

93. Kane, *Opium-Smoking in American and China*, vi.
94. Hsin-pao Chang, *Commissioner Lin and the Opium War* (Cambridge, MA: Harvard University Press, 1964), 138.
95. Kathleen L. Lodwick, *Crusaders against Opium: Protestant Missionaries in China, 1874–1917* (Lexington: University Press of Kentucky, 1996); Ian R. Tyrrell, *Reforming the World: The Creation of America's Moral Empire* (Princeton: Princeton University Press, 2010), 146–165. Yongming Zhou, *Anti-drug Crusades in Twentieth-Century China: Nationalism, History, and State Building* (Lanham, MD: Rowman & Littlefield, 1999); Su Zhiliang, *Shanghai jindu shi* (The history of narcotics control in Shanghai) (Shanghai: Shanghai sanlian shudian, 2009). They mention the demarche only in passing. Zheng Wang, "'This Is How the Chinese People Began Their Struggle': Humen and the Opium War as a Site of Memory," in *Places of Memory in Modern China: History, Politics, and Identity*, ed. Marc Andre Matten (Leiden: Brill, 2012), 167–192. On shock, trauma, and fear: Allan Young, "Suffering and the Origins of Traumatic Memory," *Daedalus* 125 (1996): 245–260. For the hiatus between traumatic experience and collective identity formation: Jeffrey C. Alexander et al., *Cultural Trauma and Collective Identity* (Berkeley: University of California Press, 2004).
96. Alexandrina Peckover, *Life of Joseph Sturge* (London: Swan Sonnenschein, 1890), 61–62.
97. Rowntree, *Imperial Drug Trade*, 16.
98. John K. Fairbank, *Trade and Diplomacy on the China Coast: The Opening of the Treaty Ports, 1842–1854* (Cambridge, MA: Harvard University Press, 1953).
99. Charles S. Leavenworth, *The Arrow War with China* (London: S. Low, Marston, 1901); Douglas Hurd, *The Arrow War: An Anglo-Chinese Confusion, 1856–1860* (London: Collins, 1967/New York: Macmillan, 1968); Desmond Christopher Martin Platt, *Finance, Trade, and Politics: British Foreign Policy, 1815–1914* (Oxford: Clarendon Press, 1968); Bruce A. Elleman,

Modern Chinese Warfare, 1795–1989 (New York: Routledge, 2001), 35–56. James L. Hevia uses both "the Opium Wars" and the "Arrow War": Hevia, *English Lessons: The Pedagogy of Imperialism in Nineteenth-Century China* (Durham, NC: Duke University Press, 2003), 29–48. Jules Davids, ed., *American Diplomatic and Public Papers: The United States and China, Ser. 1: Treaty System and the Taiping Rebellion, 1842–1860, Part 13: The Arrow War* (Wilmington, DE: Scholarly Resources, 1973).

100. John Gallagher and Ronald Robinson, "The Imperialism of Free Trade," *Economic History Review,* New Series 6 (1953): 1–15.

101. Walrond, *Letters and Journals of James, Eighth Earl of Elgin,* 209–210.

102. Joseph Esherick, *The Origins of the Boxer Uprising* (Berkeley: University of California Press, 1987), 68–75; James E. Hoare, *Embassies in the East: The Story of the British and Their Embassies in China, Japan and Korea from 1859 to the Present* (Abingdon: Routledge, 2013), 6–9; G. Patrick March, *Eastern Destiny: Russia in Asia and the North Pacific* (Westport, CT: Greenwood, 1996), 126–130; Marcel Trouche, *Le quartier diplomatique de Pékin: étude historique et juridique* (Rodez: G. Subervie, 1935). For the opposite perspective: Qi Sihe, ed., *Dierci yapian zhanzheng,* 6 vols. (Shanghai: Shanghai renmin chubanshe, 1978–1979); Paul A. Cohen, *History in Three Keys: The Boxers as Event, Experience, and Myth* (New York: Columbia University Press, 1997), 364n46.

103. Weiming Zhong, "The Roles of Tea and Opium in Early Economic Globalization: A Perspective on China's Crisis in the 19th Century," *Frontiers of History in China* 5, no. 1 (2010): 86–105, esp. 90, first published in *Zhongguo jingjishi yanjiu* 1 (2009): 96–105.

104. Zhongguo jindaishi congshu bianxiezu, ed., *Dierci yapian zhanzheng* (Shanghai: Zhongguo jindaishi congshu, 1972), with editions in 1973 and 1974; Gugong Bowuguan and Ming Qing Danganbu, *Dierci yapian zhanzheng* (Shanghai: Gugong Bowuguan, 1978); Sihe, *Dierci yapian zhanzheng.*

105. "Dainiji ahen sensō," "la seconde guerre d'opium," "der Zweite Opiumkrieg," "Segunda Guerra del Opio" (Spanish). Japanese historiography also uses "Arō senso" (Arrow War). Kan Fujisawa, *Ei-wa ōshū kindaishi gakushū kihon yōgo jiten* (English-Japanese student dictionary of European modern history) (Tokyo: Aruku, 2009); Masako Magai and Yoko Hori, *Zukai sekaishi* (Tokyo: Seitōsha, 2010), 233; Wenxiong Huang, *Chūka Teikoku no kōbō* (The rise and fall of the Chinese empire) (Tokyo: PHP Kenkyūjo, 2007), 302. For German and French examples: Albert Wissler, *Zur Geschichte der Opiumfrage* (Jena: n.p., 1930), 35; François-Xavier Dudouet, *Le grand deal de l'opium: histoire du marché légal des drogues* (Paris: Syllepse, 2009). Also W. Travis Hanes III and Frank Sanello, *The Opium Wars: The Addiction of One Empire and the Corruption of Another* (Naperville, IL: Sourcebooks, 2002); Catherine Lamour and Michel R. Lamberti, *Les grandes manoeuvres de l'opium* (Paris: Seuil, 1972) (translated as *The Second Opium War* [London: Lane, 1974]). Esteban Canales, *La Inglaterra victoriana* (Madrid: Ediciones Akal, 1999), 297; Isabel Rodríguez, *Continuidad política y cambio económica en la China del siglo XXI* (Santiago de Chile: RIL editores, 2010), 51–52.

106. J. Y. Wong, *Deadly Dreams: Opium, Imperialism, and the Arrow War (1856–1860) in China* (New York: Cambridge University Press, 1998), 37, 471; but Yuhe Huang, ed. *Liang ci yapian zhanzheng yu Xianggang ge rang: shishi he shiliao* (Taipei: Guoshiguan, 1998), 333–454, 473.

107. Wong, *Deadly Dreams*, 191, xix, 19, 31, 472. Compare David Scott, *China and the International System, 1840–1949: Power, Presence, and Perceptions in a Century of Humiliation* (New York: State University of New York Press, 2009); Fairbank, *Trade and Diplomacy on the China Coast*; Jürgen Osterhammel, "Semi-colonialism and Informal Empire' in Twentieth-Century China: Towards a Framework of Analysis," in Wolfgang J. Mommsen; Jürgen Osterhammel, ed., *Imperialism and After: Continuities and Discontinuities* (London: Allen and Unwin, 1986), 290–314.

108. One tael ("liang") approximated 1.327 ounces or 37.62 grams. Frederic Wakeman Jr., *The Great Enterprise: The Manchu Reconstruction of the Imperial Order in Seventeenth-Century China*, vol. 1 (Berkeley University of California Press, 1985), xiii. For a superb insight into the difficulties of translation: Pär Kristoffer Cassel, *Grounds of Judgment: Extraterritoriality and Imperial Power in Nineteenth-Century China and Japan* (Oxford: Oxford University Press, 2012), 58–61. For the Treaty of Tianjin: John K. Fairbank, "The Creation of the Treaty System," in *The Cambridge History of China*, vol. 10, *Late Ch'ing, 1800–1911, Part I* (Cambridge: Cambridge University Press, 1978), 249–263.

109. James Louis Hevia, *English Lessons: The Pedagogy of Imperialism in Nineteenth-Century China* (Durham, NC: Duke University Press, 2003). On "indigenous" contributions to international law under conditions of formal empire outside of Asia: Lauren A. Benton, *Law and Colonial Cultures: Legal Regimes in World History, 1400–1900* (Cambridge: Cambridge University Press, 2002); Saliha Belmessous, ed., *Native Claims: Indigenous Law against Empire, 1500–1920* (Oxford: Oxford University Press, 2012); Dong Wang, *China's unequal Treaties: Narrating National History* (Lanham, MD: Lexington Books, 2008). For a comparison with discussions of 1919: Charles S. Maier, "The Truth about the Treaties?" *Journal of Modern History* 51, no. 1 (March 1979): 56–67.

110. *First Report of the Royal Commission on Opium*, 90, 120.

111. *New York Daily Tribune*, September 20, 1858, 4 (reprinted in James Ledbetter, ed., *Dispatches for the New York Tribune: Selected Journalism of Karl Marx* [London: Penguin, 2007], 24); Shlomo Avineri, ed., *Karl Marx on Colonialism and Modernization* (Garden City, NY: Doubleday, 1968), 320.

3. Grounds of Objection: India, America, Asia

1. *Report of Annual Meeting of the Ramabai Association, Held March 11, 1892* (Boston: Press of Geo. H. Ellis, 1892), 11.

2. *Report of Annual Meeting of the Ramabai Association, Held March 11, 1890* (Boston: Press of Geo. H. Ellis, 1890), 16–17; *Report, Ramabai Association, 1892*, 18.

3. Composed of the Mukti Sadan (Home of Salvation), the Sharada Saran (Home of Learning), the Krupa Sadan (Home of Grace for Disgraced Women), Priti Sadan (Home of Love for the Aged and Infirm), Sadanand Sadan (Home for Boys), and Bartimi Sadan (Home for the Blind).

4. On Ramabai's resistance to becoming a missionary in England: Antoinette Burton, *At the Heart of Empire: Indians and the Colonial Encounter in Late-Victorian Britain* (Berkeley: University of California Press, 1998), 72–109.

5. Pandita Ramabai, *Pandita Ramabai: The Widows' Friend: An Australasian Edition of 'The High-Caste Hindu Woman'; With a Sequel by Her Daughter, Manoramabai* (Melbourne: George Robertson, 1903), 102–103.

6. Ibid., 20.

7. Elyne E. Oliver, *The Hill Station of Matheran* (Bombay: Times of India Office, 1905), 2–19.

8. *Report, Ramabai Association, 1892*, 11.

9. *Lend a Hand: A Journal of Organized Philanthropy* 4 (1889), 60; Meera Kosambi, "Multiple Contestations," 197.

10. Helen S. Dyer, *Pandita Ramabai: The Story of Her Life* (New York: Fleming H. Revell, 1900), 27.

11. Clementina Butler, *Pandita Ramabai Sarasvati: Pioneer in the Movement for the Education of the Child-Widow of India* (New York: Fleming H. Revell, 1922); Jennie Chappell, *Pandita Ramabai: A Great Life in Indian Missions* (London: Pickering and Inglis, n.d.); Mary Lucia Bierce Fuller, *The Triumph of an Indian Widow* (New York: Christian Alliance Publishing, 1928). Fuller's mother knew Ramabai personally. In Australia, the work by the president of the Australian Council of the Ramabai Mukti Mission: Bertha Todd, *Carest Thou Not? Being the Story of Pandita Ramabai and the Mukti Mission* (Melbourne: Australian Council of the Ramabai Mukti Mission, n.d.). In India: N. Macnicol, *Pandita Ramabai* (Calcutta: Association Press, 1926); Padmini Sengupta, *Pandita Ramabai Saraswati: Her Life and Work* (Bombay: Asia Publishing, 1970); S. M. Adhav, *Pandita Ramabai* (Madras: Christian Literary Society, 1979); R. K. Dongre and J. F. Patterson, *Pandita Ramabai: A Life of Faith and Prayer* (Madras: Christian Literature Society, 1963); D. N. Tilak, *Maharashtrachi Tejaswini Pandita Ramabai* (Nasik: Nagarik Prakashan, 1960); T. Sathe, *Aparajita Rama* (Pune: D. Nagarkar, 1975); Uma Chakravarti, *Rewriting History: The Life and Times of Pandita Ramabai* (Delhi: Kali for Women, 1998); Meera Kosambi, ed., *Ramabai through Her Own Words: Selected Works* (Delhi: Oxford University Press, 2000); Pandita Ramabai, *Pandita Ramabai, Inglandaca pravasa* (Mumbai: Maharashtra Rajya Sahitya ani Saskrti Mandala, 1988).

12. Caroline Healey Dall, *The Life of Dr. Anandabai Joshee: A Kinswoman of the Pundita Ramabai* (Boston: Roberts Brothers, 1888).

13. In 1890, the circles included Baltimore; Boston; Brooklyn; Bryn Mawr College; Canandaigua; Chicago; Cleveland; Concord, NH; Concordville, PA; Franklin, DE; Geneva; Germantown 1st; Germantown 2nd; Gilbertsville; Hartford; Ithaca (Cornell University); Indianapolis; Jacksonville, IL; Jamestown; Kansas City; Ingham University Leroy; London (Canada); Louisville;

Montclair, NJ; Montreal; New Haven; New Hope, PA; New York City; Niagara Falls (Canada); Smith College at Northampton; Nyack; Oswego; Philadelphia; Pawtucket, RI; Pine Bush, NY; Plainfield, NJ; Plainville; Providence, CT; Quincy, IL; the Richmond Association of Virginia; Roselle, NJ; Sherwood, NY; Sioux City; Sparkill; Springfield; Stamford; St. Louis; Toledo, OH; Toronto (Canada); Washington; Wilmington, DE; and the Branch Association of the Pacific Coast, with some twenty additional circles in addition to San Francisco. *Report, Ramabai Association, 1890,* 12–13.

14. *Report, Ramabai Association, 1892,* 22–23.
15. Shawn McHale, "Vietnamese Print Culture under French Colonial Rule: The Emergence of a Public Sphere," in *Books in Numbers: Seventy-Fifth Anniversary of the Harvard-Yenching Library,* ed. Wilt L. Idema (Cambridge, MA: Harvard-Yenching Library, Harvard University Press, 2007), 397.
16. Ramabai, *Pandita Ramabai,* 108–109.
17. Padma Anagol, *The Emergence of Feminism in India, 1850–1920* (Burlington: Ashgate, 2005), 51; Kate Storrie, *Soonderbai Powar: For 45 Years an Earnest Worker for God in India (Friend of Pandita Ramabai)* (London: Pickering and Inglis, [1924?]), 30.
18. Soonderbai H. Powar, *Hinduism and Womanhood* (London: Christian Workers' Depot, n.d.) (republished as third edition by the All Nations Missionary Union in London and the Zenana Training Home in Pune); Storrie, *Soonderbai Powar.*
19. Storrie, *Soonderbai Powar,* 31–32.
20. Maurice Gregory, *The Stand for Righteous Rule in India* (London: Dyer Brothers, 1900).
21. Soonderbai H. Powar, *An Indian Woman's Impeachment of the Opium Crime of the British Government: A Plea for Justice for her Country people* (London: Dyer, 1892).
22. Wilbur F. Crafts, Mary Leitch, Margaret W. Leitch, *Protection of Native Races against Intoxicants and Opium* (Chicago: Revell/Reform Bureau, Washington, DC, 1900), 88.
23. SOFL, "Second Report of the Committee of Urgency from July, 1892, to September, 1894," 15; Society for the Suppression of the Opium Trade Minute Book. The Minute Book dated the visit in 1891. Also Storrie, *Soonderbai Powar,* 35. Anagol claims the trip started in 1888 but dates the invitation in 1889. Anagol, *Emergence of Feminism in India,* 51–52.
24. Storrie, *Soonderbai Powar,* 31; Hudson Taylor, *The Pekin Anti-Opium Society to all Lovers of Virtue in Great Britain: With fac-simile of the original; also "Opium and the Gospel in China"* (London: Dyer Brothers, 1890).
25. Lucy E. Guinness, *Across India at the Dawn of the 20th Century* (London: The Religious Tract Society/Fleming H. Revell, 1898), 247–248.
26. *The Woman's Herald,* 14 January 1893, n.p., quoted in Anagol, *Emergence of Feminism in India,* 52; Storrie, *Soonderbai Powar,* 39–40.
27. Powar, *Indian Woman's Impeachment,* 5.
28. Ibid., 23 (original emphasis).
29. Ibid., 23–24.

30. Ibid., 12–13, 18.
31. Ibid., 22.
32. Powar, *Indian Woman's Impeachment,* 5, 23.
33. Ibid., 21. Portraits of Drs. Pandurang and Khory on p. 20.
34. Ibid., 18–19.
35. Christopher J. Virgl, *Protest in der Weltgesellschaft* (Wiesbaden: Verlag für Sozialwissenschaften, 2011), 67.
36. Religious Society of Friends Library, London (hereafter SOFL). OP M1. "Tenth Month 3rd, 1907" and "Aug 30th, 1922," *Anti-Opium Committee of the Meeting for Sufferings.*
37. Alfred S. Dyer, *The European Slave Trade in English Girls: A Narrative of Facts* (London: Dyer Brothers, 1880); Alfred S. Dyer, *Der Handel mit englischen Mädchen: Ein Bericht von Thatsachen* (Berlin: Dolfuss, 1881).
38. Jules Frédéric Pagny, *Die Organisation der weissen Sclaverei in Brüssel. Von einem Belgier. Aus dem Englischen übersetzt durch das Central-Comité des Deutschen Kulturbundes* (Berlin: Dolfuss, 1882). In French, Borel had started with *L'Etat et la moralité publique* (Neuchâtel: Bureau du Bulletin Continental, 1876), translated as *Der Staat und die öffentliche Moralität* (Neuenburg: Attinger, 1876). For Dollfuss's "public morality" series ("Die öffentliche Sittlichkeit"), regularly commissioned by the Central Committee of the *Deutscher Kulturbund.* Guillaume-Schack, *Ein Wort zur Sittlichkeitsfrage* (Berlin: Dolfuss, 1881); Alfred S. Dyer, *Der Handel mit englischen Mädchen* (Berlin: Dolfuss, 1881); *Die Organisation der weissen Sclaverei in Brüssel* (Berlin: Dolfuss, 1882); Gertrud Guillaume-Schack, *Über unsere sittlichen Verhältnisse und die Bestrebungen und Arbeiten des Britisch-Continentalen und Allgemeinen Bundes. Vortrag von Guillaume-Schack am 23. März 1882 in Darmstadt gehalten und von der Polizeibehörde daselbst verboten* (Berlin: Dolfuss, 1882), including the stenographic report of the author's trial. Also [Jules Frédéric Pagny], *Die Abschaffung der weissen Sclaverei in Brüssel. Vom Verfasser der "Organisation der weissen Sclaverei in Brüssel"* (Berlin: Dolfuss, 1882); Josephine Elizabeth Butler, *Eine Stimme in der Wüste* (Berlin: Dolfuss, 1883); Donat Sautter de Blonay, *Der Staat und die öffentliche Moralität* (Berlin: Dolfuss, 1882).
39. Gertrud Guillaume-Schack, *Ein Wort zur Sittlichkeitsfrage: Vortrag gehalten im Rathhause zu Berlin am 14. Mai 1880* (Berlin: Dolfuss, 1881).
40. For post-1899: Stephanie A Limoncelli, *The Politics of Trafficking: The First International Movement to Combat the Sexual Exploitation of Women* (Stanford: Stanford University Press, 2010).
41. Karl Marx and Frederick Engels, *Collected Works,* vol. 47: *Engels, 1883–1886* (New York: International Publishers, 1995), 311–312.
42. *Report, Ramabai Association, 1892,* 24–25; Alfred S. Dyer, *Facts for Men on Moral Purity and Health* ((London: Dyer Brothers, 1884); Alfred S. Dyer, *Safeguards against Immorality* and *Plain Words to Young Men on an Avoided Subject* (London: Dyer Brothers, 1884); Alfred S. Dyer, *British Soldiers in India in Regard to Their Morals and Health* (London: Dyer Brothers, 1897); Powar, *What Indian Women Suffer through British Greed: Women of India Commission One of Their Number* (London: Dyer Brothers, n.d.)

43. Also: *The Truth upon a Momentous Subject: An Appeal to Christian Electors against the Curse of the Opium Traffic in India. By Two Indian Missionaries. 65th thousand. Illustrated. 1d. By post, 1½ d. Britain's Crime against China: A Shorty History of the Opium Traffic. By Maurice Gregory, one of the Editors of The Banner of Asia, Bombay. With Appendix containing Letters from China by Alfred S. Dyer, Editor of The Bombay Guardian; and Appeals to the British Churches from Chinese Christians. New edition. 60th thousand. Price 1d. By post, 1½ d. A Stirring Message from Afar: Appeal from the Chinese Christian Churches at Canton to the Churches of Great Britain against the Opium Traffic. With fac-simile of the original letter.* Rev. Arthur W. Prautch. *The Black Plague amongst Indian Christians* (n.p., n.d.) *Desolation, Lamentation, Woe! Christian Women of North China to the Christian Women of England upon the Opium Iniquity. With a Chinese drawing illustrating the family misery caused by Opium* (n.p., n.d.)

44. Alfred S. Dyer, *Chinese Christians and the Ravages of the Opium Plague* (London: Dyer Brothers, 1890); Alfred S. Dyer, *The Great Plague of Asia* (London: Dyer Brothers, 1891); Maurice Gregory, *Britain's Crimes in China: A Short History of the Opium Traffic* (London: Dyer Brothers, 1892); Alfred S. Dyer, *Chinese Statesmen on Great Britain and the Opium Curse: Will the British People Permit the Infamy and Crime of a Third Opium War? Interview of the Indian Anti-Opium Deputation with the Viceroy, Li Hung Chang* (London: Dyer Brothers, 1890).

45. Zhang Jianhua, "Ershi shiji Zhongguo dui bupindeng tiaoyue gainian de qishi" (Origins of the concept of the unequal treaties in twentieth-century China) (paper presented to the Joint Conference of the History Department of Peking University and the Historical Society for Twentieth Century China, Peking University, 15–17 June 2001); Niu Daoyong, ed., *Ershi shiji de zhongguo* (Twentieth-century China) (Nanchang: Jiangxi renmin chubanshe, 2003), quoted in John Fitzgerald, "Equality, Modernity, and Gender in Chinese Nationalism," in *Performing "Nation": Gender Politics in Literature, Theater and The Visual Arts of China and Japan, 1880–1940*, ed. Doris Croissant et al. (Leiden: Brill, 2008), 29.

46. W. E. Robbins, "Opium and the Chinese Government," *Church at Home and Abroad* 8 (August 1890): 124–126.

47. Ibid.; *Chinese Recorder and Missionary Journal*, May 1890, 238–239; Alfred S. Dyer, *Word-Pictures of Chinese Life: Illustrating an Unclosed Chapter of History* (London: All Nations Missionary Union, Exeter Hall, 1905), 25.

48. Powar, *Indian Woman's Impeachment*, 30–31.

49. Ibid.

50. *The Poppy Plague in India. With Opium Map of India and other Illustrations. Contributions by the Editor of Regions Beyond; the Editor of the Bombay Guardian; one of the Editors of the Banner of Asia; and Rev. W. H. Daniels, M.A., while evangelizing in India. With the addition of a special new preface containing latest information. 50th thousand. Price 1d. By post, 1½d. Errors and Falsehoods of Opium Apologists. Illustrated. Pamphlet consisting of (a) important series of articles from the pen of Mr. Alfred S. Dyer, reprinted from The Banner of Asia; (b) important article by Dr. Wallace, Editor of The India Medical Record, re-*

printed from that paper; (c) *"My experience of the Opium Scourge in India,"* by the Rev. Colin S. Valentine, LL.D., F.R.C.S.E. & c., *Principal of the Medical Missionary Training Institution, Agra, fourteen years private physician to the late Maharajah of Jeypur, &c., &c. Price 2d. By post, 2½ d. Also The Protest of the Medical Profession of Great Britain and Ireland against the Anglo-Asiatic Opium Traffic. Full text of the declaration, the names, and titles of the five thousand medical men who have signed. 1d. By post, 1½ d.*

51. Seymour Drescher, *Abolitionism: A History of Slavery and Antislavery* (Cambridge: Cambridge University Press, 2009); Seymour Drescher and Pieter C. Emmer, eds., *Who Abolished Slavery? Slave Revolts and Abolitionism: A Debate with João Pedro Marques* (New York: Berghahn, 2010); Jürgen Osterhammel, *Sklaverei und die Zivilisation des Westens* (Munich: Carl Friedrich von Siemens Stiftung, 2000). For the political spectrum of contestation: John Chalcraft and Yaseen Noorani, eds., *Counterhegemony in the Colony and Postcolony* (Basingstoke: Palgrave Macmillan, 2007), 2. For twentieth-century chronologies: Prasenjit Duara, ed., *Decolonization: Perspectives from Now and Then* (London: Routledge, 2003), 2–3; Cemil Aydin, *The Politics of Anti-Westernism in Asia: Visions of World Order in Pan-Islamic and Pan-Asian Thought* (New York: Columbia University Press, 2007).

52. Staatsbibliothek zu Berlin. Sammlung Darmstaedter / 2 Philosophische Wissenschaften / 2d Theologie, acc. 1912.96. Christlieb to Eduard Schaer, 30 December 1878, postcard. Otto Raubenheimer, "Prof. Edward [*sic*] Schaer," *Journal of the American Pharmaceutical Association* 3 (January–December 1914): 276–277.

53. Christlieb to Eduard Schaer, 30 December 1878.

54. Ibid.

55. Don Sinibaldo de Mas, *L'Angleterre, La Chine, et l'Inde* (Paris: Lévy, 1857; Paris: Tardieu, 1858); Sinibaldo de Mas, *L'Opium* (London: n.p., 1882); also published as Sinibaldo de Mas, *L'Opium. Extrait de l'oeuvre épuisée, "L'Angleterre, la Chine, et l'Inde, etc.* (London: H. H. Sultzberger, 1882). Hartmann Henry Sultzberger, *All about Opium* (London: Wertheimer, Lea, 1884), 86–95; John King Fairbank, Katherine Frost Bruner, and Elizabeth MacLeod Matheson, eds., *The I.G. in Peking: Letters of Robert Hart, Chinese Maritime Customs, 1868–1907,* vol. 2 (Cambridge, MA: Belknap Press of Harvard University Press, 1975), 44n2; Maria da Conceiçao Meireles Pereira, "Sinibaldo de Más: el diplomatic español partidario del iberismo," *Anuario del Derecho Internacional* 17 (2001): 351–370.

56. *Church Missionary Intelligencer,* September 1876, 519; Theodor Christlieb, *Der Indobritische Opiumhandel und seine Wirkungen* (Gütersloh: C. Bertelsmann, 1878); Théodore [*sic*] Christlieb, *Le commerce Indo-britannique de l'opium et ses effets* (Paris / Neuchatel / Geneva: Sandoz et Fischbacher / J. Sandoz / Desrogis, 1879); Theodore [*sic*] Christlieb, *The Indo-British Opium Trade and Its Effect* (London: James Nisbet, 1879), 71.

57. *The Friend of China* 3, no. 9 (April 1878): 148; *Allgemeine Missionszeitschrift* (1878), 331; Gustav Warneck, *De protestantiska missionernas historia från reformationen till nuvarande tid* (Stockholm: Evangeliska

Fosterlands-Stiftelsens, 1903), 442; Warneck, *Abriss einer Geschichte der protestantischen Missionen von der Reformation bis auf die Gegenwart* (Berlin: M. Warneck, 1901) (translated as *Outline of a History of Protestant Missions from the Reformation to the Present Time* [New York: Fleming H. Revell, 1901]).

58. *Zum Gedächtnis Theodor Christliebs* (Bonn: J. Schergens, 1889); Emily Christlieb, *Theodor Christlieb, D. D. of Bonn* (New York: A. C. Armstrong, 1892), 9–88; Arno Pagel, *Theodor Christlieb: Ein Lebensbild* (Berlin: Evangelische Verlagsanstalt, 1960); Thomas Schirrmacher, *Theodor Christlieb und seine Missionstheologie* (Wuppertal: Verlag und Schriftenmission der Evangelischen Gesellschaft für Deutschland, 1985).

59. Christlieb, *Indo-British Opium Trade*, 2.

60. Ibid., 2–3.

61. Ibid., 2.

62. Christopher Leslie Brown, *Moral Capital: Foundations of British Abolitionism* (Chapel Hill: University of North Carolina Press, 2006); Seymour Drescher, "British Way, French Way: Opinion Building and Revolution in the Second French Slave Emancipation," *American Historical Review* 96, no. 3 (June 1991): 709–734; Drescher, "The Long Goodbye: Dutch Capitalism and Antislavery in Comparative Perspective," *American Historical Review* 99, no. 1 (February 1994): 44–69; Drescher, "Brazilian Abolition in Comparative Perspective," *Hispanic American Historical Review* 68, no. 3 (August 1988): 429–460. On the connected legacies: Lawrence C. Jennings, "The Interaction of French and British Antislavery, 1789–1848," *Proceedings of the Fifteenth Meeting of the French Colonial Historical Society, Martinique and Gouadeloupe, May 1989* (Lanham MD: University Press of America, 1992), 81–91.

63. The Secretaries of the Conference, ed., *Proceedings of the General Conference on Foreign Missions, held at the Conference Hall, in Mildmay Park, London, in October 1878* (London: John F. Shaw, 1879), 142.

64. Thomas Schirrmacher, "Christlieb contra Opiumhandel," in *Menschenrechte für Minderheiten in Deutschland und Europa. Vom Einsatz für Religionsfreiheit durch die Evangelische Allianz und die Freikirchen im 19. Jahrhundert*, ed. Karl Heinz Voigt and Thomas Schirrmacher (Bonn: Verlag für Kultur und Wissenschaft (Culture and Science Publications), 2004), 105–110.

65. John James Weitbrecht, *Protestant Missions in Bengal Illustrated: Being the Substance of a Course of Lectures Delivered on Indian Missions* (London: John F. Shaw, 1844), 26. Further references record the administration of opium by nurses to babies (p. 3), refer to "opium-eaters, or smokers of other narcotic drugs," as "the most abandoned profligates—a moral pestilence wherever they enter a dwelling" (p. 133), and identify opium as a "soporific," which puts the "soul and conscience fast asleep" (p. 254).

66. Rabindranath Tagore, "The Death Traffic," *Modern Review [Calcutta]* 37 (July 1925): 504.

67. Ibid., 504–505.

68. Orlando Patterson, *Slavery and Social Death: A Comparative Study* (Cambridge, MA: Harvard University Press, 1982), 38–42.

69. Diana L. Ahmad, *The Opium Debate and Chinese Exclusion Laws in the Nineteenth-Century American West* (Reno: University of Nevada Press, 2007), 41–50.

70. Tagore, "Death Traffic," 505, 507.

71. Stephen N. Hay, *Asian Ideas of East and West: Tagore and His Critics in Japan, China and India* (Cambridge, MA: Harvard University Press, 1970); Avinash M. Saklani, "Colonialism and Early Nationalist Links between India and China," *China Report* 35 (1999): 259–270; Carolien Stolte and Harald Fischer-Tiné, "Imagining Asia in India: Nationalism and Internationalism (ca. 1905–1940)," *Comparative Studies in Society and History* 54, no. 1 (2012): 65–92; Kamal Dutta, "The Tagore Wave in China: A Perspective," in *East Asian Literatures (Japanese, Chinese and Korean): An Interface with India*, ed. P. A. George (New Delhi: Northern Book Centre, 2006), 242–252; Tan Chung, ed., *Tagore and China* (Thousand Oaks, CA: Sage, 2011); Dan Ai, *Taige'er yu wu si shiqi de sixiang wenhua lunzheng* (Debate and discussion: Tagore in China) (Beijing: Renmin chubanshe, 2010).

72. Partha Chatterjee, "Tagore, China and the Critique of Nationalism," *Inter-Asia Cultural Studies* 12, no. 2 (2011): 271–283.

73. Ibid., 505.

74. Tagore, "Death Traffic," 505.

75. Ernest May, Richard Rosecrance, and Zara Steiner, "Theory and International History," in *History and Neorealism,* ed. May, Rosecrance, and Steiner (Cambridge: Cambridge University Press, 2010), 3.

76. Tagore, "Death Traffic," 505.

77. Ibid., 507.

78. Ibid., 506. Compare Syed Hussein Alatas, *The Myth of the Lazy Native: A Study of the Image of the Malays, Filipinos and Javanese from the 16th to the 20th Century and its Function in the Ideology of Colonial Capitalism* (London: F. Cass, 1977).

79. For a not dissimilar focus on food security and a concise typology of famine scenarios: Amartya Sen, *Development as Freedom* (New York: Knopf, 1999)., 161–180.

80. Compare Rudolf G. Wagner, "China 'Asleep' and 'Awakening': A Study in Conceptualizing Asymmetry and Coping with it," *Transcultural Studies* 1 (2011); Xavier Paulès, "Anti-Opium Visual Propaganda and the Deglamorisation of Opium in China, 1895–1937," *European Journal of East Asian Studies* 7, no. 2 (2008): 229–262; Xavier Paulès, "The Successful Demonization of Opium during the 1920s and 1930s in China and the End of Opium Culture," *Zeitenblicke* 9, no. 3 (2009).

81. Herbert Day Lamson, *Social Pathology in China: A Source Book for the Study of Problems of Livelihood, Health, and the Family* (Shanghai, Commercial Press, 1935); Herbert Day Lamson, *Shina shakai byōrigaku: seikatsu hoken kazoku no sho mondai ni kansuru kenkyūyō shiryōsho* (Tokyo: Seikatsusha, Shōwa 16 [1941]).

82. Christopher Bayly, *Recovering Liberties: Indian Thought in the Age of Liberalism and Empire* (Cambridge: Cambridge University Press, 2012), 33, 45–46.

83. Tagore, "Death Traffic," 507.
84. Boris Barth and Jürgen Osterhammel, eds., *Zivilisierungsmissionen: Imperiale Weltverbesserung seit dem 18. Jahrhundert* (Konstanz: UVK Verlagsgesell-schaft, 2005).
85. Editorial note, Tagore, "Death Traffic," 504. For Gandhi's early anti-opium initiative of 1918: Harumi Gotō, *Ahen to igirisu teikoku—kokusai kisei no takamari, 1906–43* (Opium and the British Empire—The rise of international control) (Tokyo: Yamagawa shuppansha, 2005), 90; Ramananda Chatterjee, *The Golden Book of Tagore: A Homage to Rabindranath Tagore from India and the World in Celebration of His Seventieth Birthday* (Calcutta: The Golden Book Committee, 1931); Nemai Sadhan Bose, *Ramananda Chatterjee* (New Delhi: Publications Division, Ministry of Information and Broadcasting, Government of India, 1974); Khsitis Roy, ed., *Ramananda Chatterjee: Selected Writings and Tributes* (New Delhi: Benson's Calcutta/Press Institute of India, 1979).
86. Dadabhai Naoroji, *Poverty of India: A Paper Read before the Bombay Branch of the East India Association on Monday the 28th February 1876* (Bombay: East India Association, 1876) (also as Dadabhai Naoroji, *Poverty of India: Papers and Statistics* [London: W. Foulger, 1888]). Also B. N. Ganguli, "Dadabhai Naoroji and the Mechanism of 'External Drain,'" *Indian Economic and Social History Review* 2 (1965): 85–102; Savak Jehangir Katrak, "Imperialism Viewed from Below: A Study of the Political and Economic Ideas of Dadabhai Naoroji" (PhD diss., Harvard University, 1972).
87. Dadabhai Naoroji, *Poverty and Un-British Rule in India* (London: Swan Sonnenschein, 1901), 203.
88. Ibid., 215.
89. Ibid., 33, 202.
90. Ibid., 215.
91. *Navavibhakar,* 29 March 1880, in *Report on the Native Press for Bengal,* 3 April 1880. *Native Opinion,* 19 June 1881; *Mahratta,* 16 April 1882, 7 December 1893; *Kesari,* 2 May 1882, all in *Report of the Native Press for Bombay,* 6 May 1882. *Samaya,* 4 June 1882, in *Report on the Native Press for Bengal,* 4 June 1882. *Sadharani,* 11 May 1884, 17 May 1884; *Hindustan,* 8 May 1884, all in *Report on the Native Press for North-West Provinces and Oudh,* 15 May 1889. Bipan Chandra, *The Rise and Growth of Economic Nationalism in India: Economic Policies of Indian National Leadership, 1880–1905* (New Delhi: New Age Printing Press/People's Publishing, 1966), 567–568n281.
92. Bayly, *Recovering Liberties,* 194.
93. Ibid., 195.
94. Ibid., 126–127.
95. R. Montgomery Martin, *China: Political, Commercial and Social; in an Official Report to Her Majesty's Government,* vol. 1 (London: James Madden, 1847), "Dedication" (n.p.), 176, 180; Bayly, *Recovering Liberties,* 194–197.
96. John Malcolm, *Political History of India,* vol. 2 (London: J. Murray, 1826), ccxlvi; "Report of the General Committee for Public Instruction," *Friend of India,* 27 October 1836.

97. Sanjay Ghildiyal, "Moral Economy and the Indigo Movement," *Economic and Political Weekly* 45 (2010): 67–72.
98. Bayly, *Recovering Liberties*, 33, 196.
99. Ibid., 126.
100. As advertised in the *Times*. Clem Seecharan, *Joseph Ruhomon's India: The Progress of Her People at Home and Abroad and How Those in British Guiana May Improve Themselves* (Kingston: University of West Indies Press, 2001), 77n36.
101. Cemil Aydin, *The Politics of Anti-Westernism in Asia: Visions of World Order in Pan-Islamic and Pan-Asian Thought* (New York: Columbia University Press, 2007), 83; Gul Karagoz-Kizilca, "'Voicing the Interests of the Public?' Contestation, Negotiation, and the Emergence of Ottoman Language Newspapers during the Financial Crises of the Ottoman Empire, 1862–1875" (PhD thesis, State University of New York at Binghamton, 2011); Philipp Zessin, *Die Stimme der Entmündigten: Geschichte des indigenen Journalismus im kolonialen Algerien* (Frankfurt: Campus, 2012); Dyala Hamzah, *The Making of the Arab Intellectual: Empire, Public Sphere and the Colonial Coordinates of Selfhood* (London: Routledge, 2012); Natascha Vittinghoff, *Die Anfänge des Journalismus in China (1860–1911)* (Wiesbaden: Harrassowitz, 2002); Mark Ravinder Frost, "Asia's Maritime Networks and the Colonial Public Sphere, 1840–1920," *New Zealand Journal of Asian Studies* 6, no. 2 (December 2004): 63–94.
102. G. Subramania Iyer, *Some Economic Aspects of British Rule in India* (Madras: Swadesamitran Press, 1903), 330.
103. Ibid., 336–337.
104. *Abstract of the Proceedings of the Council of the Governor General of India, Assembled for the Purpose of Meeting Laws and Regulations, From April 1906 to March 1907*, vol. 45 (Calcutta: Office of the Superintendent of Government Printing, India, 1907), 160, cited in M. Emdad-ul Haq, *Drugs in South Asia: From the Opium Trade to the Present Day* (London: Macmillan, 2000), 52.
105. Iyer, *Some Economic Aspects of British Rule in India*, v–vi.
106. Alfred Webb, *Alfred Webb: The Autobiography of a Quaker Nationalist* (Cork: Cork University Press, 1999), 34.
107. Ibid., 60.
108. *Parliamentary Debates*, 30 June 1893, 14, 591.
109. *Correspondence with the Government of India Respecting the Negotiations with China on the Subject of Opium* (London: HMSO, 1882).
110. *Report, Ramabai Association, 1892*, 23–24.
111. William C. King, *The World's Progress: As Wrought by Men and Women, in Art, Literature, Education, Philanthropy, Reform, Inventions, Business and Professional Life* (Springfield, MA: King-Richardson, 1896), 346. Compare Cooper-Richardson Family Papers, 1863–1977, RG 5/032, Swathmore College Special Collections, describing a similar experience by Anna C. Richardson in 1904.
112. Helen Dyer, *Pandita Ramabai*, 25–26.
113. Meera Kosambi, ed., *Pandita Ramabai's American Encounter* (Bloomington: Indiana University Press, 2003), 258.

114. King, *World's Progress*, 343.

115. Kosambi, ed., *Pandita Ramabai's American Encounter*, 205–206.

116. Ibid.

117. Leila J. Rupp, *Worlds of Women: The Making of an International Women's Movement* (Princeton, NJ: Princeton University Press, 1997).

118. King, *World's Progress*, 347.

119. Frances Willard, *Occupations for Women: A Book of Practical Suggestions, for the Material Advancement, the Mental and Physical Development, and the Moral and Spiritual Uplift of Women* (New York: Success Company/Cooper Union, 1897), 180.

120. Frances Willard, *Do Everything* (Chicago: Woman's Temperance Publication Association, 1895), 29.

121. Margaret E. Keck and Kathryn Sikkink, *Activists beyond Borders: Advocacy Networks in International Politics* (Ithaca, NY: Cornell University Press, 1998), 39–78.

122. *Chinese Recorder* 25 (April 1894): 193.

123. Kathleen L. Lodwick, *Crusaders against Opium: Protestant Missionaries in China, 1874–1917* (Lexington: University Press of Kentucky, 1996), 49–52; George Hedley, "The Anti-Opium League (Secular Radicalism)," in *The Church and Organized Movements*, ed. Randolph Crump Miller (New York: Harper, 1946), 49–81. For the ambiguity: "The Anti-Opium League Trying to Force Parliament to Stop the Trade," *New York Times*, 4 March 1893.

124. Rachel Foster Avery, ed., *Transactions of the National Council of Women of the United States, assembled in Washington, D.C., February 22 to 25, 1891* (Philadelphia: Lippincott, 1891), 51.

125. Rumi Yasutake, *Transnational Women's Activism: the United States, Japan, and Japanese Immigrant Communities in California, 1859–1920* (New York: New York University Press, 2004), 126.

126. Ibid. 29–31.

127. Ibid., 17.

128. Ibid.

129. Willard, *Do Everything*, 17; Opium-Kommission des Deutschen Zweiges der Internationalen Frauenliga für Frieden und Freiheit, ed., *Internationaler Kampf gegen Opium und Rauschgifte. 1. Konferenz in Deutschland* (Berlin: n.p., 1929); Women's International League for Peace and Freedom, Opium Commission, *Opium and Noxious Drugs: International Conference. Geneva, April 1930* (Geneva: Women's International League for Peace and Freedom, 1930).

130. Elizabeth Putnam Gordon, *Women Torch-Bearers: The Story of the Woman's Christian Temperance Union* (Evanston, IL: National Woman's Christian Temperance Union, 1924), 73; King, *World's Progress*, 347–348.

131. Ibid., 346.

132. Willard, *Occupations for Women*, 180. Most institutional features of the WWCTU are laid out in Woman's Christian Temperance Union, *The World's Woman's Christian Temperance Union, Organized 1883: What Is It? Why Is It? Who Are the Leaders? How Does It Work?* (Chicago: Woman's Christian Temperance Union, 1890).

133. King, *World's Progress,* 348; Esther Pugh, *Genesis of the World's W.C.T.U. and Our Round-the-World Missionary (Mrs. Mary Clement Leavitt)* (Chicago: National Woman's Christian Temperance Union, 1900).

134. King, *World's Progress,* 346; Gordon, *Women Torch-Bearers,* 73. The only chronologically divergent account is Willard, *Do Everything,* 11–12.

135. King, *World's Progress,* 348.

136. Frances Power Cobbe, *The Duties of Women: A Course of Lectures* (Chicago: Woman's Temperance Publication Association, 1887), 6.

137. King, *World's Progress,* 345.

138. Ibid., 354.

139. *Lend a Hand: A Journal of Organized Philanthropy* 2 (1887): 663; *Lend a Hand* 3 (1888): 62.

140. Ibid., 349.

141. Lenore Manderson, *Sickness and the State: Health and Illness in Colonial Malaya, 1870–1940* (Cambridge: Cambridge University Press, 2002), 192–193; Neil Jin Keong Khor, *The Penang Po Leung Kuk: Chinese Women, Prostitution and a Welfare Organisation* (Kuala Lumpur: Malaysian Branch of the Royal Asiatic Society, 2004). For an impressive reflection of cases and correspondences: Elizabeth Sinn, *Power and Charity: A Chinese Merchant Elite in Colonial Hong Kong* (Hong Kong: Hong Kong University Press, 2003), 232–233n124, 243–244n115).

142. King, = *World's Progress,* 345.

143. Elizabeth Andrew and Kate Bushnell, *Opium and Vice: Recent Personal Investigations* (London: Dyer Brothers, 1894; London: Kenny, 1895), 4. Citations refer to the 1895 edition.

144. Belinda Peacey, "Josephine Butler: The Great Feminist," *International Review of the Red Cross* 92 (November 1968): 555–570, here 562–563.

145. Andrew and Bushnell, *Opium and Vice,* 4. For Singapore, their sources included the *Daily Advertiser;* Andrew and Bushnell, *Opium and Vice,* 38.

146. Henry Lethbridge, "The Evolution of a Chinese Voluntary Association in Hong Kong: The Po Leung Kuk," in *Hong Kong: Stability and Change: A Collection of Essays,* ed. Lethbridge (Hong Kong: Oxford University Press, 1978), 71–103; S. W. Ng, "The Chinese Protectorate in Singapore, 1877–1900," *Journal of Southeast Asian History* 2, no. 1 (March 1961): 89–114; Angelina S. Chin, *Bound to Emancipate: Working Women and Urban Citizenship in Early Twentieth-Century China and Hong Kong* (Lanham, MD: Rowman and Littlefield, 2012), 153–212.

147. Andrew and Bushnell, *Opium and Vice,* 6.

148. Ibid., 17.

149. Andrew and Bushnell, *Opium and Vice,* 5.

150. King, *World's Progress,* 350.

151. Willard, *Do Everything,* 30.

152. Ibid., 29.

153. Ibid., 11–12.

154. Ibid., 28.

4. Britain's Last Defense: The Anti-Opium Cause on Trial

Epigraph: Geoffrey Parsons, "Royal Commission," *Punch,* 24 August 1955, 207.

1. It is indeed spelled "Pekin." "Appeal of the Pekin Anti-Opium Society to All Lovers of Virtue in Great Britain," *Sentinel* 12, no. 11 (November 1890): 136–137; *Sentinel* 12, no. 12 (December 1890): 150.
2. Jonathan D. Spence, "Opium," in *Chinese Roundabout: Essays in History and Culture,* ed. Spence (New York: Norton, 1992), 238.
3. "Appeal of the Pekin Anti-Opium Society to All Lovers of Virtue in Great Britain," 150.
4. Ibid.
5. Ibid.
6. Ibid.
7. David Edward Owen, *British Opium Policy in China and India* (New Haven, CT: Yale University Press, 1934), 314.
8. John V. Crangle, "Joseph Whitwell Pease and the Quaker Role in the Campaign to Suppress the Opium Trade in the British Empire," *Quaker History* 68, no. 2 (Fall 1979): 63–74, here 66–67.
9. Francis P. Horne, *The Condemned Opium Traffic: Shewing from Speeches delivered in the House of Commons by Members supporting the Government and from Reports of Government Officials that the System by which the Indian Opium Revenue is raised is morally indefensible* (Bombay: The Anglo-Vernacular and "Bombay Guardian" Printing Works, 1891).
10. *A Letter addressed by Sir Joseph W. Pease, Bart., M.P. to the Rt. Hon. Viscount Cross, G.C.B. on the Connection of the Indian Government with the Opium Trade* (London: Waterlow and Sons, 1892), 5.
11. Ibid., 7.
12. Ibid., 8; *Consumption of Opium in India* (London: HMSO, 1892), 33.
13. *A Letter addressed by Sir Joseph W. Pease,* 8; *Consumption of Opium in India,* 39.
14. Ibid., 43.
15. James R. Rush, *Opium to Java: Revenue Farming and Chinese Enterprise in Colonial Indonesia, 1860–1910* (Ithaca, NY: Cornell University Press, 1990).
16. *Consumption of Opium in India,* 42.
17. Imperial Maritime Customs, *II. Special Series: No. 4. Opium* (Shanghai: Inspector General of Customs, Statistical Department, 1881), 6.
18. Francis W. White, 22 August 1879, Imperial Maritime Customs, *II. Special Series: No. 4. Opium* (Shanghai: Inspector General of Customs, Statistical Department, 1881), 19.
19. C. Lenox Simpson, 20 September 1879, Imperial Maritime Customs, *II. Special Series: No. 4. Opium* (Shanghai: Inspector General of Customs, Statistical Department, 1881), 13–14.

20. Herbert Thirkell White, *A Civil Servant in Burma* (London: Edward Arnold, 1913), 55–56. Linus Pierpont Brockett, *The Story of the Karen Mission in Bassein, 1838–1890* (Philadelphia: American Baptist Publication Society, 1891), 121, 128, 157.

21. W. C. B. Purser, *Christian Missions in Burma* (Westminster: Society for the Propagation of the Gospel in Foreign Parts, 1913), 221; Erik Braun, *The Birth of Insight: Meditation, Modern Buddhism, and the Burmese Monk Ledi Sayadaw* (Chicago: University of Chicago Press, 2013). The British colonial spelling "Ledi Sadaw" differs from the established one.

22. White, *Civil Servant in Burma*, 197–199.

23. "The Humble Memorial of the Society for the Suppression of the Opium Trade," 30 July 1890, in *Consumption of Opium in India*, 110–114, here 113.

24. *A Letter addressed by Sir Joseph W. Pease*, 8; *Consumption of Opium in India*, 41.

25. Ibid., 43.

26. Mr. Birks, Lieutenant-Colonel Strover, Mr. Weidemann, Mr. Ireland, Colonel Clarke, H. E. M. James on the Northern Division, F. C. Anderson, the Commissioner of Excise of the Central Provinces, L. K. Laurie, Colonel Trevor on Ajmere Merwara, J. A. Crawford on Hyderabad, R. M. Dane on Punjab, T. D. Mackenzie and J. M. Campbell on Bombay, C. E. Frost and Rao Bahadur Munsukram Mulji, the Inspector of Police, on Ahmedabad, the Collector at Satara, K. G. Gupta on the Lower Provinces, F. C. Daukes and J. J. S. Driberg on Assam, and C. A. Galton on Madras, *A Letter addressed by Sir Joseph W. Pease*, 8–20.

27. *Consumption of Opium in India*, 12.

28. Ibid., 6.

29. Ibid., 12.

30. "Humble Memorial of the Society for the Suppression of the Opium Trade," 112–113.

31. Ibid., 114.

32. *Consumption of Opium in India*, 12.

33. Hugh McDowall Clokie, *Royal Commissions of Inquiry: The Significance of Investigations in British Politics* (Stanford: Stanford University Press, 1937), 75. The majority of Royal Commissions concerned the management of labor, family and business relations, and imperial finance. See the Table in Clokie, *Royal Commissions of Inquiry*, 76–78. The Royal Commission on Opium is not discussed in this account. For methodological issues of interpreting Royal Commissions in legal analysis and sociopolitical history: Barbara Lauriat, "'The Examination of Everything': Royal Commissions in British Legal History," *Statute Law Review* 31, no. 1 (2010): 24–46.

34. *Consumption of Opium in India*, 10.

35. *Sentinel* 12, no. 12 (December 1890): 134.

36. Ibid., 150; *Friend of China* 12 (May 1891): 92–93.

37. *Is India to Be Ruined by Opium? Alarming Spread of the Fatal Habit in That Country: The Testimony of Eye-Witnesses* (London: Dyer Brothers, 1890).

38. Maurice Gregory, *Suffering for the Truth: The Imprisonment of Missionaries in Bombay through Exposing Official Subterfuge and Criminality in*

Connection with the Iniquitous Traffic in Opium (London: Dyer Brothers, 1894), 3.

39. Ibid., 4.

40. I have not been able to ascertain the first name of Mr. Prautch.

41. Royal Commission on Opium, *Minutes of Evidence Taken before the Royal Commission on Opium from 3rd to 27th January 1894* (London: Her Majesty's Stationery Office, 1894), 299–300.

42. Man Sukh Lal, *Opium and the Gospel in Indian Villages* (London: Dyer Brothers, 1895).

43. Second Report of the Committee of Urgency from July 1892, to September 1894, 7–14; Religious Society of Friends Library, London (hereafter SOFL), TEMP MSS 150/1–2; Anti-Opium Urgency Committee, Minutes, 9 July 1894–12 August 1895.

44. Gregory, *Suffering for the Truth*, 4–5.

45. Ibid., 7.

46. Ibid., 7–8.

47. Ibid., 8.

48. "The 'Pall Mall Gazette' on the Anti-Opium Gang," *Food and Sanitation*, 22 September 1894, 298.

49. "Further Fraud by the Bombay Opium Department," *Bombay Guardian*, 20 January 1894, reprinted in Gregory, *Suffering for the Truth*, 15–16.

50. "'Pall Mall Gazette' on the Anti-Opium Gang," 298.

51. Gregory, *Suffering for the Truth*, 21. The copy available to me is of somewhat unsatisfactory quality.

52. John Anderson, *Mandalay to Momien: A Narrative of the Two Expeditions to Western China of 1868 and 1875 under Colonel Edward B. Sladen and Colonel Horace Browne* (London: Macmillan, 1876), 341.

53. On Yan: Xu Yihua, "Yanyongjing yu shenggonghui," *Jindai Zhongguo* 135–136 (2000): 193–215; Daniel H. Bays, *A New History of Christianity in China* (Malden, MA: Wiley-Blackwell, 2012), 81.

54. Second Report of the Committee of Urgency from July 1892 to September 1894, 15–20.

55. Michael R. Godley, "The Late Ch'ing Courtship of the Chinese in Southeast Asia," *Journal of Asian Studies* 34, no. 2 (February 1975): 361–385, here 366.

56. Ibid., 366–367.

57. "Report of Interview at the Tsung-Li Yamen, Peking, 2nd June, 1894," in Joseph G. Alexander, *Interviews with Chinese Statesmen with regard to the Opium Traffic* (London: Society for the Suppression of the Opium Trade, 1894), 15.

58. As per the edict of 21 December 1895 concerning the Qing's peace proposal with Japan, Zhang acted alongside Xiao Yulian, the former chargé d'affaires at St. Petersburg and governor of Formosa (Taiwan). Hosea Ballou Morse, *The International Relations of the Chinese Empire*, vol. 3, *The Period of Subjection, 1894–1911* (London: Longmans, 1918), 40, 86. For a biographical sketch of Zhang: Fang Chao-Ying, "Chang Yin-huan," in *ECCP*, 60.

59. "Report of Interview at the Tsung-Li Yamen, Peking, 2nd June, 1894," 13.
60. Ibid., 14.
61. Royal Commission on Opium, vol. 6, *Final Report of the Royal Commission on Opium. Part I: The Report*, 231–232.
62. Ibid., 14–15.
63. Ibid., 15.
64. "Report of Interview with Li Hung-Chang," in Alexander, *Interviews with Chinese Statesmen*, 18.
65. Virginia Berridge and Griffith Edwards, *Opium and the People: Opiate Use in Nineteenth-Century-England* (London: Lane, 1981); Kathleen L. Lodwick, *Crusaders against Opium: Protestant Missionaries in China, 1874–1917* (Lexington: University Press of Kentucky, 1996); Paul C. Winther. *Anglo-European Science and the Rhetoric of Empire: Malaria, Opium, and British Rule in India, 1756–1895* (Lanham, MD: Lexington, 2003). Compare John F. Richards, "Opium and the British Indian Empire: The Royal Commission of 1895," *Modern Asian Studies* 36, no. 2 (2002): 375–420; Frank Dikötter, Lars Peter Laamann, and Zhou Xun, *Narcotic Culture: A History of Drugs in China* (Chicago: University of Chicago Press, 2004).
66. Horace B. Alexander, *Joseph Gundry Alexander* (London: Swarthmore, 1920), 63–64.
67. Winther, *Anglo-European Science and the Rhetoric of Empire*, 185.
68. J. A. Baines (Secretary to the Commission), "On the Course of the Movement in England against the Opium Trade, with especial reference to the Action taken in connexion with it in Parliament (July, 1894)," in Royal Commission on Opium, vol. 6, *Final Report of the Royal Commission on Opium*, 171.
69. "The Export of Indian Opium to China and the Straits," in Royal Commission on Opium, vol. 6, *Final Report of the Royal Commission on Opium*, 48.
70. Royal Commission on Opium, vol. 6, *Final Report of the Royal Commission on Opium*, 22.
71. Baines, "On the Course of the Movement in England against the Opium Trade," 171.
72. War Office Memorandum, October 10, 1906, quoted in Stanley A. Wolpert, *Morley and India 1906–1910* (Berkeley: University of California Press, 1967), 216.
73. Baines, "On the Course of the Movement in England against the Opium Trade," 163–171. Baine's report referenced seven parliamentary debates on "the Second Opium War" between 1870 and 1895, by Gladstone, Sir M. Steward, Sir Joseph Pease, Mr. S. Smith and others: *Parliamentary Debates*, vol. 201, par. 516; vol. 225, par. 375; vol. 252, pars. 1232 and 1252; vol. 335, par. 1146; vol. 144, par. 1421; vol. 144, par. 1846. Margin note in Baines, "On the Course of the Movement in England against the Opium Trade," 164.
74. Frederick Cooper, *Colonialism in Question: Theory, Knowledge, History* (Berkeley: University of California Press, 2005), 163–168.
75. Joshua Rowntree, *An Analysis of the Opium Commission Report Showing Some of the Misstatements, Evasions and Garbled Quotations* (London: The

Society for the Suppression of the Opium Trade, 1896), 9, excerpted from Rowntree, *The Opium Habit in the East.*

76. Royal Commission on Opium, vol. 6, *Final Report of the Royal Commission on Opium,* 94.

77. Owen, *British Opium Policy,* 328.

78. See the doubtful qualifications of witnesses: Royal Commission on Opium, *Correspondence Regarding the Report by the Royal Commission on Opium* (London: Her Majesty's Stationery Office, 1896); Royal Commission on Opium, vol. 7, *Final Report of the Royal Commission on Opium. Part 2: Historical Appendices; Together with an Index of Witnesses and Subjects . . .* (London: Her Majesty's Stationery Office, 1895), 217–229.

79. *Correspondence Regarding the Report by the Royal Commission on Opium* (London: HMSO, 1896), 49–59.

80. Joseph Alexander, *Interviews with Chinese Statesmen with regard to the Opium Traffic*; Arnold Foster, *The Wresting of Medical Evidence: A Criticism of the Report of the Royal Commission on Opium* (Shanghai: American Presbyterian Mission Press, 1896) (pamphlet was reprinted from the *China Medical Missionary Journal*); Arnold Foster, *The Report of the Royal Commission on Opium Compared with the Evidence from China That Was Submitted to the Commission* (P. S. King, 1899), drawing liberally on writings by Zhang Zhidong and evidence by a Chinese general, a clerk, a former student, an intendant, a writer, an interpreter (Gu), and a sub-prefect.

81. Royal Commission on Opium, *Proceedings,* vol. 5, *Appendices; together with Correspondence on the Subject of Opium with the Straits Settlements and China* (London: HMSO, 1894), 148.

82. Royal Commission on Opium, *Proceedings,* vol. 5, *Appendices,* 153–154.

83. Ibid.

84. Ibid., 154.

85. Ibid.

86. Ibid., 151.

87. *Straits Times,* 21 July 1877, 2.

88. *Straits Times,* 26 January 1883, 2. Also *Straits Times Weekly Issue,* 12 February 1883, 7; *Sentinel* 12, no. 12 (December 1890): 150; "Free Speech in the Pulpit," *Straits Times Weekly Issue,* 25 June 1890), 12; *Straits Times Weekly Issue,* 26 December 1893), 2; "Opium and Charity," *Straits Times,* 7 March 1894, 2; "Anti-Opium Agitation," *Mid-day Herald,* 25 June 1895, 3; *Straits Times,* 23 October 1895, 3; "The Opium Question," *Straits Times,* 1 July 1898, 2; "Legislative Council," *Straits Times,* 18 April 1900, 3; "Legislative Council," *Straits Times,* 30 October 1901, 3.

89. "The "Straits Times" and the Truth," *Daily Advertiser,* 8 March 1894, 2; "A Singapore Phonograph: Startling Disclosures," *Daily Advertiser,* 10 March 1894, 2; *Daily Advertiser,* 17 May 1894, 2.

90. "Notes and Extracts," *Friend of China* 12, no. 2 (March 1891): 74. The number of 11,000 residents reported in the "Anti-Opium Notes," *Sentinel* 12, no. 12 (December 1890): 150, has to be considered a typo.

91. Yen Ching Hwang, *The Overseas Chinese and the 1911 Revolution* (Kuala Lumpur: Oxford University Press, 1976), 41–42.

92. Eng Hee Khor, "The Public Life of Dr. Lim Boon Keng" (bachelor's thesis, University of Malaya, 1958); Seow Leng Ang and Bonny Tan, *Lim Boon Keng: A Life to Remember, 1869–1957; A Select Annotated Bibliography* (Singapore: National Library Board, 2007); Li Yuanjin, *Lin Wenqing de sixiang: Zhongxi wenhua de huiliu yu maodun* (Lin Wenqing's thought: Convergence and divergence between Chinese and Western culture) (Singapore: Xinjiapo Yazhou yanjiu xuehui, 1991). For his clash with Lu Xun: Wang Gungwu, "Lu Xun, Lim Boon Keng and Confucianism," *Papers on Far Eastern History* 39 (1989): 75–91.

93. *Straits Times,* 14 October 1903, 6.

94. Wu Lien-teh, *A Short Autobiography* (n.p., n.d.); Carsten Flohr, "The Plague Fighter: Wu Lien-teh and the Beginning of the Chinese Public Health System," *Annals of Science* 53 (1996): 361–380.

95. "Grandmotherly Legislation," *Straits Times,* 8 May 1896, 2; "The Municipal Bill," *Straits Times,* 15 May 1896, 3; "The Government of Johore: Alleged Tyrannous Treatment of a Chinaman; A Case for British Inquiry," *Straits Times,* 30 August 1897, 3; "Opiomaniacs," *Straits Times,* 1 July 1898, 3; "Legislative Council," *Straits Times,* 22 January 1902, 5; "Legislative Council," *Straits Times,* 15 November 1902, 5; *Straits Chinese Magazine* 1, no. 1 (1897): 2.

96. Mark Ravinder Frost, "Transcultural Diaspora: The Straits Chinese in Singapore, 1819–1918," (Working Paper Series No. 10, Asia Research Institute, National University of Singapore, August 2003), 22–23.

97. Lim Boon Keng, "The Attitude of the State towards the Opium Habit," *Straits Chinese Magazine* 2, no. 6 (1898): 48, 50.

98. J. B. Brown, "Politics of the Poppy: The Society for the Suppression of the Opium Trade, 1874–1916," *Journal of Contemporary History* 8, no. 3 (July 1973): 97–111.

99. Lim, "Attitude of the State," 48.

100. Lim was nevertheless critical enough to realize that "modern science" had also introduced hypodermic morphine injections as a mass phenomenon in China: Lim, "Attitude of the State," 51. Henrietta Harrison has studied this process in-depth: "Narcotics, Nationalism and Class in China: The Transition from Opium to Morphine and Heroin in early 20th Century Shanxi," *East Asian History* 32/33 (2006/2007): 151–176.

101. Lim, "Attitude of the State," 50.

102. Ibid., 52–53. Since Karl Marx's famous critique in 1848, the monotony of everyday life has been more prominently associated with high industrial than with non-industrial routines. Of the former, Marx wrote: "It exhausts the nervous system to the uttermost.... It ... confiscates every atom of freedom." Karl Marx, *Manifesto of the Communist Party [1848]* (Beijing: Foreign Language Press, 1976), 58. E. P. Thompson, "Time, Work-Discipline, and Industrial Capitalism," *Past and Present* 38 (December 1967): 56–97.

103. Lim, "Attitude of the State," 52–53.
104. *Report of the Commission Appointed to Enquire into Matters Relating to the Use of Opium in the Straits Settlements and Federated Malay States* (Singapore: Government Printing Office, 1908), vol. 2, questions 743, 750.
105. Peter Toohey, *Boredom: A Lively History* (New Haven, CT: Yale University Press, 2011), 152; Peter A. Horton, "Padang or Paddock: A Comparative View of Colonial Sport in Two Imperial Territories," *International Journal of the History of Sport* 14, no. 1 (January 1997): 1–20; Ng Aplin and Quek Jin Jong, "Celestials Touch: Sport and the Chinese in Colonial Singapore," *International Journal of the History of Sport* 19, no. 2/3 (February 2002): 67–98; Andrew Morris, "'To Make the Four Hundred Million Move': The Late Qing Dynasty Origins of Modern Chinese Sport and Physical Culture," *Comparative Studies in Society and History* 42, no. 4 (October 2000): 876–906.
106. Frances E. Willard, *Glimpses of Fifty Years: The Autobiography of an American Woman* (Chicago: Woman's Temperance Publication Association, 1889), title page.
107. Jabez Thomas Sunderland, *India in Bondage: Her Right to Freedom and a Place among the Great Nations* (New York: 1932).
108. Reinhard Frank, *Englands Herrschaft in Indien* (Berlin: Erich Zander, 1940), 73.
109. Ibid., 74.
110. Reinhard Frank, *British Tyranny in India* (Berlin: n.p., 1940). Translated by Agostino Toso for *Quaderni di politica e di economia contemporanea*: Reinhard Frank, *Il dominio inglese nell'India* (Rome: Artiganato Grafico, 1941) and also as Reinhard Frank, *La dominazione inglese in India* (n.p., n.p., 1940). Translated by Allan Ekberg-Hedqvist into Swedish: Reinhard Frank, *England och Indien: En historisk återblick* (Stockholm: Svea Rike, 1940). Also Reinhard Frank, *La Domination de l'Angleterre sur l'Inde* (Berlin: n.p., 1940). In Slovenian as Rajnchard Frank, *Gospodstvoto na Anglija v Indija* (Berlin: n.p., 1940). The opium chapter was also published separately as *Opium in Indien* (Berlin: Europa-Verlag, 1940). Reinhard Frank, *L'opium aux Indes* (Paris: Éditions Européennes, 1940). Reinhard Frank, *Opium in India* (London: European Publishers, 1940). In Romanian for the *Colecţia informativă* series as Reinhard Frank, *Opiul în India* (Berlin: Europa-Verlag, 1941).
111. *Pittsburgh Press*, 13 September 1941, 2.
112. Deutsche Verwaltung für Volksbildung in der sowjetischen Besatzungszone, *Liste der auszusondernden Literatur. Vorläufige Ausgabe nach dem Stand vom 1. April 1946* (Berlin: Zentralverlag, 1946), 3, 117.

5. The Japanese Blueprint and Its American Discovery

1. Shunzo Sakamaki, "Japan and the United States, 1790–1853," *Transactions of the Asiatic Society of Japan*, 2nd ser., 18 (1939): 144; Sakamaki, "Japan and the United States, 1790–1853," plate 3, "Complete map of all countries of

the globe," between 112 and 113; and plate 6, "Complete map of 31 states of the Republican Government," between 142 and 143.

2. Sakamaki, 126–127, quoting *Suzuki dai zasshū* 4 (Tokyo, 1918), 347–348, and *Kaei yonen yori ansei yonen ni itaru fūsetsugaki* (n.p., n.d.).

3. Ibid., 127.

4. William Speiden, *With Commodore Perry to Japan: The Journal of William Spelden Jr., 1852–1855* (Annapolis: Naval Institute Press, 2013).

5. *The Complete Journal of Townsend Harris: First American Consul and Minister to Japan* (Tokyo: Charles E. Tuttle, 1959), 33–34; James Hogg, *The Uncollected Writings of Thomas de Quincey*, vol. 1 (London: Swan Sonnenschein, 1892), 300.

6. "Account of an interview with the American ambassador in the 10th month of the 4th year of Ansei (December, 1857)," in *Papers Relating to the Foreign Relations of the United States,* 46th Cong., 2d sess. (Washington, DC: Government Printing Office, 1879), 627.

7. *The Complete Journal of Townsend Harris,* 484; "Account of an interview with the American ambassador," 628.

8. "Account of an interview with the American ambassador," 628.

9. Hayashi Shihei, *Kaikoku heidan* (Tokyo: Daiichi Shobo, 1979), 82, quoted in Hung Yueh Lan, "Facing the sea, Becoming the West: The Imagination of Maritime Nation and Discourses of Asia in Japan," in *European-East Asian Borders in Translation,* ed. Joyce C. H. Liu and Nick Vaughan-Williams (New York: Routledge, 2014), 100.

10. "Account of an interview with the American ambassador," 628–629.

11. Fūkō Mineta, *Kaigai shinwa,* 5 vols. (n.p., 1849); Bob Tadashi Wakabayashi, "Opium, Expulsion, Sovereignty: China's Lessons for Bakumatsu Japan," *Monumenta Nipponica* 47, no. 1 (Spring 1992); 1–25.

12. Anonymous, *Afuyo Ibun* (A collection of opium tales) (n.p., n.d.).

13. "Treaty of Amity and Commerce, between the United States of America and the Empire of Japan, concluded at the City of Yedo, July 29, 1858, Art. IV. Ratifications exchanged at Washington May 22, 1860. Proclaimed May 23, 1860," in *Treaties and Conventions Concluded between the United States of America and Other Powers, since July 4, 1776* (Washington, DC: Government Printing Office, 1873), 518.

14. Pär Kristoffer Cassel, *Grounds of Judgment: Extraterritoriality and Imperial Power in Nineteenth-Century China and Japan* (Oxford: Oxford University Press, 2012), 90.

15. Townsend Harris to Catherine Drinker, 1 November 1858, in *Some Unpublished Letters of Townsend Harris,* ed. Sakanishi Shio (n.p.).

16. Ibid.

17. Marquis de Moges, *Souvenirs d'une ambassade en Chine et au Japon en 1857 et 1858* (Paris: Hachette, 1860).

18. Art. VIII of Treaty of Friendship and Commerce between the United States and Siam, dated 29 May 1856; S. J. Smith, *The Siam Repository, containing a Summary of Asiatic Intelligence,* vol. 4, nos. 1, 2, 3, 4 (Bangkok: At S. J. Smith's Place, 1872), 153–154; Sinthanun Chuvongs, "Addiction Policies

and Siam Nation-Making Process," *Journal of the Graduate School of Asia-Pacific Studies (Waseda University)*, 30, 2015.9, 221–236; Michael R. Auslin, *Negotiating with Imperialism: The Unequal Treaties and the Culture of Japanese Diplomacy* (Cambridge, MA: Harvard University Press, 2004), 22–24.

19. *Friends' Review: A Religious, Literary and Miscellaneous Journal* 40 (1886–1887): 580.

20. *Report of the Committee Appointed by the Philippine Commission to Investigate the Use of Opium and the Traffic Therein, and the Rules, Ordinances, and Laws Regarding such Use and Traffic in Japan, Formosa, Shanghai, Hongkong, Saigon, Singapore, Burmah, Java and the Philippine Islands* (Washington, DC: Bureau of Insular Affairs, War Department, 1905), 58 (hereafter "POC Report").

21. Ibid., 58.

22. Madeline Duntley, "Confucianism, Internationalism, Patriotism and Protestantism: The Ecclesiological Matrix of Japanese Christian Activists in Japan and the US Diaspora," in *Ecumenical Ecclesiology,* ed. Gesa Elsbeth Thiessen (New York: Continuum, 2009), 230–231.

23. Yukiko Kimura, *Issei: Japanese Immigrants in Hawaii* (Honolulu: University of Hawai'i), 170, 133; George J. Tanabe Jr., "Grafting Identity: The Hawaiian Branches of the Bodhi Tree," in *Buddhist Missionaries in the Era of Globalization,* ed. Linda Learman (Honolulu: University of Hawai'i, 2005), 82.

24. Edward D. Beechert, *Working in Hawaii: A Labor History* (Honolulu: University of Hawai'i), 99; Dennis M. Ogawa, *Kodomo no tame ni—for the Sake of the Children: The Japanese American Experience in Hawaii* (Honolulu: University of Hawai'i), 47.

25. Kasahara Yōko, "Firipin repōto to Chūgoku no kinen undo" (The Philippine report and the anti-opium campaign in China), *Ningen bunka ronshū (Ochanomizu joshi daigaku)* 9 (2006): 141–150; Gotō Harumi, *Ahen to Igirisu teikoku* (Opium and the British empire) (Tokyo: Yamakawa shuppansha, 2005), 21–24. Anne L. Foster, "Prohibition as Superiority: Policing Opium in South-East Asia, 1898–1925," *International History Review* 22, no. 2 (June 2000): 253–273; Anne L. Foster, "Models for Governing: Opium and Colonial Policies in Southeast Asia, 1898–1910," in *The American Colonial State in the Philippines: Global Perspectives,* ed. Julian Go and Anne L. Foster (Durham, NC: Duke University Press, 2003), 92–117; Su Zhiliang, *Quanqiu jindu de kaiduan: 1909 nian Shanghai wanguo jinyanhui* (The beginning of global drug prohibition: The 1909 Shanghai International Opium Conference] (Shanghai: Shanghai sanlian shudian, 2009), 40–47, 73–75.

26. The argument of Arnold H. Taylor, "American Confrontation with the Opium Problem in the Philippines," *Pacific Historical Review* 36, no. 3 (August 1967): 307–324.

27. POC Report, 55.

28. Henry Knox Sherrill, "Charles Henry Brent (1862–1929)," *Proceedings of the American Academy of Arts and Sciences* 70, no. 10 (March 1936): 501–503; Alexander C. Zabriskie, *Bishop Brent: Crusader for Christian Unity* (Philadelphia: Westminster Press, 1948); Pedro S. de Achutegui and Miguel A. Bernad, "Brent, Herzog, Morayta and Aglipay," *Philippine Studies* 8, no. 3 (1960):

568–583; "The Philippines in 1902," *New York American and Journal*; Hearst's *Chicago American*; *San Francisco Examiner*, *The American Almanac, Year-Book, Cyclopedia and Atlas 1903* (Chicago: W. R. Hearst, 1902), 404–405; John Bancroft Devins, *An Observer in the Philippines, or Life in Our New Possessions* (Boston: American Tract Society, 1905), 312.

29. Edward Champe Carter, *The Lone Scout: A Tale of the United States Public Health Service* (Boston: Cornhill, 1920); Edward Champe Carter, *"A Marine, Sir!"* (Boston: Cornhill, 1921); Edward Champe Carter, *Eight Bells* (Boston: Cornhill, 1923), Edward Champe Carter, "Some Observations concerning the Controling [sic] of Epidemics," *Journal of the Association of Military Surgeons of the United States* 18, no. 1 (January 1906): 89–95.

30. Paul Brouardel, *Opium, Morphine et Cocaïne: Intoxication aigue par l'opium. Mangeurs et Fumeurs d'opium. Morphinomanes et Cocaïnomanes* (Paris: Librairie J.-B. Baillière et Fils, 1906).

31. In Japan, the commission was assisted by Mr. Usawa, a barrister-at-law, and occasionally Mr. Imai as translators. POC Report, 2, 56.

32. *Havre Daily News*, 16 January 1925, 2. For the obituary: *Kalispell Daily Inter Lake*, 15 January 1925, 2; *Saratogian*, 15 January 1925, 11; *Singapore Free Press and Mercantile Advertiser*, 18 February 1925, 12; *Morning Sun*, 20 February 1925, 2; *Ogden Standard-Examiner*, 18 January 1925, 4; Government of the Philippine Islands. Philippine Civil Service Board, *Official Roster of the Officers and Employees in the Civil Service of the Philippine Islands, Jan. 1, 1901* (Manila: Bureau of Public Printing, 1904), 22.

33. "Proceedings of the Opium Committee," POC Report, 1.

34. POC Report, 54.

35. William Howard Taft to Edward C. Carter, 8 August 1903, POC Report, 54.

36. Ibid.

37. On the Spanish opium regime: Jan F. Gamella and Elisa Martin, "Las Rentas de Anfión: El Monopolio Español del opio en Filipinas (1844–1898) y su rechazo por la administración norteamericana," *Revista de Indias* 52, no. 194 (1992): 61–106. On the security aspects: Alma N. Bamero, "Opium: The Evolution of Policies, the Tolerance of the Vice, and the Proliferation of Contraband Trade in the Philippines, 1843–1908," *Social Science Diliman* 3, no. 1–2 (January–December 2006): 49–83. On the parallel case of the private tobacco monopoly in Spain: Eugenio Torres Villanueva, "Intervención del Estado, propiedad y control en las empresas gestoras del Monopolio de Tabacos de España," *Revista de Historia Económica* 18, no. 1 (2000): 139–173.

38. José Maria Alvarez, *Descripción geográfica de la Isla de Formosa* (Madrid: Imprenta del Patronato de Huérfanos de Intendencia é Intervención Militares, 1915), 5–6, 230, 337, 462.

39. POC Report, 2. For a vivid description of Harris's reception: Townsend Harris in his correspondence with Catherine Drinker, 16 July 1858, in *Some Unpublished Letters of Townsend Harris*, ed. Sakanishi Shio (New York: Japan Reference Library, 1941) (n.p.).

40. POC Report, 55.

41. Ibid.

42. For McKim's reaction: *An Historical Sketch of the Japan Mission of the Protestant Episcopal Church in the U.S.A.* (New York: Domestic and Foreign Missionary Society of the Protestant Episcopal Church in the United States of America, 1891), 33.

43. On Chiba Takasaburō's grueling experience of seeking refuge at Nicolai's church: Irokawa Daikichi, *The Culture of the Meiji Period* (Princeton: Princeton University Press, 1988), 84–87; Dallas Finn, *Meiji Revisited: The Sites of Victorian Japan* (New York: Weatherhill, 1995), 88–89; Mitsuo Naganawa, "The Japanese Orthodox Church in the Meiji Era," in *A Hidden Fire: Russian and Japanese Cultural Encounters, 1868–1926,* ed. J. Thomas Rimer (Stanford: Stanford University Press/Woodrow Wilson Center, 1995), 158–169.

44. J. T. Gracey, "An Account of Bishop Nicolai and the Present Crisis," *Missionary Review of the World,* July 1904, 518; Alfred Stead, *Great Japan: A Study of National Efficiency* (London: John Lane, 1906). 82; Michael van Remortel, "Historical Introduction," in Michael van Remortel and Peter Chang, eds., *St. Nikolai Kasatkin and the Orthodox Mission in Japan* (Point Reyes Station, CA: Divine Ascent Press, 2003), 15.

45. Donald Keene, "The Diaries of Niijima Jō," in *Modern Japanese Diaries: The Japanese at Home and Abroad as Revealed through Their Diaries* (New York: Columbia University Press, 1998), 233–234; Carl Munzinger, *Japan 1900* (Bremen: Europäischer Hochschulverlag, 2010), 115.

46. Kathleen L. Lodwick, *Crusaders against Opium: Protestant Missionaries in China, 1874–1917* (Lexington: University Press of Kentucky, 1996); Huang Zhiqi, *Yi you ren yi: jidu jiao chuan jiao shi yu yapian maoyi de douzheng* (Hong Kong: Xuandao chubanshe, 2004); Ian R. Tyrrell, *Reforming the World: The Creation of America's Moral Empire* (Princeton, NJ: Princeton University Press, 2010).

47. The letters by Luís Fróis, Organtino Gnecchi-Soldo, Giovanni Francesca Stephanoni, and Francisco Cabral from 1566 and 1577 were first published as Luigi Froes and Francesco Cabral, *Lettere del Giappone dell'anno M. D. LXXVII. Scritte dalli Reverendi Padri della Compagnia di Giesù* (Roma: Francesco Zanetti, 1579). Also published in Brescia by Giacomo & Policreto Turlini, in Palermo by Mayda & Giovan Pietro Sartoia, in Naples by Matthio Cancer, in Venice by Antonio Ferrari, or in the French version: Francisco Cabral and Louys Froès, *Lettres de Jappon, de l'an M.D. LXXX. Envoyées par les prestres de la Compagnie de Jésus, vacans à la conversion des infideles audit lieu* (Paris: Thomas Brumen, 1580). Golownin, *Recollections of Japan* (London: Henry Colburn, 1819), 33.

48. Daikichi, *Culture of the Meiji Period,* 81. On Golovnin's influence: J. Thomas Rimer, introduction to *A Hidden Fire: Russian and Japanese Cultural Encounters, 1868–1926* (Stanford: Stanford University Press, 1995), 3; Captain Golovnin, *Narrative of My Captivity in Japan, during the Years 1811, 1812 & 1813* (London: Henry Colburn, 1818); Captain Golovnin, *Japan and the Japanese: Comprising the Narrative of a Captivity in Japan, and an Account of British Commercial Intercourse with that Country,* 2 vols. (London: Colburn,

1852). For the French version by Jean Baptiste Benoît Eyriès: V. M. Golovnin, *Begebenheiten des Capitains von der Russisch-Kaiserlichen Marine. Golownin in der Gefangenschaft bei den Japanern in den Jahren 1811, 1812 und 1813: nebst seinen Bemerkungen über das japanische Reich und Volk* (Leipzig: Gerhard Fleischer d. J., 1817–1818); V. M. Golovnin, *Voyage de M. Golovnin, contenant le récit de sa captivité chez les Japonais, pendant les années 1811, 1812, et 1813, et ses observations sur l'Empire du Japon; suivi de la relation du voyage de M. Ricord aux côtes du Japon en 1812 et 1813, etc. traduit sur la version Allemande* (Paris: Gide, 1818).

49. Nakamura Kennosuke, *Senkyōshi Nikorai to Meiji Nippon* (Tokyo: Iwanami, 1996); Nakamura Kennosuke, "Some Aspects of the Life and Work of St. Nikolai Kasatkin," in *St. Nikolai Kasatkin and the Orthodox Mission in Japan,* ed. Michael van Remortel and Peter Chang, 94–97; Michael van Remortel, historical introduction to *St. Nikolai Kasatkin,* 1–36.

50. Kyoto ethnologist Umesao Tadao claims that "the idea that Japanese civilization began in 1868 is generally accepted." "Japanese Civilization in the Modern World," in *Japan in Global Context: Papers Presented on the Occasion of the Fifth Anniversary of the German Institute for Japanese Studies, Tōkyō,* ed. Josef Kreiner (Munich: Iudicium, 1994), 31.

51. Diaries, vol. 1 (1901–1910), 172, Brent Papers, box 53, Library of Congress.

52. Ibid., 173, Brent Papers, box 53, Library of Congress.

53. POC Report, 55.

54. Joachim Winsmann, *Die "Heimat" des Sergei M. Wolkonsky* (n.p., n.d.), 226–227.

55. "Findings and Recommendations of the Opium Investigation Committee Appointed under the Provisions of Act No. 800, as Amended by Act No. 812 of the Philippine Commission," 15 June 1904, in POC Report, 11.

56. Nakamura Kennosuke et al., ed., *Senkyōshi Nikorai no zenniki, vol. 7 (1901 nen 7 gatsu—1903 nen)* (Tokyo: Kyōbunkan, 2007), 308. The original Russian edition is titled *Dnevniki Sviatogo Iaponskogo v 5 tomakh* (St. Petersburg: Giperion, 2004). On Nicolai and the Anglo-American clergy in Japan: Nakamura, "Some Aspects of the Life and Work of St. Nikolai Kasatkin," 98–101.

57. POC Report, 55. On McKim: William Wilkinson, *A History of the General Convention of the Protestant Episcopal Church in the United States, held in Gethsemane Church, Minneapolis, in October, 1895, with Biographical Sketches of its Members, also a Chapter on the History of the Church in the Early Days of Minnesota, and a Chapter on the Work of the Woman's Auxiliary in the United States* (Minneapolis: William Wilkinson, 1895), 643–644; Domestic and Foreign Missionary Society of the Protestant Episcopal Church in the U.S. of America, Secretaries of the Board of Managers, *The Spirit of Missions,* vol. 48 (New York: Nos. 22 and 23 Bible House, 1883), 54. On Awdry: Frederick Sawrey Archibald Lowndes, *Bishops of the Day: A Biographical Dictionary of the Archbishops and Bishops of the Church of England, and of All Churches in Communion Therewith throughout the World* (London:

Grant Richards, 1897), 213; Mandeville B. Phillips, *Church and Queen. Diamond Jubilee Lambeth Conference* (London: Church Newspapers Company, 1897), 59. On Brinkley: Donald Keene, *Emperor of Japan: Meiji and His World, 1852–1912* (New York: Columbia University Press, 2002), 820n41; J. E. Hoare, "Captain Francis Brinkley (1841–1912): Yatoi, Scholar and Apologist," in *Britain and Japan: Biographical Portraits*, vol. 3, ed. Hoare (Richmond: Surrey, 1999), 99–107; Ellen P. Conant, "Captain Frank Brinkley Resurrected," in *The Nasser D. Khalili Collection of Japanese Art*, ed. Oliver Impey and Malcolm Fairley (London: Kibo Foundation, 1995), 124–151.

58. S. A. Rachinskii's introduction to S. Shōji, "Kaki a stal khristaninom," *Ruskii viestnik*, 217 (1891), quoted in Konishi, "Translation and Conversion," 240n12, 239n11; Remortel and Chang, *St. Nikolai Kasatkin and the Orthodox Mission in Japan*, 14.

59. Remortel, historical introduction to *St. Nikolai Kasatkin*, 12–13.

60. Sho Konishi, "Translation and Conversion beyond Western Modernity: Tolstoian Religion in Meiji Japan," in *Converting Cultures: Religion, Ideology and Transformations of Modernity*, ed. Dennis Charles Vashburn and A. Kevin Reinhart (Leiden: Brill, 2007), 240.

61. T. Gracey, "An Account of Bishop Nicolai and the Present Crisis," 517; *Japan Weekly Mail*, 12 November 1904, 541; *Mission News: A Journal of Religious and Social Progress; with Especial Reference to the Work of the American Board in Japan* 7, no. 1 (26 September 1903): 18. Nicolai commissioned the article written by Ishikawa, "The Eastern Church in Japan," *Japan Christian Year Book* 5 (1907): 276–278. On the *Fukuin Shimpo*: Board of Foreign Missions of the Presbyterian Church in the U.S.A., *The 68th Annual Report* (New York: Presbyterian Building, 1905), 209–212; *Reformed Church Review*, 4th ser., 9, 1905, 265.

62. Nakamura Kennosuke et al., *Senkyōshi Nikorai no zenniki*, 309.

63. Erwin Baelz, *Awakening Japan: The Diary of a German Doctor* (Bloomington: Indiana University Press, 1974), 255–256. Entry for 7 September 1905, in *A Diary of the Russo-Japanese War: Being an account of the War as published daily in the "Kobe Chronicle,"* vol. 2 (Kobe: "Chronicle" Office, 1904), 339. On Orthodox opposition to Nicolai: *Zeitschrift für Missionskunde und Religionswissenschaft* 18 (1908), 28; *Allgemeine Missionszeitschrift* 32, no. 1 (January 1905): 549–552; Carl Munzinger, *Die Japaner: Wanderungen durch das geistige, soziale und religiöse Leben des japanischen Volkes* (Berlin: A. Haack, 1898), 301.

64. Henry Lansdell, *Through Siberia* (London: Sampson Low, Marston, Searle and Rivington, 1882), 359–360.

65. POC Report, 56.

66. Ibid., 55.

67. James L. Amerman, *Shinseiron: kan* (n.p.: Beikoku seikyō shorui gaisha, 1885); Commission on Christian Education in Japan, *Christian education in Japan, being the report of a Commission on Christian Education in Japan, representing the National Christian Council of Japan, the National Christian Education Association of Japan, the Foreign Missions Conference of North America and the International Missionary Council* (New York: International Missionary Council, 1932); Margaret Prang, *A Heart at Leisure from Itself: Caroline Macdonald of Japan* (Vancouver: UBC Press, 1995), 44–45.

68. "Is Japan Turning Moslem?" and Kajinosuke Ibuka to W. H. T. Gairdner and D. M. Thornton, 18 February 1907, in *Blessed by Egypt* 8 (1906): 41.

69. Diaries, vol. 1 (1901–1910), 174, Brent Papers, box 53.

70. Alice Mabel Bacon, *Japanese Girls and Women* (Cambridge, MA: The Riverside Press/Houghton, 1891); Barbara Rose; *Tsuda Umeko and Women's Education in Japan* (New Haven, CT: Yale University Press, 1992), 82, 84; Kinuko Kameda, *Tsuda Umeko hitori no meikyōshi no kiseki* (Tsuda Umeko: One woman's fame and path) (Tokyo: Sōbunsha Shuppan, 2005); Masako Iino, Kinuko Kameda, and Yūko Takahashi, *Tsuda Umeko wo sasaeta hitobito* (The supporters of Tsuda Umeko) (Tokyo: Tsudajuku Daigaku/Hatsubaijo Yūhikaku, 2000). On Japanese participation in the WCTU's anti-geisha, anti-smoking, and anti-drinking agendas: Elizabeth Dorn Lublin, *Reforming Japan: The Woman's Christian Temperance Union in the Meiji Period* (Vancouver: UBC Press, 2010).

71. Compare Fujita's credit for the Law for the Prevention of Prostitution and the Drunkards' Law in the 1960s. Taki Fujita, "Women and Politics in Japan," *Annals of the American Academy of Political and Social Sciences, 375: Women around the World* (January 1968), 91–95. Both cited in Sally A. Hastings, "Women's Education and the World: Fujita Taki (1898–1993)," *Asian Cultural Studies* 39 (2013): 49–64, here 51, 61.

72. POC Report, 56–57.

73. Ibid., 13.

74. Marius B. Jansen, *Japan and Its World: Two Centuries of Change* (Princeton, NJ: Princeton University Press, 1995), 36.

75. POC Report, 13–14.

76. David S. Spencer, "Temperance and Christianity in Japan," *Gospel in All Lands*, January 1896, 375. One koku equaled 40 gallons.

77. "Quantities of imports of selected agricultural products, 1851–1908," *Yearbook of the United States Department of Agriculture 1908* (Washington, DC: Government Printing Office, 1909), 775.

78. On this documentary problem: Peter Andreas, *Smuggler Nation: How Illicit Trade Made America* (Oxford: Oxford University Press, 2013).

79. POC Report, 15.

80. Ibid., 16.

81. Ibid.

82. Ibid., 33.

83. Ibid., 14–15.

84. Marius Jansen, "Japan and the World," in *New Directions in the Study of Meiji Japan*, ed. Helen Hardacre and Adam L. Kern (Leiden: Brill, 1997), 287.

85. POC Report, 69.

86. Ibid.

87. Ibid., 63.

88. Ibid., 22.

89. Committee of the Formosan Special Census Investigation, *The Special Population Census of Formosa: 1905* (Tokyo: Imperial Printing Bureau), 24; *Rinji Taiwan Kyūkan chōsakai dai nibu chōsa keizai shiryō hōkoku* (Taihoku: Taiwan Sōtokufu, 1905); Taiwan Sōtokofu, *Rinji Taiwan kokō chōsa shūkei*

genpyō (Taihoku: Rinji Taiwan kokō chōsabu, 1907); *Rinji Taiwan kokō chōsa kekkahyō* (Taihoku: Rinji Taiwan kokō chōsabu, 1908).

90. POC Report, 9.

91. Committee of the Formosan Special Census Investigation, *1905*, 166–167.

92. Matsuda Yoshiro, "Formation of the Census System in Japan: 1871–1945—Development of the Statistical System in Japan Proper and Her Colonies," *Hitotsubashi Journal of Economics* 21, no. 2 (February 1981): 55–56.

93. Grant K. Goodman, "Filipino Secret Agents, 1896–1910," *Philippine Studies* 46, no. 3 (1998): 376–387, here 381.

94. Irene B. Taeuber and Edwin G. Beal, "The Demographic Heritage of the Japanese Empire," *Annals of the American Academy of Political and Social Science* 237 (January 1945): 70; Yao Jen-to, "The Japanese Colonial State and Its Form of Knowledge in Taiwan," *Taiwan under Japanese Colonial Rule, 1895–1945: History, Culture, Memory*, ed. Liao Ping-hui and David Der-wei Wang (New York: Columbia University Press, 2006), 37–61.

95. Committee of the Formosan Special Census Investigation, 167.

96. Ibid., 167.

97. Ibid., 165, 173. For a table of "Opium Eaters and Smokers Classified by Race" (Formosans, including Aggregate Chinese, Fukienese Chinese, Cantonese Chinese, Other Chinese, Ripe Savages, and Raw Savages and "regular Chinese"), 175.

98. Ibid., 169–170.

99. Ibid., 170.

100. Kelly B. Olds, "Female Productivity and Mortality in Early-20th-Century Taiwan," *Economics and Human Biology* 4 (2006): 206–221.

101. Hui-yu Caroline Ts'ai, "Engineering the Social or Engaging "Everyday Modernity"? Interwar Taiwan Reconsidered," in *Becoming Taiwan: From Colonialism to Democracy*, ed. Ann Heylen and Scott Sommers (Wiesbaden: Harrassowitz, 2010), 84–93; Meguro Gorō and Jiang Tingyuan, *Genkō hokō seido sōsho* (Collection of books concerning the current baojia system) (Taichū: Hokō seido sōsho fukyūsho, 1936).

102. "The Shimonoseki Negotiations," *Peking and Tientsin Times*, 13 July 1895, in *Verbal Discussions during Peace Negotiations, between the Chinese Plenipotentiary Viceroy Li Hung-Chang and the Japanese Plenipotentiaries Count Ito and Viscount Mutsu, at Shimonoseki, Japan, March-April, 1895* (Tientsin: Tientsin Press, 1895), ii. Also published as *History of the Peace Negotiations, Documentary and Verbal, between China and Japan, March-April, 1895, with text of the Treaty of Peace and Portrait of the Viceroy Li Hung-Chang* (Tientsin: Tientsin Press, 1895).

103. For a comparison of Japan's rapid industrialization since the mid-1880s, combined with high literacy and high savings rates as one of the relative advantages compared to India: Natalie McPherson, "India and Japan: Laissez-Faire and Economic Development from 1850 to 1939," *Canadian Journal of*

Development Studies/Revue canadieene d'études du développement 6, no. 2 (1985): 289–308.

104. *Bulletin of the American Geographical Society* 44, no. 1 (1912): 59.

105. "Countries, Populations, Areas," *Social Progress: A Year Book and Encyclopedia of Economic, Industrial, Social and Religious Statistics*, 1905, 2.

106. Representative Board of the Anti-Opium Societies, Meeting on 3rd June 1896, TEMP MSS 150/1–2, Anti-Opium Urgency Committee, Minutes 9 July 1894–12 August 1895. SOFL.

107. POC Report, 93.

108. Ibid., 94.

109. Ibid., 100.

110. "Findings and Recommendations of the Opium Investigation Committee Appointed under the Provisions of Act No. 800, as Amended by Act No. 812 of the Philippine Commission," 15 June, 1904, in POC Report, 12.

111. POC Report, 42.

112. Ibid., 16.

113. Ibid., 33.

114. Ibid.

115. Ibid., 40.

116. Lim Boon Keng, "The Attitude of the State towards the Opium Habit," *Straits Chinese Magazine* 2, no. 6 (1898): 50; POC Report, 100.

117. Ye Zhongling, *Wong Nai Siong and the Nanyang Chinese: An Anthology* (Singapore: Singapore Society of Asian Studies, 2001); Liu Zizheng, *Huang Naishang yu xin Fuzhou* (Huang Naishang and the new Fuzhou) (Singapore: Nanyang xuehui, 1979); Cheng Lau Tzy, *Wong Nai Siong yu Xinfuzhou* (Wong Nai Siong and the new Fuzhou) (Singapore: Nanyang xuehui congshu di ershi zhong, 1979).

118. Ibid., 105.

119. POC Report, 100.

120. Ibid.

121. Ibid.

122. Ibid., 85.

123. Ibid., 104–105.

124. Blackstone also appeared at the Seventh Annual Convention of the Woman's Christian Temperance Union in Queensland. *Brisbaine Courier,* 21 September 1892, 3.

125. POC Report, 100.

126. Ibid., 29, 88, 91, 105.

127. "Philippine Opium Commission in Singapore," *Straits Times,* 11 December 1903, 5.

128. POC Report, 30.

129. Ibid., 12.

130. Ibid., 45.

131. John Bancroft Devins, *An Observer in the Philippines, or Life in Our New Possessions* (Boston: American Tract Society, 1905), 138–141.

132. POC Report, 46–47.
133. Taylor, "American Confrontation with the Opium Traffic in the Philippines," 319–321.
134. Ibid., 47.
135. Ibid.
136. POC Report, 44–45.
137. Goldsworthy Lowes Dickinson, *Letters from John Chinaman: Being an Eastern View of Western Civilization* (London: R. Brimley Johnson and York Buildings, Adelphi, 1901); Christopher A. Bayly, "The Boxer Uprising and India: Globalizing Myths," in *The Boxers, China, and the World,* ed. Robert Bickers and R. G. Tiedemann (Lanham, MD: Rowman and Littlefield, 2007), 149.
138. David Edward Owen, *British Opium Policy in China and India* (New Haven, CT: Yale University Press, 1934), 327–332.
139. Royal Commission on Opium, vol. 6, *Final Report of the Royal Commission on Opium. Part I: The Report* (London: Her Majesty's Stationery Office, 1895), 244, 296–298, especially references to entries 1702 and 1750.
140. POC Report, 12.

6. Activists into Diplomats: Toward the International Opium Commission

1. Louis T. Sigel, "T'ang Shao-yi (1860–1938): The Diplomacy of Chinese Nationalism" (PhD diss., Harvard University, 1972).
2. Ibid., 98.
3. Arthur W. Hummel Jr., "Yuan Shih-k'ai as an official under the Manchus" (master's thesis, Department of Oriental Languages and Literatures, 1949); Stephen R. Mackinnon, "Liang Shih-i and the Communications Clique," *Journal of Asian Studies* 29, no. 3 (May 1970): 581–602.
4. Sigel, "T'ang Shao-yi," 155.
5. Louis T. Sigel, "Ch'ing Tibetan Policy, 1906–1910," *Papers on China* 19 (December 1965): 177–201.
6. Sigel, "T'ang Shao-yi," 156. For the British understanding of Qing policy: "Memorandum (28 April, 1912)," ML MSS 312–194, Morrison Papers, State Library of New South Wales, Sydney.
7. Morrison to Valentine Chirol, 14 May 1907) in *The Correspondence of G. E. Morrison,* vol. 1, *1895–1912,* ed. Hui-min Lo (Cambridge: Cambridge University Press, 1976), 410; Sigel, "T'ang Shao-yi," 151; Clare E. Harris, *The Museum on the Roof of the World: Art, Politics, and the Representation of Tibet* (Chicago: Chicago University Press, 2012), 49–78.
8. Dhara Anjaria, "Curzon and the Limits of Viceregal Power: India, 1899–1905" (PhD diss., Royal Holloway College, University of London, 2009).
9. Sigel, "T'ang Shao-yi," 207–209.
10. Guo Wu, *Zheng Guanying: Merchant Reformer of Late Qing China and His Influence on Economics, Politics, and Society* (Amherst, NY: Cambria Press, 2010), 38; Yuru Wang, "Capital Formation and Operating Profits of the

Kailuan Mining Administration (1903–1937)," *Modern Asian Studies* 28, no. 1 (1994), 99–128; Kwang-ching Liu, "Tang Tingshu zhi maiban shidai," *Qinghua xuebao* 2, no. 2 (June 1961): 143–180.

11. Sigel, "T'ang Shao-yi," 172, 207.

12. Jordan, 30 September 1906, and Jordan to Grey, 22 January 1907, both in COD/C46 Confidential Despatches from Secretary of State to the Straits Settlements, COD/C45 [microfilm NL 4349], National Archives of Singapore.

13. *Japan Daily Mail* 44 (18 November 1905): 540.

14. According to the Imperial Edict of 10 August 1907. Murata Yujiro, "Dynasty, Nation, and Society: The Case of Modern China," in *Imagining the People: Chinese Intellectuals and the Concept of Citizenship, 1890–1920*, ed. Joshua A. Fogel and Peter Gue Zarrow (Armonk, NY: M. E. Sharpe, 1997), 113–141, here 132.

15. W. W. Rockhill to Secretary of State, 19 September 1905, *FRUS*, 59th Cong., 1st sess. (Washington, DC: Government Printing Office, 1906), 182. The *North China Daily News* commented that the abolition of the examination system raised hopes that the current "dearth of statesmen in China" would soon be alleviated. "The disappearance of the literary examinations," *North China Daily News*, 12 September 1905; Enclosure in Rockhill to Secretary of State, 19 September 1905, *FRUS*, 59th Cong., 1st sess., 183–184.

16. Kathleen L. Lodwick, *Crusaders against Opium: Protestant Missionaries in China, 1874–1917* (Lexington: University Press of Kentucky, 1996), 161.

17. Rev. Donald MacGillivray, "China's Present Relation to the Opium Traffic," *Missionary Review of the World* 20 (New Series) or 30 (Old Series) (January–December 1907), 119–120. The same MacGillivray compiled *A Mandarin-Romanized Dictionary of Chinese* (Shanghai: Presbyterian Mission Press, 1905).

18. *China Times*, 16 January 1906.

19. "Report of the Anti-Opium Committee: To the Meeting for Suffering," *Extracts from the Minutes and Proceedings of the Yearly Meeting of Friends Held in London* (London: Office of the Society of Friends, 1906), 170.

20. *China and the Gospel: An Illustrated Report of the China Inland Mission 1906* (London: China Inland Mission, n.d.); Kwanha Yim, "Yuan Shih-k'ai and the Japanese," *Journal of Asian Studies* 24, no. 1 (November 1964): 63–73.

21. "The Anti-Opium League: Annual Report," *North China Herald and Supreme Court and Consular Gazette*, 30 August 1907, 499.

22. Hampden C. DuBose, *The Last Days of the Poppy* (Shanghai: Methodist Publishing House, 1909), 3.

23. Ibid.

24. "Anti-Opium League: Annual Report," 499.

25. Zhao's younger brother, Zhao Erfeng, was the imperial resident in Tibet, who, as the *New Zealand Herald* aptly put it, "to the astonishment of India, established China's authority at Lhasa, and caused the flight of the Dalai Lama." "New Viceroy of Manchuria," *New Zealand Herald* 48, no. 14697 (3 June 1911): 6; "Memorial submitted by the Board of Finance, containing Proposals for the Provision of Funds to meet the Annual Expenditure for the

Administration of the Tibetan Marches," Enclosure to Stephen Leech, "Despatch from Sir J. Jordan to Sir Edward Grey, dated Peking, 9th April, 1908," Great Britain, *Further Papers relating to Tibet* (London: HMSO, 1910), 149–150.

26. "Conversation with Dr. T. J. N. Gatrell," ML MSS 312–194. Morrison Papers; Paul S. Reinsch, "Diplomatic Affairs and International Law, 1909," *American Political Science Review* 4 (1910): 16–51, here 28–29; Li Xizhu, "Provincial Officials in 1911–12: Their Backgrounds and Reactions to Revolution—an Inquiry into the Structure of the "Weak Center, Weak Regions" in the late Qing," in *China: How the Empire Fell*, ed. Joseph W. Esherick and C. X. George Wei (New York: Routledge, 2014), 160.

27. Lancelot Carnegie to Edward Grey, 16 July 1906, FO 371–22. UKNA.

28. Hampden C. DuBose, *Are Missionaries in Any Way Responsible for the Present Disturbances in China?* (n.p., 1900), 8.

29. Ibid.

30. Ibid.

31. Brent Diary, 7 November 1903, Papers of Charles H. Brent, box 53, Library of Congress.

32. "The Rev. Griffith John, D. D., on Opium in China," *Chinese Recorder* 25 (April 1894): 194–200.

33. Alan Baumler, *Worse Than Floods and Wild Beasts: The Chinese and Opium under the Republic* (New York: State University of New York Press, 2007), 50–51.

34. Goodnow to Secretary of State, 24 December 1902, in Anti-Opium League, *The Report of the American Consuls on Opium in China* (Shanghai: American Presbyterian Mission Press, 1904), 3; Consul James W. Ragsdale (Tianjin) to Hill, 25 August 1902, in Anti-Opium League, *Report of the American Consuls on Opium in China*, 10.

35. C. R. Edwards to John T. Morgan, 28 January 1905, and Morgan to DuBose, 31 January 1905, in Anti-Opium League, *Opium in the Orient: Report of the Philippine Commission* (Shanghai: North China Herald Office, 1905), 1; "Anti-Opium League: Annual Report," 501.

36. A. P. Wilder to Clementi, 2 December 1908, MSS. Ind. Ocn. s. 352/46–4, Clementi Papers, University of Oxford.

37. "Anti-Opium League: Annual Report," 499.

38. Copy of a letter sent to Mr. Adams from D. H. C. DuBose (Soochow, 26 November 1906), MS Box R1/2/20, SOFL; DuBose, *Last Days of the Poppy*, 4.

39. "Extract from the 'Peking Gazette' of September 20, 1906, Enclosure in Jordan to Grey, 30 September 1906, FO 371–37, UKNA.

40. "Constitutional Government in China: Imperial edict of September 1, 1906," *FRUS*, 350.

41. *Monthly Consular and Trade Reports*, December 1906, 39.

42. Jordan to Grey, 30 September 1906, FO 371–337, UKNA.

43. Arthur Godley to Lancelot Carnegie, 20 September 1906, FO 371–337, UKNA.

44. Newman, "India and the Anglo-Chinese Opium Agreements, 1907–14."

45. Sun Yat-sen, "A Plea to Li Hung-chang (June 1894)," in *Prescriptions for Saving China: Selected Writings of Sun Yat-sen,* ed. Julie Lee Wei, Ramon H. Myers, and Donald G. Gillin (Stanford: Hoover Institution Press, 1994), 16–17. Note, by contrast, Sun, the anti-opium crusader: David Strand, *An Unfinished Republic: Leading by Word and Deed in Modern China* (Berkeley: University of California Press, 2011), 336n58.

46. "Memorandum read by Alexander, 12th June, 1894," in Society for the Suppression of the Opium Trade, Minute Book, SOFL; *Anti-Opium Committee of the Meeting for Sufferings,* OP M1, SOFL; Jordan to Grey, 30 September 1906, FO 371–37.

47. "Anti-Opium League: Annual Report," 500.

48. Ibid.

49. William Hector Park, *Opinions of over 100 Physicians on the Use of Opium in China* (Shanghai: American Presbyterian Mission Press, 1899).

50. Ibid., iii.

51. On DuBose: Nettie DuBose, *"For the Glory of God:" Memoirs of Dr. and Mrs. H. C. DuBose* (Lewisburg, VA: Children of Dr. and Mrs. DuBose, 1910).

52. For the response of the State Department's Bureau of Foreign Commerce to DuBose: Christopher Alan Morrison, "A World of Empires: United States Rule in the Philippines, 1898–1913" (PhD diss., Department of History, Georgetown University, 2009), 115–119.

53. Madeleine Zelin, *The Magistrate's Tael: Rationalizing Fiscal Reform in Eighteenth-Century Ch'ing China* (Berkeley: University of California Press, 1984), 62–65; Man Bun Kwan, *The Salt-Merchants of Tianjin: State-Making and Civil Society in Late Imperial China* (Honolulu: University of Hawai'i Press, 2001), 29–49; Chao Ho Hsu, "The Salt Gabelle in Chinese Finance" (master's thesis, University of California, 1929).

54. Introduction to Park, *Opinions of over 100 Physicians,* vii.

55. "Anti-Opium League: Annual Report," 500.

56. Ibid.

57. Ibid. Copy of a letter sent to Mr. Adams from D. H. C. DuBose (Soochow, 26 November 1906); MS Box R1/2/20, SOFL.

58. "Anti-Opium League. Annual Report," 500.

59. J. T. Gracey, "The Fight against Opium in China," *Missionary Review of the World* 21 (New Series) or 31 (Old Series) (January–December 1908): 921–923.

60. "Anti-Opium League: Annual Report," 500.

61. Alan Baumler, *Worse Than Floods and Wild Beasts: The Chinese and Opium under the Republic* (New York: State University of New York Press, 2007), 50–51.

62. "Appendix B—No. 1. Regulations Prohibiting Opium Smoking, Compiled by the Government Council," in "Memorandum on Opium from China," in International Opium Commission, *Report of the International Opium Commission, Shanghai, China, February 1 to February 26, 1909,* vol. 1, *Reports of the Proceedings* (Shanghai: North China Daily News and Herald, 1909), 79–82 (hereafter IOC 1). For a summary: "Appendix I. Chinese Regulations in Brief,

Issued at Peking, November 22nd, 1906," in "The Opium Question: A Lecture by E. W. Thwing," Papers of Sir Cecil Clementi (hereafter "Clementi Papers"), MSS. Ind. Ocn. s.352/46–4.

63. "Anti-Opium League: Annual Report," 500.
64. Ibid., 501.
65. "Hong Kong, 17, XI, 1906," in *Journal Letter No. 7*, 11, Joseph Alexander Gundry's journal, MS Box 1/2/7–9. SOFL.
66. "Anti-Opium League: Annual Report," 501.
67. On Duan Fang: Patrick Taveirne, *Han-Mongol Encounters and Missionary Endeavors: A History of Scheut in Ordos (Hetao), 1874–1911* (Leuven: Leuven University Press, 2004), 538; Yuzhang Wu, *Recollections of the Revolution of 1911: A Great Democratic Revolution of China* (Honolulu: University Press of the Pacific, 1981).
68. "Anti-Opium League: Annual Report," 500.
69. Ibid.
70. Ibid.
71. Ibid.
72. Ibid. Copy of a letter sent to Mr. Adams from D. H. C. DuBose (Soochow, 26 November 1906), MS box R1/2/20, SOFL.
73. Jordan to Grey, 20 October 1906, FO 371–322.
74. Sigel, "T'ang Shao-yi," 211.
75. Ibid., 210; Journal Letter No. 10, MS box R1/2/10–12, SOFL, 2–3.
76. For the complete proceedings: *Records: China Centenary Missionary Conference, Held at Shanghai, April 25 to May 8, 1907* (Shanghai: Centenary Conference Committee, 1907).
77. Joseph Alexander, "Journal No. 17. Nanking, 25/4, 1907," 1, Joseph Alexander Gundry's journal, MS box R 1/2/1–3, SOFL.
78. "Anti-Opium League: Annual Report," 501. The pamphlet in question was prefaced by the Archbishop of Canterbury and published by the "Printers to the Queen's Most Excellent Majesty." Arnold Foster, *The Report of the Royal Commission on Opium Compared with the Evidence from China that was Submitted to the Commission* (London: Eyre and Spottiswoode, 1899). A shorter version in the *China Medical Missionary Journal* was reprinted as Arnold Foster, *The Wresting of Medical Evidence: A Criticism of the Report of the Royal Commission on Opium* (Shanghai: American Presbyterian Mission Press, 1896); Arnold Foster, *The International Commission for the Investigation of the Opium Trade and the Opium Habit in the Far East to Be Held in Shanghai, February 1909: A Warning and an Appeal* (London: Hodder and Stoughton, 1909), distributed by the Society of Friends; "Minutes of Meeting of Representative Board, Held 28th Jan. 1909," in *Opium Traffic Committee. Anti-Opium Committee, c. 1920–23*, OP M1, SOFLl "Fifth of the Seventh Month, 1906," "Copy of Minutes of Meeting held 7th June 1906 of Representative Board to which were invited the Friends Anti-Opium Committee, the Women's Anti-Opium Committee and the Committee of the Society for the Suppression of the Opium Traffic and the Christian Union, for the purpose of conferring with Joseph Allen Baker, M.P."

Anti-Opium Committee of the Meeting for Sufferings, OP M1, SOFL. Foster's favorable response had been received and discussed in September 1906. "9th Month, 6th, 1906," *Anti-Opium Committee of the Meeting for Sufferings,* OP M1, SOFL.

79. "Ss. Tayuen, on the Yangtse, 27. XII. 1906," in *Journal Letter No. 11,* 3, Joseph Alexander Gundry's journal, MS box R 1/2/10–12, SOFL.

80. "Hankow, 24. XII," in *Journal Letter No. 10,* 15, Joseph Alexander Gundry's journal, MS box R 1/2/10–12, SOFL. On Foster being overworked and as a result unable to organize a local anti-opium rally in Hankou: "Ss. Tayuen, on the Yangtse, 27. XII. 1906," in: *Journal Letter No. 11,* 1, Joseph Alexander Gundry's journal, MS box R 1/2/10–12, SOFL.

81. Joseph Alexander, "Journal 18. SS Kosai Maen [*sic*], 11/5/07, 4, Joseph Alexander Gundry's journal, MS box R 1/2/1–3, SOFL.

82. Richard H. Immerman, *John Foster Dulles: Piety, Pragmatism, and Power in U.S. Foreign Policy* (Lanham, MD: Rowman and Littlefield, 1998), 4; Tingfang Wu, *America through the Spectacles of an Oriental Diplomat* (London: Anthem Press, 2007), 29–30.

83. "Journal Letter No. 7. Hong Kong, 17, XI, 1906," MS box R 1/2/7–9, 11–12; Joseph Alexander Gundry Journal, SOFL.

84. Ibid.

85. Norman Miners, *Hong Kong under Imperial Rule, 1912–1941* (New York: Oxford University Press, 1987), 209; Carl Trocki, *Opium, Empire and the Global Political Economy: A Study of the Asian Opium Trade 1750–1950* (London: Routledge, 1999), 128.

86. *The Parliamentary Debates: Authorised Edition. Fourth Series. First Session of the Twenty-eight Parliament of the United Kingdom of Great Britain and Ireland. 6 Edward VII.* vol. 158, Seventh Volume of Session 1906 (London: His Majesty's Stationery Office, 1906), 516.

87. *International Investigation of Opium Evil: Message from the President of the United States.* 60th Cong., 1st sess., Doc. 926, 1.

88. J. F. Scheltema. *De Opiumpolitiek der regeering en de vrijheid der drukpers* ('s Gravenhage: W. P. van Stockum, 1903).

89. Sir Edward Grey received word of Tang's understanding of Baker's indications on 17 November 1906 through the British minister in Beijing, Sir John Jordan. Jordan to Grey, 30 September 1906, FO 371–337, UKNA.

90. Benjamin Broomhall, *The Truth about Opium-Smoking* (London: Hodder and Stoughton, 1882); Broomhall, *The Opium Question from a New Point of View* (London: Morgan and Scott, 1906).

91. Henry Cotton to Edward Grey, 9 June 1906, FO 371–337, UKNA.

92. *Restrictions on Opium-Smoking in China,* "The Anti-Opium Propaganda," *North China Herald,* 25 May 1906, FO 371–337, UKNA.

93. Ibid.; Joseph Alexander, "Journal No. 17. Nanking, 25/4, 1907," 6, Joseph Alexander Gundry's journal, MS box R 1/2/1–3, SOFL.

94. Carnegie to Grey, 2 July 1906, FO 371–337.

95. Ibid. The correspondence was circulated widely in British imperial correspondence. Carnegie to Grey, 21 July 1906, in *Confidential Despatches from*

Secretary of State to the Straits Settlements. COD/C45 [microfilm NL 4349], National Archives of Singapore. Also Jordan to Grey, 30 September 1906, in Great Britain, *China No. 1 (1908): Correspondence Respecting the Opium Question in China* (London: HMSO, 1908).

96. Carnegie to Grey, 21 July 1906, FO 371–337.
97. Journal No. 17, Nanking, 25/4, 1907, SOFL, 4–5.
98. "Anti-Opium League: Annual Report," 500.
99. Ibid.
100. For a thorough summary of the positive British response to the Chinese successful suppression: Niels Petersson. *Imperialismus und Modernisierung: Siam, China und die europäischen Mächte 1895–1914* (Munich: Oldenbourg, 2000), 268–275.
101. Ibid.
102. The German government approved Beijing's Regulations for the Abolition of Opium and consented to its enforcement under German extraterritoriality in Qingdao in March 1907. "Opium Prohibition at Tsingtao," *North China Herald and Supreme Court and Consular Gazette* 82 (8 March 1907): 503; Von Rex to DuBose, 8 September 1909, in DuBose, *Last Days of the Poppy*.
103. "Anti-Opium League: Annual Report," 501.
104. Ibid., 500–501.
105. Ibid., 501.
106. Ibid. For the imperial morphine regulations: "Appendix B—No. 7," "Memorial by the Board of Laws and the Imperial Commissioners for Law Reform reporting on a Memorial by the Governor of Kiangsu recommending the enactment of special penal laws against the sale of morphia," IOC 1, 92–94.
107. DuBose to Morrison, 30 January 1908, ML MSS 312–320, Morrison Papers, State Library of New South Wales, Sydney.
108. Joseph Alexander, "Journal 18, SS Kosai Maen [sic], 11/5/07, 4, Joseph Alexander Gundry's journal, MS box R 1/2/1–3, SOFL.
109. "Anti-Opium League: Annual Report," 501.
110. Wilbur Fisk Crafts, *A Primer of Internationalism: With Special Reference to University Debates* (Washington, DC: International Reform Bureau, 1908), 6, with a biographical sketch up to 1902.
111. Ibid.
112. "Anti-Opium League," *Hawaiian Gazette,* 27 October 1908, 3.
113. Brent Diary, 21 October 1902, Papers of Charles H. Brent, box 53.
114. Stuntz to Crafts, 2 May 1903, quoted in Ian Tyrrell, "The Regulation of Alcohol and Other Drugs in a Colonial Context: United States Policy Towards the Philippines, c. 1898–1910," *Contemporary Drug Problems* 35 (Winter 2008): 559.
115. For the hotel's own vademecum: Palace Hotel, *Guide to Shanghai* (Shanghai: The Hotel, 1909).
116. For example, *Dongfang zazhi (Far Eastern Miscellany)* 6, no. 2 (25 February 1909). For one of the first histories of modern Chinese journalism: Yutang Lin, *A History of the Press and Public Opinion in China* (London:

Oxford University Press, 1937), published with the support of the China Council of the Institute of Pacific Relations.

117. Edward Denison, "The Peace Hotel," *Architectural Design* 75, no. 6 (November–December 2005): 124–126.

118. Algernon Sydney Thelwall, *The Iniquities of the Opium Trade with China: Being a Development of the Main Causes which Exclude the Merchants of Great Britain from the Advantages of an Unrestricted Commercial Intercourse with that Vast Empire. With Extracts from Authentic Documents* (London: Wm. H. Allen, 1839). *Compendium of Facts relating to the Opium Trade* (n.p., 1840). For several versions of Lin Zexu's protest compared: Lydia Liu, *Clash of Empires: The Invention of China in Modern World Making* (Cambridge, MA: Harvard University Press, 2004), 229–241.

119. "The Opium Question: A Lecture by E. W. Thwing," 11, Oxford University, Rhodes House, Papers of Sir Cecil Clementi, MSS Ind. Ocn. s. 352, box 46–4; Edward Thwing, *The New-National Anti-Opium Movement in China* (Beijing: n.p., 1910), 3; Ryan Dunch, *Fuzhou Protestants and the Making of a Modern China, 1857–1927* (New Haven, CT: Yale University Press, 2001), 50. On continuities: Joyce A. Madancy, *The Troublesome Legacy of Commissioner Lin: The Opium Trade and Opium Suppression in Fujian Province, 1820s to 1920s* (Cambridge, MA: Harvard University Asia Center, 2003).

120. "Supreme Court, Calcutta. Ramsabuck Mulcik versus de Souza and others," enclosure of Mr. Trevelyan to Viscount Canning, 18 December 1841, in *Correspondence Relative to the Actual Value of the Opium Delivered Up to the Chinese Authorities in 1839* (London: T. R. Harrison, 1843), 2–3. On the ensuing debate: *Opinions of the London Press Respecting the Amount of Opium Compensation Offered by Her Majesty's Government* (London: W. Clarke, 1843); Rabindranath Tagore, "The Death Traffic," *Modern Review (Calcutta)* 37 (July 1925): 504–507.

121. Anne L. Foster, "Models for Governing: Opium and Colonial Policies in Southeast Asia, 1898–1910," in *The American Colonial State in the Philippines: Global Perspectives,* ed. Julian Go and Anne L. Foster (Durham, NC: Duke University Press, 2003), 92–117; Anne L. Foster, "Prohibition as Superiority: Policing Opium in South-East Asia, 1898–1925," *International History Review* 22, no. 2 (June 2000): 253–273.

122. IOC 1, 9.

123. Ibid.

124. Michael R. Godley, "China's World Fair of 1910: Lessons from a Forgotten Event," *Modern Asian Studies* 12, no. 3 (1978): 503–522; Susan R. Fernsebner, "Objects, Spectacle, and a Nation on Display at the Nanyang Exposition of 1910," *Late Imperial China* 27, no. 2 (December 2006): 99–124; Zhang Jun, "Spider Manchu: Duanfang as Networker and Spindoctor of the Late Qing New Policies" (PhD diss., Department of History, University of California, San Diego, 2008), 210–211.

125. DuBose, *Last Days of the Poppy,* 12.

126. International Opium Commission, *Report of the International Opium Commission, Shanghai, China, February 1 to February 26, 1909*, vol. 2, *Reports of the Delegations* (Shanghai: North China Daily News and Herald, 1909), 352–354 (hereafter IOC 2).

127. IOC 2, 347–351.

128. IOC 1, 84.

129. William Lyon Mackenzie King, *Report on the Need of Suppression of Opium Traffic in Canada* (Ottawa: S. E. Dawson, 1908).

130. James Thompson, *British Political Culture and the Idea of "Public Opinion," 1867–1914* (Cambridge: Cambridge University Press, 2013).

131. *Report by W. L. Mackenzie King, C.M.G., Deputy Minister of Labour, on the Need for the Suppression of the Opium Traffic in Canada* (Ottawa: S. E. Dawson, 1908), 10.

132. Ibid., 11–13.

133. Ibid., 13.

134. Peter Hing to Mackenzie King, 29 May 1908, in *Report by W. L. Mackenzie King*, 5.

135. *Report by W. L. Mackenzie King*, 9.

136. Ibid. King mistakenly identified the article as having been published on 9 May 1908; in fact, it was published on 8 May 1908, as "The Opium Question," *Times of India*, 6.

137. Morrison to Hosie, 19 February 1909, ML MSS 312–220, Morrison Papers, State Library of New South Wales, Sydney.

138. Ibid.

139. Ibid.

140. Rössler to Bethmann-Hollweg, 29 April 1910, GSPK, GSPK, Ministerium für Handel und Gewerbe, *Akten betreffend die international Opiumkonferenz*, I. HA. Rep. 120. C XIII, 1 no. 84, vol. 1, 7–8.

141. IOC 1, 20. For the Japanese adoption of U.S. rhetoric, K. Midzuno, *Japan's Crusade on the Use of Opium in Formosa* (New York: North American Review, 1909); John R. Shepherd, "Trends in Mortality and Causes of Death in Japanese Colonial Period Taiwan," in *Death at the Opposite Ends of the Eurasian Continent: Mortality Trends in Taiwan and the Netherlands*, ed. Theo Engelen, John Robert Shepherd, and Yang Wen-Shan (Amsterdam: Aksant Academic, 2011), 45–80.

142. IOC 1, 79.

143. Charles E. Terry and Mildred Pellens, *The Opium Problem* (New York: Committee on Drug Addictions/Bureau of Social Hygiene, 1928), 629.

144. IOC 1, 9.

145. Charles Henry Brent to General Leonard Wood, 28 May 1909, Papers of Charles H. Brent, box 64, Library of Congress.

146. Morrison to Jordan, 16 February 1909, ML MSS 312–220, Morrison Papers. Original emphasis.

147. Charles Henry Brent to General Leonard Wood, 29 January 1909, 2, Papers of Charles H. Brent, box 64, Library of Congress.

148. Ibid.

149. Ibid.
150. Ibid.
151. Morrison to Hosie, 19 February 1909, ML MSS 312–220, Morrison Papers.
152. "Memorandum on Affairs in China (3 April, 1909), not for publication," ML MSS 312–193, Morrison Papers.
153. Charles Henry Brent to General Leonard Wood, 28 May 1909, Papers of Charles H. Brent, box 64, Library of Congress.
154. Ibid.
155. Ibid.
156. Bryna Goodman and David S. G. Goodman, eds., *Twentieth-Century Colonialism and China: Localities, the Everyday and the World* (Abingdon: Routledge, 2012); Turan Kayaoğlu, *Legal Imperialism: Sovereignty and Extraterritoriality: In Japan, the Ottoman Empire, and China* (Cambridge: Cambridge University Press, 2010), 149–190; Pär Kristoffer Cassel, *Grounds of Judgment: Extraterritoriality and Imperial Power in Nineteenth-Century China and Japan* (Oxford: Oxford University Press, 2012).
157. Howard Padwa, *Social Poison: The Culture and Politics of Opiate Control in Britain and France, 1821–1926* (Baltimore: Johns Hopkins University Press, 2012).
158. Friends' Association for Abolishing State Regulation of Vice, *France: The Failure of a Century of Regulated Vice in France (with an Appendix Giving the Medical Reasons Why Regulation Has Always Failed, and Always Must Fail* (London: Friends' Association for Abolishing State Regulation of Vice, 1901). On the notable colonial and transnational connections of Forbes to Uganda and Francophone Canada: Raynald Pelletier, *Monseigneur John Forbes (1864–1926). Vicaire apostolique coadjuteur de l'Ouganda* (n.p.: Société des Missionaries d'Afrique, n.d.); Guy Laperrière, *Les Congrégations Religieuses: De la France au Québec, 1880–1914* (2 Vols.) (Saint Nicolas (Québec): Les Presses de l'Université Laval, 1999); Méthode Gahungu, *Former les Prêtres en Afrique: Le Rôle des Pères Blancs (1879–1936)* (Paris: L'Harmattan, 2007).
159. Carl Hartwich, *Das Opium als Genussmittel* (Zurich: Zürcher und Furrer, 1898).

7. The Drugs of War: Germany, Japan, and the Morphine Threat

1. Georges della Sudda, *Monographie des opiums de l'Empire ottoman envoyés à l'exposition universelle de Paris, par le colonel Fayk Bey* (Paris: Poitevin, 1867).
2. Hermann Hager, ed., *Commentar zur Pharmacopoea Germanica*, vol. 2 (Berlin: Julius Springer, 1874), 519; Nicolas Jean-Baptiste Gaston Guibourt, *Mémoire sur le dosage de l'opium et sur la quantité de morphine que l'opium*

doit contenir. Observation sur le laudanum liquid de Sydenham (Paris: Thunot, 1862).

3. Abdolonyme Ubicini, *La Turquie actuelle* (Paris: Hachette, 1855), v, 278. Ubicini also edited the French edition of the Ottoman constitution: *La Constitution ottomane du 7 zilhidje 1923* (23 decembre 1876) (Paris: Cotillon, 1877).

4. "Opium-Culture," *Medical Times and Register,* 1 February 1871, 159. On desperate institutional efforts at market transparency in the United States and western Europe: Hartmut Berghoff, "Markterschließung und Risikomanagement. Die Rolle der Kreditauskunfteien und Rating-Agenturen im Industrialisierungs- und Globalisierungsprozess des 19. Jahrhunderts," *Vierteljahresschrift für Sozial- und Wirtschaftsgeschichte* 92, no. 2 (2005): 141–162.

5. Pierre Belon, *Les observations de plusieurs singularitez et choses mémorables trouvées en Grece, Asie, Iudée, Egypte, Arabie, & autres pays estranges, redigées en trois liures* (Paris: Hierosme de Marnef, & la veufue Guillaume Cauellar, au mont S. Hilaire, à l'enfeigne du Pelican, 1588), 404–405, first published in 1553.

6. Ubicini, *La Turquie actuelle.*

7. Hager, *Commentar zur Pharmacopoea Germanica,* 520.

8. "Verzeichnis der Pharmakopöen mit den dafür im Texte gewählten Abkürzungen," in Wilhelm Mitlacher, *Die offizinellen Pflanzen und Drogen. Eine systematische Übersicht über die in sämtlichen Staaten Europas sowie in Japan und den Vereinigten Staaten von Amerika offizinellen Pflanzen und Drogen mit kurzen erläuternden Bemerkungen* (Vienna and Leipzig: Kaiserliche und königliche Hof-Buchdruckerei und Hof-Verlags-Buchhandlung Carl Fromme, 1912). For differences in pharmaceutical use and distribution as defined by the two contrasting consortia in Germany and France: *Pharmaceutische Rundschau: Eine Monatsschrift* 13, no. 1 (January 1895): 10–11.

9. Charles Issawi, *The Economic History of Turkey 1800–1914* (Chicago: University of Chicago Press, 1980), 261–263.

10. Hager, *Commentar zur Pharmacopoea Germanica,* 520.

11. Meyer, "Japan and the World Narcotics Traffic," in *Consuming Habits: Drugs in History and Anthropology,* ed. Jordan Goodman, Paul E. Lovejoy, and Andrew Sherratt (Abingdon: Routledge, 1995), 198.

12. Hager, *Commentar zur Pharmacopoea Germanica,* 519.

13. Ibid., 529.

14. "Das einheimische Opium von 1871," *Archiv der Pharmacie: Eine Zeitschrift des allgemeinen deutschen Apotheker-Vereins, Abtheilung Norddeutschland,* 22 (Apotheker-Verein/Buchhandlung des Waisenhauses in Halle a. S., 1872), 81–83.

15. Hager, *Commentar zur Pharmacopoea Germanica,* 529–530.

16. David T. Courtwright, "Opiate Addiction as a Consequence of the Civil War," *Civil War History* 24, no. 2 (June 1978): 101–111.

17. Julius Jobst, "The Salicylate and Carbolate of Quinia," *American Journal of Pharmacy* August 1875, 350–351, first published in *Neues Repertorium für Pharmacie. Year-Book of Pharmacy, comprising Abstracts of Papers relating to*

Pharmacy, Materia Medica, and Chemistry, contributed to British and Foreign Journals, from July 1, 1873, to June 30, 1874, with the Transactions of the British Pharmaceutical Conference at the Eleventh Annual Meeting held at London, August, 1874 (London: J. & A. Churchill, 1874), 10, 19–23, 152; "Opium-Culture," *Medical Times and Register,* 1 February 1871, 159.

18. *Guide through the Exhibition of the German Chemical Industry. Columbian Exposition in Chicago 1893* (Berlin: Julius Sittenfeld, 1893), 52–54, 10; Volker Ziegler, *Die Familie Jobst und das Chinin: Materialienwarenhandel und Alkaloidproduktion in Stuttgart 1806–1927* (Berlin: Verlag für Geschichte der Naturwissenschaften und der Technik, 2003).

19. Rößler to Bethmann Hollweg, 11 October 1909, Geheimes Staatsarchiv Preußischer Kulturbesitz (GSPK), Ministerium für Handel und Gewerbe, *Akten betreffend die international Opiumkonferenz,* I. HA. Rep. 120, C XIII, 1 no. 84, vol. 1, 3.

20. Remy to Bethmann Hollweg, 24 August 1910, Graf von Luxburg to Bethmann Hollweg, 19 April, GSPK, Ministerium für Handel und Gewerbe, *Akten betreffend die international Opiumkonferenz,* I. HA. Rep. 120, C XIII, 1 no. 84, vol. 1.

21. On the scope of this largely neglected empire: Sebastian Conrad, *German Colonialism: A Short History* (Cambridge: Cambridge University Press, 2011).

22. Kaiserliches Gouvernement von Kamerun, Buea to Staatssekretär des Reichs-Kolonialamts Berlin, 19 May 1910. Kaiserlicher Gouverneur von Deutsch-Südwestafrika to Staatssekretär des Auswärtigen Amts, 23 August 1910. Kaiserlich Deutsche Gesandschaft Teheran (A. Quandt) to Bethmann Hollweg, 28 August 1910. Kaiserlich Deutsche Botschaft Pera, 5 January 1911, to Bethmann Hollweg. For German New Guinea, the Customs Regulation of 10 June 1908 (§3). Kaiserlicher Gouverneur von Deutsch-Neu-Guinea to Staatssekretär des Reichs-Kolonialamts Berlin, 22 June 1910, GSPK, I. HA Rep. 120, C VIII 1, no. 2, vol. 12.

23. *Die Chemische Industrie* 40 (1917): 178.

24. Kaiserlich Deutsche Gesandtschaft in den Niederlanden to Bethmann Hollweg, 29 December 1910, GSPK, I. HA Rep. 120, C VIII 1, no. 2, vol. 12.

25. Steven B. Karch, "Japan and the Cocaine Industry of Southeast Asia, 1864–1944," in *Cocaine: Global Histories,* ed. Paul Gootenberg (Abingdon: Routledge, 1999), 149.

26. Kathryn Steen, *The American Synthetic Organic Chemicals Industry: War and Politics, 1910–1930* (Chapel Hill: University of North Carolina Press, 2014), 50–51.

27. *Pharmaceutische Rundschau: Eine Monatsschrift,* 13, no. 1 (January 1895).

28. Karch, "Japan and the Cocaine Industry of Southeast Asia," 149–150.

29. Hoshi has become the subject of cultural diplomacy for the Embassy of Japan in Germany. Botschaft von Japan, Persönlichkeiten des Austausches zwischen Japan und Deutschland (1): Hajime Hoshi (1873–1951)," *Neues aus Japan* 87 (February 2012), http://www.de.emb-japan.go.jp/NaJ/NaJ1202/hoshi.html.

30. "Peruvian Cinchona for Japanese," *Drug and Chemical Markets,* 14 April 1920, 700.

31. Hager, *Commentar zur Pharmacopoea Germanica,* 520.
32. Meyer, "Japan and the World Narcotics Traffic," 200.
33. Karch, "Japan and the Cocaine Industry of Southeast Asia," 154.
34. Rössler to Bethmann Hollweg, 13 May 1910, GSPK, I. HA Rep. 120, C VIII 1, no. 2, vol. 12.
35. Ibid.
36. Der Minister des Innern to Grossherzoglich Hessische Ministerium des Innern in Darmstadt, 5 September 1917, GSPK, I. HA Rep. 120, C VIII 1, no. 2, vol. 12.
37. Präsident des Kaiserlichen Gesundheimtsamts, "Betrifft die geplante international Opiumkonferenz," 15 April 1911, GSPK, I. HA Rep. 120, C VIII 1, no. 2, vol. 12, 5.
38. As the president of the Imperial Health Office explained early: Bumm to Staatssekretär des Innern, 15 April 1911, GSPK, I. HA Rep. 120, C VIII 1, no. 2, vol. 12, 3.
39. "Bestimmungen über den Verkehr mit Opium, Morphium und Kokain," GSPK, I. HA Rep. 120, C VIII 1, no. 2, vol. 12.
40. Rössler to Bethmann Hollweg (no exact date, July 1911), GSPK, I. HA Rep. 120, C VIII 1, no. 2, vol. 12, 4–5.
41. F. May to Bonar Law, 30 November 1915, in "Further Correspondence Respecting Opium," Part X, no. 1, *TOT,* vol. 3: 1913–1916, 1.
42. Luxburg to Bethmann Hollweg, 22 April 1911, GSPK, I. HA Rep. 120, C VIII 1, no. 2, vol. 12.
43. Metternich to Bethmann Hollweg, 20 January 1911; Graf Bernstorff to Bethmann Hollweg, 18 March 1911, GSPK, I. HA Rep. 120, C VIII 1, no. 2, vol. 12.
44. Grey to Baron Gericke, 31 January 1911, GSPK, I. HA Rep. 120, C VIII 1, no. 2, vol. 12.
45. W. Collins to W. Langley, 21 February 1916, in *Further Correspondence Respecting Opium,* Part X, January–December 1916, *TOT,* 13. Also Wu Lien-Teh, "The Menace of Morphine to China," *Lancet,* 9 June 1917, 874–875.
46. Collins to Langley, 14.
47. On opium: University of Oxford, Bodleian Library, MS. Harcourt 502, fols. 42–61.
48. Collins to Langley, 14.
49. "Question asked in the House of Commons, February 26, 1917," in Great Britain, Foreign Office, *Further Correspondence Respecting Opium,* Part XI, Confidential (11265), F.O. 415, no. 10 (hereafter COROP).
50. W. Collins to W. Langley, 21 February 1916, in *Further Correspondence Respecting Opium,* Part X, January–December 1916, *TOT,* 14.
51. George Ernest Morrison, "Japan's Morphia Trade with China: From a Correspondent," 4, GEMP, ML MSS 312–205. On the growing wartime problem of Russian border control: Andrey Shlyakhter, "La contrebande aux frontières de l'URSS dans les années 1920: méthodes d'évaluation et mesures de lutte." Sophie Cœuré et Sabine Dullin, eds., *Frontières du communisme. Mythologies et réalités de la division de l'Europe de la révolution d'Octobre au mur de Berlin* (Paris: La Decouverte, 2007), 406–427.

52. Records of the Japanese Ministry of Foreign Affairs (hereafter JFMA), Miscellanies Related to the Imperial Diet, Bills introduced by the Government, *Ahen "moruhine" nado torihiki kinatsu hō ni kansuru sotchi buri ni tsuki kakugi seikyū no ken* (Demand of measures for the prohibition of opium and morphine etc. to the cabinet council), 1919.01.18–1919.03.29.

53. Taichirō Mitani, *Nihon Seitō Seiji No Keisei: Hara Takashi No Seiji Shidō No Tenkai* (The formation of party politics in Japan: The development of Hara Takashi's leadership) (Tokyo: Tokyo Daigaku Shuppankai, 1967); Taiichirō Mitani, *Taishō Demokurashii Ron* (Essays on Taishō Democracy) (Tokyo: Chuō Kōronsha, 1974); Jung-Sun N. Han, *An Imperial Path to Modernity: Yoshino Sazuko and a New Liberal Order in East Asia, 1905–1937* (Cambridge, MA: Harvard University Press, 2013).

54. Kikuchi Toraji, *Ahen mondai ne kenkyū* (Tokyo: Kokusai renmei kyōkai, 1928).

55. Morrison, "Japan's Morphia Trade with China: From a Correspondent," 2–3.

56. Peter Duus, "Introduction: Japan's Informal Empire in China, 1895–1937: An Overview," in *The Japanese Informal Empire in China, 1895–1937,* ed. Peter Duus, Ramon H. Myers, and Mark R. Peattie (Princeton: Princeton University Press, 1989), xi–xxix.

57. On simulacrum as a narrative strategy of investigative journalism: Johannes Ehrat, *Power of Scandal: Semiotic and Pragmatic in Mass Media* (Toronto: University of Toronto Press, 2011), 54–59.

58. *Prominent Americans Interested in Japan and Prominent Japanese Interested in America: Supplement to the January Number of "Japan and America"* (1903), 51; "Directors Record Sorrow at the Death of Mr. Webb," in *Greater New York: Bulletin of the Merchants' Association of New York* 8, no. 26 (30 June 1919): 3; Morrison to Gull, 8 September 1915, in GEMP, MSS 312–205.

59. Morrison to Gull, 8 September 1915.

60. On Japanese nongovernmental drug activities on the Asian continent: Motohiro Kobayashi, "Drug Operations by Resident Japanese in Tianjin," in *Opium Regimes: China, Britain, and Japan, 1839–1952,* ed. Timothy Brook and Bob Tadashi Wakabayashi (Berkeley: University of California Press, 2000), 152–166. Historians have recognized this leitmotif of Chinese anti-opium movements in the period of sinicized opposition since the late 1920s, but have neglected its international origins and international force in the formative decades before. Bob Tadashi Wakabayashi, "'Imperial Japanese' Drug Trafficking in China: Historiographic Perspectives," *Sino-Japanese Studies* 13 (2000): 3–19. It is not uncommon in Chinese historiography to emphasize on Tokyo's full control, oversight, and knowledge of imperial, nongovernmental activities, a trope that itself is indebted to its anti-imperial provenance. Lee En-han, "Jiu yi ba shibian qian hou riben dui dongbei (wei manzhouguo) de duihua zhengce," in *Bulletin of the Institute of Modern History, Academia Sinica* 25 (January 1996): 269–310. For a broad comparative perspective in the core area of Japanese formal expansion: Norman Smith, *Intoxicating Manchuria: Alcohol, Opium, and Culture in China's Northeast* (Vancouver: UBC Press, 2012).

61. Keizai Chōsakai Mantetsu and Dai-Go-Bu, *Chōsen ahen mayaku seido chōsa hōkoku* (Report on the investigation of the Korean opium and narcotics system), National Diet Library, Tokyo, mimeograph report marked "secret," 30 June 1932, 3–4; Chōsen Sōtokufu Senbaikyoku, *Chōsen senbai shi* (The history of monopolies in Korea) 3 (Seoul: Chōsen Sōtokufu Senbaikyoku, 1936), 482–483, quoted in John M. Jennings, "The Forgotten Plague: Opium and Narcotics in Korea Under Japanese Rule, 1910–1945," *Modern Asian Studies* 29 (1995): 795–815.

62. Michael Adas, "Contested Hegemony: The Great War and the Afro-Asian Assault on the Civilizing Mission Ideology," in *Journal of World History* 15, no. 1 (2004): 31–63; Frederick R. Dickinson, *War and National Reinvention: Japan in the Great War, 1914–1919* (Cambridge, MA: Harvard University Asia Center, 1999); Thomas W. Burkman, *Japan and the League of Nations: Empire and World Order, 1914–1938* (Honolulu: University of Hawai'i Press, 2008), 1–103; Xu Guoqi, *China and the Great War: China's Pursuit of a New National Identity and Internationalization* (Cambridge: Cambridge University Press, 2005); Erez Manela, *The Wilsonian Moment: Self-Determination and the International Origins of Anticolonial Nationalism* (New York: Oxford University Press, 2007).

63. Frank Giles, *A Prince of Journalists: The Life and Times of Henri Stefan Opper de Blowitz* (London: Faber and Faber, 1962), 7. For Blowitz's own reflections: A. Opper de Blowitz, *My Memoirs* (London: Edward Arnold, 1903).

64. George Herbert Perris. *The War Traders: An Exposure* (London: National Peace Council, 1914), 17; "George H. Perris, Journalist, Dies at 53," *New York Times*, 24 December 1920. Original emphasis.

65. Morrison to Luxburg, 13 April 1911, GSPK, I. HA Rep. 120, C VIII 1, no. 2, vol. 12.

66. Morrison, "Japan's Morphia Trade with China: From a Correspondent," 1. Original typescript. On the domestic dimension of Japanese prostitution: Garon, "The World's Oldest Debate? Prostitution and the State in Imperial Japan, 1900–1945," *American Historical Review* 98 (1993): 710–732.

67. "Death by Morphia," *Australasian*, 5 July 1884, 28; "Morphia Habit Increasing," *New Zealand Graphic and Ladies' Journal*, 6 February 1897, 171. Judge Poupardin would earn more criticism than fame among the French and American public, who ridiculed the case as "such hilarious bonhomie." "Trial of Comtesse Hugo," *New York Times*, 13 March 1898.

68. "The Morphia Trade in Hongkong," *Straits Times Weekly Issue*, 29 August 1893, 8; "A Rival to Opium-Smoking," *British Medical Journal*, 7 October 1893, 803; "Morphine in the Far East," *Chemist and Druggist*, 26 September 1896, 479; "The Morphia-Habit in China," *Chemist and Druggist*, 21 October 1893, 592; "Morphine in China," *Chemist and Druggist*, 20 September 1902, 528, and 27 September 1902, 560; "Morphine in China," *Chemist and Druggist*, 11 October 1902, 630; "The Trade in Morphine to the East," *British Medical Journal*, 22 January 1910, 240; "Export of Morphia from Great Britain," *Pharmaceutical Journal*, 3 December 1910, 658; "The Passing of the Chinese Opium Trade," *British Medical Journal*, 17 May 1913, 1078; quoted in

Terry M. Parssinen, *Secret Passions, Secret Remedies: Narcotic Drugs in British Society, 1820–1930* (Philadelphia: Institute for the Study of Human Issues/Manchester: Manchester University Press, 1983), 144–163; Paul Brouardel, *Opium, morphine et cocaïne: intoxication aigue par l'opium, mangeurs et fumeurs d'opium, morphinomanes et cocaïnomanes* (Paris: Baillière, 1906). Hélène Gispert (ed.) *«Par la science, pour la patrie»: L'association française pour l'avancement des sciences* (Rennes: Presses Universitaires de Rennes, 2002).

69. Samuel Merwin, *Drugging a Nation: The Story of China and the Opium Curse: A Personal Investigation, during an Extended Tour, of the Present Conditions of the Opium Trade in China and Its Effects upon the Nation* (New York: F. H. Revell, 1908).

70. Morrison, "Japan's Morphia Trade with China: From a Correspondent," 2–3.

71. Ibid., 4.

72. Ibid., 3; Morrison to Gull, 8 September 1915.

73. Morrison to Gull, 8 September 1915; Memorandum by Cecil Arthur Verner Bowra, 15 January 1915; Bowra to Morrison, 21 January 1915, all in GEMP, ML MSS, 312–205. Morrison to Taylor, 13 August 1917, in GEMC 2, 624; Morrison to Wearne, 6 September 1917, in GEMC 2, 629. For further biographical information, see the first chapters of Leslie George Mitchell, *Maurice Bowra: A Life* (Oxford: Oxford University Press, 2009).

74. Morrison to Gull, 8 September 1915; Morrison. "Japan's Morphia Trade with China: From a Correspondent," 5–6.

75. Morrison to Gull, 8 September 1915. On Gull: GEMC 2, 403, no. 1. Eugene Lubot, "Modern Chinese History as Reflected in the North China Herald," *Social Studies* 65, no. 3 (1974): 126–129.

76. Morrison to Gull, 8 September 1915; Morrison Diary, 11 December 1918, in GEMP, ML MSS 312/2–27. On Green: GEMC 2, 64, no. 1.

77. Morrison to Gull, 8 September 1915.

78. Morrison to Gray, 4 February 1915, in GEMP, ML MSS 312–205.

79. Enclosure to letter from Green to Morrison, 19 December 1918?, in GEMC 1, 723. Editor Lo Hui-min misdates the article's publication date as 17 December 1918, a Tuesday, but the *North China Herald* published only on Saturdays. See the original edition in the *North China Herald*, 21 December 1918, 764–765. Lo also erroneously refers to Green's letter as dating from 19 December 1918, but as the letter refers to the article of 21 December, it must have been written shortly after that date.

80. Green to Morrison, 19 December 1918?, in GEMC 2, 722.

81. Luxburg to Bethmann Hollweg, 22 April 1911, GSPK, I. HA Rep. 120, C VIII 1, no. 2, vol. 12.

82. "Kaiser a Wreck: Slave to Drugs; In Dread of Assassination, His Chauffeur Tells Women," *Washington Post*, 26 February 1917.

83. Annika Hoffmann, "'Keineswegs nur eine Frage der Medizin': Opiate und Kokain in den 1910er und 1920er Jahren in Deutschland," in *Biopolitik und Sittlichkeitsreform. Kampagnen gegen Alkohol, Drogen und Prostitution 1880–1950*, ed. Judith Große, Francesco Spöring, and Jana Tschurenev (Frankfurt:

Campus, 2014), 148. For the international scientific debate about morphine addiction therapies: Oscar Jennings, "On Chronic Morphinism and Its Treatment," *Lancet,* 31 October 1908, 1324–1326. For a glimpse of the U.S. debate: Jeannette Marks, "Narcotism and the War," *North American Review* 206, no. 745 (December 1917): 879–884.

8. Toward International Accountability for Transnational Harm

1. *Medical Register for 1946,* 320; "Obituary," *British Medical Journal,* 21 December 1946, 967.
2. International Anti-Opium Association, Peking, *The War against Opium* (Tientsin: Tientsin Press, 1922), vi. This echoed an analogy first evoked by William Collins in 1914: Great Britain, *Correspondence Respecting the Third International Opium Conference, Held at The Hague, June 1914* [Cd. 7813], 13; S. K. Chatterjee, *Legal Aspects of International Drug Control* (The Hague: Martinus Nijhoff, 1981), 47, 49.
3. William Job Collins, "Aetiology of the European Conflagration," *Scientia (Rivista di scienzia),* 17 (1915): 276–285. Reprinted under the same title by Nicola Zanichelli in Bologna in 1915.
4. Mr. King and Mr. Mitchell-Thomson, *House of Commons Debates,* 27 November 1911, 32, cc 4–5.
5. *Report of the British Delegates to the International Opium Conference, Held at the Hague, December, 1911, to January, 1912* (London: His Majesty's Stationery Office, 1912) [Cd. 6448], 26. The Hague conferences did spur domestic, regulative antidrug legislation: the U.S. Harrison Narcotics Tax Act of 1914, Britain's DORA 40B of 1916, and the Dangerous Drugs Act of 1920.
6. Société des Nations, *Convention Internationale de l'Opium* / League of Nations, *International Opium Convention.* O.C. 1 (I), 27 (Art. 5).
7. This working definition of "globalization" borrows some elements from Jürgen Osterhammel and Niels P. Petersson, *Globalization: A Short History* (Princeton, NJ: Princeton University Press, 2005), vii–x.
8. Jonathan D. Spence, "Opium," in *Chinese Roundabout: Essays in History and Culture* (New York: Norton, 1992), 238.
9. *George Ernest Morrison Papers: George Morrison Diaries,* ML MSS 312, item 111 [microfilm], n.d.
10. January–June 1912, in *COROP, Part V, Confidential,* no. 118.
11. Ibid., no. 89; July–December 1912, in *COROP, Part VI, Confidential,* no. 124.
12. Xu Guoqi, *China and the Great War* (Cambridge: Cambridge University Press, 2005), 62; Zhang Yongjin, *China in the International System 1918–20: The Middle Kingdom at the Periphery* (Basingstoke: Macmillan, 1991).
13. "Sir J. Jordan to Mr. Balfour. Peking, December 5, 1918," in *COROP, Part XIII, Confidential (11628),* no. 7.
14. William O. Walker. "'A Grave Danger to the Peace of the East': Opium and Imperial Rivalry in China, 1895–1920," in *Drugs and Empires: Essays in*

Modern Imperialism and Intoxication, c. 1500–c. 1930, ed. James H. Mills and Patricia Barton (Basingstoke: Palgrave Macmillan, 2007), 197.

15. *COROP, Part XIV, Confidential,* no. 13.

16. See the documentation in FO 371–3687.

17. "Sir J. Jordan to Mr. Balfour. December 30, 1918," in *COROP, Part XIII, Confidential (11628),* no. 9.

18. Countermeasures were not taken until 1925, when the Geneva conferences introduced a certificate system that required the authentication of shipments from both the exporter and the importer. Chatterjee, *Legal Aspects of International Drug Control,* 121–123.

19. Elise McCormick, *Audacious Angles of China* (New York: Appleton, 1923), 198.

20. *Missionary Review of the World* 43 (January 1920): 1088.

21. "Mr. Davis to Earl Curzon, January 27, 1919," in *COROP, Part XIII, Confidential (11628),* no. 5.

22. "Mr. Davis to Earl Curzon, February 13, 1919," in *COROP, Part XIII, Confidential (11628),* no. 8.

23. *George Ernest Morrison Papers: George Morrison Diaries,* ML MSS 312, item 111 [microfilm], n.d.

24. William B. McAllister, *Drug Diplomacy in the Twentieth Century* (London: Routledge, 2000), 36.

25. W. W. Yen [Yan Huiqing], *East-West Kaleidoscope, 1877–1944: An Autobiography* (New York: St. John's University Press, 1974), 86.

26. Chatterjee, *Legal Aspects of International Drug Control,* 49.

27. Joyce A. Madancy, *The Troublesome Legacy of Commissioner Lin: The Opium Trade and Opium Suppression in Fujian Province, 1820s to 1920s* (Cambridge, MA: Harvard University Asia Center, 2003).

28. As a response to rising anti-Americanism in China, which had been ignited over the 1882 exclusion act for Chinese immigrants and culminated in the anti-American boycott of 1905, many American missionaries allied themselves with American and Chinese anti-opium movements. They upheld an increasingly benevolent American image of China, which found expression in the American Opium Exclusion Act of 1909, rendering the racial reasoning of the 1882 act untenable in the face of burgeoning Anglo-American opium consumption. Diana L. Ahmad, *The Opium Debate and Chinese Exclusion Laws in the Nineteenth-Century American West* (Reno: University of Nevada Press, 2007), 89. Canada instituted racist and exclusionist opium policies toward Chinese overseas addicts, which resulted in over a thousand Chinese men being deported from Canada to China between 1922 and 1940. Catherine Carstairs, *Jailed for Possession: Illegal Drug Use, Regulation, and Power in Canada, 1920–1961* (Toronto: University of Toronto Press, 2006), 64.

29. Compare Paul A. Cohen, "The Asymmetry in Intellectual Relations between China and the West in the Twentieth Century," in *Er shi shiji de zhongguo yu shi jie lunwen yuanji* (China and the world in the twentieth century), vol. 1, ed. Chang Chi-hsiung (Taipei: Zhongyang yanjiuyuan, Jindai shi yanjiu suo, 2001), 61–93; William C. Kirby, "The Internationalization of China: Foreign

Relations at Home and Abroad," in "Reappraising Republican China," special issue, *China Quarterly* 150 (June 1997): 433–458.

30. Akira Iriye, *Global Community: The Role of International Organizations in the Making of the Contemporary World* (Berkeley: University of California Press, 2002).
31. "The War against Opium," *British Bulletin of the Society for the Suppression of the Opium Trade* 12 (October 1922), Library of the Religious Society of Friends Library, London (SOFL), box OP M1, Opium Traffic Committee, Anti-Opium Committee, Associated Documents, c. 1920–23.
32. International Anti-Opium Association Peking, *The War against Opium* (Tientsin: Tientsin Press, 1922), i–vi.
33. Susan Pedersen has recently pointed out these largely unexplored dimensions of the League of Nations. Pedersen, "Back to the League of Nations," *American Historical Review* (October 2007): 1091–1117, here 1092.
34. "Letter from Arthur Sowerby (International Anti-Opium Association Peking) to Sir John Jordan, April 14th, 1919," CO 323/801, 176.
35. Ibid., 177.
36. Arnold H. Taylor, *American Diplomacy and the Narcotics Traffic, 1900–1939: A Study in International Humanitarian Reform* (Durham, NC: Duke University Press, 1969), 141.
37. FO 371–3687, 2–3.
38. William Hector Park, *Opinion of over 100 Physicians on the Use of Opium in China* (Shanghai: American Presbyterian Mission Press, 1899).
39. CO 323/801, 171–175. For subsequent legislative efforts: CO 323/839. The important monopoly in Hong Kong had been adjusted to the requirements of the Hague Convention in 1913: *Agreement between the United Kingdom and Portugal for the Regulation of the Opium Monopolies in the Colonies of Hong Kong and Macao* (London: Her Majesty's Stationery Office, 1913).
40. Walker, "'Grave Danger to the Peace of the East,'" 197.
41. Yen [Yan Huiqing], *East-West Kaleidoscope,* 87.
42. Taylor, *American Diplomacy and the Narcotics Traffic,* 142.
43. Yan Huiqing, *Yan Huiqing riji,* vol. 1 (Beijing: Zhongguo dang an chu ban she, 1996), 164.
44. The summa summarum of the British delegation in Paris as of 26 March 1919. "Memorandum Respecting the Enforcement of the 1912 Convention for the Suppression of the Opium Traffic," FO 374–20.
45. Taylor, *American Diplomacy and the Narcotics Traffic,* 142.
46. U.S. Department of State, *Foreign Relations of the United States: Paris Peace Conference,* vol. 4 (Washington, DC: Government Printing Office, 1970), 552–553 (hereafter *FRUS*).
47. Thomas W. Burkman. *Japan and the League of Nations: Empire and World Order, 1914–1938* (Honolulu: University of Hawai'i Press, 2008), 80; Naoko Shimazu. *Japan, Race and Equality: The Racial Equality Proposal of 1919* (London: Routledge, 1998); Frederick R. Dickinson, *War and National Reinvention: Japan in the Great War, 1914–1919* (Cambridge, MA: Harvard University Asia Center, 1999).

48. *COROP, Part XIII, Confidential,* no. 16; *COROP, Part XV,* January–June 1921, nos. 6, 78, and enclosures; 79 and enclosures.

49. Quoted in Xu, *China and the Great War,* 116.

50. Wang Zhengting in his autobiographic sketch, box no. 1, folder 10, 239, Chengting Thomas Wang Papers, Yale University Archives.

51. Ibid., 252–254.

52. David Hunter Miller, *My Diary at the Conference of Paris,* vol. 16 (New York: Printed for the author by the Appeal Printing Company, 1924), 24.

53. Comparison between the draft covenant and the final text: International Intermediary Institute, The Hague, *Documents on the League of Nations* (Leiden: A. W. Sijthoff's Uitgeversmaatschappij, 1920), 61. For the negotiations, Miller, *My Diary at the Conference of Paris,* 22–24, 51–53, 90–91.

54. Chatterjee, *Legal Aspects of International Drug Control,* 67. Analogous opium provisions were included in the other peace treaties as well: in Article 247 of the Treaty of St. Germain with Austria, 10 September 1919; Article 174 of the Treaty of Neuilly with Bulgaria, 27 November 1919; Article 230 of the Treaty of Trianon with Hungary, 4 June 1920; and Article 280 of the Treaty of Sèvres with Turkey, 10 August 1920. The result was thirty-four additional ratifications to the 1912 convention. *FRUS: Paris Peace Conference,* vol. 13, 580.

55. Participants in the Third International Opium Conference without major interests in the opium trade included Argentine, Austria-Hungary, Belgium, Bolivia, Bulgaria, Brazil, Chile, Colombia, Costa Rica, Cuba, Denmark, Dominica, Ecuador, Greece, Guatemala, Haïti, Honduras, Italy, Luxemburg, Mexico, Montenegro, Nicaragua, Norway, Panama, Paraguay, Peru, Romania, Russia, Salvador, Serbia, Spain, Sweden, Uruguay, and Venezuela.

56. U.S. Congress, *Treaty of Peace with Germany: Hearings before the Committee on Foreign Relations,* 66th Cong., 1st Sess., 1919, LVIII, part 7, 698–700; Taylor, *American Diplomacy and the Narcotics Traffic,* 144–145.

57. William O. Walker. *Opium and Foreign Policy: The Anglo-American Search for Order in Asia, 1912–1954* (Chapel Hill: University of North Carolina Press, 1991), 31.

58. League of Nations Archives, United Nations Office at Geneva (hereafter UNOG), *Special Supplement 1920–1921: Resolutions Adopted by the Assembly during Its First Session (November 15th to December 18th 1920),* Ref SDN 2026, 21–22. The "countries chiefly concerned" were those who had dominated the International Opium Commission of 1909 and the Hague opium conferences.

59. League of Nations Archives, UNOG, "Appointment of Advisory Committee on Traffic in Opium. Report by Mr. Wellington Koo, adopted by the Council on February 21st, 1921," *Council Sessions 12 (February, 1921): Annex 147,* 55–56.

60. Wunsz King, *China at the Washington Conference* (New York: St. John's University Press, 1963), 53–54.

61. Xu, *China and the Great War,* 273.

Conclusion

1. Chao-Hsin Chu, "The World Campaign against Opium," *Asiatic Review 18* (July 1922): 447.
2. Ibid., 442–447.
3. Admiral Pierre Lacoste, "Summary Session," in *The Intelligence Revolution: A Historical Perspective,* ed. Walter T. Hitchcock (Washington, DC: U.S. Air Force Academy, 1991), 310.
4. Chao-Hsin Chu, "China after the War," *Scientific Monthly* 8, no. 4 (Apr., 1919): 305–308, here 306.
5. Chao-Hsin Chu, "The Geographical Principle and the League of Nations," *National Review* 84 (Sept. 1924–Feb. 1925): 63–67; Chao-Hsin Chu, "Asia and the League of Nations," *The Nineteenth Century and After,* vol. 95, *January–June 1924* (London: Constable, 1924), 335–340; Chao-Hsin Chu, *Revision of Unequal Treaties: China Appeals to the League of Nations* (London: Caledonian Press, 1926).
6. Chu, "China after the War," 308.
7. Herman Theodore Bussemaker, *Paradise in Peril: Western Colonial Power and Japanese Expansion in South-East Asia, 1905–1941* (PhD diss., Universiteit van Amsterdam, 2001).
8. For reflections in our time, see Sudhir Anand et al., ed., *Public Health, Ethics, and Equity* (Oxford: Oxford University Press, 2006).
9. Robert A. Bickers and Jeffrey N. Wasserstrom, "Shanghai's 'Dogs and Chinese Not Admitted' Sign: Legend, History and Contemporary Symbol," *China Quarterly* 142 (1995): 444–466; Judith Wyman, "The Ambiguities of Chinese Antiforeignism: Chongqing, 1870–1900," *Late Imperial China* 18 (1998): 86–122; Peter Zarrow, "Historical Trauma: Anti-Manchuism and Memories of Atrocity in Late Qing China," *History and Memory* 16 (2004): 67–107.

Acknowledgments

Like poets, composers, and other artists, historians sustain themselves through the kindness of others. Their international projects, in particular, rely on an embarrassing wealth of intellectual generosity, material assistance, professional backing, and personal support. That alone is cause for humility. Since, however, gratitude has rarely fit on the printed page, I have chosen to keep my thanks unmercifully short. Any reader mentioned here and in doubt over the reasons for my gratitude will be welcome to ask for further elaboration in private.

I had the great fortune to be taught by a series of superb mentors, starting with Jürgen Osterhammel at the University of Konstanz, who introduced me to East Asian and global history in combination. His early and original encouragement, boundless support, and rigor have left a deep impression. At Yale University, Jonathan Spence, Peter Perdue, and Patrick Cohrs affirmed the possibility and the promise of my interests conjointly, despite their being so awkwardly divided between distinct fields of thought, research, and teaching. In the PhD program at Harvard University, where an early version of this project was submitted, Erez Manela, Charles Maier, and Akira Iriye were not only mentors but benefactors and examples of the profession. The best teachers are those who teach you more than method. They proofread your thoughts, test your logic, and ask questions that you cannot immediately answer. In graduate school, this project, in a premature form, also benefited from early comments and extensive criticism by the late Ernest May and conversations with David Armitage, Sugata Bose, Andrew Gordon, Maya Jasanoff, Cemal Kafadar, William Kirby, and Mary Lewis. Jacqueline Bhabha alerted me to the parallels and relations between drug trafficking and human trafficking at the Seminar on History and Policy at the Kennedy School of Government. I am very grateful to Moshik Temkin for organizing this opportunity. To the Weatherhead

Center for International Affairs at Harvard University, I am grateful for supportive working conditions round the clock; thanks in particular to Clare Putnam. Among the librarians at Harvard, Ryan Wheeler at Harvard's Houghton Library deserves special thanks.

I express my utmost gratitude to librarians and archivists on four continents for invaluable access: Harvard University (Phillips Reading Room at Widener Library; Harvard-Yenching; Andover-Harvard; Baker at Harvard Business School; Center for the History of Medicine at the Countway Library of Medicine at Harvard Medical School; Fung Library; Harvard Law School; Tozzer Library; Harvard University Archives and Interlibrary Loan Services); Yale (Sterling Memorial Library, Divinity School Special Collections; Yale Law School; Beinecke, Mudd and Yale University Archives for access to the Chengting Thomas Wang Papers); Princeton (Firestone); Columbia (East Asian Library, Rare Book and Manuscript Library, Burke); Stanford (Hoover Institution); the Library of Congress in Washington, DC, for access to the Charles H. Brent papers; the New York Public Library on Fifth Avenue; the League of Nations Archives of the United Nations Office in Geneva; the university libraries of Konstanz, Tübingen (also Institut für Erziehungswissenschaften and Institut für Kriminologie) and Leiden; the University of Oxford (Bodleian Library, New Bodleian Library, and the Bodleian Library of Commonwealth and African Studies at Rhodes House for access to the Papers of Sir Cecil Clementi); the Geheimes Staatsarchiv Preußischer Kulturbesitz in Berlin; the Staatsbibliothek zu Berlin for access to the Sammlung Darmstaedter; the National Archives of the United Kingdom in Kew; the British Library; the Library of the Religious Society of Friends in London; the Senate House Library of the University of London; in Australia, the Mitchell Library of the State Library of New South Wales for access to the George Ernest Morrison Papers; in Asia, the National Central Library in Taipei; the National University of Singapore (Malaysia Collection of the Central Library, Chinese Library and Medical/Science Library); the National Library of Singapore; the National Archives of Singapore; the National Archives of Japan; the Foreign Ministry Archives of Japan; the National Diet Library; the main university libraries at Peking University; National Taiwan University; National Taiwan Normal University; the Chinese University of Hong Kong; Waseda University; the Institute for Advanced Studies on Asia (Tōyō Bunka Kenkyūjo) library at the University of Tokyo; and finally the now dissolved library of the Koninklijk Instituut voor de Tropen in Amsterdam.

My academic peregrinations led me back to Yale, where I thank John Lewis Gaddis as director of International Security Studies for his invitation and Amanda Behm, Igor Biryukov, Kathleen Galo, and Liz Vastakis for their support. Paul Kennedy, Adam Tooze, and Patrick Cohrs shared liberally their wide-ranging reflections in weekly seminar discussions. At the University of Oxford, Nigel Bowles, then director of the Rothermere American Institute, welcomed me together with Jay Sexton and Jane Rawson, all of whom made my stay such a productive and rewarding one. I am most grateful to Sho Konishi, director of the Nissan Institute of Japanese Studies, for his memorable welcome at St. Antony's College and for being an astute, knowledgeable, and versatile interlocutor. The Nissan Institute became a home away from home. As director of the China Centre, Rana Mitter offered time, space, and inspiration at the China Centre seminar and helped with invaluable library access. I thank Henrietta Harrison for illuminating conversations and help with precious library access, Aimee Collis for her assistance in the St. Antony's College Library, Toby Garfitt at Magdalen College for shepherding me into relevant Francophone literature, Yuen Foong Khong at Nuffield College just before his departure for Singapore, Andrew Hurrell at Balliol College, Neil MacFarlane at St. Anne's College, and Liz Fisher at the Faculty of Law. Rana Mitter, Pete Millwood, Helena Ferreira Santos Lopes, and other participants offered criticism at the Oxford International History of East Asia Research Seminar.

At the Weatherhead East Asian Institute of Columbia University, I thank Charles Armstrong, Robert Barnett, Gerald Curtis, Carol Gluck, Eugenia Lean, and Andrew Nathan, as well as Rattana Bounsouaysana, Waichi Ho, Sarah Kirsch, and Kara Hélène Lightman, who made my year much more than a spell. Chengzhi Wang at the East Asian Library offered great encouragement in stressful times.

At the International Institute for Asian Studies in Leiden, I offer thanks to director Philippe Peycam and deputy director Willem Vogelsang, and for support and good cheer to Wai Cheung, Erica van Bentem, Mary Lynn van Dijk, Sandra van der Horst, Titia van der Maas, Heleen van der Minne, Paul van der Velde, Sonja Zweegers, and Grizzly. Mamie Gourmande offered gastronomic consolation. Leonard Blussé, Remco Breuker, Giles Scott-Smith, and Nira Wickramasinghe offered more support than was ever expected. Further institutional support and academic hospitality were offered by the Institute of Asia-Pacific Studies of Waseda University in Tokyo, where I owe deep thanks to Hatsue Shinohara. Despite best efforts to avoid teleologies of any kind, my chronology of thanks ends on a high note. I had the great fortune to complete this book in Tokyo, where Masashi Haneda received me most graciously at the venerable Institute for Advanced Studies on Asia (Tōyō Bunka Kenkyūjo) at the University of Tokyo, organized a presentation, assembled his team, and granted access to Tobunken's outstanding library and several eye-opening conversations. For all of this, I am in his debt. Further questions and comments by Professor Khohchahar Chuluu, Professor Naofumi Abe, Professor Yijiang Zhong, Professor Noriko Berlinguez-Kono, Claire Cooper, Pierre-Emmanuel Bachelet, and other seminar participants gave me new points of discursive orientation in the global academe. Yuka Tomomatsu taught me more about history than any other anthropologist. At Tobunken, I also wish to thank Kaori Araki, Saeko Hanasaka, and Miho Sugimoto for their flawless service, their courtesy, and their forbearance.

For financial support, I thank the Andrew W. Mellon Foundation; the Columbia University Libraries Research Award; the Harvard Committee for Australian Studies and its chair, David Haig; the Department of History at Harvard; the Harvard University Asia Center; the Fairbank Center for Chinese Studies; the Clive Fellowship Fund; the American Philosophical Society; and the Transregional Research Junior Scholar Fellowship of the InterAsia program of the Social Science Research Council (SSRC).

Seminars and conferences with their individual vintages and vistas helped orient and focus my thinking: at Harvard, the East-West Center in Hawai'i, Oxford, Geneva, Yale, Princeton, Columbia, the London School of Hygiene and Tropical Medicine, EHESS in Paris, the Royal Academies for Science and the Arts of Belgium,

Konstanz, the German Historical Institute in London, the conferences of SHAFR, AHA, and the European Social Science History Conference (ESSHC) in Vienna. Colleagues who helped refine my arguments and see them in relation to others' work were Timothy Brook, Patricia Clavin, Patrick Cohrs, Linda Colley, John Dower, Benjamin Elman, Selçuk Esenbel, Sheldon Garon, Akira Iriye, Paul Kennedy, Sandrine Kott, Amandine Lauro, Khiun Kai Liew, Erez Manela, Patrick Manning, Bill McAllister, Francine McKenzie, Jürgen Osterhammel, Susan Pedersen, Peter C. Perdue, Daniel Rodgers, Davide Rodogno, Emmanuelle Saada, Martin Thomas, and Ashley Wright. Daniel Headrick, Daniel Rodgers, Lee Ting Wong, and Benedikt Neueder valiantly read versions of the manuscript. Many more friends gave me the opportunity to test premature arguments, air contradictory ones, and learn which ones persuaded them or not. I pledge to thank each one individually.

Whatever errors, inaccuracies, and inadequacies remain in this book are my responsibility and mine alone. The communication of any errors that have escaped my attention will be welcome. At Harvard University Press, Joyce Seltzer, Kathleen Drummy, Stephanie Vyce, and Michael Higgins were models of professionalism, courtesy, and intelligence. I am also thankful to Mary Ribesky and Jamie Thaman at Westchester Publishing Services. Like this superb team, Stephen Ullstrom produced an admirable index. The family should not come last, although in most acknowledgments they do. I am most grateful for the trust, ceaseless encouragement, and moral support of my parents, my brothers, my nephew, and my three nieces. Sadly, my father passed away as I finished the manuscript. This book is dedicated to my parents, who supported me more than I know and perhaps more than they know.

INDEX